THE
BEST
OF
Gourmet

THE
BEST
OF

Gourmet

1999

FROM THE EDITORS OF GOURMET

PHOTOGRAPHS BY ROMULO A. YANES

CONDÉ NAST BOOKS · RANDOM HOUSE, NEW YORK

Random House website address:
www.atrandom.com

Most of the recipes in this work were published previously in *Gourmet* Magazine.

Printed in the United States of America
on acid-free paper

98765432
First Edition

Informative text in this book was written
by Diane Keitt and Caroline A. Schleifer.

The text of this book was set in Times
Roman by Media Projects Incorporated.
The four-color separations were done by
American Color and Applied Graphic
Technologies. The book was printed and
bound at R. R. Donnelley and Sons. Stock
is Citation Web Gloss, Westvāco.

Front Jacket: Seafood Paella with Lemon
Garlic Mayonnaise (page 272).
Back Jacket: Berry Tart with Mascarpone
Cream (page 209).
Frontispiece: Peach Raspberry Top-Crust
Pie (page 215).

For Condé Nast Books
Lisa Faith Phillips, Vice President and
  General Manager
Tom Downing, Associate Direct
  Marketing Director
Lucille Friedman, Fulfillment Manager
Colleen P. Shire, Assistant Direct
  Marketing Manager
Angela Lee, Direct Marketing Associate
Meredith L. Peters, Direct Marketing
  Assistant
Serafino J. Cambareri, Quality Control
  Manager

For *Gourmet* Books
Diane Keitt, Director
Caroline A. Schleifer, Editor

For *Gourmet* Magazine
Gail Zweigenthal, Editor-in-Chief

Zanne Early Stewart, Executive Food
  Editor
Kemp Miles Minifie, Senior Food Editor
Alexis M. Touchet, Associate Food Editor
Lori Walther Powell, Food Editor
Elizabeth Vought, Food Editor
Katy Massam, Food Editor
Shelton Wiseman, Food Editor
Alix Palley, Food Editor

Romulo A. Yanes, Photographer
Marjorie H. Webb, Style Director
Nancy Purdum, Senior Style Editor

Produced in association with
Media Projects Incorporated

Carter Smith, Executive Editor
Anne B. Wright, Project Editor
John W. Kern, Production Editor
Marilyn Flaig, Indexer
Karen Salsgiver, Design Consultant

ACKNOWLEDGMENTS

The editors of Gourmet Books would like to thank all those who contributed to this volume, especially our consultants—Zanne Early Stewart, *Gourmet*'s Executive Food Editor, Kemp Minifie, *Gourmet*'s Senior Food Editor, and Penelope Casas, the well-known cookbook and travel writer who specializes in Spain.

Spanish menus for our Cuisines of the World section were developed and styled by Alexis Touchet (A Tapas Party), Liz Vought (A Spring Family Dinner), and Lori Walther Powell (Summer Lunch by the Sea). Lori also styled her paella for the jacket. Penelope Casas reviewed our primers and menus and generously shared her own recipes—several of our dishes are based on those found in her cookbooks, *Tapas* (Knopf), *Delicioso* (Knopf), and *Paella!* (Holt). Gerald Asher, *Gourmet's* Wine Editor, selected wines for each of the menus. Romulo Yanes and Jeannie Oberholtzer, respectively, photographed and styled this year's exceptional jacket and menus; while Romulo, Julian Nieman, and Tina Gehring contributed photos of Spain. Throughout are lovely photographs of Spanish tiles by Jane Strong and line drawings by Laura Hartman Maestro.

Our Addendum, Easy One-Dish Dinners, offers 24 clever recipes by Katy Massam, Shelly Wiseman, and Alix Palley. They are accompanied by Agni Saucier's fine drawings.

The Recipe Compendium is embellished with line drawings by Jean Chandler, Suzanne Dunaway, Maurie Harrington, Vicky Gonis, Tina Lang, Elisa Mambrino, Jeanne Meinke, Bob Palevitz, Rowena Perkins, Kristen Reilly, Agni Saucier, Jim Saucier, Alexis Seabrook, and Meg Shields. Special thanks to Beverly Charlton, who sent a box of fabulous drawings, which we intend to use for some time to come.

And finally, thanks to Anne Wright and John Kern of Media Projects, Karen Salsgiver, who, once again, designed a great new look for this series, and to Jane Daniels Lear, Hobby McKenney Coudert, and Kathleen Duffy Freud, who kept us editorially correct.

CONTENTS

INTRODUCTION

Just outside our test kitchens and studio, we keep a "photo wall" of menu photographs that have appeared in the last twelve issues of *Gourmet*. This gives everyone, including me, a collective view of what has been published during the past year—Romulo Yanes, our photographer, keeps track of camera angles and lighting; food editors see what dishes have been developed and how they were styled; and prop stylists note color schemes, etc. Recently it became obvious (as you'll notice in the Menu Collection of this volume) that during 1998 we often moved our parties out of the dining room. We chose menu themes that appealed to our sense of ease and created meals that not only could, but *should*, be served buffet-style or, at least, in less formal settings. At the suggestion of our art director, Felicity Keane, we stacked dishes and loosened the feel of a menu by moving it to a television room, the beach, a porch, poolside.... Even our Christmas Dinner was served before a roaring fire with a camelback sofa pulled up to a beautifully set long table. The look is cozy and comfortable, but sophisticated and stylish at the same time.

In keeping with the tone of this collection, our Cuisines of the World section turns to the simple flavors of Spain. Three brand-new menus include a spring family dinner with asparagus and lamb specialties; an hors d'oeuvres *tapas* party highlighting many classic dishes from around the country; and an alfresco summer lunch featuring everyone's favorite, seafood paella. Exquisite full-color photographs and three informative primers bring the regional tastes of Spain to life. And, 24 more brand-new recipes appear in this year's Addendum—Easy One-Dish Dinners. Dishes like Chili Lime Chicken Salad with Mango, and Pork and Pinto Bean Chili add new spark to everyday meals.

In all, you'll find 27 menus and over 400 recipes to help you plan everything from tonight's quick dinner to next week's party. The very best of 1998 awaits—and that certainly bodes well for relaxed entertaining at its best.

Gail Zweigenthal, Editor-in-Chief

THE MENU
COLLECTION

Dancing flames reflected in slender champagne flutes at an intimate Fireside Dinner ...sturdy earth-toned ceramic plates illuminated by ivory pillar candles for a Rustic Italian Dinner...cheery gingham napkins and glass pitchers at a sunny Summer Brunch—at *Gourmet*, we know that just the right lighting, glasses, plates, and linens make our delicious menus even more tantalizing. Today, more than ever, comfortable settings and colorful everyday tableware set a relaxed tone, while china and starched linens, luxurious and always inviting, are reserved for extra-special occasions. Here, then, are over 70 pages of *Gourmet*'s best menus from 1998 to enliven your imagination *and* your table.

This year, *Gourmet*'s informal parties move out of the dining room—to the kitchen, the backyard, even the television room—but meals remain as stylish as ever. At our country-kitchen Sunday Dinner, guests help themselves to grilled flank steak, sautéed mushrooms, twice-baked potatoes, and later, to Lemon Blueberry Ice-Cream Cake. Our little Lunch among the Hydrangeas, set in a sun-dappled garden, captures the freshness of the season with fig and prosciutto salad, poached salmon with tarragon sauce, and a tart piled high with summer berries.

For true pampering, travel with us to Necker Island, a Caribbean paradise where three delightful menus await. A Brunch in the Shade features asparagus and morels with poached eggs and hollandaise; a Buffet by the Sea includes island cocktails and plenty of tropical dishes like Coconut Tempura Shrimp on Banana Caper Relish; and a Lazy Day Lunch boasts Grilled Mahimahi with Crushed Potatoes, Orange Vinaigrette, and Cilantro Pesto. Home and hearth (of all kinds) beckon for holiday fare. Our Grill-Roasted Brined Turkey with Anaheim Chile Salsa Verde is a great reason to fire up the barbecue for a Southwestern Thanksgiving. And a cozy Christmas Dinner concludes the year with table and chairs (even a sofa) pulled fireside for heartwarming Rib Roast with Roasted-Garlic Thyme Sauce. For dessert, our tipsy finale, Prune Kumquat Sticky Pudding with Armagnac Toffee Sauce, is divine.

Whether casual or grand, homey or chic—however *you* want to entertain—24 outstanding *Gourmet* menus are now at your fingertips. As you leaf through this album of entertaining ideas, look for the little touches that make them so special.

FIRESIDE DINNER

BEET CHIPS, P. 90

Poire William Champagne Cocktails, p. 233

CARAMELIZED LEEK SOUP, P. 111

RACLETTE CHEESE TOASTS, P. 111

Germanier Balavaud Fendant Vétroz les Terrasses '96

CRISP DUCK BREAST
WITH PINK PEPPERCORN SAUCE, P. 145

MASHED-POTATO CAKES, P. 175

SAUTÉED KOHLRABI AND WATERCRESS, P. 172

Saint-Estèphe Château Cos d'Estournel '94

GINGER CAKES WITH
MOLTEN CHOCOLATE CENTERS AND
GINGER CRÈME ANGLAISE, P. 204

Emilio Lustau Rare Cream "Solera Reserva" Sherry

Serves 4

Top left: Caramelized Leek Soup. Top right: Raclette Cheese Toasts.
Below: Crisp Duck Breast with Pink Peppercorn Sauce, Mashed-Potato Cake,
and Sautéed Kohlrabi and Watercress. Opposite: Ginger Cakes with
Molten Chocolate Centers and Ginger Crème Anglaise

SUPERBOWL SUNDAY BUFFET

HERBED BEAN SPREAD WITH BAGUETTE TOASTS, P. 97

Schneider Weisse beer

MEATBALLS IN WINTER TOMATO SAUCE, P. 132

ITALIAN BREAD

BAKED ZITI WITH MUSHROOMS, PEPPERS,
AND PARMESAN, P. 165

MAKE-YOUR-OWN SALAD
WITH LEMON GARLIC DRESSING, P. 187

Cartlidge & Browne Chardonnay '96

D'Angelo Aglianico del Vulture '94

SPICED PECAN PIE, P. 216

CHOCOLATE PEANUT BUTTER CHIP COOKIES, P. 206

Serves 8 to 10

BRUNCH IN THE SHADE ON NECKER ISLAND

FRUIT SALAD

MIXED GREENS, ASPARAGUS, AND MORELS
TOPPED WITH POACHED EGGS
AND HOLLANDAISE, P. 154

Tropical Juices, Coffee, Tea

Serves 6

Buffet by the Sea on Necker Island

Necker "Sunrises", p. 235

Rum "Lemonade", p. 233

COCONUT TEMPURA SHRIMP
ON BANANA CAPER RELISH, P. 126

SPICED CHICKEN BREASTS
WITH COUSCOUS SALAD, P. 141

PICKLED RED CABBAGE
WITH TOASTED SESAME SEEDS, P. 189

CELERY ROOT AND APPLE SALAD
WITH CREAMY MUSTARD DRESSING, P. 189

FENNEL CONFIT AND TOMATO SALAD, P. 190

Veuve Clicquot La Grande Dame '89

SAMBUCA SOUFFLÉS
WITH WHITE CHOCOLATE ICE CREAM, P. 230

Sambuca

Serves 8 to 10

LAZY DAY LUNCH ON NECKER ISLAND

CHILLED PUMPKIN AND LEMONGRASS SOUP
WITH CRAB MEAT, P. 114

Dom Pérignon '90

GRILLED MAHIMAHI WITH
CRUSHED POTATOES, ORANGE VINAIGRETTE,
AND CILANTRO PESTO, P. 116

Louis Latour Corton-Charlemagne '94

Domaine Dujac Clos Saint-Denis Pinot Noir '92

FROZEN PASSION-FRUIT PARFAITS
WITH KIWIFRUIT-PINEAPPLE SALSA,
STRAWBERRY COULIS,
AND COCOA SPIRALS, P. 222

Château d'Yquem '88

Serves 6

A Rustic Italian Dinner

ARTICHOKE AND PANCETTA FETTUCCINE. P. 162

CIABATTA. P. 103
ITALIAN "SLIPPER" BREAD

Feudi di San Gregorio Greco di Tufo '96

PAN-ROASTED VEAL WITH SALSA VERDE. P. 133

POTATO, TOMATO, AND ROSEMARY GRATIN. P. 178

SWISS CHARD WITH GARLIC. P. 179

SAVOY CABBAGE AND ARUGULA SALAD. P. 186

Falesco "Vitiano" '96

LATTICE-TOPPED APRICOT CROSTATA. P. 210

Nuova Agricultura Passito di Pantelleria '93

Serves 6

Above: Artichoke and Pancetta Fettuccine. Opposite: Potato, Tomato, and Rosemary Gratin, Pan-Roasted Veal with Salsa Verde, and Swiss Chard with Garlic

A Cheese Tasting Party

EXOTIC MUSHROOM BROTH, P. 115

GOAT CHEESES

RED GLOBE AND RIBIER GRAPES

MEDJOOL DATES

OATCAKES, P. 108

Lucien Crochet Sancerre '96

SOFT CHEESES

CELERY, FENNEL, AND RED PEAR SALAD, P. 191

Michel Tête Juliénas "Cuvée Prestige" '96

FIRM/HARD CHEESES

PICKLED PEPPERS AND ONIONS, P. 198

Chapoutier Cornas '95

BLUE CHEESES

MESCLUN AND RADICCHIO SALAD
WITH SHALLOT VINAIGRETTE, P. 186

Château Suduiraut Sauternes '89

APPLE, APRICOT, AND PRUNE TART, P. 208

Serves 12

GOAT CHEESES

SOFT CHEESES

BLUE CHEESES

FIRM/HARD CHEESES

Opposite/Top left. Goat cheeses (clockwise from top left): Pouligny-Saint-Pierre, Chabichou du Poitou, Picandine Chèvre, and Valençay. Top right. Soft cheeses (clockwise from top left): Muenster, Hudson Valley Camembert, Taleggio, and Pierre Robert. Bottom right. Firm/hard cheeses (clockwise from top): Dry Jack, Farmhouse Cheddar, Vermont Shepherd, and Parmigiano-Reggiano. Bottom left. Blue cheeses (clockwise from top left): Maytag Blue, Gorgonzola Dolce, Roquefort, and Cabrales. This page: Apple, Apricot, and Prune Tart with Crème Fraîche

Easter Sunday

RADISHES WITH GOAT CHEESE. P. 96

SEARED SCALLOPS
WITH VEGETABLE CONFETTI. P. 124

Château Smith Haute-Lafitte '95

RACK OF LAMB WITH SPINACH PINE-NUT
CRUST AND MINTED PEA SAUCE. P. 137

BABY CARROTS AND ASPARAGUS. P. 171

MASHED JERUSALEM ARTICHOKES. P. 171

Franciscan Estate Selections Quintessa '94

PINEAPPLE RUM TRIFLE CAKE. P. 205

PISTACHIO BISCOTTI THINS. P. 208

Château Lafaurie-Peyraguey Sauternes '90

Serves 6

Above: Rack of Lamb with Spinach Pine-Nut Crust and Baby Carrots
and Asparagus. Opposite: Pineapple Rum Trifle Cake

34

A BARBECUE AT THE PHOENICIAN

PUMPKIN-SEED SPREAD, P. 100

MINI CHAPATIS, P. 100

Prickly Pear Margaritas, p. 234

GRILLED SQUID SALAD, P. 184

GRILLED LEMON GARLIC CHICKEN THIGHS
ON ARUGULA SALAD, P. 144

BABY BACK RIBS
WITH CHIPOTLE HONEY SAUCE, P. 136

GRILLED RED POTATO AND SMOKED HAM
SALAD WITH TOMATO DRESSING, P. 193

SWEET-POTATO FOCACCIA
WITH ANCHO CHILES, P. 104

SOUTHWESTERN CORN STICKS, P. 105

Dos Cabezas Cochise County (Arizona) Pinot Gris '96

Marchese di Gresy "Martinenga" Barbaresco '85

CHOCOLATE BANANA CREAM PIE, P. 211

ROASTED PINEAPPLE AND MACADAMIA
NUT TART, P. 218

Serves 12

Below: Roasted Pineapple and Macadamia Nut Tart and Chocolate Banana Cream Pie. Opposite: Baby Back Ribs with Chipotle Honey Sauce, Grilled Red Potato and Smoked Ham Salad with Tomato Dressing, Grilled Lemon Garlic Chicken Thigh on Arugula Salad, Sweet-Potato Focaccia with Ancho Chiles, and Grilled Squid Salad

MOTHER'S DAY AT THE RITZ-CARLTON, CHICAGO

FRISÉE AND WATERCRESS SALAD
WITH BALSAMIC THYME VINAIGRETTE
AND ARTICHOKE RAGOUT, P. 185

SLOW-ROASTED SALMON
WITH MUSTARD PARSLEY GLAZE, P. 119

WARM POTATO SALAD
WITH CAVIAR DRESSING, P. 192

STEAMED ASPARAGUS

J. Fritz Winery "Dutton Ranch" '95

STRAWBERRY LIME TART
WITH SPUN SUGAR, P. 219

Far Niente "Dolce" Late Harvest Table Wine '94

Serves 8

Above: Frisée and Watercress Salad with Balsamic Thyme Vinaigrette and
Artichoke Ragout. Opposite: Strawberry Lime Tart with Spun Sugar

TO THE LIGHTHOUSE

SPICY CRUNCH MIX, P. 96

Southsides, p. 234

LOBSTER SALAD WITH CORN, SUGAR SNAP
PEAS, AND BASIL-MINT OIL, P. 182

GINGERED WATERMELON
AND YELLOW TOMATO SALAD, P. 194

PEPPERED PITA CRISPS, P. 107

Domaine Weinbach Riesling Grand Cru Schlossberg '96

NECTARINE LIME CURD TART
WITH A BROWN-SUGAR CRUST, P. 214

Doisy-Védrines Barsac '90

Serves 4

SUNDAY DINNER

ASPARAGUS, CUCUMBER, AND SUGAR
SNAP PEAS WITH HERB GARLIC DIP, P. 98

BROCCOLI RABE, BLACK OLIVE,
AND SMOKED MOZZARELLA PIZZA, P. 90

Joseph Phelps Vineyards Grenache Rosé '96

SPINACH AND SPROUT SALAD, P. 188

GRILLED FLANK STEAK WITH SAUTÉED
PORTABELLA AND CREMINI MUSHROOMS, P. 130

TWICE-BAKED POTATOES WITH BASIL
AND SOUR CREAM, P. 175

Château Fortia Châteauneuf-du-Pape '94

LEMON BLUEBERRY ICE-CREAM CAKE, P. 202

Domaine des Coyeux Muscat de Beaumes-de-Venise

Serves 8

Above: Spinach and Sprout Salad, Grilled Flank Steak with Sautéed
Portabella and Cremini Mushrooms, and Twice-Baked Potatoes with Basil
and Sour Cream. Opposite: Lemon Blueberry Ice-Cream Cake

LUNCH AMONG THE HYDRANGEAS

FRESH FIG, PROSCIUTTO, AND ARUGULA SALAD
WITH PARMESAN SHAVINGS, P. 184

Mormoraia Vernaccia di San Gimignano '96

POACHED SALMON WITH TARRAGON SAUCE
AND FINGERLING POTATOES, P. 120

Qupé Bien Nacido Reserve Chardonnay '96

BERRY TART WITH MASCARPONE CREAM, P. 209

Serves 6

Above: Berry Tart with Mascarpone Cream. Opposite: Poached Salmon
with Tarragon Sauce and Fingerling Potatoes

Summer Brunch

BLUEBERRIES WITH YOGURT
AND MAPLE-BLUEBERRY SYRUP, P. 159

CORN AND BASIL EGG ROULADE
WITH YELLOW TOMATO COULIS, P. 155

SLICED BLACK FOREST HAM

BAKING POWDER BISCUITS, P. 105

Honeydew Mimosas, p. 234

Serves 8

GRILLING BY THE POOL

HERBED KALAMATA OLIVES, p. 96

GRILLED EGGPLANT SPREAD, p. 98

SPICED PITA TOASTS, p. 99

Domaine Maravenne Côtes de Provence Rosé '97

SHRIMP AND ONION KEBABS, p. 125

LAMB AND RED PEPPER KEBABS, p. 138

GRILLED CORN WITH
CUMIN SCALLION BUTTER, p. 173

BULGUR, PARSLEY, AND MINT SALAD, p. 195

Bodegas Montecillo Viña Combrero Rioja '94

FROZEN PISTACHIO HALVAH PIE, p. 216

PLUMS IN WHITE PEPPERCORN AND
VANILLA SYRUP, p. 225

Serves 8

FLAVORS OF JAPAN

EDAMAME, P. 94
SOYBEANS IN THE POD

CRAB AND EGG MAKI WITH TOBIKO, P. 92

Mumm de Cramant Champagne Blanc de Blancs Brut

TERIYAKI-GLAZED SEA BASS, P. 121

SPICY EGGPLANT, P. 174

UMEBOSHI AND RICE SALAD WITH
PICKLED GINGER AND SUGAR SNAP PEAS, P. 196

VINEGARED CUCUMBER SALAD, P. 191

Sake or White Wine

WATERMELON ICE, P. 224

Green Tea

Serves 6

Above: Watermelon Ice. Opposite: Umeboshi and Rice Salad with Pickled Ginger and Sugar Snap Peas, Spicy Eggplant, Vinegared Cucumber Salad, and Teriyaki-Glazed Sea Bass

FAMILY REUNION

Orangeade, p. 235

GOAT CHEESE AND TOMATO TART
IN A CORNMEAL CRUST, p. 94

ROASTED GARLIC-PEA PURÉE ON
SOURDOUGH CROÛTES, p. 93

Rodney Strong Charlotte's Home Sauvignon Blanc '97

GRILLED SPICED DOUBLE-THICK
PORK CHOPS, p. 134

PICKLED PLUMS AND RED ONIONS, p. 198

POTATO, GREEN BEAN, AND
CORN SALAD, p. 192

Pellegrini Carignane '95

PEACH RASPBERRY TOP-CRUST PIES, p. 215

VANILLA BEAN ICE CREAM, p. 223

BUTTERMILK CUPCAKES WITH
TWO FROSTINGS, p. 202

Serves 12

Above: Spiced Double-Thick Pork Chop, Pickled Plums and Red Onions, and Potato, Green Bean, and Corn Salad. Opposite: Buttermilk Cupcakes with Two Frostings, Peach Raspberry Top-Crust Pie, and Vanilla Bean Ice Cream

A SOUTHWESTERN
THANKSGIVING

SPICED PUMPKIN-SEED FLATBREAD, P. 107

Pine Ridge Winery Chenin Blanc Viognier '97

GRILL-ROASTED BRINED TURKEY WITH
ANAHEIM CHILE SALSA VERDE, P. 147

CHORIZO, ROASTED CORN, AND
CURRANT DRESSING, P. 148

ANCHO SWEET-POTATO PURÉE, P. 180

CREAMED CHAYOTE WITH CHIVES, P. 173

JÍCAMA, CARROT, AND RED CABBAGE SLAW
WITH ANISE AND LIME, P. 194

Qupé Los Olivos Cuvée '96

DRIED-APPLE TART WITH
CRISP CRUMBLE TOPPING, P. 212

Arrowood Winery "Hoot Owl Creek Vineyard"
Special Select Late Harvest Riesling '97

Serves 6

Above: Dried-Apple Tart with Crisp Crumble Topping.
Opposite: Grill-Roasted Brined Turkey

69

THANKSGIVING IN THE CITY

VINE LEAF—WRAPPED SHEEP'S-MILK RICOTTA WITH
FENNEL AND OLIVES, P. 102

Taittinger Domaine Carneros "Le Rêve" '92

RED CURRANT—GLAZED TURKEY WITH SAGE AND
RED CURRANT GRAVY, P. 149

WHEAT-BERRY STUFFING WITH PEARL ONIONS, P. 150

CRANBERRY APRICOT COMPOTE, P. 198

ROASTED ACORN SQUASH AND CHESTNUTS, P. 178

STEAMED SAVOY CABBAGE AND MUSTARD GREENS
WITH BACON, P. 173

Marimar Torres Estate "Don Miguel Vineyard" '96

CARAMEL NUT TART, P. 212

GINGER ICE CREAM, P. 221

CINNAMON NUTMEG TUILES, P. 206

Henriques & Henriques 10-Year-Old Malmsey Madeira

Serves 8

Red Currant–Glazed Turkey with Sage, Red Currant Gravy, Cranberry Apricot Compote, Wheat-Berry Stuffing with Pearl Onions, Roasted Acorn Squash and Chestnuts, and Steamed Savoy Cabbage and Mustard Greens with Bacon

CHRISTMAS DINNER

CRAB WITH DILL ON CAYENNE TOASTS, P. 93

ROQUEFORT DIP WITH APPLE, ENDIVE,
AND CELERY HEARTS, P. 101

Bollinger Spécial Cuvée Brut NV

RIB ROAST WITH ROASTED-GARLIC
THYME SAUCE, P. 128

ROASTED BEETS WITH PARSLEY, P. 172

CREAMY CABBAGE, PARSNIP, AND POTATO
CASSEROLE WITH ROBIOLA, P. 170

Château La Croix du Casse '94

PRUNE KUMQUAT STICKY PUDDING WITH
ARMAGNAC TOFFEE SAUCE, P. 229

ARMAGNAC ICE CREAM, P. 220

Cossart-Gordon 10-Year-Old Malmsey Madeira

Serves 8

HOLIDAY BRUNCH

Blood-Orange Mimosas, p. 235

POPOVER PUDDING WITH IRISH BACON, p. 157

ARUGULA, ENDIVE, AND RADICCHIO SALAD, p. 186

ROASTED SPICED PEARS AND FIGS
WITH ALMONDS, p. 224

Serves 8

Above: Roasted Spiced Pears and Figs with Almonds.
Opposite: Popover Pudding with Irish Bacon

GRILLED PORK TENDERLOIN CUTLETS
WITH CHILI MAPLE GLAZE, P. 135

PAPAYA AND RED ONION SALSA, P. 200

GRILLED ZUCCHINI
AND BELL PEPPER COUSCOUS, P. 161

WHITE-GRAPE GRANITAS, P. 220

Serves 4

Each serving about 497 calories and 8 grams fat

SPINACH AND ENDIVE SALAD WITH
LEMON-GINGER DRESSING AND
CRISP WON TON STRIPS, P. 187

RED SNAPPER WITH SPICY SOY
GLAZE ON SAUTÉED VEGETABLES
AND SWEET POTATO, P. 118

Serves 4

Each serving about 466 calories and 5 grams fat

CILANTRO-STUFFED CHICKEN BREASTS
WITH POBLANO CHILE SAUCE, P. 140

RICE, BEAN, AND CORN SALAD, P. 195

PINEAPPLE WITH BASIL, P. 225

Serves 4

Each serving about 473 calories and 10 grams fat

A RECIPE COMPENDIUM

Whether you need an easy snack for a relaxed get-together, a quick meal when you're on the run, a fancy hors d'oeuvre to pamper guests, or the perfect cake for a pot-luck supper, you're sure to find the right dish in this collection of *Gourmet*'s best recipes from 1998. In addition to all the recipes that make up our menus, we've included hundreds more from *Gourmet*'s monthly food columns—in all, you'll find over 400 irresistible options.

In keeping with today's hectic schedules, nearly half of these recipes can be prepared in 45 minutes or less. From our Quick Kitchen column come hearty "one-pot" suppers, such as Smoked Sausage Jambalaya, and Chicken, Polenta, and Red Pepper Ragout. Or mix and match dishes to create your own easy little dinners, like Sautéed Shrimp with Caraway Seeds, Wilted Red Cabbage with Balsamic Vinegar, and perhaps Gingersnap Ice-Cream Sundaes with Rum Syrup for dessert. (Quick recipes are indicated by a clock symbol ◔ throughout the book *and* in the index.)

Other recipes, culled from columns that explore seasonal harvests, offer maximum freshness. This summer, plan a trip to the farmers market to buy heirloom tomatoes for Smashed-Potato Tomato Gratin or Chilled Lemongrass-Tomato Soup; and next autumn, when beets are abundant, prepare Beet and Beet Green Risotto with Horseradish, or Golden and Red Beet Soup. When it comes to creative ideas using everyday ingredients, The Last Touch column offers some inventive twists: Yesterday's bread is transformed into garlicky Skillet-Toasted Mini Croutons to toss into salads or soups, while salted capers add piquancy to an inspired topping—Caper, Raisin, and Lemon Pesto—for grilled chicken or sautéed scallops.

More tasty treats from our Less is More column are sprinkled throughout this section. Zesty salsas (Spicy Pineapple, Apricot, and Jícama Salsa), hearty salads (Grilled Chicken and Chick-Pea Salad with Carrot-Cumin Dressing), exotic main courses (Moroccan turkey pie), even fabulous finales (White-Grape Granitas) satisfy cravings without excess fat or calories. (Lighter recipes are marked with a feather symbol ☞ throughout the book *and* in the index.)

Plenty of choices guarantee endless possibilities for any occasion. Come enjoy the variety, the flavor, and the excitement of *Gourmet*'s newest and best recipes.

APPETIZERS

BEET CHIPS ◔

6 medium beets (about ¾ pound)
¼ cup cornstarch
about 4 cups safflower or vegetable oil
    for deep-frying

Peel beets. Using a *mandoline* or other manual slicer cut beets into paper-thin slices and transfer to a large bowl. Add cornstarch and toss well to coat.

In a 3-quart saucepan heat oil until a deep-fat thermometer registers 350° F. Working in batches of 8 to 10 slices, separating them from one another, fry beets, turning once or twice, until crisp and beginning to shrivel, 30 seconds to 1 minute, making sure oil returns to 350° F. before adding next batch. Transfer chips as fried with a large slotted spoon to paper towels to drain and season with salt. *Beet chips may be made 12 hours ahead and kept, uncovered, at room temperature.* Serves 4.

BROCCOLI RABE, BLACK OLIVE, AND SMOKED MOZZARELLA PIZZA

1 puff pastry sheet (from one 17¼-ounce package
    frozen puff pastry sheets), thawed
½ pound broccoli rabe
⅓ cup drained Kalamata or other brine-cured
    black olives
2 garlic cloves
1 tablespoon fresh lemon juice
6 ounces smoked mozzarella
1 tablespoon extra-virgin olive oil

Line a baking sheet with parchment paper. On a lightly floured surface unfold pastry sheet and gently roll out to a 14- by 12-inch rectangle. Transfer pastry to baking sheet and prick all over with a fork. *Chill pastry, covered, at least 30 minutes and up to 1 day.*

Preheat oven to 400° F.

Have ready a bowl of ice and cold water. Trim 1 inch from bottoms of broccoli rabe stems. In a saucepan of boiling salted water blanch broccoli rabe 30 seconds and transfer with tongs to ice water to stop cooking. Drain broccoli rabe well in a colander and pat dry. Cut broccoli rabe into ½-inch pieces and transfer to a bowl. Pit and chop olives. Mince garlic. Add olives, garlic, lemon juice, and salt and pepper to taste to broccoli rabe and toss well. Into another bowl coarsely grate mozzarella and chill, covered.

Bake pastry in middle of oven until golden, 15 to 20 minutes. Sprinkle cheese evenly over pastry, leaving a ½-inch border on all sides. Spread broccoli rabe mixture evenly on top of cheese and bake in middle of oven 10 minutes, or until heated through. Drizzle oil over pizza.

Cut pizza into small serving pieces. Serves 8 as an hors d'oeuvre.

PHOTO ON PAGE 47

CORN CAKES WITH SALMON ROE ◔

5 tablespoons yellow cornmeal
2 tablespoons all-purpose flour
¼ teaspoon baking soda
¼ teaspoon salt
a pinch sugar
⅓ cup thawed frozen corn
1 large egg
¼ cup well-shaken buttermilk
2 tablespoons finely chopped fresh chives
1 tablespoon clarified butter
    (procedure follows)
½ cup sour cream
about 4 ounces salmon roe

Garnish: slivered red onion

In a bowl whisk together cornmeal, flour, baking soda, salt, and sugar. Chop corn and in another bowl stir together with egg, buttermilk, and chives. Stir in cornmeal mixture. Let batter stand 15 minutes.

In a 10-inch nonstick skillet heat 1 teaspoon butter over moderate heat until foam subsides and drop batter by teaspoon measures into skillet, without crowding (about 10). Cook cakes until golden, about 1 minute on each side, transferring to paper towels to drain, and make more cakes in same manner.

Top warm cakes with sour cream and salmon roe and garnish with slivered red onion. Makes about 30 hors d'oeuvres.

To Clarify Butter

unsalted butter

Cut butter into 1-inch pieces and in a heavy saucepan melt over low heat. Remove pan from heat and let butter stand 3 minutes. Skim froth and slowly pour butter into a measuring cup, leaving milky solids in bottom of pan. Discard milky solids and pour clarified butter into a jar or crock. *Butter keeps, covered and chilled, indefinitely.* When clarified, butter loses about one fourth of its original volume.

Curried Cheddar Date Bites

⅓ cup walnuts
2 tablespoons vegetable oil
1 Granny Smith apple
⅓ cup pitted dates
2 cups grated extra-sharp Cheddar
¼ cup mayonnaise
2 tablespoons chopped fresh flat-leafed
    parsley leaves
2 tablespoons fresh lemon juice
1 tablespoon apricot preserves
¾ teaspoon curry powder
three 5-inch pita loaves

Chop walnuts and in a small skillet cook in oil over moderate heat, stirring, until lightly toasted. Cool nuts slightly.

Preheat broiler.

Coarsely grate apple and finely chop dates. In a bowl stir together all ingredients except pitas until combined well.

Horizontally split pitas and arrange, cut sides down, on a large baking sheet. Broil pitas about 4 inches from heat until golden and crisp, 1½ to 2 minutes. Remove baking sheet from oven and turn pitas over. Divide Cheddar mixture among pitas, spreading evenly. Broil pitas until cheese mixture begins to bubble, about 2 minutes. Cut each pita into 6 wedges. Makes 36 hors d'oeuvres.

Caviar and Smoked Salmon on Toasted Brioche Cubes

five ¾-inch-thick slices brioche loaf or challah
½ pound thinly sliced smoked salmon
5 tablespoons unsalted butter
about 2.5 ounces caviar
⅓ cup *crème fraîche* or sour cream

Cut bread slices into about thirty 1-inch cubes. Cut salmon lengthwise into ½-inch-wide strips and crosswise into 4-inch-long pieces. In a large nonstick skillet heat 3 tablespoons butter over moderate heat until foam subsides and brown half of cubes on 2 opposite sides until golden, about 2 minutes, transferring to a platter. Brown remaining cubes in same manner, adding remaining 2 tablespoons butter.

Top each cube decoratively with salmon, caviar, and *crème fraîche* or sour cream. Makes about 30 hors d'oeuvres.

CRAB AND EGG MAKI WITH TOBIKO

½ pound lump crab meat (about 1 packed cup)
1 teaspoon seasoned rice vinegar
For nori egg sheets
1½ cups lightly beaten eggs (5 to 6 large)
1 tablespoon *mirin** (sweet rice wine)
1 tablespoon water
½ teaspoon salt
vegetable oil for brushing skillet
three 8- by 7½-inch sheets toasted *nori**
   (dried laver)
For dipping sauce
⅓ cup Japanese soy sauce such as Kikkoman
2 tablespoons *mirin** (sweet rice wine)
2 tablespoons water

3 ounces (total) plain *tobiko** (flying-fish roe),
   flavored/seasoned *tobiko***, and/or golden
   whitefish caviar**

*available at Japanese markets and by mail order
   from Uwajimaya, (800) 889-1928
**available at some specialty foods shops and by
   mail order in 1-ounce containers from Collins
   Caviar Co., (800) 226-0342

Pick over crab to remove any bits of cartilage and
shell and stir together with vinegar and salt to taste.
Chill crab, covered.

Make nori egg sheets:

In a 2-cup measure stir together eggs, *mirin*,
water, and salt until just combined. Lightly brush a
12-inch nonstick skillet with oil and heat over
moderately low heat until just hot. (A drop of egg
mixture should set without sizzling or browning.)
Pour ½ cup egg mixture into skillet, tilting to coat
bottom evenly. Cook egg mixture until set on underside but still slightly wet on top, about 1 minute, and
center 1 *nori* sheet on top, pressing gently with
fingers to adhere *nori* to egg. Cook sheet until egg
under *nori* is set, about 30 seconds more (egg not
covered by *nori* may not be completely set) and
invert onto a sheet of wax paper. Invert *nori* egg
sheet onto a cutting board and discard wax paper.
Trim egg even with *nori*, discarding excess, and
halve sheet crosswise. Stack halves and cover with a
damp paper towel. Make and halve 2 more *nori* egg
sheets in same manner, using a fresh sheet of wax
paper for each.

Have ready 6 rinsed and squeezed-dry paper
towels. On a work surface put 1 *nori* egg sheet half,
nori side up and with a long side close to you.
Spread 2½ tablespoons crab mixture over *nori*,
leaving a ¾-inch-wide *nori* border along far edge of
sheet. Beginning with long side closest to you,
tightly roll up sheet and wrap in 1 damp paper towel.
Make 5 more rolls in same manner. *Rolls may be
made 1 day ahead and chilled, wrapped in damp
paper towels in a sealable plastic bag.*

Make dipping sauce:

In a bowl stir together soy sauce, *mirin*, and water.

Gently unwrap rolls from paper towels and put,
seam sides down, on cutting board. With a sharp
knife trim ends and halve rolls crosswise. Cut each
half into 3 pieces and top each piece with a small
mound of *tobiko* and/or caviar.

Serve rolls with dipping sauce. Makes 36 rolls.

PHOTO ON PAGE 59

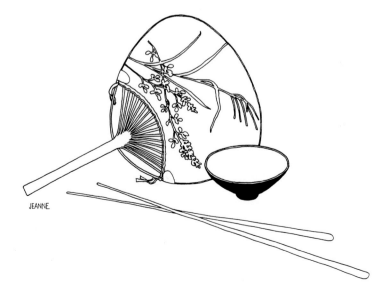

JEANNE

ROASTED GARLIC-PEA PURÉE ON SOURDOUGH CROÛTES

1 sourdough baguette
¼ cup extra-virgin olive oil
2 large heads garlic
a large piece Parmigiano-Reggiano (about
    ¾ pound)
two 10-ounce packages frozen peas,
    thawed
3 tablespoons water
2 teaspoons fresh lemon juice,
    or to taste
24 small arugula leaves

Preheat oven to 400° F.

Diagonally cut twenty-four ¼-inch-thick slices from baguette with a serrated knife and arrange in one layer on a large baking sheet. Lightly brush tops of slices with about 1 tablespoon oil total and season with salt and pepper. Bake baguette slices in middle of oven 5 minutes, or until golden, and transfer to a rack to cool.

Separate garlic heads into cloves, discarding loose papery outer skin but keeping skin on cloves intact, and wrap together in foil, crimping seams to seal tightly. Roast garlic in middle of oven 30 minutes, or until soft. Unwrap garlic and cool slightly. Peel skin from each clove. Finely grate enough Parmigiano-Reggiano to measure ¼ cup and chill remainder, wrapped in plastic wrap.

In a saucepan cook peas in water, stirring, until just tender and heated through. In a food processor purée warm peas, garlic, grated cheese, lemon juice, 1 tablespoon oil, and salt and pepper to taste until smooth. Transfer garlic-pea purée to a bowl and cool completely. *Garlic-pea purée may be made 1 day ahead and chilled, covered. Bring purée to room temperature before using and season with salt and pepper to taste.*

With a vegetable peeler shave 24 thin slices from chilled piece of Parmigiano-Reggiano. Spread about 1 heaping tablespoon garlic-pea purée on each toast and top with an arugula leaf and a Parmigiano-Reggiano shaving.

Serve toasts drizzled with remaining oil. Makes 24 hors d'oeuvres.

PHOTO ON PAGE 62

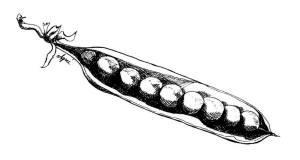

CRAB WITH DILL ON CAYENNE TOASTS

For toasts
6 slices firm white sandwich bread
3 tablespoons unsalted butter
⅛ teaspoon cayenne
¼ teaspoon salt

6 ounces jumbo lump crab meat
1 tablespoon minced shallot
1 tablespoon chopped fresh dill leaves
2 tablespoons mayonnaise
2 tablespoons sour cream
2 teaspoons fresh lemon juice

Garnish: 24 fresh dill sprigs

Make toasts:
Preheat oven to 350° F.

Stack bread slices and cut off crusts. Quarter slices to make twenty-four 1½-inch squares and arrange squares on a baking sheet. In a small saucepan melt butter and stir in cayenne and salt. Brush tops of squares with butter mixture and bake in middle of oven until pale golden, about 10 minutes. Cool toasts on a rack. *Toasts may be made 1 day ahead and kept in an airtight container at room temperature.*

Pick over crab meat to remove any bits of shell and cartilage (being careful not to break up lumps). In a bowl stir together remaining ingredients with salt to taste and gently stir in crab. *Crab mixture may be made 6 hours ahead and chilled, covered.*

Just before serving, mound about ½ tablespoon crab mixture on each toast and garnish with dill. Makes 24 canapés.

PHOTO ON PAGE 74

EDAMAME ◗

SOYBEANS IN THE POD

Sweet, delicious young soybeans, which appear fresh in markets in Japan throughout the summer (they are available frozen in the U.S.), make great hors d'oeuvres. They are packed with protein and fun to eat—the slightly fuzzy green pods tickle your lips as you gently suck the beans into your mouth. Provide bowls for the empty pods.

a 1-pound bag frozen *edamame** (soybeans
   in the pod)
coarse salt to taste

*available at Japanese markets and by mail order
   from Uwajimaya, (800) 889-1928

Fill a 5-quart kettle three fourths full with water and bring to a boil. Have ready a bowl of ice and cold water. Cook frozen *edamame* in boiling water until bright green, 2 to 3 minutes, and transfer with a slotted spoon to ice water to stop cooking. Drain *edamame* well and trim stem ends of pods for easier eating. *Edamame may be prepared 4 hours ahead and kept in a bowl, covered with a damp paper towel and plastic wrap, at cool room temperature.*

Just before serving, toss *edamame* with salt. Serves 6 as an hors d'oeuvre.

PHOTO ON PAGE 59

GOAT CHEESE AND TOMATO TART
IN A CORNMEAL CRUST

For crust
1½ sticks (¾ cup) cold unsalted butter
1 cup all-purpose flour
¾ cup yellow cornmeal
1 teaspoon salt
3 tablespoons ice water
pie weights or raw rice for
   weighting crust
For custard
½ cup packed fresh basil leaves
7 ounces mild soft goat cheese,
   softened
¾ stick (6 tablespoons) unsalted butter,
   well softened
½ cup sour cream
2 large eggs

¾ pound vine-ripened cherry tomatoes
   (preferably red)

Make crust:
Cut butter into pieces.

In a food processor pulse together flour, cornmeal, and salt. Add butter and pulse until mixture resembles coarse meal. Add ice water and pulse until incorporated and mixture just forms a dough. Press dough evenly into bottom and up sides of a 10½- by 7- by 1-inch rectangular tart pan with a removable fluted rim or a 10- by 1-inch round tart pan with a removable rim and roll a rolling pin over rim of pan to trim dough flush with rim. *Chill crust about 20 minutes, or until firm.*

While crust is chilling, preheat oven to 375° F.

Line crust with foil and fill with pie weights or raw rice. Bake crust in lower third of oven until edge is set, 10 minutes. Carefully remove foil and weights or rice and bake crust 5 minutes more, or until just dry. Leave oven on and cool crust in pan on a rack (crust may crack slightly). *Crust may be made 1 day ahead and kept, loosely covered with plastic wrap, at room temperature.*
Make custard:

Chop basil. In a bowl whisk together basil and remaining custard ingredients and season with salt and pepper.

Pour custard into crust, spreading evenly. Halve tomatoes and arrange, cut sides up, in one layer on custard, pressing lightly into custard. Season tomatoes with salt and pepper and bake tart in lower third of oven until custard is just set, about 25 minutes. Cool tart to warm in pan on rack. *Tart may be made 1 day ahead and cooled completely before being chilled, covered, in tart pan. Reheat tart, uncovered, in a 350° F. oven or bring to room temperature before serving.*

Carefully remove rim from pan. Cut tart into roughly 2-inch pieces and serve warm or at room temperature. Makes about 36 hors d'oeuvres.

PHOTO ON PAGE 62

Herbed Goat Cheese Toasts ◌

1 small garlic clove
⅛ teaspoon salt, or to taste
½ teaspoon minced fresh rosemary leaves
½ cup soft mild goat cheese
1½ tablespoons extra-virgin olive oil
freshly ground black pepper
   to taste
2 slices country-style bread (about
   6½ by 3 inches each)

Mince garlic and mash to a paste with salt. In a small bowl stir together garlic paste, rosemary, goat cheese, olive oil, and pepper. Toast bread and cut each slice into 4 pieces. Spread herbed goat cheese on toasts. Serves 2 as an hors d'oeuvre.

Portabella Mushroom and Dried Tomato Bruschetta ◌

¼ cup dried tomatoes
1 cup water
1 teaspoon balsamic vinegar
2 portabella mushroom caps (about ¾ pound)
2 garlic cloves
3 tablespoons olive oil
2 slices crusty Italian bread

In a small saucepan simmer tomatoes in water, uncovered, until tender, about 10 minutes. In a blender purée tomatoes, cooking liquid, and vinegar until smooth (use caution when blending hot liquids) and season with salt and pepper.

Cut mushrooms into ¼-inch-thick slices and mince garlic. In a large skillet heat 2 tablespoons oil over moderate heat until hot but not smoking and cook mushrooms and garlic with salt and pepper to taste, stirring, until liquid mushrooms give off is evaporated, about 5 minutes. Remove skillet from heat and toss mushrooms with remaining tablespoon oil. Keep mushrooms warm, covered.

Toast bread and spread with tomato purée. Top purée with mushrooms. Serves 2 generously as an hors d'oeuvre.

Fried Okra Poppers ◌

24 Ritz crackers (about 3 ounces)
¼ cup all-purpose flour
1 large egg
2 ounces chilled pepper Jack cheese
12 medium okra
2 cups corn oil or other vegetable oil
   for frying

Accompaniment: prepared salsa

In a food processor finely grind crackers. In a shallow bowl whisk together cracker crumbs, flour, and salt to taste. In another shallow bowl beat egg. Cut pepper Jack cheese into twelve 1½- by ½- by ¼-inch pieces.

With a sharp knife cut a 2-inch slit lengthwise on side of each okra. With fingers gently pull slit slightly open and insert a slice of cheese. Transfer okra to a plate and chill 5 minutes.

Working in batches of 4, dip stuffed okra in egg to coat, letting excess drip off, and roll in cracker crumb mixture, shaking off excess. Arrange okra in one layer on plate as coated and chill 5 minutes.

In a deep 10-inch heavy skillet heat oil over moderate heat until hot but not smoking and fry okra, 4 at a time, turning them, until golden brown, 1 to 2 minutes. With a slotted spoon transfer okra as fried to paper towels to drain.

Season okra with salt and serve immediately with salsa. Makes 12 poppers.

Jícama and Cucumber Chili Spears ◔

Jícama spears with lime juice and chili powder are a popular street snack in Mexico—crunchy, sour, and spicy.

a ½-pound piece *jícama*
½ English cucumber
2 teaspoons fresh lime juice
⅛ teaspoon chili powder
a pinch cayenne
coarse salt to taste

Peel *jícama* and seed cucumber. Cut *jícama* and cucumber into roughly 2½- by ¼-inch spears and in a bowl toss with remaining ingredients. Serves 2 as an hors d'oeuvre.

Green Olives Stuffed with Chili Almonds ◔

a 10-ounce jar pitted large green olives (about 24)
2 tablespoons olive oil
1¼ teaspoons chili powder
24 whole almonds with skins (about ¼ cup)

Preheat oven to 375° F.

In a large sieve rinse olives and drain well. In a bowl stir together ½ teaspoon oil and ½ teaspoon chili powder and add almonds, tossing to coat. Transfer almonds to a baking sheet and toast in middle of oven until fragrant and a couple of shades darker, 8 to 10 minutes. Cool almonds just until they can be handled and stuff each olive with an almond. In bowl toss olives with remaining oil and chili powder. *Olives may be made 1 day ahead and kept, covered, at cool room temperature (almonds will begin to soften after 4 hours).* Makes about 1½ cups.

Herbed Kalamata Olives ◔+

1 teaspoon coriander seeds
two 7-ounce jars Kalamata or other brine-cured
  black olives (about 3 cups)
½ lemon
8 fresh thyme sprigs
1½ cups olive oil

In a dry small heavy skillet toast seeds over moderate heat, shaking skillet, until fragrant, about 1 minute, and cool. With a mortar and pestle or with bottom of a heavy skillet coarsely crush seeds. Drain olives and thinly slice lemon. With flat side of a large knife lightly bruise thyme and in a bowl stir together all ingredients. *Marinate olives, covered and chilled, at least 3 days and up to 1 week. Bring olives to room temperature, about 15 minutes, before serving.* Makes about 3 cups.

Radishes with Goat Cheese ◔

½ cup soft mild goat cheese, softened
3 tablespoons heavy cream
12 large radishes with tops

Garnish: 24 small fresh chervil sprigs

In a small bowl stir together goat cheese, cream, and salt and pepper to taste until combined and transfer to a pastry bag fitted with a ¼-inch tip. (Alternatively, transfer mixture to a small heavy-duty sealable plastic bag and press out excess air. Snip off 1 corner, making a small hole.) *Cheese mixture may be made 2 days ahead and chilled in bag. Bring cheese mixture to room temperature before proceeding.*

Trim radish tops to ½ inch and halve radishes lengthwise. Pipe mixture onto radish halves.

Garnish hors d'oeuvres with chervil. Makes 24 hors d'oeuvres.

PHOTO ON PAGE 33

Spicy Crunch Mix ◔

6 large shallots (about ½ pound)
2 cups vegetable oil
¼ teaspoon cayenne, or to taste
½ teaspoon ground cumin
1 cup unseasoned freeze-dried peas*
1 cup unseasoned dry-roasted soybeans*

*available at specialty foods shops, some natural
  foods stores and supermarkets, and by mail
  order from Just Tomatoes, (800) 537-1985

Cut shallots crosswise into ¼-inch-thick slices. In a deep 12-inch heavy skillet heat oil over moderately high heat until hot but not smoking and fry shallots, stirring occasionally, until golden brown, about 7 minutes. Transfer shallots with a slotted spoon to paper towels to drain and season with salt. Pour off all but about 1½ tablespoons oil from skillet and into skillet stir cayenne and cumin. Cook spices over moderate heat, stirring, until fragrant, about 10 seconds. Remove skillet from heat and cool seasoned oil to room temperature.

Add shallots, peas, soybeans, and salt and pepper to taste to seasoned oil, tossing to combine. *Mix may be made 1 day ahead and kept in an airtight container at room temperature.* Makes about 3 cups.

DIPS AND SPREADS

CHICKEN LIVER PÂTÉ ◔

1 small onion
½ pound chicken livers
⅓ cup chicken broth
¼ teaspoon ground allspice
3 tablespoons unsalted butter, softened
½ teaspoon Cognac, or to taste
½ teaspoon salt
3 tablespoons well-chilled heavy cream

Accompaniment: crackers or toasts

Thinly slice onion. In a small saucepan combine onion, chicken livers, broth, and allspice and simmer, stirring occasionally, 10 minutes, or until chicken livers are cooked through. Drain liver mixture in a sieve and in a food processor purée with butter, Cognac, and salt until smooth. To facilitate cooling, transfer pâté to a plate and spread. Chill pâté in freezer, its surface covered with plastic wrap, 10 minutes.

In a small bowl whisk cream until it holds stiff peaks and fold in pâté. Transfer pâté to a ramekin and chill in freezer, covered, 15 minutes.

Serve pâté with crackers or toasts. Serves 2 as an hors d'oeuvre.

HERBED BEAN SPREAD WITH BAGUETTE TOASTS ◔

For toasts
1 baguette (about 22 inches)
½ stick (¼ cup) unsalted butter
For spread
two 19-ounce cans white beans such as *cannellini*
1 cup packed fresh flat-leafed parsley leaves
2 large garlic cloves
1 teaspoon salt
2 teaspoons minced fresh thyme leaves
2 teaspoons drained capers
3 tablespoons fresh lemon juice
6 tablespoons extra-virgin olive oil

Make toasts:
Preheat oven to 375° F.
Cut baguette crosswise into ¼-inch-thick slices. In a saucepan melt butter with salt to taste over moderate heat and brush butter on one side of each slice. Arrange baguette slices, buttered sides up, on 2 large baking sheets and toast in upper and middle thirds of oven until golden, about 12 minutes. *Toasts may be made 2 days ahead and kept in an airtight container.*

Make spread:
Drain beans in a colander. Gently rinse beans and drain well. Mince parsley. In a food processor blend together all spread ingredients except oil until smooth. With motor running, add oil in a slow stream, blending until incorporated, and season spread with salt and pepper. *Spread may be made 1 day ahead and chilled, covered. Bring spread to room temperature before serving.* Makes about 3½ cups spread and about 75 toasts.

PHOTO ON PAGE 17

ASPARAGUS, CUCUMBER, AND SUGAR SNAP PEAS WITH HERB GARLIC DIP ☺+

For dip
2½ cups plain yogurt (about 24 ounces)
1 cup fresh flat-leafed parsley leaves
1 tablespoon chopped fresh tarragon leaves
½ teaspoon minced garlic
2 tablespoons fresh lemon juice

1 pound thin asparagus
½ pound sugar snap peas
3 Kirby cucumbers
1 tablespoon extra-virgin olive oil

Make dip:
In a cheesecloth-lined sieve or colander set over a bowl drain yogurt, covered and chilled, at least 8 hours and up to 1 day. Discard liquid in bowl and in a food processor pulse yogurt with remaining dip ingredients and salt and pepper to taste until herbs are finely chopped and yogurt is pale green. *Dip may be made 1 day ahead and chilled, covered.*

Have ready a bowl of ice and cold water. Trim asparagus and peas. In a large saucepan of boiling salted water blanch asparagus 1 minute and transfer with tongs to ice water to stop cooking. Drain asparagus well in a colander and pat dry. Return water in saucepan to a boil and blanch peas 30 seconds. Drain peas in a sieve and plunge into ice water to stop cooking. Drain peas well and pat dry. *Asparagus and peas may be blanched 1 day ahead and chilled in a sealable plastic bag.* Cut cucumbers lengthwise into spears.

Drizzle oil over dip and serve with vegetables. Serves 8 as an hors d'oeuvre.

PHOTO ON PAGE 47

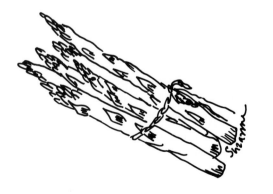

AVOCADO AND WHITE BEAN SALSA ☺

a 16-ounce can small white beans
    such as navy
1 firm-ripe California avocado
1 vine-ripened tomato
½ medium red onion
2 tablespoons fresh lime juice
1 teaspoon extra-virgin olive oil

Accompaniment: tortilla chips

Rinse and drain enough beans to measure ½ cup and reserve remainder for another use. Halve, pit, and peel avocado. Finely chop avocado, tomato, and onion and fold together with beans, lime juice, oil, and salt to taste.

Serve salsa with chips. Serves 2.

GRILLED EGGPLANT SPREAD

4 pounds medium eggplants
1 small red onion
2 large garlic cloves
⅔ cup packed fresh flat-leafed parsley leaves
⅓ cup extra-virgin olive oil
3 tablespoons white-wine vinegar
3 tablespoons mayonnaise

Accompaniment: spiced pita toasts (recipe
    follows)

Prepare grill.

Pierce eggplants in several places with a fork and grill on a rack set 5 to 6 inches over glowing coals, turning them occasionally, until very soft, 30 to 40 minutes. (Alternatively, broil eggplants under a broiler about 6 inches from heat 30 to 40 minutes. Broiled eggplant will not have a smoky flavor.)

Transfer eggplants to a colander and, when cool enough to handle, quarter lengthwise. With a small knife remove and discard as many seeds as possible. Scrape flesh into a large sieve set over a bowl, discarding skin. *Drain eggplant, covered and chilled, 1 day.* Discard any juices from eggplant.

Mince onion and garlic and finely chop parsley. In a food processor pulse eggplant with onion, garlic, parsley, and remaining ingredients until coarsely puréed. Transfer spread to a bowl and season with salt and pepper. *Chill spread, covered, at least 3 hours and up to 3 days.*

Serve spread with pita toasts. Makes about 3 cups.

SPICED PITA TOASTS ☉

4 teaspoons cumin seeds
1 teaspoon kosher salt
2 teaspoons paprika
½ cup olive oil
six 6-inch pitas with pockets

Preheat oven to 400° F.

In a dry small heavy skillet toast seeds over moderate heat, shaking skillet, until fragrant, about 1 minute, and cool. In an electric coffee/spice grinder finely grind seeds with salt and paprika and in a bowl stir together with oil.

Split each pita into 2 rounds and brush rough sides with cumin oil. Cut each round into 8 wedges and arrange, rough sides up, on 2 large baking sheets. Bake wedges in upper and lower thirds of oven, switching position of sheets halfway through baking, until golden brown and crisp, about 8 minutes total. Cool pita toasts on racks. *Pita toasts keep in an airtight container at room temperature 5 days.* Makes 96 pita toasts.

GRILLED ZUCCHINI AND YOGURT DIP ☉

2 medium zucchini (about ¾ pound total)
1 small garlic clove
½ teaspoon salt
¼ cup plain yogurt
2 tablespoons mayonnaise
1 tablespoon minced fresh mint leaves
1 teaspoon fresh lemon juice

Accompaniment: tomato-rubbed *bruschetta*
   (recipe follows)

Prepare grill.
Cut zucchini lengthwise into ¼-inch-thick slices and grill on an oiled rack set 5 to 6 inches over

glowing coals until very tender, about 5 minutes on each side.

Mince garlic with salt and mash to a paste. Finely chop zucchini and stir into garlic paste with remaining ingredients.

Serve dip with *bruschetta*. Serves 2.

TOMATO-RUBBED BRUSCHETTA ☉

four ½-inch-thick diagonal slices Italian bread
   or baguette
1½ tablespoons extra-virgin olive oil
1 garlic clove
1 small vine-ripened tomato
¼ teaspoon paprika
kosher salt to taste

Prepare grill.
Brush bread slices on both sides with oil and grill on a rack set 5 to 6 inches over glowing coals until golden, about 1 minute on each side. While bread is grilling, halve garlic and tomato crosswise. Rub grilled bread with garlic and tomato to moisten it (you may have tomato left over) and sprinkle with paprika and salt. Serves 2.

CHEDDAR DIP ☉

2 pickled jalapeño chiles
3 cups grated sharp Cheddar
   (about 12 ounces)
⅔ cup beer (not dark)
⅓ cup sour cream
2 tablespoons mayonnaise
¾ teaspoon caraway seeds

Accompaniment: assorted crudités or crackers

Wearing rubber gloves, seed chiles if desired and finely chop. In a blender pulse Cheddar, beer, sour cream, mayonnaise, and caraway seeds, scraping down side occasionally, until smooth and creamy. Transfer dip to a bowl and stir in chiles. *Dip keeps, covered and chilled, 2 days.*

Serve dip with crudités or crackers. Makes about 2 cups.

PUMPKIN-SEED SPREAD ◐+

3½ cups hulled green pumpkin seeds*
    (about 1 pound)
2 dried *ancho* chiles* (about 1 ounce)
½ tablespoon cumin seeds
¼ teaspoon whole allspice
¼ teaspoon whole cloves
3 large garlic cloves
½ tablespoon dried oregano, crumbled
½ cup cider vinegar
1 cup olive oil
½ tablespoon kosher salt, or to taste

Accompaniment: mini *chapatis* (recipe follows)
    or whole-wheat pitas

*available at Latino markets, specialty foods
    shops, some supermarkets, and by mail order
    from Kitchen Market, (888) 468-4433

Heat a dry large heavy skillet (preferably cast iron) over moderate heat until hot and toast pumpkin seeds, stirring constantly, until they puff and begin to pop but do not brown, 3 to 5 minutes. Transfer pumpkin seeds to a plate to cool. In skillet toast *anchos*, pressing down with tongs, a few seconds on each side to make more pliable and transfer to a bowl. Remove skillet from heat. Cover chiles with hot water and soak, turning them occasionally, until softened, about 30 minutes.

While chiles are soaking, heat skillet over moderate heat. Cook cumin seeds, allspice, and cloves, stirring, until fragrant, about 1 minute, and transfer to another plate to cool. In an electric coffee/spice grinder grind spice mixture to a powder.

Transfer soaked chiles with tongs to a cutting board and reserve ½ cup soaking liquid. Wearing rubber gloves, remove stems and seeds and finely chop chiles. Mince garlic. In a food processor purée chiles, garlic, pumpkin seeds, spice mixture, oregano, vinegar, oil, salt, and reserved soaking liquid until smooth. *Spread may be made 3 days ahead and chilled, its surface covered with plastic wrap. Bring spread to room temperature before serving.*

Serve pumpkin-seed spread with mini *chapatis* or pitas. Makes about 4 cups.

PHOTO ON PAGE 36

MINI CHAPATIS
INDIAN WHOLE-WHEAT FLATBREAD

Chapatis, unleavened breads from India, are generally torn into pieces and used to scoop up cooked food.

1½ cups whole-wheat flour
¾ cup all-purpose flour plus additional
    if necessary
½ teaspoon salt
5 tablespoons cold unsalted butter (preferably
    clarified; procedure on page 91)
⅔ cup plus 3 tablespoons warm water
    (105°–115° F.)

In a bowl stir together whole-wheat flour, ¾ cup all-purpose flour, and salt. Cut 1 tablespoon butter into small pieces and with your fingertips rub into flour mixture until combined well. Add ⅔ cup warm water, stirring to form a dough, and if necessary stir in enough remaining water, 1 tablespoon at a time, to make dough pliable but not sticky. On a work surface knead dough, adding some additional flour if it becomes sticky or adding remaining water, 1 tablespoon at a time, if too dry, until very smooth, about 5 minutes. Form dough into a ball and put in a lightly oiled bowl, turning to coat. *Chill dough, covered with plastic wrap, at least 2 hours and up to 1 day. Let dough stand, still covered, at room temperature 15 minutes.*

Divide dough into 4 pieces and roll each piece into a ¾-inch-wide log (10 inches long). Cut each log crosswise into ¾-inch-thick pieces (about 13 pieces per log) and roll each into a ball. Transfer balls to a platter and cover with a damp kitchen towel.

On a lightly floured surface with a rolling pin roll out 5 balls, keeping remaining balls covered with towel, into 2½-inch rounds (about ⅛ inch thick). In a small saucepan melt remaining 4 tablespoons butter over low heat and keep warm.

Heat a well-seasoned cast-iron skillet or griddle over moderately low heat until hot. Brush skillet or griddle with some melted butter and cook rounds, turning them once or twice, until blistered and golden brown (bread will puff in spots), about 3 minutes total. Transfer *chapatis* to a large sheet of foil as cooked and wrap in foil. Roll out and cook more *chapatis* in same manner, wiping skillet or griddle clean between batches and stacking *chapatis* in foil as cooked. *Chapatis may be made 1 day ahead and chilled, wrapped well in foil. Reheat chapatis, wrapped in foil, in a 300° F. oven.* Makes about 52 *chapatis*.

PHOTO ON PAGE 36

ROQUEFORT DIP WITH APPLE, ENDIVE, AND CELERY HEARTS ◐

This dip is attractive served in a hollowed-out head of Castelfranco radicchio, a white and pink radicchio.

4 ounces *fromage blanc* or softened cream
    cheese (about ½ cup)
3 tablespoons milk
2 teaspoons medium-dry Sherry
4 ounces Roquefort (about 1 cup crumbled)
2 Belgian endives
12 inner celery ribs with leaves
1 medium head white *radicchio** (optional)
1 crisp red apple such as Gala or Fuji

*available at some specialty produce shops

If using *fromage blanc*, in a bowl stir together with milk and Sherry until smooth. If using cream cheese, with an electric mixer beat together with milk and Sherry until smooth. Crumble Roquefort and gently stir into mixture (being careful not to break up lumps). *Dip may be made 1 day ahead and chilled, covered.*

Have ready a large bowl of ice and cold water. Trim root ends of endives and separate leaves. Trim celery ribs to 4- to 6-inch lengths. Remove any discolored outer leaves from *radicchio* and trim root end slightly so *radicchio* stands upright. Put vegetables in bowl of ice water to crisp (and to help *radicchio* leaves open). *Let vegetables stand at least 15 minutes and up to 2 hours.*

In a colander drain *radicchio* and shake to remove water. Twist and pull out center leaves to form a "bowl." Spoon dip into *radicchio* or a small bowl.

In colander drain endive and celery and pat dry. Quarter apple and remove core. Cut quarters into thin wedges. Put some ice cubes in each of 2 wineglasses and stand endive, celery, and apple over ice.

Serve dip with apple, endive, and celery. Serves 8 as an hors d'oeuvre.

PHOTO ON PAGE 74

VINE LEAF—WRAPPED SHEEP'S-MILK RICOTTA WITH FENNEL AND OLIVES

Although we prefer the taste and texture of sheep's-milk ricotta, this recipe can be made using (whole-milk) cow's-milk ricotta, which should first be drained overnight in a cheesecloth-lined sieve set over a bowl. The grapevine leaves make for a beautiful presentation, but, because they haven't been softened in water, they should not be eaten.

1 large fennel bulb (about 1 pound)
2 tablespoons extra-virgin olive oil
⅓ cup pine nuts
⅓ cup golden raisins
⅓ cup Kalamata olives
¾ teaspoon salt
1 pound sheep's-milk ricotta* (about 2 cups; see note, above)
about 15 leaves from a 1-pound jar brine-packed grape leaves**

Accompaniments:
toasted thinly sliced rustic Italian bread
assorted brine-cured olives

*available at some specialty foods shops and by mail order from Old Chatham Sheepherding Company, (888) 743-3760

**available at specialty foods shops and some supermarkets

Trim fennel stalks flush with bulb, discarding stalks, and remove core. With a *mandoline* or other hand-held manual slicer cut bulb into very thin slices and coarsely chop. In a large skillet cook fennel in oil over moderate heat, stirring occasionally, until tender, about 10 minutes. In a dry small skillet toast pine nuts over moderately low heat, stirring occasionally, until just pale golden, about 5 minutes. Coarsely chop toasted pine nuts and raisins. Pit and chop olives.

In a bowl combine fennel, pine nuts, raisins, olives, salt, and pepper to taste. Add ricotta and gently toss together.

Drain grapevine leaves and pat dry. Line bottom and side of a 9-inch pie plate with a layer of overlapping leaves, leaving a 2-inch overhang. Spread ricotta mixture over leaves and fold overhang in toward center. Use more leaves to cover exposed ricotta. *Chill spread at least 1 hour and up to 3 days.*

Invert a platter over pie plate and invert leaf-covered spread onto platter. Peel back center leaves and serve spread chilled or at room temperature with toasts and olives. Serves 8 as an hors d'oeuvre.

PHOTO ON PAGE 71

BREADS

CIABATTA
ITALIAN "SLIPPER" BREAD

The inspiration for this recipe comes from Carol Field's ciabatta in The Italian Baker. *The ciabatta requires a simple sponge, but it takes only a few minutes to put together the day before making the bread. Though the dough is very wet and sticky, resist the temptation to add more flour. Note: For this recipe you will need a baking stone or unglazed "quarry" tiles, available at cookware shops and by mail order from The Baker's Catalogue, (800) 827-6836.*

For sponge
⅛ teaspoon active dry yeast
2 tablespoons warm water (105°–115° F.)
⅓ cup room-temperature water
1 cup bread flour*
For bread
½ teaspoon active dry yeast
2 tablespoons warm milk (105°–115° F.)
⅔ cup room-temperature water
1 tablespoon olive oil
2 cups bread flour*
1½ teaspoons salt

*available at many supermarkets and by mail order
   from The Baker's Catalogue, (800) 827-6836

Make sponge:
In a small bowl stir together yeast and warm water and let stand 5 minutes, or until creamy. In a bowl stir together yeast mixture, room-temperature water, and flour and stir 4 minutes. Cover bowl with plastic wrap. *Let sponge stand at cool room temperature at least 12 hours and up to 1 day.*

Make bread:
In a small bowl stir together yeast and milk and let stand 5 minutes, or until creamy. In bowl of a standing electric mixer fitted with dough hook blend together milk mixture, sponge, water, oil, and flour on low speed until flour is just moistened and beat dough on medium speed 3 minutes. Add salt and beat 4 minutes more. Scrape dough into an oiled bowl and cover with plastic wrap. *Let dough rise at room temperature until doubled in bulk, about 1½ hours. (Dough will be sticky and full of air bubbles.)*

Have ready a rimless baking sheet and 2 well-floured 12- by 6-inch sheets parchment paper. Turn dough out onto a well-floured work surface and cut in half. Transfer each half to a parchment sheet and form into an irregular oval about 9 inches long. Dimple loaves with floured fingers and dust tops with flour. Cover loaves with a damp kitchen towel. *Let loaves rise at room temperature until almost doubled in bulk, 1½ to 2 hours.*

At least 45 minutes before baking *ciabatta*, put a baking stone or 4 to 6 unglazed "quarry" tiles (see headnote) arranged close together on oven rack in lowest position in oven and preheat oven to 425° F.

Transfer 1 loaf on its parchment to baking sheet with a long side of loaf parallel to far edge of baking sheet. Line up far edge of baking sheet with far edge of stone or tiles, and tilt baking sheet to slide loaf with parchment onto back half of stone or tiles. Transfer remaining loaf to front half of stone or tiles in a similar manner. Bake *ciabatta* loaves 20 minutes, or until pale golden. With a large spatula transfer loaves to a rack to cool. Makes 2 loaves.

PHOTO ON PAGE 24

POPPY-SEED ONION CHEDDAR BREAD

2 medium onions
½ stick (¼ cup) unsalted butter
1½ teaspoons salt
2 cups all-purpose flour
1 cup yellow cornmeal
1 tablespoon dry mustard
1 tablespoon baking powder
3 tablespoons poppy seeds
3½ cups grated sharp Cheddar
   (about 14 ounces)
3 large eggs
1½ cups milk

Preheat oven to 350° F. Grease and flour a 9- by 5- by 3-inch loaf pan, knocking out excess flour.

Chop onions and in a large skillet cook in butter with ½ teaspoon salt over moderate heat, stirring occasionally, until softened and pale golden, about 15 minutes. Cool onions.

Into a bowl sift together flour, cornmeal, mustard, baking powder, and remaining teaspoon salt. Stir in poppy seeds and Cheddar. In a small bowl lightly beat eggs and stir in milk. Add milk mixture and onion mixture to flour mixture, stirring until just combined.

Pour batter into loaf pan. Bake bread 1¼ hours, or until a tester inserted in center comes out clean. Cool bread in pan on a rack 10 minutes. Turn out bread onto rack and cool completely. Makes 1 loaf.

SWEET-POTATO FOCACCIA WITH ANCHO CHILES

¾ pound sweet potato (about 1 large)
3½ to 4 cups bread flour
1½ teaspoons table salt
2 dried *ancho* chiles* (about 1 ounce)
two ¼-ounce packages active dry yeast
   (about 5 teaspoons total)
¾ cup warm water (105°–115° F.)
2½ tablespoons olive oil
½ cup freshly grated Parmesan
   (about 1½ ounces)
2 teaspoons coarse sea salt

*available at specialty foods shops and by mail
   order from Kitchen Market, (888) 468-4433

Halve sweet potato crosswise. In a saucepan cover potato with salted cold water by 1 inch and simmer until tender, about 30 minutes. Drain potato. Cool potato just until it can be handled and peel. In a bowl with a fork mash potato until smooth.

In another bowl whisk together 3½ cups flour and table salt. In a bowl cover *anchos* with hot water and soak, turning them occasionally, until softened, about 30 minutes. Transfer chiles with tongs to a cutting board and discard soaking liquid. Wearing rubber gloves, remove stems and seeds and finely chop chiles.

In bowl of a standing electric mixer stir yeast into ¾ cup warm water and let stand until foamy, about 5 minutes. Stir in potato, flour mixture, chiles, and 1½ tablespoons oil, stirring until a soft, slightly sticky dough forms. With dough hook attachment knead dough on moderate speed 8 minutes, or until smooth and elastic, adding remaining ½ cup flour, 2 tablespoons at a time, if dough is too sticky. (Alternatively, knead dough on a lightly floured surface until smooth and elastic, about 10 minutes.)

Move a rack to lowest position in oven and preheat oven to 400° F.

Form dough into a ball and transfer to a lightly oiled bowl, turning it to coat. Let dough stand, loosely covered with a kitchen towel, in a warm draft-free place until almost doubled in bulk, 20 to 30 minutes.

Lightly oil a 13- by 9- by 2-inch metal baking pan. Flatten dough to eliminate air bubbles and stretch and pat out to fit bottom of pan. Drizzle dough with remaining tablespoon oil and sprinkle with Parmesan and coarse salt. With your fingertips make small indentations all over dough and bake in oven 15 minutes, or until golden brown. Cool *focaccia* in pan on a rack. Serves 12.

PHOTO ON PAGE 38

BAKING POWDER BISCUITS ◯

These tender biscuits are especially light when made with cake flour.

2 cups cake flour (not self-rising) or
    all-purpose flour
1 tablespoon baking powder
½ teaspoon salt
¾ stick (6 tablespoons) cold unsalted
    butter
⅓ cup whole milk
⅔ cup heavy cream

Accompaniment: butter

Preheat oven to 425° F.

Into a large bowl sift together flour, baking powder, and salt. Cut butter into bits and with your fingertips or a pastry blender blend butter into flour mixture until mixture resembles coarse meal. Add milk and heavy cream, stirring with a wooden spoon until just combined (mixture will be wet).

Transfer dough to a well-floured surface and with floured hands turn dough to coat evenly. Knead dough gently 4 to 6 times, or just until smooth (do not overwork dough), and pat or roll out dough into an 8-inch round (slightly more than ½ inch thick).

Using a floured 2- to 2½-inch star-shaped or round cutter, cut out biscuits and arrange about 1 inch apart on baking sheets. Gently pat out or roll out dough scraps and cut out more biscuits in same manner.

Bake biscuits, 1 sheet at a time, in middle of oven until pale golden and cooked through, 10 to 12 minutes. Transfer biscuits as baked to a basket lined with a cloth and cover to keep warm and moist.

Serve biscuits with butter. Makes 16 to 24 baking powder biscuits.

PHOTO ON PAGE 54

SOUTHWESTERN CORN STICKS

For these tender corn sticks we used 2 cast-iron corn-stick pans, available at cookware shops and by mail order from Bridge Kitchenware, (800) 274-3435 or (212) 838-1901. Be sure to season the pans according to the manufacturer's instructions before using.

vegetable-oil cooking spray
1 stick (½ cup) unsalted butter,
    softened
½ cup sugar
4 large eggs
1 cup all-purpose flour
1 cup yellow cornmeal
2 tablespoons baking powder
½ cup drained canned diced green chiles
1½ cups (one 14¾-ounce can) canned
    creamed corn
½ cup grated Cheddar (about 2 ounces)
½ cup grated Monterey Jack cheese
    (about 2 ounces)
½ cup finely chopped dried tart cherries
    (about 2 ounces)

Preheat oven to 400° F. Generously spray 2 corn-stick pans (each with seven 5- by 1½-inch molds; see note, above) with cooking spray.

On a baking sheet heat corn-stick pans in middle of oven until hot, about 10 minutes.

While pans are heating, in a bowl with an electric mixer beat together butter and sugar until light and fluffy. Add eggs 1 at a time, beating well after each addition.

Into a bowl sift together flour, cornmeal, and baking powder and add to egg mixture, beating until just combined. Beat in chiles, corn, cheeses, and cherries until just combined (do not overbeat).

Carefully remove hot pans from oven and spoon a scant ¼ cup batter into each mold, spreading evenly. Bake corn sticks on baking sheet in middle of oven until golden brown, about 15 minutes. Cool corn sticks in pans on racks 15 minutes. Gently loosen edges of corn sticks with a sharp small knife and remove from pans, transferring to racks to cool. Clean pans and make about 10 more corn sticks in same manner. Makes about 24 corn sticks.

PHOTO ON PAGE 37

BLUEBERRY LEMON CORN MUFFINS ☺

paper muffin cup liners
½ stick (¼ cup) unsalted butter
¾ cup all-purpose flour
1½ teaspoons baking powder
½ cup yellow cornmeal
½ cup plus 1 tablespoon sugar
1 tablespoon freshly grated lemon zest
½ cup whole milk
2 large egg yolks
½ cup blueberries

Preheat oven to 375° F. and line six ⅓-cup muffin cups with paper liners.

Melt butter and cool. Into a bowl sift together flour and baking powder and whisk in cornmeal, ½ cup sugar, zest, and a generous pinch salt. In a bowl whisk together butter, milk, and yolks and add to flour mixture with half of blueberries, gently stirring until just combined.

Divide batter evenly among cups (batter will fill cups) and press remaining blueberries into tops of muffins. Sprinkle tops of muffins evenly with remaining tablespoon sugar. Bake muffins in middle of oven about 15 minutes, or until tops are golden and a tester comes out clean. Remove muffins from cups and cool on a rack. *Muffins keep in an airtight container at room temperature 2 days.* Serves 2.

CINNAMON SUGAR MUFFINS ☺

For cinnamon sugar topping
¼ cup sugar
1 teaspoon cinnamon

1 cup all-purpose flour
1½ teaspoons baking powder
½ teaspoon salt
¼ teaspoon freshly grated nutmeg
½ stick (¼ cup) unsalted butter, softened
⅓ cup sugar
1 large egg
⅓ cup milk

Make topping:
In a small bowl stir together sugar and cinnamon.

Preheat oven to 375° F. and butter six ⅓-cup muffin cups.

Into a bowl sift together flour, baking powder, salt, and nutmeg. In a bowl with an electric mixer beat together butter and sugar until light and fluffy. Beat in egg until combined well. Beat in flour mixture and add milk, beating until mixture is just combined.

Divide batter evenly among cups and sprinkle with topping. Bake muffins in middle of oven 15 to 20 minutes, or until a tester comes out clean. Remove muffins from cups and cool on a rack. *Muffins keep in an airtight container at room temperature 2 days.* Makes 6 muffins.

MUSTARD CHEDDAR CRACKERS

1 pound sharp Cheddar
2 sticks (1 cup) unsalted butter, softened
1 large egg yolk
¼ cup Dijon mustard
2 tablespoons dry mustard
¼ cup black* or yellow mustard seeds
2 teaspoons salt
2 cups all-purpose flour

*available at East Indian markets and by mail order from Kalustyan's, (212) 685-3451

Coarsely grate Cheddar. In a food processor blend butter and cheese until smooth. Add remaining ingredients, pulsing until just combined. In a bowl chill dough, covered, 15 minutes.

Halve dough and on a lightly floured surface roll into two 12-inch logs. *Chill logs, wrapped in wax paper and foil, until firm, at least 2 hours, and up to 1 week; or freeze logs up to 2 months.*

Preheat oven to 350° F.

With a sharp thin knife cut dough into ⅛-inch slices and arrange about 1 inch apart on greased baking sheets. Bake slices in batches in middle of oven until golden, about 12 minutes. Transfer crackers to racks to cool. *Crackers keep in an airtight container at room temperature 1 week.* Makes about 120 crackers.

SPICED PUMPKIN-SEED FLATBREAD

1 cup lukewarm water (about 100° F.)
1 tablespoon sugar
1 teaspoon active dry yeast
¾ stick (6 tablespoons) cold unsalted butter
2½ cups all-purpose flour
⅓ cup cornmeal
1 tablespoon pure chile powder* (preferably
   red New Mexican)
1 teaspoon table salt
1 cup hulled green pumpkin seeds* (about
   5 ounces)
1 large egg
2 tablespoons cold water
kosher salt for sprinkling

*available at Latino markets, natural foods stores,
   and some supermarkets and by mail order from
   Kitchen Market, (888) 468-4433

In a large bowl stir together lukewarm water,
sugar, and yeast and let stand until foamy, about 5
minutes. Cut butter into bits and stir into yeast
mixture with flour, cornmeal, chile powder, and
table salt, stirring until mixture just forms a dough.
On a lightly floured surface knead dough until
smooth and butter is incorporated, about 5 minutes.
Form dough into a ball and put in a lightly oiled
bowl, turning it to coat. *Chill dough, covered with
plastic wrap, 1 hour.*

Preheat oven to 400° F. and lightly flour 2 large
baking sheets.

Chop pumpkin seeds. (The finer they are chopped,
the thinner the flatbread will be.) In a small bowl
with a fork beat together egg and cold water until
combined well to make an egg wash. Divide dough
in half and chill one half, covered. On a lightly
floured surface with a floured rolling pin roll out
remaining half of dough into an ⅛-inch-thick rough
oval and sprinkle with half of pumpkin seeds. With
rolling pin press seeds into dough and roll dough as
thin as possible. Brush dough with some egg wash
and cut into irregular long thin wedges (about 6 by
1 inch). With a spatula transfer wedges to baking
sheets and sprinkle with kosher salt to taste.

Bake wedges in upper and lower thirds of oven,
switching position of sheets halfway through baking,
until crisp, 10 to 15 minutes total, and transfer
to racks to cool. Make more flatbread wedges in
same manner with chilled dough. *Flatbread wedges
may be made 3 days ahead and kept in an airtight
container at room temperature.* Makes about 50 flatbread wedges.

PHOTO ON PAGE 66

PEPPERED PITA CRISPS

two 10-inch very thin pitas with pockets or
   four 6-inch pitas with pockets
1 tablespoon Sichuan peppercorns*
¾ stick (6 tablespoons) unsalted butter
1 teaspoon coarse salt (preferably sea salt)

*available at Asian markets, some specialty foods
   shops, and by mail order from Uwajimaya,
   (800) 889-1928

Preheat oven to 400° F.

Split each pita into 2 rounds. With a mortar and
pestle or in an electric coffee/spice grinder finely
grind peppercorns. In a small saucepan melt butter
with peppercorns and salt and brush rough sides of
rounds with butter mixture. Cut rounds into long
narrow triangles and arrange, rough sides up, in
one layer on 2 large baking sheets. Bake pita triangles in upper and lower thirds of oven, switching
position of sheets halfway through baking, until
golden brown and crisp, about 5 minutes total. Transfer crisps to racks to cool. *Crisps may be made 1 day
ahead and kept in an airtight container at room
temperature.* Makes about 24 to 32 crisps, depending
on size of pitas.

PHOTO ON PAGE 45

BREAD CRUMBS FOR PASTA ☺

In parts of Italy these crumbs are sprinkled on pasta. They can also be used as a topping for vegetable dishes.

3 cups 1-inch cubes day-old bread
    (preferably whole-grain)
1 tablespoon extra-virgin olive oil

In a blender pulse bread cubes in 2 batches until coarsely ground. In a dry large cast-iron skillet toast bread over moderately low heat, stirring constantly, until golden and crisp, 10 to 20 minutes. In a bowl toss bread crumbs with oil and salt to taste. *Bread crumbs keep in an airtight container at room temperature 1 week.* Makes about 2 cups.

OATCAKES

These Scottish wafers are usually served with cheese, but they are also delicious with orange marmalade or honey.

2 cups old-fashioned rolled oats
2 sticks (1 cup) cold unsalted butter
2 cups whole-wheat flour
2 teaspoons baking powder
1½ tablespoons packed light brown sugar
1 teaspoon salt
½ cup milk

Preheat oven to 350° F. Butter 2 baking sheets.
In a food processor pulse oats until finely chopped. Cut butter into bits. Add butter to oats with all remaining ingredients except milk and pulse until mixture resembles coarse meal. Add milk and pulse until mixture just forms a dough.
On a lightly floured surface halve dough and wrap 1 half in plastic wrap. Roll out remaining dough ⅛ inch thick (about a 14-inch round) and with a 3-inch fluted round cutter cut out about 18 oatcakes.

On baking sheets arrange oatcakes about ¾ inch apart and bake in upper and lower thirds of oven, switching position of sheets halfway through baking, until pale golden, about 20 minutes total. Transfer oatcakes to a rack to cool completely. Make more oatcakes with remaining dough in same manner. *Oatcakes may be made 1 week ahead and kept in an airtight container at room temperature.* Makes about 36 oatcakes.

PHOTO ON PAGE 30

SKILLET-TOASTED MINI CROUTONS ☺

2 garlic cloves
1 cup olive oil
3 cups ¼-inch cubes day-old bread

Halve garlic cloves. In a 12-inch skillet heat oil with garlic over moderate heat until hot but not smoking and cook bread, stirring, until golden, about 5 minutes. With a slotted spoon transfer croutons to paper towels to drain and discard garlic. Season croutons with salt. *Croutons keep in an airtight container at room temperature 1 week.* Makes about 3 cups.

OVEN-BAKED PARMESAN CROUTONS ☺

3 cups ¼-inch cubes day-old bread
¼ cup olive oil
⅔ cup freshly grated Parmesan

Preheat oven to 350° F.
In a shallow baking pan toss bread with oil. Toss bread with Parmesan and bake in middle of oven, stirring occasionally, 30 minutes, or until golden. *Croutons keep in an airtight container at room temperature 1 week.* Makes about 3 cups.

SOUPS

CHEDDAR POTATO SOUP WITH BACON

4 bacon slices
1 large onion
1 pound boiling potatoes
¼ cup all-purpose flour
1¾ cups water
1½ cups chicken broth
¼ cup dry white wine
2 cups grated sharp Cheddar (about
   8 ounces)
2 tablespoons chopped fresh chives

Chop bacon and in a large heavy saucepan cook over moderate heat, stirring occasionally, until crisp. Transfer bacon with a slotted spoon to paper towels to drain, reserving fat in pan.

While bacon is cooking, finely chop onion. Peel potatoes and cut into ½-inch cubes. Cook onion in reserved bacon fat over moderate heat, stirring occasionally, until softened. In a measuring cup stir together flour and water and add to onion with potatoes and broth. Simmer mixture 5 minutes, or until potatoes are just tender. Add wine and simmer 1 minute.

Reduce heat to low and gradually stir in Cheddar (do not let boil).

Divide soup among 4 bowls and sprinkle with bacon and chives. Makes about 5 cups.

CURRIED BLACK-EYED PEA SOUP

1¼ cups dried black-eyed peas
5 bacon slices
1 medium onion
2 celery ribs
¼ teaspoon cayenne
½ teaspoon curry powder
½ teaspoon ground cumin
¼ teaspoon dried hot red pepper flakes

6 cups chicken broth
3 tablespoons chopped fresh cilantro leaves

Quick-soak black-eyed peas (procedure follows).
Coarsely chop bacon and finely chop onion. Thinly slice celery.

In a 5-quart kettle cook bacon over moderate heat, stirring occasionally, until golden, about 10 minutes. Add onion, celery, and spices and cook, stirring occasionally, until onion is softened. Add peas and broth and simmer, uncovered, until peas are tender, about 20 minutes. Season soup with salt and pepper.

In a blender purée 2 cups soup until smooth (use caution when blending hot liquids). Stir purée and cilantro into soup in kettle. Makes about 8 cups.

TO QUICK-SOAK DRIED BLACK-EYED PEAS

Pick over peas and in a saucepan cover with cold water by 2 inches. Bring water to a boil and boil peas 2 minutes. Remove pan from heat. *Soak peas 1 hour.* Drain peas in a sieve.

GOLDEN AND RED BEET SOUP

3 medium golden beets (about 1 pound with greens)
3 medium red beets (about 1 pound with greens)
1 large onion
2 tablespoons unsalted butter
4 cups water
2 teaspoons salt
2½ cups milk
6 tablespoons *crème fraîche* or sour cream
3 tablespoons chopped fresh dill leaves

Garnish: fresh dill sprigs

Trim beets (reserve greens for another use) and peel. Separately cut golden and red beets into ¼-inch-thick slices. Finely chop onion. In each of two 3-quart saucepans melt 1 tablespoon butter over moderate heat. Add red beets and half of onion to butter in one pan and golden beets and remaining onion to other. Cook beet mixtures, stirring, 5 minutes. Add 2 cups water and 1 teaspoon salt to each beet mixture and simmer, uncovered, 40 minutes, or until beets are very tender.

In a blender or food processor purée each mixture separately with 1¼ cups milk until smooth (use caution when blending hot liquids). Return soups to pans and reheat over moderate heat.

In a small bowl whisk together *crème fraîche* or sour cream and dill. Divide soups among 6 bowls, pouring them simultaneously into opposite sides of each bowl.

Serve soup topped with cream mixture and garnished with dill. Makes about 6 cups, serving 6.

CHICKEN SOUP WITH AVOCADO AND CRISPY TORTILLA STRIPS

1 small onion
2 garlic cloves
½ fresh jalapeño chile, or to taste
½ cup packed fresh cilantro leaves
2 chicken breast halves with bones and skin (about 1 pound)
3½ cups chicken broth
3 cups water
4 corn tortillas
½ cup vegetable oil
2 firm-ripe California avocados
2 tablespoons fresh lime juice

Coarsely chop onion and garlic. Wearing rubber gloves, finely chop jalapeño. Chop cilantro. Remove and discard skin from chicken.

In a 3-quart saucepan cook chicken with onion, garlic, jalapeño, 1 tablespoon cilantro, broth, and water at a bare simmer until just cooked through, about 15 minutes.

Transfer chicken to a cutting board with tongs and, when cool enough to handle, shred meat, discarding bones. Pour broth mixture through a fine sieve into a bowl and return to cleaned pan.

Halve tortillas and cut crosswise into ⅛-inch-wide strips. In an 8-inch skillet heat oil over moderately high heat until hot but not smoking and, working in 3 batches, fry tortilla strips, stirring gently, until golden. With tongs transfer strips as fried to paper towels to drain.

Halve, pit, and peel avocados and cut flesh into ½-inch cubes. Add chicken to broth and heat over moderate heat until hot. Add remaining cilantro, avocado, lime juice, and salt to taste.

Serve soup garnished with tortilla strips. Serves 6 as a first course or 4 as a main course.

NEW ENGLAND CLAM CHOWDER ◕

18 small hard-shelled clams such as littlenecks (less than 2 inches in diameter)
¾ cup cold water
1 bacon slice
½ small onion
1 medium boiling potato
1 tablespoon unsalted butter
½ cup half-and-half
1 tablespoon packed chopped fresh flat-leafed parsley leaves

Scrub clams well and put in a saucepan with water. Steam clams, covered, over moderately high heat 5 to 8 minutes, checking them every minute after 5 minutes and transferring them with tongs as they open to a bowl. Discard any clams that are unopened after 8 minutes and reserve cooking liquid. When clams are cool enough to handle, remove from shells and coarsely chop. Carefully pour reserved cooking liquid through a fine sieve into a small bowl, leaving any grit in pan.

Separately chop bacon and onion. Peel potato and cut into ¼-inch dice. In cleaned pan cook bacon in butter over moderate heat, stirring, until golden. Add onion and cook, stirring, until softened. Stir in potatoes and cooking liquid. Simmer mixture, covered, until potatoes are tender, about 3 minutes. Stir in clams, half-and-half, and pepper to taste and cook over moderate heat until heated through, about 1 minute (do not let boil). Stir in parsley. Serves 2.

CARAMELIZED LEEK SOUP

2 pounds leeks (about 2 bunches; use white
   and pale green parts only)
3 tablespoons unsalted butter
1¼ teaspoons sugar
¼ cup vermouth
3½ cups chicken broth

Garnish: 4 teaspoons finely sliced fresh chives
Accompaniment: raclette cheese toasts
   (recipe follows)

Halve leeks lengthwise and thinly slice crosswise. In a large bowl of cold water wash leeks well and lift from water into a large sieve to drain. In a 6-quart heavy kettle cook leeks in butter over moderately low heat, stirring occasionally, until some begin to turn golden, about 40 minutes. Stir in sugar and cook, stirring occasionally, 10 minutes. Stir in vermouth and cook, stirring occasionally, until liquid is evaporated and most leeks are golden, 10 to 15 minutes. Deglaze kettle with ½ cup broth and cook, stirring occasionally, 10 minutes more, until liquid is evaporated and leeks are deep golden. Add remaining 3 cups broth and bring soup just to a boil. Season soup with salt and pepper.

Serve soup, garnished with chives, with raclette cheese toasts. Makes about 5 cups, serving 4 as a first course.

PHOTO ON PAGE 14

RACLETTE CHEESE TOASTS ◔

a whole-grain baguette or other whole-grain
   country-style loaf
8 ounces cold raclette cheese*
4 teaspoons whole-grain mustard

*available at specialty foods shops and
   cheese stores

Preheat broiler.

Diagonally cut eight ½-inch-thick slices from bread, reserving remainder for another use. On a baking sheet toast one side of bread slices under broiler about 4 inches from heat and leave broiler on. Using a cheese plane thinly slice raclette. Turn bread over and spread ½ teaspoon mustard on untoasted side of each slice. Top toasts with cheese and broil until cheese is just melted, about 2 minutes. Makes 8 cheese toasts.

PHOTO ON PAGE 14

CHILLED LEMONGRASS-TOMATO SOUP

3 stalks fresh lemongrass*
6 cups tomato water (recipe follows)
1½ teaspoons unflavored gelatin
a 1-inch-thick slice watermelon
1 tablespoon finely chopped fresh chives
2 teaspoons finely chopped fresh mint leaves

*available at Southeast Asian markets, some
   specialty foods shops and supermarkets, and by
   mail order from Uwajimaya, (800) 889-1928

Discard 1 or 2 outer leaves of lemongrass and
trim root ends. Finely chop enough lemongrass from
lower 6 inches of stalks to measure ¼ cup total.

In a small saucepan combine lemongrass and 1 cup
tomato water and simmer, uncovered, 10 minutes.
Pour mixture through a fine sieve into another small
saucepan, discarding solids, and stir in gelatin. Heat
mixture over low heat, stirring, until gelatin is
dissolved. In a large bowl stir gelatin mixture into
remaining 5 cups tomato water. *Chill tomato-water
mixture, covered, at least 8 hours and up to 1 day.*
Discard rind and seeds from watermelon and finely
chop enough fruit to measure ¾ cup.

Divide soup among 6 bowls and just before
serving add watermelon, chives, and mint. Serves 6
as a first course.

TOMATO WATER

*In addition to using this pale-orange liquid as a base for
soup, add a dash to any summer recipes that call for a little
extra zest—its flavor is the very essence of tomato.*

4 pounds vine-ripened red tomatoes
   (about 10 medium)
1½ tablespoons kosher salt
two 18-inch-square pieces cheesecloth

Quarter tomatoes and in a food processor purée
with salt until smooth. Line a large sieve set over a
tall nonreactive kettle with cheesecloth and carefully
pour tomato purée into center of cheesecloth. Gather
sides of cheesecloth up over purée to form a large
sack and, without squeezing purée, gently gather
together upper thirds of cheesecloth to form a neck

(see drawings on this page). Carefully tie neck
securely with kitchen string. Tie sack to a wooden
spoon longer than diameter of kettle and remove
sieve. Put spoon across top of kettle, suspending
sack inside kettle and leaving enough room underneath sack so that it will not sit in tomato water that
accumulates. *Let sack hang in refrigerator at least
8 hours.*

Without squeezing sack, discard it and its con-
tents and transfer tomato water to a bowl. *Tomato
water keeps, covered and chilled, 4 days.* Makes
about 6 cups.

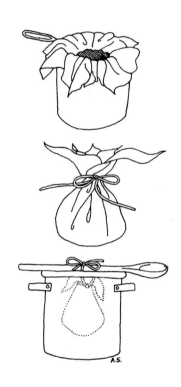

HAM AND BLACK-EYED PEA SOUP
WITH COLLARD GREENS ◐

1 medium onion
1 garlic clove
a 4-ounce piece cooked ham
2 tablespoons olive oil
½ pound collard greens
1 cup chicken broth (8 fluid ounces)
3 cups water
a 16-ounce can black-eyed peas (about
   1½ cups)
1 teaspoon cider vinegar

Chop onion and garlic and cut ham into ¼-inch dice. In a 3-quart saucepan cook onion, garlic, and ham in oil over moderate heat, stirring occasionally, until onion is pale golden.

While onion mixture is cooking, discard stems and center ribs from collards and finely chop leaves. Add collards, broth, and water to onion mixture and simmer until collards are tender, about 20 minutes.

Rinse and drain black-eyed peas. In a bowl mash half of peas with a fork. Stir mashed and whole peas into soup and simmer 5 minutes. Season soup with salt and pepper and stir in vinegar. Makes about 4 cups, serving 2 as a main course.

LOBSTER BISQUE

a 3-pound live lobster
1 medium onion
1 celery rib
1 carrot
1 vine-ripened tomato
1 head garlic
2 tablespoons olive oil
2 tablespoons chopped fresh tarragon leaves
2 tablespoons chopped fresh thyme leaves
1 bay leaf
8 black peppercorns
½ cup brandy
½ cup dry Sherry
4 cups fish stock*
¼ cup tomato paste
½ cup heavy cream
1½ tablespoons cornstarch
2 tablespoons water

*available at fish markets and some specialty
 foods shops

Fill a 6-quart kettle three fourths full with salted water and bring to a boil. Plunge lobster headfirst into water and cook, covered, over high heat 8 minutes. Transfer lobster with tongs to a large bowl and in a measuring cup reserve 2 cups cooking liquid. Let lobster stand until cool enough to handle. Working over a bowl to catch the juices, twist off tail and claws. Reserve tomalley and discard head sacs and any roe. Remove meat from claws and tail,

reserving shells and lobster body. (Lobster will not be cooked through.) Coarsely chop meat and transfer to bowl with juices. Chill lobster, covered.

Chop onion, celery, carrot, and tomato and halve garlic head crosswise. In a 6-quart heavy kettle heat oil over moderately high heat until hot but not smoking and sauté reserved lobster shells and body, stirring occasionally, 8 minutes. Add vegetables, garlic, herbs, peppercorns, brandy, and Sherry and simmer, stirring, until almost all liquid is evaporated, about 5 minutes. Add stock and reserved tomalley and cooking liquid. Simmer mixture, uncovered, stirring occasionally, 1 hour.

Pour mixture through a fine sieve into a large saucepan, pressing on and discarding solids. Whisk in tomato paste and simmer until reduced to about 3 cups, about 10 minutes. Add cream and simmer bisque 5 minutes. In a small bowl stir together cornstarch and water and whisk into bisque. Simmer bisque, stirring, 2 minutes. (Bisque will thicken slightly.) Add lobster meat with any reserved juices and simmer bisque 1 minute, or until lobster meat is just cooked through. Season bisque with salt and pepper. Makes about 5 cups, serving 4.

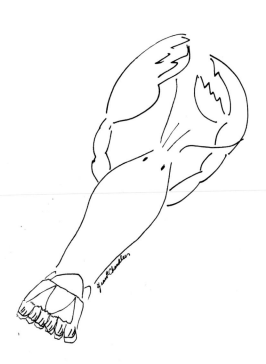

Sherried Cream of Portabella Mushroom Soup

¾ pound portabella mushrooms
1 small onion
1 tablespoon unsalted butter
1½ cups water
½ cup heavy cream
2 tablespoons medium-dry Sherry
2 tablespoons thinly sliced fresh chives

Quarter and thinly slice mushrooms and chop onion. In a heavy saucepan cook mushrooms and onion in butter over moderate heat, stirring occasionally, until softened and any liquid mushrooms give off is evaporated. Add water and cream and simmer 15 minutes. In a blender purée half of mixture (use caution when blending hot liquids) and stir purée, Sherry, and salt and pepper to taste into mixture remaining in pan. Heat soup until hot and stir in chives. Makes about 2½ cups, serving 2 as a first course.

Chilled Pumpkin and Lemongrass Soup with Crab Meat

a 2-pound piece pumpkin or butternut squash
1 onion
2 garlic cloves
1 large carrot
⅓ cup packed fresh cilantro leaves
2 fresh lemongrass stalks*
3 tablespoons vegetable oil
2 teaspoons Thai red curry paste*
1⅓ cups unsweetened coconut milk* (from a
    13½- to 14-ounce can)
7 cups chicken stock (recipe follows) or broth
3 fresh or thawed frozen *kaffir* lime leaves*
⅓ cup Asian fish sauce*, or to taste
For crab mixture
1 pound jumbo lump crab meat
½ cup packed fresh cilantro leaves
1 tablespoon fresh lemon juice

Garnish: 6 fresh cilantro sprigs

*available at Southeast Asian markets, some

specialty foods shops and supermarkets, and by mail order from Adriana's Caravan, (800) 316-0820, or Uwajimaya, (800) 889-1928

Peel pumpkin or squash with a sharp knife and discard seeds and stringy pulp. Cut pumpkin or squash into 1-inch pieces. Coarsely chop separately onion, garlic, carrot, and cilantro. Discard outer leaves from lemongrass and trim root ends. Finely chop enough of lower 6 inches of stalks to measure ⅓ cup, reserving remainder for another use.

In a large heavy kettle heat oil over moderately low heat until hot but not smoking and cook onion, garlic, lemongrass, and curry paste, stirring, until onion is softened. Add pumpkin or squash and carrot and cook, stirring, 3 minutes. Add coconut milk, stock or broth, cilantro, and lime leaves and simmer 30 minutes, or until vegetables are tender. Cool soup slightly and in a blender purée in batches (use caution when blending hot liquids), transferring to a large bowl. Stir in fish sauce and salt and pepper to taste and cool soup completely. *Chill soup, covered, until cold, at least 3 hours, and up to 2 days.*

Make crab mixture:

Pick over crab meat and transfer to a bowl. Finely chop ½ cup cilantro and stir into crab meat with lemon juice and salt and pepper to taste.

Ladle soup into 6 bowls and mound crab meat in center. Garnish each serving with a cilantro sprig. Makes about 14 cups, serving 6.

PHOTO ON PAGE 22

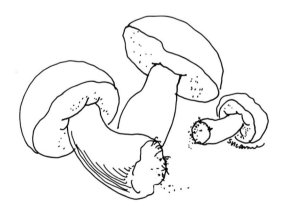

CHICKEN STOCK

2 onions
1 celery rib
2 carrots
3 pounds chicken wings, backs, necks,
    and/or bones
14½ cups cold water
2 whole cloves
½ teaspoon dried thyme, crumbled
4 garlic cloves, unpeeled
1 teaspoon salt
6 long fresh parsley sprigs
12 black peppercorns
1 bay leaf

Peel and halve onions. Halve celery rib and carrots. If using wings, cut each wing at joints into 3 pieces. In a stockpot or kettle (at least 6 quarts) combine chicken parts with 14 cups water and bring to a boil, skimming froth. Add remaining ½ cup water and bring chicken mixture to a simmer, skimming froth.

Stick 2 onion halves with 1 clove each and add to stockpot or kettle with celery, carrots, and remaining ingredients. Cook stock, partially covered, at a bare simmer, skimming froth, 3 hours.

Pour stock through a fine sieve into a large heatproof bowl and discard solids. If a more concentrated flavor is desired, in a large saucepan boil stock until reduced to desired concentration. Cool stock, uncovered. *Chicken stock keeps, covered and chilled 1 week, or frozen in an airtight container 3 months. Remove fat before using.* Makes about 10 cups.

EXOTIC MUSHROOM BROTH

5 shallots
2 garlic cloves
10 cups beef broth
6 cups water
1 cup dried morel mushrooms*
    (about 1 ounce)
1 cup dried *porcini* mushrooms*
    (about 1 ounce)
1 teaspoon fresh thyme leaves
8 ounces fresh *shiitake* mushrooms
¼ cup packed fresh flat-leafed parsley
    leaves
¼ cup medium-dry Sherry

*available at specialty foods shops and
    by mail order from Marché aux Delices,
    (888) 547-5471

Chop shallots and slice garlic. In a 6-quart kettle bring broth and water to a boil with shallots, garlic, dried mushrooms, and thyme and cook at a bare simmer 1 hour. Line a large sieve with a double thickness of cheesecloth or dampened paper towels and pour liquid through sieve into a large bowl. Press hard on solids and discard. *Broth may be made 3 days ahead and chilled, covered.*

Discard *shiitake* stems and thinly slice caps. In cleaned kettle simmer broth, *shiitake* caps, parsley, and Sherry, stirring occasionally, 10 minutes, or until mushrooms are tender, and season with salt and pepper. Makes about 12 cups.

PHOTO ON PAGE 29

FISH AND SHELLFISH

FISH

BAKED FLOUNDER FILLETS IN
LEMON-SOY VINAIGRETTE ◯

two 6-ounce flounder fillets
1 garlic clove
2 tablespoons fresh lemon juice
2 teaspoons soy sauce
½ teaspoon sugar
¼ teaspoon salt
2 tablespoons olive oil

Preheat oven to 450° F.

Arrange fillets in a ceramic or glass baking dish just large enough to hold them in one layer. Mince garlic and in a small bowl combine with lemon juice, soy sauce, sugar, and salt. Whisk in oil until emulsified and pour vinaigrette over fish.

Bake fish in middle of oven until just cooked through and no longer translucent, 5 to 7 minutes. Serves 2.

GRILLED MAHIMAHI WITH CRUSHED POTATOES,
ORANGE VINAIGRETTE, AND CILANTRO PESTO

This dish is photographed with honey-cumin plantain chips and steamed vegetables.

For orange vinaigrette
½ cup fresh orange juice
½ small fresh red or green Thai chile
   or ¼ fresh jalapeño chile
1 tablespoon fresh lime juice
1½ teaspoons red-wine vinegar
1 tablespoon chopped red onion
1 small garlic clove
½ teaspoon Dijon mustard
½ teaspoon chili powder

¼ cup extra-virgin olive oil
freshly ground black pepper to taste
For cilantro pesto
1 cup packed fresh cilantro leaves
1 tablespoon hulled green pumpkin seeds*
1 tablespoon fresh lime juice
1 garlic clove
1 teaspoon salt, or to taste
2 teaspoons freshly ground black pepper
2½ tablespoons olive oil
3 tablespoons water

six 6-ounce pieces skinless *mahimahi* fillet
about 2 tablespoons olive oil

Accompaniment: crushed potatoes (recipe follows)

*available at natural foods stores, specialty foods shops, Latino markets, and by mail order from Kitchen Market, (888) 468-4433

Make vinaigrette:

In a small saucepan simmer orange juice until reduced to a glaze (about 2 tablespoons), about 5 minutes. Wearing rubber gloves, discard seeds and ribs from chile. In a blender blend orange glaze, chile, lime juice, vinegar, onion, garlic, mustard, and chili powder 1 minute. With motor running, add oil in a stream and blend until smooth. Season vinaigrette with pepper and salt and transfer to a squeeze bottle or sealable plastic bag. *Vinaigrette may be made 1 day ahead and chilled, covered. Bring vinaigrette to room temperature before using.*

Make pesto:

In a blender combine cilantro, pumpkin seeds, lime juice, garlic, salt, and pepper. With motor running, add oil and water in a stream and purée until smooth. Transfer pesto to a squeeze bottle or a sealable plastic bag. *Cilantro pesto may be made 1 day ahead and chilled, covered. Bring pesto to room temperature before using.*

Pat *mahimahi* pieces dry. Season fish with salt and pepper and rub with oil to coat. Heat a well-seasoned ridged grill pan over moderate heat until hot and grill 3 pieces 4 minutes on each side, or until just cooked through. Transfer fish to a plate and keep warm, loosely covered. Grill remaining 3 pieces in same manner.

Mound potatoes on 6 heated large plates and top with fish. Cut a small hole in 1 corner of sealed plastic bags of vinaigrette and pesto, if using. Squeeze or drizzle vinaigrette and pesto decoratively over each serving. Serves 6.

PHOTO ON PAGE 23

CRUSHED POTATOES

2 russet (baking) potatoes (about 1¼ pounds total)
6 scallions
1 cup packed fresh flat-leafed parsley leaves·
¾ cup extra-virgin olive oil

Peel potatoes and quarter. In a saucepan cover potatoes with cold salted water by 1 inch and simmer 15 minutes, or until just tender. Drain potatoes in a colander and let stand 5 minutes. Finely chop white and light green parts of scallions. Finely chop parsley. In saucepan heat oil and chopped scallions over moderate heat until oil begins to sizzle and add potatoes. With a fork lightly crush potatoes into scallion oil (do not mash potatoes completely). Season potatoes with salt and pepper and stir in parsley. Serves 6.

GRILLED SALMON KEBABS WITH DILL

two 10-inch bamboo or metal skewers
a 10-ounce piece center-cut salmon fillet, skinned
1 medium zucchini
¼ cup dry white wine
2 tablespoons olive oil
1 tablespoon chopped fresh dill leaves
1 teaspoon minced garlic
6 vine-ripened cherry tomatoes

Prepare grill. If using bamboo skewers, soak in warm water 15 minutes.

Pat salmon dry and cut into 8 cubes. Cut zucchini into ¾-inch-thick rounds. In a bowl stir together wine, oil, dill, and garlic. Add salmon, zucchini, and tomatoes, tossing to coat, and let stand, covered, at room temperature 15 minutes.

Alternately thread salmon, zucchini, and tomatoes onto skewers and season with salt and pepper. Grill kebabs on an oiled rack set 5 to 6 inches over glowing coals, turning kebabs, until salmon is just cooked through, 6 to 8 minutes. (Alternatively, kebabs may be broiled under a preheated broiler 3 to 4 inches from heat.) Serves 2.

RED SNAPPER WITH SPICY SOY GLAZE ON SAUTÉED VEGETABLES AND SWEET POTATO

2 medium carrots
1 yellow bell pepper
3 ounces snow peas (about ¾ cup)
1 cup fresh cilantro sprigs
a ¾-pound sweet potato
¾ cup spicy soy glaze (recipe follows)
2 teaspoons vegetable oil
four 4-ounce red snapper or grouper fillets
   with skin
2 cups thinly sliced Napa cabbage
¼ cup thinly sliced red onion
1 tablespoon seasoned rice vinegar

Garnish: lime wedges

Separately cut carrots and bell pepper into thin strips and diagonally cut snow peas into ½-inch pieces. Chop cilantro. Peel sweet potato and, if desired, with a channel knife cut 4 lengthwise grooves (one every quarter turn). Cut potato crosswise into 12 slices (about ¼ inch thick) and in a steamer set over 1 inch boiling water steam slices, in one layer if possible, covered, until just cooked through but not falling apart, about 8 minutes.

Remove steamer from heat and season potato with salt and pepper. Keep potato warm in steamer, covered. In a small saucepan heat glaze and keep warm, covered.

Preheat oven to 275° F.

In a nonstick skillet heat ½ teaspoon oil over moderately high heat until hot but not smoking and sauté 2 fillets, skin sides down, pressing on fish with a metal spatula to help skin brown evenly, until skin is golden brown, about 1 minute. With spatula turn fillets over and sauté until golden, about 30 seconds more. Transfer fillets, skin sides up, to a nonstick baking pan and sauté remaining 2 fillets in ½ teaspoon oil in same manner. Bake fish in middle of oven until just cooked through, about 3 minutes.

While fish is baking, in a large nonstick skillet heat ½ teaspoon remaining oil over moderately high heat until hot but not smoking and sauté carrots until barely tender, about 2 minutes. Add remaining ½ teaspoon oil, bell pepper, and snow peas and sauté vegetables, stirring, until just tender, about 30 seconds. Add cabbage and onion and sauté, stirring, until just tender, about 1 minute. Immediately transfer sautéed vegetables to a bowl and toss with cilantro, vinegar, and salt and pepper to taste.

Divide potato among 4 plates and top with vegetables. Put fillets, skin sides up, on vegetables and drizzle with some glaze.

Garnish plates with lime wedges and serve remaining glaze on the side. Serves 4.

PHOTO ON PAGE 85

☞ each serving, without skin, about 390 calories
and 4 grams fat

SPICY SOY GLAZE ◑

½ pound shallots (about 5 large)
½ teaspoon vegetable oil
½ cup soy sauce
¼ cup water
3 tablespoons sugar
2 tablespoons plum or apricot jam
1 tablespoon finely grated peeled fresh gingerroot
2 teaspoons minced garlic
⅛ teaspoon ground allspice
¼ teaspoon dried hot red pepper flakes
1 tablespoon fresh lime juice
½ teaspoon freshly grated lime zest

Chop enough shallots to measure 1 cup. In a heavy saucepan cook shallots in oil over moderate heat, stirring, until softened, about 3 minutes. Stir in soy sauce, water, sugar, jam, gingerroot, garlic, allspice, and red pepper flakes and simmer, stirring occasionally, until reduced to about ¾ cup, about 20 minutes. Stir in lime juice and zest. *Glaze may be made 2 days ahead and cooled completely before being chilled, covered.* Makes about ¾ cup.

☞ each 3-tablespoon serving about 129 calories
and 1 gram fat

SAUTÉED SALMON WITH FIVE-SPICE LIME BUTTER ◑

two 6-ounce pieces center-cut salmon fillet
    with skin
1 tablespoon vegetable oil
1 tablespoon unsalted butter
a scant ½ teaspoon five-spice powder*
2 teaspoons fresh lime juice

*available at Asian markets and many
    supermarkets

Pat salmon pieces dry and season with salt and pepper. In a 10- to 12-inch nonstick skillet heat oil over moderately high heat until hot but not smoking and sauté salmon, skin sides down, 2 minutes. Reduce heat to moderate and cook salmon 3 minutes more. Turn salmon over and sauté over moderately high heat 2 minutes. Reduce heat to moderate and cook salmon until just cooked through, about 2 minutes more.

Transfer salmon to 2 plates. Pour off oil from skillet and carefully wipe out skillet with paper towels. In skillet melt butter with five-spice powder and salt to taste, stirring. Stir in lime juice and spoon lime butter over salmon. Serves 2.

SLOW-ROASTED SALMON WITH MUSTARD PARSLEY GLAZE

Slow roasting gives a firm-bodied fish like salmon such a tender texture that it practically melts in your mouth. When you test for doneness, do not look for flakiness but rather a change in appearance—from translucent to opaque.

For glaze
1 tablespoon drained candied lime zest
    (procedure follows)
¾ stick (6 tablespoons) unsalted butter, softened
3 tablespoons fine dry bread crumbs
2 tablespoons chopped fresh flat-leafed parsley
    leaves
1 tablespoon mustard seeds
1 tablespoon fresh lime juice
2 teaspoons Dijon mustard
1 teaspoon honey

eight 5-ounce pieces skinless center-cut
    salmon fillet
½ teaspoon freshly ground white pepper

Preheat oven to 225° F.
Make glaze:
Finely chop enough candied lime zest to measure 1½ teaspoons. In a bowl stir together zest with remaining glaze ingredients until combined well.

Trim any dark flesh from skinned sides of salmon. In a large roasting pan arrange salmon, skinned sides down, without crowding, and season with white pepper and salt. Spread glaze over salmon and roast in middle of oven 25 to 30 minutes, or until fish is just cooked through (see headnote). Serves 8.

PHOTO ON PAGE 41

CANDIED LIME ZEST ◑

1 lime
½ cup water
½ cup sugar

With a vegetable peeler remove zest from lime in long ½-inch-wide pieces. Diagonally cut pieces crosswise into very thin julienne strips.

In a small saucepan bring water and sugar to a boil, stirring until sugar is dissolved. Add zest and simmer 10 minutes. Cool zest in syrup. *Candied zest may be made 1 week ahead and chilled in an airtight container.* Makes about 2 tablespoons.

POACHED SALMON WITH TARRAGON SAUCE AND FINGERLING POTATOES

This dish may be served warm or at room temperature.

For sauce
2 large bunches fresh tarragon
1 large bunch fresh chives (about ⅔ ounce)
1 large shallot
¾ cup fresh flat-leafed parsley leaves
1 cup mayonnaise
⅓ cup rice vinegar (not seasoned)
2 teaspoons Dijon mustard

2½ cups dry white wine
2½ cups water
a 2½- to 3-pound salmon fillet with skin
1½ pounds pink fingerling or other new potatoes

Garnish: ½ pound cooked sugar snap peas, diagonally cut into thirds

Make sauce:
Pick enough tarragon leaves to measure ½ cup (do not pack). Chop enough chives to measure ⅓ cup. Coarsely chop shallot. In a food processor purée tarragon, chives, and shallot with remaining sauce ingredients until smooth and season with salt and pepper. *Sauce may be made 1 day ahead and chilled, covered. Bring sauce to cool room temperature before serving.*

In a deep 10-inch skillet bring wine and water to a simmer, covered. Cut salmon into 6 pieces and season with salt and pepper. Submerge 3 salmon pieces, skin sides down, in simmering liquid (add hot water if necessary to just cover salmon) and poach at a bare simmer, covered, 8 minutes, or until just cooked through. Transfer cooked salmon with a slotted spatula to a platter to cool and poach remaining salmon in same manner. When salmon is cool enough to handle, peel off skin and if desired with a sharp knife scrape off any dark meat. *Salmon may be cooked 1 day ahead and chilled, covered. Bring poached salmon to cool room temperature before serving.*

Cut potatoes lengthwise into ⅛-inch-thick slices. In a steamer set over boiling water steam potatoes until just tender, 4 to 5 minutes.

Spoon sauce onto 6 plates and arrange some potatoes in a circle, overlapping slightly, on top of sauce. Season potatoes with salt and arrange salmon on top of potatoes. Garnish salmon with sugar snap peas. Serves 6.

PHOTO ON PAGE 52

PAN-SEARED SEA BASS WITH BEET SAUCE AND BEET GREENS

1 pound red beets with greens (about 3 medium)
1 cup water
1½ tablespoons soy sauce (preferably Kikkoman)
1 tablespoon balsamic vinegar
3 tablespoons unsalted butter
1 teaspoon minced peeled fresh gingerroot
4 sea bass fillets (about ½ pound each)
½ teaspoon ground coriander

Preheat oven to 450° F.

Trim red beets, leaving about 1 inch of stems attached, and reserve greens with stems. Wrap beets tightly in foil and in a baking pan roast in middle of oven until tender, about 1 hour. Unwrap beets carefully. When beets are cool enough to handle, slip off skins and stems.

In a blender or food processor purée beets with water, soy sauce, vinegar, and salt and pepper to taste until smooth. Transfer sauce to a small saucepan and keep warm, covered.

Cut reserved greens into ½-inch-wide slices and chop stems. In a 12-inch nonstick skillet heat 1½ tablespoons butter over moderate heat until foam subsides and cook gingerroot, stirring, 30 seconds. Add greens and cook, stirring occasionally, until tender, about 10 minutes. Season greens with salt and pepper and keep warm, covered.

Pat sea bass fillets dry. Sprinkle fillets with coriander and season with salt and pepper. In a large nonstick skillet heat remaining 1½ tablespoons butter over moderately high heat until foam subsides and sauté fillets, skin sides down, pressing gently with a spatula if fillets curl, until skin is golden, about 3 minutes. Turn fish over and sauté about 2 minutes more, or until just cooked through.

Serve sea bass with beet greens and beet sauce. Serves 4.

TERIYAKI-GLAZED SEA BASS

⅓ cup soy sauce (preferably Kikkoman)
⅓ cup *mirin** (sweet rice wine)
⅓ cup *sake*
1 tablespoon sugar
six 4-ounce sea bass fillets
½ pound fresh *enoki* mushrooms* (about
    200 grams; optional)
1 tablespoon vegetable oil

Garnish: fresh Japanese chives or regular chives

*available at Japanese markets and by mail order
    from Uwajimaya, (800) 889-1928

In a 1-cup measure stir together soy sauce, *mirin*, and *sake* and reserve ¼ cup. In a small saucepan simmer remaining ¾ cup soy sauce mixture and sugar until reduced to a glaze (about ¼ cup) and remove pan from heat.

Using tweezers, remove any bones from sea bass. Trim spongy root ends from mushrooms. Have ready a shallow baking pan lined with paper towels. In a 12-inch nonstick skillet heat oil over moderately high heat until it just begins to smoke and sauté fillets, skin sides down, pressing gently with a spatula if fillets curl, until skin is golden, about 3 minutes. Turn fillets over and sauté 2 minutes more, or until almost cooked through. Add reserved (uncooked) soy sauce mixture to fish and simmer until fish is just cooked through, about 1 minute. Transfer fillets, skin sides down, with a slotted spatula to baking pan to drain and add mushrooms

to liquid remaining in skillet. Cook mushrooms, stirring frequently, until tender, about 1 minute, and remove skillet from heat.

Arrange fish and mushrooms on 6 plates. Brush fish with glaze and garnish with chives. Serves 6.

PHOTO ON PAGE 60

SEARED SEA BASS WITH
FRESH HERBS AND LEMON ☺

⅓ cup mixed fresh herbs such as parsley, dill,
    and chives
2 sea bass fillets with skin (each about 7 ounces)
1 teaspoon olive oil
1½ tablespoons unsalted butter
⅓ cup dry white wine
1 tablespoon fresh lemon juice

Chop herbs. Using tweezers, remove any bones from sea bass. Pat fillets dry and score just through skin in 4 places. Diagonally cut each fillet in half and season with salt and pepper. In a heavy skillet heat oil and 1 tablespoon butter over moderately high heat until foam subsides and sear fish, skin sides down, about 3 minutes, or until skin is golden. Turn fish over and cook 2 minutes more, or until just cooked through. Transfer fish to 2 plates.

Remove skillet from heat and add white wine to deglaze, scraping up any brown bits with a wooden spoon. Stir in lemon juice, chopped herbs, remaining ½ tablespoon butter, and salt and pepper to taste. Spoon sauce over fish. Serves 2.

SHELLFISH

Clams with Zucchini and Jalapeño

4 dozen small hard-shelled clams such as
    littlenecks (less than 2 inches in diameter)
2 small zucchini
1 fresh jalapeño chile
1 small onion
3 tablespoons unsalted butter
1 cup dry white wine

Accompaniment: crusty Italian or French bread

Scrub clams well and in a large bowl cover with salted cold water. Cut zucchini into 2- by ¼-inch sticks. Wearing rubber gloves, halve jalapeño lengthwise and discard seeds from one half. Finely chop jalapeño and onion. In a large saucepan heat 2 tablespoons butter over moderately high heat until foam subsides and sauté zucchini, jalapeño, and onion, stirring, until zucchini is crisp-tender, about 5 minutes. Transfer zucchini mixture to a bowl.

In pan melt remaining tablespoon butter over moderately high heat and add clams and wine. Steam clams, covered, over moderately high heat 5 to 8 minutes, checking them every minute after 5 minutes and transferring them with tongs as they open to a serving bowl. Reserve cooking liquid in pan. (Discard clams that are unopened after 8 minutes.) Stir zucchini mixture into reserved cooking liquid and pour over clams.

Serve clams with bread. Serves 2 as a main course.

Deviled Crab Tart

pastry dough (page 217)
pie weights or raw rice for weighting shell
1 medium onion
1 medium green bell pepper
2 celery ribs
½ stick (¼ cup) unsalted butter
1½ pounds jumbo lump crab meat
a 7-ounce jar roasted peppers
⅔ cup packed fresh flat-leafed parsley leaves
1 bunch scallions
½ cup plus 1 tablespoon mayonnaise
1½ teaspoons Worcestershire sauce
½ cup plus 3 tablespoons fine fresh
    bread crumbs
¼ teaspoon cayenne

Preheat oven to 375° F.

On a lightly floured surface with a floured rolling pin roll out dough into a 14-inch round (about ⅛ inch thick) and fit into an 11-inch round tart pan with a removable rim. Roll rolling pin over top of shell to trim dough flush with rim and lightly press dough up side of pan. With a fork prick bottom and side of shell all over. *Chill shell 30 minutes, or until firm.*

Line shell with foil and fill with pie weights or raw rice. Bake shell in middle of oven 25 minutes and carefully remove foil and weights or rice. Bake shell until just pale golden, about 8 minutes more. *Shell may be made 8 hours ahead and kept in pan, loosely covered, at room temperature.*

Finely chop onion, bell pepper, and celery and in a heavy skillet cook in butter over moderately low heat, stirring, until bell pepper is softened.

Increase temperature to 425° F.

Pick over crab meat and drain roasted peppers. Finely chop roasted peppers, parsley, and scallion greens, reserving whites for another use. In a large bowl whisk together mayonnaise, Worcestershire sauce, and ½ cup fresh bread crumbs and gently stir in onion mixture, crab, roasted peppers, parsley, scallion, cayenne, and salt to taste.

Spoon filling into shell, smoothing top, and sprinkle with remaining 3 tablespoons bread crumbs. Bake tart in middle of oven until top is golden, 20 to 25 minutes. Serve tart warm or at room temperature. Serves 6 as a main course.

STEAMED MUSSELS WITH SOFRITO ⊙

Sofrito is a sautéed vegetable mixture used as a seasoning in Latin America.

4 dozen mussels (preferably cultivated)
2 red bell peppers
1 small onion
4 large garlic cloves
¼ cup packed fresh cilantro sprigs
1 teaspoon dried oregano, crumbled
½ teaspoon cumin seeds
1 tablespoon olive oil
½ cup dry white wine
½ cup chicken broth
2 tablespoons fresh orange juice, or to taste

Accompaniment: crusty bread

Scrub mussels well and remove beards. Cut bell peppers into ½-inch pieces and transfer half to a blender, reserving remaining half in a bowl. Chop onion and garlic. Add onion, garlic, cilantro, oregano, and cumin to blender and purée until smooth.

In a 4-quart kettle heat oil over moderate heat until hot but not smoking and cook purée, stirring, 2 minutes. Add mussels, reserved bell peppers, wine, and broth and simmer, covered, 4 to 8 minutes, checking mussels occasionally after 4 minutes and transferring them as they open to a bowl. (Discard any unopened mussels after 8 minutes.) Season sauce with orange juice and salt and pepper.

Serve mussels with sauce and bread. Serves 2.

LOUISIANA MUSSEL "SAUCE PIQUANTE" WITH GARLIC BREAD ⊙

2 pounds mussels (preferably cultivated)
1 medium onion
1 celery rib
1 small green bell pepper
2 tablespoons unsalted butter
2 tablespoons all-purpose flour
2 teaspoons tomato paste
1 cup chicken broth
a 14- to 16-ounce can whole tomatoes
   including juice
½ teaspoon cayenne
For garlic bread
1 small garlic clove
2 tablespoons unsalted butter
a 12-inch piece French or Italian bread

Scrub mussels well and remove beards. Finely chop onion, celery, and bell pepper. In a 6- to 8-quart heavy kettle melt butter over moderately low heat and stir in flour. Cook *roux*, stirring constantly, until color of peanut butter, about 6 minutes. Stir in chopped vegetables and cook, covered, until soft. Stir in tomato paste, broth, tomatoes with juice, and cayenne and bring to a boil, breaking up tomatoes. Simmer sauce, uncovered, stirring occasionally, 15 minutes, or until thickened.

Make garlic bread while sauce is simmering:
Preheat broiler.

Mince garlic and mash to a paste with a pinch salt. In a small saucepan melt butter over moderate heat and stir in garlic paste. Halve bread horizontally and brush garlic butter on cut sides. On a baking sheet broil bread about 4 inches from heat until golden, 1 to 2 minutes.

Stir mussels into sauce and simmer, covered, 4 to 8 minutes, or until mussels are opened. (Discard any unopened mussels after 8 minutes.) Divide mussels between 2 bowls.

Season sauce with salt and ladle over mussels. Serve bread on the side. Serves 2 as a main course.

CREAMED OYSTERS AND MUSHROOMS ON TOAST ◐

¼ pound mushrooms
1 large shallot
1 tablespoon unsalted butter
2 tablespoons dry white wine
¾ cup whole milk
1 tablespoon all-purpose flour
½ cup heavy cream
a pinch cayenne
two ¾-inch-thick slices bread (preferably brioche)
12 shucked oysters (preferably Belon)
2 teaspoons chopped fresh parsley leaves

Cut mushrooms into ¼-inch-thick slices and finely chop shallot. In a 2-quart saucepan cook mushrooms and shallot with salt to taste in butter over moderate heat, stirring occasionally, until liquid mushrooms give off is evaporated and they are golden. Add wine and bring to a boil. In a measuring cup vigorously stir together milk and flour and add to mushroom mixture with cream and cayenne. Simmer cream mixture, stirring occasionally, until mixture is slightly thickened, about 3 minutes.

Toast bread. Add oysters and parsley to cream mixture, stirring gently, and cook at a bare simmer until edges of oysters curl, about 3 minutes. Arrange toast on 2 plates and spoon creamed oysters and mushrooms on top. Serves 2.

COCONUT SCALLOPS ◐

1½ cups sweetened flaked coconut
2 cups boiling-hot water
¼ teaspoon cayenne
½ teaspoon salt
10 medium sea scallops (about ½ pound)
½ cup all-purpose flour
1 large egg
½ cup vegetable oil

Accompaniment: lime wedges

Preheat oven to 350° F.

In a small bowl stir together coconut and water. Drain coconut in a sieve and pat dry. On a baking sheet spread coconut in one layer and bake in middle of oven until pale golden, about 10 minutes. In a bowl stir together coconut, cayenne, and salt.

Remove tough muscle from side of each scallop if necessary. Pat scallops dry and season with salt and pepper. In 2 separate shallow bowls have ready flour and lightly beaten egg. Dredge scallops in flour, shaking off excess. Dip each scallop in egg, letting excess drip off, and coat well with coconut.

In a 10-inch skillet heat oil over moderate heat until hot but not smoking and cook scallops until golden and just cooked through, about 1½ minutes on each side. Drain scallops on paper towels.

Serve scallops with lime wedges. Serves 2.

SEARED SCALLOPS WITH VEGETABLE CONFETTI

For vegetables
¼ pound *haricots verts* or regular green beans
3 scallions
1 medium zucchini
1 large yellow bell pepper
2 cups water
1 cup sugar
1 tablespoon olive oil
2 teaspoons fresh lemon juice

9 large sea scallops (about 9 ounces)
1 tablespoon olive oil
½ cup dry white wine
2 tablespoons unsalted butter
2 teaspoons fresh lemon juice

Garnish: chopped fresh chives

Prepare vegetables:
Cut beans and scallions crosswise into ¼-inch pieces and transfer to a bowl. Cut zucchini and bell pepper into ¼-inch dice and add to bean mixture. In a 3-quart saucepan bring water and sugar to a boil. Blanch vegetables 30 seconds in sugar water and drain in a sieve. In a bowl stir together vegetables, oil, and salt and pepper to taste and cool. *Vegetables may be prepared 1 day ahead and chilled, covered. Bring vegetables to room temperature before proceeding.* Add lemon juice to vegetables, tossing to combine.

Remove tough muscle from side of each scallop if necessary and horizontally halve each scallop to form 2 rounds. Pat scallops dry and season with salt and pepper. In a 10-inch skillet heat ½ tablespoon oil over moderately high heat until hot but not smoking. Arrange half of scallops in skillet, without crowding, and sauté until golden and just cooked through, about 15 seconds on each side. Transfer scallops to a plate and keep warm, covered. Wipe skillet clean and repeat procedure with remaining ½ tablespoon oil and scallops. To drippings remaining in skillet add wine, butter, lemon juice, and any juices that have accumulated from scallops on plate and simmer, stirring and scraping up brown bits, until reduced to about ¼ cup.

Divide vegetable confetti, mounding it, among 6 plates and top with scallops. Spoon 2 teaspoons sauce over each serving and sprinkle with chives. Serves 6.

PHOTO ON PAGE 32

SHRIMP AND ONION KEBABS

16 pearl onions (about 1 inch in diameter)
1¼ cups herb-garlic marinade (recipe follows)
24 jumbo shrimp (about 1½ pounds)
eight 10-inch wooden skewers

In a large saucepan of boiling water boil onions until tender, 3 to 4 minutes, and drain in a colander. When onions are just cool enough to handle, peel, leaving root ends intact. While onions are still warm, in a bowl stir together with ¼ cup marinade. *Marinate onions, covered and chilled, stirring occasionally, 1 day.*

If desired, shell shrimp. (Note: shrimp grilled in shells will be more succulent.) In a large heavy-duty sealable plastic bag combine shrimp with ¾ cup marinade and seal bag, pressing out excess air. *Marinate shrimp, chilled, at least 1 hour and up to 4.*

Prepare grill. *Soak wooden skewers in warm water 30 minutes.*

Drain shrimp, discarding marinade. In a sieve set over a bowl drain onions and reserve marinade for basting. Thread 3 shrimp and 2 onions, alternating shrimp with onions, onto each skewer. *Kebabs may be assembled 1 hour ahead and chilled, covered.*

Grill kebabs on a lightly oiled rack set 5 to 6 inches over glowing coals, basting with reserved marinade and turning them occasionally, until just cooked through, about 3 minutes on each side. (Alternatively, broil kebabs under a preheated broiler 2 to 3 inches from heat about 2½ minutes on each side.) Drizzle kebabs with remaining ¼ cup marinade. Serves 8.

PHOTO ON PAGE 56

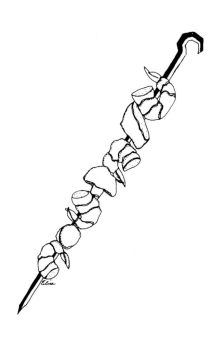

HERB-GARLIC MARINADE

6 large garlic cloves
⅓ cup packed tender fresh thyme sprigs
¼ cup packed fresh rosemary leaves
1½ tablespoons kosher salt
1 cup fresh lemon juice
1½ cups olive oil
freshly ground black pepper
    to taste

Mince together garlic, thyme sprigs, and rosemary with salt and mash to a coarse paste. In a bowl whisk together garlic paste and remaining ingredients until emulsified. *Marinade may be made 1 day ahead and chilled, covered.* Makes about 2½ cups.

COCONUT TEMPURA SHRIMP ON BANANA CAPER RELISH

2 pounds large shrimp (about 40)
For batter
1 cup cornstarch
1 cup all-purpose flour
1 cup shredded fresh coconut (procedure follows)
    or unsweetened desiccated coconut*
1 teaspoon salt, or to taste
3 large egg whites
1 cup well-stirred canned unsweetened
    coconut milk*
¼ cup club soda plus additional if necessary
For relish
1 medium red onion
2 garlic cloves
1 stick (½ cup) unsalted butter
4 firm-ripe medium bananas (about 1¼ pounds)
¼ cup drained capers
2 to 3 tablespoons fresh lemon juice, or to taste
2 tablespoons white-wine Worcestershire sauce
    or regular Worcestershire sauce
2 tablespoons chopped fresh flat-leafed parsley

about 6 cups vegetable oil for deep-frying

Garnish if desired: julienne strips of seeded
    peeled tomato

*available at Southeast Asian markets,
    some specialty foods shops and supermarkets,
    and by mail order from Adriana's Caravan,
    (800) 316-0820, or Uwajimaya, (800) 889-1928

Shell shrimp, leaving tail and connecting shell segment intact, and devein.
Make batter:
In a bowl stir together cornstarch, flour, coconut, and salt. Whisk in whites, coconut milk, and ¼ cup club soda until combined well. (Add additional club soda if batter is too thick to coat a spoon without clumping.)
Make relish:
Halve onion and cut into thin slices. Finely chop garlic. In a large heavy skillet cook onion and garlic in butter over moderately low heat, stirring, until softened. Diagonally cut bananas into ¼-inch-thick slices. To onion mixture add bananas, capers, lemon juice, and Worcestershire sauce and cook, stirring gently, until bananas are heated through, 2 to 3 minutes. Stir in parsley and season with salt and pepper. Keep relish warm.

In a 3-quart saucepan heat 2 inches oil until a deep-fat thermometer registers 350° F. Working in batches of 4, dip shrimp in batter and fry until golden, about 3 minutes, transferring to brown paper or paper towels to drain.

Serve shrimp over relish, garnished with tomato. Serves 8 to 10 as part of a buffet.

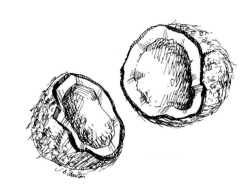

SHREDDED FRESH COCONUT

1 heavy coconut, without any cracks and
    containing liquid

Preheat oven to 400° F.
Pierce softest eye of coconut with a metal skewer or small screwdriver and drain liquid. Bake coconut in oven 15 minutes. With a hammer or back of a heavy cleaver break shell and with point of a strong knife remove flesh, levering it out carefully. Remove brown membrane with a sharp paring knife or vegetable peeler. *Fresh coconut keeps, chilled in a sealable plastic bag, 1 week.*

Shred coconut meat on small teardrop-shaped holes of a four-sided grater. Makes about 2½ cups.

LEMON-GARLIC BAKED SHRIMP ◒

3 garlic cloves
¾ pound medium shrimp (16 to 20)
¼ cup packed fresh flat-leafed parsley leaves
¼ cup extra-virgin olive oil
2 tablespoons fresh lemon juice

Accompaniment: hot crusty bread

Preheat oven to 450° F.
Thinly slice garlic and shell shrimp. Very coarsely chop parsley.
In an 8-inch shallow baking dish bake garlic in oil in middle of oven 5 minutes, or until garlic is lightly colored. Add shrimp, 1 tablespoon juice, and salt and pepper to taste and toss to combine. Bake shrimp, turning them once, until just cooked through, 6 to 8 minutes. Stir in remaining tablespoon juice.
Sprinkle parsley over shrimp and serve with bread. Serves 2.

SAUTÉED SHRIMP WITH CARAWAY SEEDS ◒

¾ pound large shrimp (about 15)
1 garlic clove
¾ teaspoon caraway seeds
1 tablespoon olive oil

Accompaniments:
lemon wedges
wilted red cabbage with balsamic
    vinegar (page 171)

Shell shrimp. Mince garlic and with a mortar and pestle coarsely grind caraway seeds. In a 10- to 12-inch heavy skillet heat oil over moderately high heat until hot but not smoking and sauté shrimp, stirring, 2½ minutes. Add garlic and caraway seeds and sauté, stirring, until shrimp are just cooked through, about 30 seconds more.
Serve shrimp with lemon and cabbage. Serves 2.

FRIED SQUID WITH AÏOLI

For aïoli
1 cup mayonnaise
¼ cup sour cream
2 tablespoons fresh lemon juice
1 tablespoon chopped fresh flat-leafed
    parsley leaves
1 teaspoon minced garlic

24 Ritz crackers (about 3 ounces)
¾ cup all-purpose flour
1½ teaspoons salt
1 teaspoon sugar
1 pound small squid, cleaned
about 5 cups vegetable oil for
    deep-frying

Accompaniment: lemon wedges

Make aïoli:
In a small bowl stir together mayonnaise, sour cream, lemon juice, chopped parsley, and garlic until combined well and season with salt and pepper to taste. *Aïoli may be made 2 days ahead and chilled, covered.*
In a food processor pulse crackers with flour, salt, and sugar until finely ground and transfer to a bowl.
Cut flaps from squid sacs if attached. Cut flaps into ¼-inch-thick strips and halve tentacles crosswise if large. Cut sacs crosswise into ¼-inch-thick rings. Pat squid dry with paper towels and season with salt and pepper.
In a 3-quart heavy kettle heat 2 inches oil over moderate heat until a deep-fat thermometer registers 375° F. While oil is heating, toss squid in flour mixture to coat, shaking off excess. Fry squid in small batches, turning them, until crisp and golden, about 1 minute, transferring with a slotted spoon to paper towels to drain. Make sure oil returns to 375° F. between batches.
Serve squid with *aïoli* and lemon wedges. Serves 4 as a first course.

MEAT

RIB ROAST WITH ROASTED-GARLIC THYME SAUCE

a 7- to 8-pound trimmed prime beef rib roast*
   (3 or 4 ribs)
1 tablespoon vegetable oil
2 heads garlic
3 tablespoons chopped fresh thyme leaves
¼ cup minced shallot
2 tablespoons red-wine vinegar
1½ cups dry red wine
1 bay leaf
3 cups veal or beef *demiglace*** or 4 cups
   beef broth
1½ tablespoons unsalted butter, softened
1½ tablespoons all-purpose flour if using
   beef broth

*available by request from butchers
**available at specialty foods shops and by
   mail order from Citarella, (800) 588-0383
   or (212) 874-0383

Preheat oven to 475° F.

Put roast, ribs side down, in center of a 13- by 9-inch flameproof roasting pan and rub all over with ½ tablespoon oil. Cut about ½ inch from tops of garlic heads to expose cloves and discard tops. Rub beef all over with cut sides of garlic and sprinkle with 2 tablespoons thyme, pressing to adhere. Season beef generously with salt and pepper. Put garlic heads on a double layer of foil and drizzle with remaining ½ tablespoon oil. Wrap garlic tightly in foil.

Roast beef in middle of oven 30 minutes. Remove beef from oven and with a bulb baster skim all but about ½ cup fat from pan. Baste beef with fat remaining in pan.

Reduce temperature to 375° F.

Add garlic to oven. Roast beef, with garlic, 1¼ to 1½ hours more, or until a meat thermometer inserted into center of meat registers 115° F. Transfer garlic in foil to a rack and transfer beef to a platter, reserving pan juices. Let beef stand 25 minutes. (Meat will continue to cook, reaching about 130° F. for medium-rare.)

While beef is standing, remove all but about 2 tablespoons fat from pan. Add shallot to pan and on top of stove cook over moderate heat, stirring, 2 minutes. Unwrap garlic. Protecting your hand with a doubled paper towel, squeeze roasted garlic into shallot mixture and discard skins. Add vinegar, wine, bay leaf, and remaining tablespoon thyme and boil mixture, scraping up brown bits and mashing garlic with a wooden spatula against bottom of pan, until reduced to about ½ cup, about 5 minutes.

If using *demiglace*, stir into garlic mixture and boil sauce until reduced to about 2 cups, about 5 minutes. Whisk in butter. (If using beef broth, in a small bowl mash together butter and flour to make a *beurre manié*. Stir beef broth into garlic mixture and boil sauce until reduced to about 2 cups. Whisk *beurre manié* into broth mixture and cook over moderate heat, whisking, until sauce is smooth and slightly thickened, about 3 minutes.) Pour sauce through a fine sieve into a bowl, pressing hard on solids. Season sauce with salt and pepper.

Cut rib roast into slices and serve with sauce. Serves 8.

PHOTO ON PAGE 75

BEEF WELLINGTONS WITH GORGONZOLA

four 1½-inch-thick center-cut filets mignons
   (about 6 ounces each)
4 large mushrooms (about ¼ pound total)
1 tablespoon unsalted butter
1 tablespoon finely chopped shallot

1 tablespoon minced garlic

1 large egg

1 puff pastry sheet (from a 17¼-ounce package frozen puff pastry), thawed

4 tablespoons Gorgonzola cheese (about 2½ ounces)

For sauce

1 cup veal or beef demiglace*

2 tablespoons Sercial Madeira

*available at specialty foods shops and by mail order from Citarella, (800) 588-0383 or (212) 874-0383

Preheat oven to 425° F.

Pat filets mignons dry and season with salt and pepper. In a shallow roasting pan roast filets in middle of oven 12 minutes, or until a meat thermometer registers 110° F. for rare, and cool (filets will be baked again after being wrapped in pastry). *Chill filets, covered, until cold, about 1 hour.*

Thinly slice mushrooms and in a heavy skillet cook in butter with shallot, garlic, and salt and pepper to taste over moderate heat, stirring, until mushrooms are lightly browned. Transfer mushroom mixture to a bowl to cool completely. In a small bowl lightly beat egg to make an egg wash.

On a lightly floured surface roll out puff pastry sheet into a 14-inch square. Trim edges to form a 13-inch square and cut square into four 6½-inch squares.

Put 1 tablespoon Gorgonzola in center of 1 square and top with one fourth mushroom mixture. Top mushroom mixture with a filet mignon, pressing it down gently, and wrap 2 opposite corners of puff pastry over filet, overlapping them. Seal seam with egg wash. Wrap remaining 2 corners of pastry over filet and seal in same manner. Seal any gaps with egg wash and press pastry around filet to enclose completely. Arrange beef Wellington, seam side down, in a non-stick baking pan. Make 3 more beef Wellingtons in same manner. Chill remaining egg wash for brushing on pastry just before baking. *Chill beef Wellingtons, loosely covered, at least 1 hour and up to 1 day.*

Preheat oven to 425° F.

Brush top and sides of each beef Wellington with some remaining egg wash and bake 20 minutes, or until pastry is golden.

Make sauce while beef Wellingtons are baking:

In a saucepan boil *demiglace* and Madeira 1 minute and keep sauce warm.

Serve beef Wellingtons with sauce. Serves 4.

GARLIC DIJON SKIRT STEAK

2 garlic cloves

2 tablespoons Dijon mustard

1 tablespoon fresh lime juice

a 10-ounce skirt steak (about ¾ inch thick)

Accompaniments if desired:

cumin coleslaw (page 189)

spicy French fries (page 176)

Mince garlic and in a bowl stir together with mustard and lime juice. Trim steak if necessary. Rub steak with mixture and marinate 15 minutes.

Heat a well-seasoned ridged grill pan over moderately high heat until just smoking and grill steak 3 minutes on each side. (Alternatively, broil steak on rack of a broiler pan about 4 inches from heat.) Transfer steak to a platter and let stand, uncovered, 5 minutes.

With a sharp knife diagonally cut steak into ⅓-inch-thick slices and serve with coleslaw and fries. Serves 2.

Grilled Flank Steak with Sautéed Portabella and Cremini Mushrooms

3½ pounds flank steak
4 large shallots
⅓ cup balsamic vinegar
¼ cup sugar
¼ cup soy sauce

Accompaniment: sautéed portabella and *cremini* mushrooms (recipe follows)

Pat steak dry and cut crosswise at a 45° angle into 4 equal pieces. Season steaks with salt and pepper and transfer to a large sealable heavy-duty plastic bag. Chop shallots and in a bowl stir together with vinegar, sugar, and soy sauce. Pour marinade into bag. *Marinate steaks, covered and chilled, turning plastic bag over at least once, at least 2 hours and up to 2 days.*

Prepare grill.

Remove steaks from bag and discard marinade. Grill steaks on a lightly oiled rack set 5 to 6 inches over glowing coals 7 to 9 minutes on each side for medium-rare. (Alternatively, grill steaks in 2 batches in a hot lightly oiled well-seasoned ridged grill pan over moderately high heat.) Transfer steaks as cooked to a cutting board and let stand 10 minutes.

Cut steak at a 45° angle across grain into thin slices. Serve steak with mushrooms. Serves 8.

PHOTO ON PAGE 48

Sautéed Portabella and Cremini Mushrooms

1½ pounds portabella mushrooms
1½ pounds *cremini* mushrooms
3 large shallots
1 stick (½ cup) unsalted butter
4 scallions (green parts only)
½ cup balsamic vinegar
5 tablespoons soy sauce
¼ cup sugar

Halve portabellas and cut into ¼-inch-thick slices. Cut *cremini* into ¼-inch-thick slices. Chop shallots and in a 12-inch heavy skillet cook half of shallots in half of butter over moderate heat, stirring, 1 minute. Add portabellas and salt and pepper to taste and cook, stirring occasionally, until liquid mushrooms give off is evaporated, about 15 minutes. Transfer portabellas to a bowl and keep warm, covered. Cook remaining shallots in remaining butter over moderate heat, stirring, 1 minute. Add *cremini* and salt and pepper to taste and cook, stirring occasionally, until liquid mushrooms give off is evaporated, about 10 minutes. Add portabellas to *cremini* and keep warm, covered. *Mushrooms may be prepared up to this point 1 day ahead and chilled, covered.*

Diagonally cut scallions into thin slices. In a bowl whisk together vinegar, soy sauce, and sugar. Heat mushrooms over moderately high heat until hot and add vinegar mixture. Boil mixture 3 minutes, or until liquid is reduced slightly, and stir in scallions. Serves 8.

Pot Roast with Root Vegetables

1 medium onion
3 garlic cloves
¾ pound carrots
½ pound parsnips
½ pound turnips
6 ounces mushrooms
a 3-inch piece fresh gingerroot

a 28- to 32-ounce can whole tomatoes
a 3-pound boneless beef chuck roast
2 tablespoons olive oil
¾ cup Tawny Port
¾ cup dry red wine
2 cups beef or chicken broth
2 tablespoons Worcestershire sauce
1 tablespoon packed brown sugar
3 bay leaves
1 teaspoon dried thyme, crumbled
1 teaspoon dried oregano, crumbled
3 tablespoons cornstarch
3 tablespoons water

Chop onion and mince garlic. Peel carrots and parsnips and diagonally cut into ¾-inch-thick slices. Peel turnips and cut into ¾-inch-thick wedges. Cut mushrooms into ½-inch-thick slices. Peel gingerroot and mince enough to measure ¼ cup. Drain tomatoes and chop.

Pat chuck roast dry and season with salt and pepper. In a 5-quart heavy kettle heat oil over moderately high heat until hot but not smoking and brown roast on all sides. Transfer roast to a plate and pour off all but 1 tablespoon fat from kettle. Add onion to kettle and cook over moderate heat, stirring, until golden. Add garlic and cook, stirring, 1 minute. Add Port and red wine and simmer, scraping up any brown bits on bottom of kettle, 5 minutes. Stir in broth, Worcestershire sauce, brown sugar, gingerroot, tomatoes, bay leaves, thyme, and oregano and bring mixture to a boil. Add roast, carrots, parsnips, turnips, and mushrooms and simmer, covered, turning roast over halfway through cooking time, 3 hours total, or until tender. *Pot roast may be made up to this point 3 days ahead. Cool roast, uncovered, before chilling, covered, and remove any solidified fat before reheating.*

Transfer roast with tongs to a cutting board and let stand 10 minutes. If necessary skim fat from cooking liquid and bring cooking liquid and vegetables to a boil over moderate heat. In a cup stir together cornstarch and water until smooth and stir enough into sauce to thicken to desired consistency. Simmer sauce, stirring occasionally, 2 minutes.

Cut roast crosswise into ½-inch-thick slices and arrange on a deep platter. Spoon vegetables and sauce over meat. Serves 4 to 6.

MOROCCAN SPICED BEEF ☻

1 teaspoon ground cumin
1 teaspoon ground coriander
  seeds
¾ teaspoon ground cinnamon
⅛ teaspoon salt
⅛ teaspoon freshly ground black
  pepper
2 teaspoons olive oil
two ¾-inch-thick boneless sirloin steaks
  (about 1 pound total)

Accompaniment: creamy mint-cilantro "chutney"
  (recipe follows)

Prepare grill.
In a shallow bowl stir together all ingredients except steaks. Add steaks and rub with spice mixture. Let steaks stand, covered, at room temperature 15 minutes.

Grill steaks on an oiled rack set 5 to 6 inches over glowing coals about 3 minutes on each side for medium-rare. (Alternatively, broil steaks under a preheated broiler 3 to 4 inches from heat.)

Serve steaks with chutney. Serves 2.

CREAMY MINT-CILANTRO "CHUTNEY" ☻

This fresh chutney is an excellent condiment for beef, chicken, and fish.

⅓ cup sliced almonds
¾ cup packed fresh mint leaves
¾ cup packed fresh cilantro sprigs
3 tablespoons sour cream
2 teaspoons honey
½ teaspoon minced garlic

Preheat oven to 325° F.
On a small baking sheet toast almonds in one layer in middle of oven until golden, about 10 minutes, and cool. In a food processor finely grind almonds. Add herbs, sour cream, honey, garlic, and salt and pepper to taste and blend until combined well. *Chutney may be made 1 day ahead and chilled, covered.* Makes about ⅔ cup.

GRILLED RIB-EYE STEAKS WITH CHILI CUMIN SPICE RUB ◑

1 tablespoon fresh lime juice
1¼ teaspoons chili powder
½ teaspoon ground cumin
two ½-inch-thick rib-eye steaks
    (each about 6 ounces)

In a bowl stir together lime juice, chili powder, cumin, and salt and pepper to taste. Pat steaks dry and spread spice rub on both sides of each steak.

Heat a well-seasoned ridged grill pan over high heat until hot but not smoking and grill steaks about 2 minutes on each side for medium-rare. Serves 2.

MEATBALLS IN WINTER TOMATO SAUCE

For meatballs
1 cup fine fresh bread crumbs
1½ cups milk
2 medium onions
2½ pounds ground round
1½ pounds ground pork
1 large egg
½ teaspoon freshly grated nutmeg
2½ teaspoons salt
¾ teaspoon freshly ground black pepper
¼ cup minced fresh flat-leafed parsley leaves

about ½ cup olive oil for browning meatballs
a 28- to 32-ounce can whole plum tomatoes
    including juice
1 tablespoon minced garlic
1½ teaspoons dried oregano, crumbled
2 tablespoons minced fresh flat-leafed
    parsley leaves

Make meatballs:
In a large bowl soak bread crumbs in milk 10 minutes. Finely chop onions. Add onions and remaining meatball ingredients to bread crumb mixture and with your hands blend together until just combined well (do not overmix). Form mixture into walnut-size balls and arrange on large trays.

In a large heavy skillet heat 2 tablespoons oil over moderately high heat until hot but not smoking and brown meatballs in batches without crowding, shaking skillet to maintain round shape and adding remaining oil as necessary. Transfer meatballs as browned (and any browned onions that fall from meatballs) with a slotted spoon to a 7- to 8-quart heavy kettle.

In a large sieve set over a bowl drain tomatoes, reserving juice, and chop. To meatballs add chopped tomatoes with reserved juice, garlic, and oregano and simmer, covered, 30 minutes. Transfer meatballs with a slotted spoon to a bowl and keep warm, loosely covered with foil. Briskly simmer sauce until reduced to about 2 cups, about 25 minutes. Season sauce with salt and pepper and gently stir in meatballs. *Meatballs in tomato sauce may be made 3 days ahead and cooled completely, uncovered, before being chilled, covered. Reheat meatballs in sauce before serving.*

Gently stir parsley into meatballs and sauce. Makes about 110 meatballs, serving 8 to 10.

PHOTO ON PAGE 16

VEAL AND OTHER MEATS

BUFFALO AND PANCETTA MEAT LOAF

1 pound sliced *pancetta* (Italian
    unsmoked cured bacon)
2 medium onions
4 garlic cloves
2 celery ribs
1 carrot
½ cup fresh flat-leafed parsley
    leaves
¾ cup ketchup
¾ teaspoon salt
¼ teaspoon freshly ground black pepper
1 tablespoon Worcestershire sauce
1¾ cups fine fresh bread crumbs
2 pounds ground buffalo* or ground
    beef sirloin
2 large eggs

Accompaniment: olive oil and garlic whipped
    potatoes (page 177)

*available at some butcher shops and
supermarkets and by mail order from
Denver Buffalo Company, (800) 289-2833
or (303) 831-1299

Preheat oven to 375° F.

Coarsely chop three fourths *pancetta* and in a large heavy skillet cook over moderate heat until crisp and golden, transferring to paper towels to drain. Cool *pancetta* and reserve fat in skillet. Finely chop cooked *pancetta*. Finely chop onions and mince garlic. Cut celery and carrot into ¼-inch dice.

In skillet cook onions, garlic, celery, and carrot in reserved fat over moderate heat, stirring occasionally, until onions are softened. While onion mixture is cooking, coarsely chop parsley.

In a large bowl stir together chopped *pancetta*, onion mixture, parsley, ½ cup ketchup, salt, pepper, Worcestershire sauce, bread crumbs, buffalo or beef, and eggs until just combined (do not overmix). In a shallow 13- by 9-inch baking pan form mixture into a 10- by 5-inch oval loaf and spread remaining ¼ cup ketchup onto it. Drape remaining *pancetta* over loaf.

Bake meat loaf in middle of oven 1 hour and 10 minutes, or until a meat thermometer inserted 2 inches into center registers 160° F. Let meat loaf stand 10 minutes.

Slice meat loaf and serve with whipped potatoes. Serves 6 to 8.

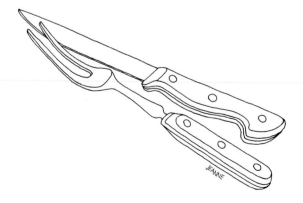

PAN-ROASTED VEAL WITH SALSA VERDE

Here the veal is roasted on top of the stove. Unlike braising, this method uses only a small amount of liquid and results in meat that is succulent and tender but not falling apart. Pan roasting also renders a caramelized coating and savory pan juices. Surprisingly, the anchovies do not impart a strong fishy flavor to the dish but rather add rich depth. Do not salt the meat before browning it, as the anchovies have plenty.

2 large garlic cloves
5 bottled flat anchovy fillets
a 3-pound boneless veal shoulder roast,
    rolled and tied
2 tablespoons olive oil
¾ cup dry white wine
1 to 2 cups water

Accompaniment: salsa verde
    (page 134)

Mince garlic with anchovies. If veal is encased in a net, remove net and with kitchen string tie veal crosswise at 1-inch intervals.

Pat veal dry. In a heavy kettle just large enough to hold veal heat oil over moderate heat until hot but not smoking and brown veal well, turning it. Transfer veal to a plate. In oil remaining in kettle cook anchovy mixture, stirring, 1 minute. Add wine and boil 1 minute.

Return veal to kettle and simmer, partly covered, turning veal every 20 minutes and adding water as needed (about 3 tablespoons at a time; do not let liquid completely evaporate—there should always be just enough to keep veal from sticking to kettle), 1½ to 2 hours, or until an instant-read thermometer inserted in thickest part registers 155° F. for medium meat.

Transfer veal to a cutting board and let stand 10 minutes. Skim any fat from liquid in kettle. Add ⅓ cup water and simmer, scraping up brown bits from bottom and side of kettle, until liquid has consistency of thin gravy.

Transfer pan juices to a platter. Cut veal crosswise into ½-inch-thick slices and discard string. Arrange slices over pan juices and spoon *salsa verde* over meat. Serves 6.

PHOTO ON PAGE 27

Salsa Verde ◉
Caper and Parsley Sauce

3 tablespoons capers (preferably packed in salt)
   or drained bottled capers
½ cup packed fresh flat-leafed parsley leaves
⅓ cup extra-virgin olive oil
2 tablespoons chopped shallot
1 teaspoon Dijon mustard
½ teaspoon chopped garlic
1 tablespoon red-wine vinegar

If using capers packed in salt, in a small bowl soak in water to cover by 2 inches for 15 minutes and drain. In a food processor combine all ingredients except vinegar and finely chop. *Salsa verde may be prepared up to this point 1 day ahead and chilled, covered. Bring salsa verde to room temperature before proceeding.* Just before serving, stir in vinegar. Makes about ⅔ cup.

PORK

Grilled Spiced Double-Thick Pork Chops

The brine in this recipe is based on one that appears in Mark Peel and Nancy Silverton's Food of Campanile.

For brine
9 large garlic cloves
3 quarts water
½ cup kosher salt
¼ cup plus 2 tablespoons black peppercorns
¼ cup plus 2 tablespoons sugar
1½ tablespoons dried thyme, crumbled
1 teaspoon whole allspice
½ bay leaf

twelve 1½-inch-thick rib pork chops
For spice rub
½ cup plus 2 tablespoons packed
   light brown sugar
2½ tablespoons ground cumin
1 tablespoon kosher salt
½ teaspoon cayenne

Make brine:
Lightly mash garlic with flat side of a large heavy knife. In a kettle bring water to a boil with garlic and remaining brine ingredients and simmer 15 minutes. Cool brine completely.

Working over a bowl, divide pork chops and brine among 3 large heavy-duty sealable plastic bags and seal bags, pressing out any excess air. *Marinate pork chops in bags in a large bowl, chilled, turning them once, 2 days.*

Make spice rub:
In a small bowl whisk together all spice rub ingredients.

Prepare grill.

Remove pork chops from brine, discarding brine and any spices still adhering to chops, and pat dry. Season chops with salt and pepper and sprinkle each side of each chop with about ½ tablespoon spice rub, patting it into meat.

Grill chops on an oiled rack set 5 to 6 inches over glowing coals 10 to 12 minutes on each side, or until a meat thermometer diagonally inserted 2 inches into centers registers 155° F. (Alternatively, arrange chops in 2 lightly oiled shallow baking pans. Roast chops in upper and lower thirds of a preheated 450° F. oven, switching position of pans halfway through roasting, about 20 minutes, or until a meat thermometer registers 155° F.) Transfer pork chops to a platter and let stand 5 minutes before serving. Serves 12.

PHOTO ON PAGE 64

Teriyaki Pork Chops ◉

1 large garlic clove
⅓ cup soy sauce
2 tablespoons *mirin* (sweet rice wine)
   or cream Sherry
2½ tablespoons cider vinegar
1½ tablespoons packed light brown sugar
1½ tablespoons minced peeled fresh
   gingerroot
two 1-inch-thick rib pork chops
1 tablespoon vegetable oil

Finely chop garlic. In a saucepan bring soy sauce, *mirin* or Sherry, and vinegar to a boil with garlic, brown sugar, and gingerroot, stirring until brown sugar is dissolved. Transfer marinade to a metal bowl set in a large bowl of ice and cold water and cool, stirring occasionally, to room temperature.

In a small dish arrange pork chops in one layer and pour marinade over them, turning chops to coat well. Marinate chops at room temperature, turning them once, 15 minutes.

Pour marinade into a small saucepan and simmer 5 minutes. In a 10- to 12-inch heavy skillet heat oil over moderate heat until hot but not smoking and cook chops 6 to 8 minutes on each side, or until just cooked through.

Serve chops drizzled with marinade. Serves 2.

GRILLED PORK TENDERLOIN CUTLETS WITH CHILI MAPLE GLAZE

2 pork tenderloins (about
   1½ pounds total)
2 cups water
1½ tablespoons salt
1½ tablespoons pure maple syrup
1 tablespoon chili powder

In a bowl large enough to hold pork covered with water stir together salt and water until salt is dissolved and add pork, making sure it is completely covered by brine. *Marinate pork, covered and chilled, 1 day.*

Prepare grill.

In a small bowl stir together syrup and chili powder. Discard brine and diagonally cut pork into ¾-inch-thick pieces. Put pork between sheets of plastic wrap and pound with a rolling pin to flatten into ¼-inch-thick cutlets. Pat pork dry and season with salt.

Grill pork on a lightly oiled rack set 5 to 6 inches over glowing coals until just cooked through, 2 to 3 minutes on each side. Brush pork with glaze and grill 15 seconds more on each side. (Alternatively, pork may be grilled in a hot well-seasoned ridged grill pan over moderately high heat in same manner.) Serves 4.

PHOTO ON PAGE 83

🍂 each serving about 217 calories and 5 grams fat

BONELESS PORK CHOPS WITH GINGER, FIG, AND LEMON COMPOTE ◔

1 lemon
1 medium shallot
4 dried figs (preferably Calimyrna)
two 1¼-inch-thick boneless pork loin chops
   (about ¾ pound)
1 tablespoon olive oil
1 teaspoon grated peeled fresh gingerroot
⅓ cup water
2 tablespoons dry white wine
1 tablespoon unsalted butter

Garnish: lemon slices

With a vegetable peeler cut 3 lengthwise strips of zest from lemon and cut strips crosswise into enough very thin slices to measure 1 packed teaspoon. Squeeze 2 tablespoons juice from lemon. Mince shallot and cut figs into ¼-inch-thick slices.

Pat pork dry and season with salt and pepper. In a skillet heat oil over moderately high heat until hot but not smoking and sauté pork until browned, about 1 minute on each side. Transfer pork to a plate and in fat remaining in skillet cook shallot and gingerroot, stirring, until fragrant, about 30 seconds. Add pork, water, wine, zest, lemon juice, and figs and simmer, covered, 10 minutes, or until pork is just cooked through.

Transfer pork to 2 plates and if fig mixture is too liquid boil until reduced to a sauce-like consistency, about 1 minute. Whisk butter into fig mixture until incorporated.

Garnish pork with lemon slices and serve with compote. Serves 2.

BABY BACK RIBS WITH CHIPOTLE HONEY SAUCE

We used a 22½-inch kettle grill and cooked the ribs in 2 batches. Your oven, though, will be able to accommodate the ribs in 1 batch, and roasting them that way is a delicious (and less time-consuming) option.

4 racks baby back pork ribs (about 6 pounds)
For marinade
two 12-ounce bottles dark beer
1 cup red-wine vinegar
¼ cup Worcestershire sauce
2 tablespoons chopped garlic
2 tablespoons freshly ground black pepper
1 tablespoon dried hot red pepper flakes
1 tablespoon dried thyme
1 tablespoon dried rubbed sage
1 tablespoon kosher salt
For chipotle honey sauce
½ cup honey
¼ cup cider vinegar
2 tablespoons Creole mustard*
1 tablespoon minced canned *chipotle* chiles
    in *adobo**

2 cups hickory wood chips**
132 briquettes
grill drip pan** or other heavy-duty
    aluminum pan

*available at specialty foods shops and by mail
    order from Adriana's Caravan, (800) 316-0820
**available at some hardware stores and by mail
    order from Weber, (800) 446-1071

On a work surface invert ribs so that white membrane sides are up. With a sharp small knife cut across center of lengths of racks to aid removal of membrane. Pull membrane off and discard. Put ribs in a large bowl.

Make marinade:

In a large bowl stir together marinade ingredients.

Pour three fourths marinade over ribs and reserve remainder, chilled, for basting. *Marinate ribs, covered and chilled, turning them if necessary to keep covered with marinade, 24 hours.*

Make sauce:

In a blender blend all sauce ingredients until emulsified. *Sauce may be made 1 day ahead and chilled, covered.*

Soak wood chips in 2 cups water 2 hours.

Open vents in lid and bottom of grill and put 50 briquettes in bottom of grill. Light briquettes. As soon as they are lightly coated with gray ash, in about 30 minutes, divide briquettes in half, pushing halves to opposite sides of bottom of grill. Put drip pan or other aluminum pan between mounds of coals. Drain wood chips well, shaking off excess water. Spread 1 cup wood chips evenly on top of coals. When chips begin to smoke, in about 2 minutes, grill is ready.

Drain ribs and discard marinade. Grill half of ribs in one layer, covered, on a rack over pan, basting them every 15 minutes with reserved marinade and turning them, 45 minutes. Add 8 briquettes to each mound of coals and continue to cook ribs, covered, without basting, until done, 45 minutes more. Transfer ribs to a platter and keep warm, loosely covered with foil. Grill remaining ribs in same manner. (Alternatively, in foil-lined large roasting pans arrange ribs in one layer and roast in upper and lower thirds of a 350° F. oven, basting every 15 minutes with reserved marinade, turning them and switching position of pans halfway through roasting, 1 hour total. Continue to roast ribs, without basting, 15 minutes more.) Discard any unused basting marinade and with a clean brush coat ribs with some sauce. *Ribs may be made 1 day ahead and chilled, covered. Reheat ribs in a 350° F. oven until just heated through, about 15 minutes.*

Transfer ribs to a cutting board and cut ribs between bones. Serve ribs with remaining sauce. Serves 12 as part of a buffet.

PHOTO ON PAGE 38

SMOKED SAUSAGE JAMBALAYA ☽

½ pound smoked pork sausage
   such as kielbasa
1 small onion
1 small red bell pepper
1 celery rib
1 teaspoon vegetable oil
⅔ cup long-grain white rice
1⅓ cups chicken broth
⅛ teaspoon cayenne
2 scallions

Cut sausage into ¼-inch-thick slices and chop onion, bell pepper, and celery. In a dry 2- to 2½-quart heavy saucepan brown sausage over moderately high heat, stirring frequently, and with a slotted spoon transfer to paper towels to drain. Pour off any fat from pan and in pan cook vegetables in oil over moderate heat, stirring occasionally, until onion is softened. Stir in rice, broth, and cayenne and bring to a boil. Cover pan and cook rice over low heat 15 minutes.

Remove pan from heat and let rice stand, covered, 5 minutes. Thinly slice scallions. Fluff rice with a fork and stir in sausage, scallions, and salt and pepper to taste. Serves 2 as a main course.

LAMB

RACK OF LAMB WITH SPINACH PINE-NUT CRUST AND MINTED PEA SAUCE

For crust mixture
½ cup pine nuts (about 3 ounces)
1 pound spinach (about 2 bunches)
¼ pound sliced smoked ham
1 cup packed fresh flat-leafed parsley leaves
½ stick (¼ cup) unsalted butter, softened
2 cups fine fresh bread crumbs
1 whole large egg
1 large egg yolk
1 teaspoon finely grated fresh lemon zest
½ teaspoon salt
¼ teaspoon freshly ground black pepper

3 racks of lamb (8 ribs and about 1½ pounds
   each), frenched to eye of meat and, if desired,
   leaving a 1-inch-wide strip of fat along top of
   eye of rack*
1 tablespoon vegetable oil
2 tablespoons Dijon mustard

Accompaniment: minted pea sauce
   (page 138)

*available by request from butchers

Make crust mixture:
Preheat oven to 350° F.

In a baking pan toast pine nuts in middle of oven until golden, about 10 minutes, and cool.

Discard stems from spinach and coarsely chop spinach. Rinse spinach and drain in a colander. In a large heavy kettle cook spinach in water clinging to leaves, covered, 1 minute, or until just wilted. Drain spinach well in colander, pressing out excess liquid with back of a large spoon, and cool. Tear ham into pieces. In a food processor pulse spinach with nuts, parsley, ham, and butter until finely chopped and transfer to a large bowl. Stir in remaining crust ingredients until combined well. *Crust mixture may be made 1 day ahead and chilled, covered.*

Increase temperature to 425° F.

If leaving strip of fat on racks, score a diamond pattern on fat with tip of a sharp thin knife. Halve lamb racks to form six 4-rib pieces. Pat lamb dry and season with salt and pepper.

In a large heavy skillet heat oil over moderately high heat until hot but not smoking and lightly brown pieces 2 at a time, on all sides, about 1 minute total for each batch. Transfer pieces as browned to a large shallow roasting pan and arrange meaty sides up. Spread meaty side of each piece with 1 teaspoon mustard. Divide crust mixture into 6 portions and pat over mustard coating on each piece, gently pressing to help adhere.

Roast lamb in middle of oven 25 minutes, or until a thermometer inserted 2 inches into center registers 135° F. for medium-rare. Transfer lamb to a cutting board and let stand 10 minutes.

Cut lamb into individual chops and serve with sauce. Serves 6.

PHOTO ON PAGE 34

MINTED PEA SAUCE ☾

1½ cups chicken broth (12 fluid ounces)
2¼ cups frozen peas (about a 10-ounce package)
¾ cup packed fresh mint leaves
2 tablespoons unsalted butter

In a 3-quart saucepan bring broth to a boil. Add 2 cups peas, mint, and butter to broth and simmer, uncovered, 5 minutes, or until peas are tender. In a blender purée mixture until smooth (use caution when blending hot liquids) and pour through a fine sieve into cleaned pan. Add remaining ¼ cup peas and simmer until peas are just tender, about 2 minutes. Season sauce with salt and pepper. Makes about 2½ cups.

CORIANDER LAMB CHOPS ☾

1 tablespoon coriander seeds
2 garlic cloves
½ teaspoon salt
2 teaspoons olive oil
6 rib lamb chops (about 1⅓ pounds total)

Preheat broiler.
With a mortar and pestle or in an electric coffee/spice grinder grind coriander seeds. Mince garlic and mash to paste with salt. In a bowl stir together coriander, garlic paste, and oil and rub onto lamb chops.
Arrange chops on rack of a broiler pan and broil 3 inches from heat 3 minutes on each side for medium-rare. Serves 2.

LAMB AND RED PEPPER KEBABS

a 2-pound piece trimmed boneless leg of lamb
1¼ cups herb-garlic marinade (page 125)
4 large red bell peppers
eight 10-inch wooden skewers

Cut lamb into 32 pieces, each about 1¼ inches. In a large heavy-duty sealable plastic bag combine lamb and ¾ cup marinade and seal bag, pressing out excess air. *Marinate lamb, chilled, 1 day.*
Cut bell peppers into thirty-two 2- by 1½-inch pieces and blanch in a large saucepan of boiling water 30 seconds. Drain peppers in a colander and, while still hot, in a bowl stir together with ¼ cup marinade. *Marinate bell peppers, covered and chilled, 1 day.*
Prepare grill. *Soak wooden skewers in warm water 30 minutes.*
Drain lamb, discarding marinade. In a sieve set over a bowl drain peppers and reserve marinade for basting. Thread 4 pepper pieces and 4 lamb pieces, alternating pepper with lamb, onto each skewer. *Lamb and pepper kebabs may be assembled 1 hour ahead and chilled, covered.*
Grill kebabs on a lightly oiled rack set 5 to 6 inches over glowing coals, basting with reserved marinade and turning them occasionally, about 12 minutes total for medium-rare meat. (Alternatively, broil kebabs under a preheated broiler 2 to 3 inches from heat about 4 minutes on each side.) Drizzle kebabs with remaining ¼ cup marinade. Serves 8.

PHOTO ON PAGE 56

TANDOORI SPICED LAMB CHOPS ☾

2 shoulder lamb chops (each about
    ¾ inch thick)
2 tablespoons *tandoori* paste such as
    Pataks brand*

Accompaniment: cucumber and celery salad
    with yogurt (page 191)

*available at many supermarkets and by mail
    order from Kalustyan's, (212) 685-3451

Preheat broiler and lightly brush a shallow baking pan with oil.
Pat lamb chops dry and spread with *tandoori* paste. Season chops with pepper. In baking pan broil chops 3 to 4 inches from heat 6 minutes for medium.
Serve lamb chops with salad. Serves 2.

POULTRY

CHICKEN

CHICKEN AND FENNEL PIE WITH BACON-BISCUIT CRUST

For filling
4 cups water
1¾ cups chicken broth
1 large whole chicken breast (about 1 pound)
1 chicken leg (about ½ pound)
1 teaspoon black peppercorns
1 bay leaf
2 small fennel bulbs (about 1 pound)
3 carrots
1 medium boiling potato
1 medium onion
2 garlic cloves
½ cup packed fresh flat-leafed parsley leaves
¾ teaspoon fennel seeds
½ stick (¼ cup) unsalted butter
¼ cup all-purpose flour

For crust
6 bacon slices
2¾ cups all-purpose flour
1 tablespoon baking powder
1 teaspoon salt
1⅓ cups heavy cream
1 large egg yolk
1 tablespoon whole milk

Make filling:
In a 4- to 5-quart heavy kettle combine water, broth, chicken breast and leg, peppercorns, and bay leaf and bring to a boil. Simmer mixture, covered, until breast is just cooked through, about 12 minutes, and transfer breast with tongs to a bowl. Simmer mixture 5 minutes more, or until leg is just cooked through, and transfer leg with tongs to bowl. When chicken is cool enough to handle, remove meat in large pieces, discarding skin and bones, and put in a large bowl. Pour broth through a fine sieve into a bowl and return to cleaned kettle.

Trim fennel stalks flush with bulbs, discarding stalks, and halve bulbs lengthwise. Thinly slice fennel crosswise and cut carrots into ½-inch-thick slices. Peel potato and cut into ½-inch cubes. Thinly slice onion. Simmer vegetables in broth until just tender, 8 to 10 minutes, and with a slotted spoon add to chicken. Measure out 2 cups stock and reserve remainder for another use. Mince garlic and finely chop parsley. Add garlic, parsley, and fennel seeds to chicken mixture.

In a heavy saucepan melt butter over moderately low heat and stir in flour. Cook *roux*, stirring, 3 minutes and whisk in 2 cups stock in a stream. Bring mixture to a boil, whisking, and simmer sauce, whisking, 5 minutes. Season sauce with salt and pepper and pour over chicken mixture, stirring gently to combine. *Filling may be made 1 day ahead and cooled completely before being chilled, covered. Reheat filling before proceeding.* Spoon filling into a 12-inch (10-cup) round baking dish.

Preheat oven to 450° F.

Make crust:
Chop bacon and in a heavy skillet cook over moderate heat, stirring, until crisp. Transfer bacon with a slotted spoon to paper towels to drain, reserving 1 tablespoon bacon fat, and mince.

Into a bowl sift together flour, baking powder, and salt. Add cream, bacon, and reserved fat and with a fork stir until mixture just forms a dough. Gather dough into a ball and on a lightly floured surface with a floured rolling pin roll out into a 12½-inch round (about ½ inch thick). Trim dough to create a 12-inch round and with a large knife cut dough into 12 wedges. Arrange wedges on filling in overlapping pairs. In a small bowl whisk together yolk and milk and lightly brush onto crust.

Bake pie in middle of oven until crust is puffed and golden and filling is bubbling, 20 to 25 minutes. Serve pie warm. Serves 6 as a main course.

E.M.

CHICKEN PICCATA WITH NIÇOISE OLIVES

¼ cup Niçoise olives (about 2 ounces)
4 small skinless boneless chicken breast halves
    (about 1½ pounds total)
2 tablespoons olive oil
½ stick (¼ cup) unsalted butter
¼ cup dry white wine
1 tablespoon fresh lemon juice
2 tablespoons minced fresh flat-leafed parsley
    leaves

In a sieve rinse olives and drain well. Pit olives and cut into slivers. With a knife butterfly each chicken breast half by horizontally cutting through meat, keeping 1 long side intact, and opening like a book. With a rolling pin lightly pound chicken between sheets of plastic wrap to about ⅛ inch thick. Pat chicken dry and season with salt and pepper.

In a 12-inch heavy skillet heat olive oil and 2 tablespoons butter over moderately high heat until foam subsides and sauté chicken, 1 piece at a time, until golden and just cooked through, about 30 seconds on each side. Transfer chicken as sautéed with tongs to a platter and keep warm, loosely covered with foil.

Pour off any fat in skillet. Add wine and deglaze skillet over moderately high heat, scraping up brown bits. Stir in lemon juice and remaining 2 tablespoons butter and heat sauce, swirling skillet, until butter is just incorporated. Remove skillet from heat and stir in olives, parsley, and salt and pepper to taste.

Spoon sauce over chicken. Serves 4.

CILANTRO-STUFFED CHICKEN BREASTS WITH POBLANO CHILE SAUCE

1 teaspoon vegetable oil
1 garlic clove
3 tablespoons finely chopped fresh cilantro leaves
¼ teaspoon salt
4 small skinless boneless chicken breast halves
2 cups *poblano* chile sauce (recipe follows)

Preheat broiler and lightly brush a shallow baking pan with some oil. Finely chop garlic and in a small bowl stir together with cilantro and salt. Pat chicken dry and trim any fat.

To form a pocket in chicken for cilantro filling: Put a chicken breast half on a cutting board and, beginning in middle of 1 side of breast half, horizontally insert a sharp thin knife three fourths of the way through center, moving knife in a fanning motion to create a pocket. (Opening will only be about 1 inch wide.) Make pockets in remaining chicken breast halves in same manner. Put about ½ tablespoon filling into each pocket and with finger spread evenly. Transfer chicken to baking pan and brush with remaining oil. Season chicken with salt and pepper and broil 5 to 6 inches from heat 7 minutes. Turn chicken over and broil until just cooked through, 3 to 5 minutes more.

Serve chicken with *poblano* chile sauce. Serves 4.

PHOTO ON PAGE 87

each serving, including sauce, about 276 calories and 8 grams fat

POBLANO CHILE SAUCE

This sauce can be prepared with poblano chiles or yellow bell peppers—both peppers complement the chicken.

¾ pound fresh *poblano* chiles* (4 to 6) or
    yellow bell peppers (2 to 3)
2 garlic cloves
1 large onion
2 teaspoons vegetable oil
1 cup chicken broth (8 fluid ounces)

*available at Latino markets, specialty produce
    markets, and many supermarkets

Lay whole peppers on their sides on racks of gas stove burners (preferably 1 to a burner) and turn flame on high. Roast peppers, turning them, until skins are blistered and have brown patches, 3 to 6 minutes. Do not overchar bell peppers; they will lose their bright color. (Alternatively, peppers may be roasted in same manner on rack of a broiler pan under a preheated broiler about 2 inches from heat.) Transfer peppers to a bowl and let stand, covered, until cool enough to handle. Peel peppers (wear rubber gloves when handling chiles). Cut off tops and discard seeds and ribs. Chop peppers. *Peppers may be prepared 1 day ahead and chilled, covered.*

Chop garlic and chop enough onion to measure 1 cup. In a nonstick skillet cook garlic and onion in oil over moderately low heat, stirring, until softened. Skim fat from broth. Stir in broth and peppers and simmer 1 minute. In a blender purée mixture until completely smooth (use caution when blending hot liquids) and season with salt. Makes 2 cups.

☞ each ½-cup serving about 78 calories and 2.8 grams fat

SPICED CHICKEN BREASTS
WITH COUSCOUS SALAD

For marinade
½ cup sour cream
2 tablespoons olive oil
2 tablespoons fresh lime juice
2 tablespoons fresh orange juice
2 tablespoons fresh lemon juice
2 tablespoons chili powder

2 tablespoons paprika
1 teaspoon cayenne
½ teaspoon freshly ground black pepper
½ teaspoon salt

10 skinless boneless chicken breast halves
(about 5 pounds total)
2 cups packed fresh cilantro sprigs
1 teaspoon fresh thyme leaves

Accompaniment: couscous salad
(page 142)

Make marinade:
In a blender blend together marinade ingredients until smooth.

Pat chicken breast halves dry. Trim any fat from chicken and arrange chicken in a shallow glass or ceramic dish just large enough to hold it in one layer. Chop cilantro sprigs and thyme leaves. Add marinade and herbs to chicken and toss to coat. *Marinate chicken, covered and chilled, at least 6 hours and up to 1 day.*

Prepare grill.

Remove chicken from marinade, letting excess drip off, and discard marinade. Grill chicken on an oiled rack set 5 to 6 inches over glowing coals until just cooked through, about 5 minutes on each side. (Alternatively, broil chicken.) Transfer chicken as grilled with tongs to a serving platter.

Serve chicken with couscous salad. Serves 8 to 10 as part of a buffet.

PHOTO ON PAGE 20

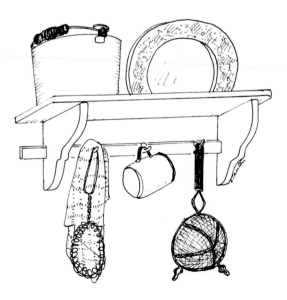

COUSCOUS SALAD

¾ pound thin asparagus stalks (about 1 bunch)
1 red bell pepper
1 yellow bell pepper
7 scallions (about 1 bunch)
1 medium red onion
2 fresh jalapeño chiles
1 tablespoon minced garlic
1 teaspoon cinnamon
1 teaspoon freshly grated nutmeg
2¾ cups couscous (from about 2 boxes)
3½ cups water
1 cup packed fresh basil leaves
1 cup packed fresh mint leaves
1 cup packed fresh cilantro sprigs
½ cup olive oil
2 tablespoons fresh lemon juice
3 tablespoons fresh lime juice

Trim asparagus and chop. Finely chop bell peppers, scallions, and onion. Wearing rubber gloves, seed jalapeños and finely chop.

In a large bowl stir together asparagus, bell peppers, scallions, onion, jalapeños, garlic, cinnamon, nutmeg, and couscous. Bring 3 cups water to a boil. Stir boiling water into couscous mixture and tightly cover bowl with plastic wrap. *Let couscous stand at room temperature 1 hour.*

Bring remaining ½ cup water to a boil and chop all herbs.

With a fork stir boiling water, herbs, and remaining ingredients into couscous until just combined well and tightly cover bowl with plastic wrap. *Let couscous stand at room temperature 30 minutes more.* Fluff salad with a fork and season with salt and pepper. Serves 8 to 10.

CHICKEN FRICASSEE WITH BLACK-EYED PEAS AND SPINACH

1 cup dried black-eyed peas
1 medium onion
2 garlic cloves
10 ounces white mushrooms
2 tablespoons olive oil
½ teaspoon dried thyme

¼ cup dry Sherry
4 skinless boneless chicken breast halves
    (about 1½ pounds total)
2 tablespoons all-purpose flour
2¼ cups chicken broth
1 pound spinach
½ cup heavy cream
1 tablespoon Dijon mustard

Quick-soak dried black-eyed peas (procedure on page 109).

Chop onion and mince garlic. Cut mushrooms into ¼-inch-thick slices.

In a 4-quart heavy kettle cook onion and garlic in 1 tablespoon oil over moderate heat, stirring occasionally, until onion is softened. Add mushrooms and thyme and cook, stirring, until mushrooms are tender and liquid from mushrooms is evaporated. Stir in Sherry and simmer 1 minute. Transfer mushroom mixture to a bowl.

Pat chicken dry and cut crosswise into ½-inch-thick slices. Season chicken with salt and pepper. In kettle heat remaining tablespoon oil over moderately high heat until hot but not smoking and cook chicken, stirring, until browned. Add flour, stirring to coat chicken evenly. Add broth and bring to a boil, stirring. Stir in mushroom mixture and drained peas and simmer, covered, 20 minutes, or until peas are tender.

While mixture is simmering, discard coarse stems from spinach and cut leaves crosswise into ¼-inch-wide strips.

Stir spinach, cream, mustard, and salt and pepper to taste into fricassee and simmer, stirring, 2 minutes. Serves 4.

CHICKEN, POLENTA, AND RED PEPPER RAGOUT ☺

1 leek (white and pale green part only)
1 medium onion
1 red bell pepper
1 large garlic clove
2 tablespoons olive oil
2 skinless boneless chicken breast halves
    (about ¾ pound total)
a ½-pound piece store-bought plain polenta roll*
    (from a 1½-pound roll)

1 cup canned chopped tomatoes
⅛ teaspoon dried thyme, crumbled
1 tablespoon chopped fresh flat-leafed
   parsley leaves

*available at specialty foods shops, natural foods
   stores, and many supermarkets

Halve leek lengthwise and cut crosswise into ½-inch pieces. In a bowl of cold water wash leek well and with a slotted spoon transfer to a sieve to drain. Chop onion and cut bell pepper into 1-inch pieces. Mince garlic.

In a 12-inch nonstick skillet cook leek, onion, bell pepper, and garlic in 1 tablespoon oil over moderate heat, stirring occasionally, until onion is softened and pepper is tender, about 15 minutes. Transfer vegetables to a bowl. Pat chicken dry and cut crosswise into ½-inch-thick strips. Season chicken with salt and pepper and cut polenta into ¾-inch cubes.

In skillet heat remaining tablespoon oil over moderately high heat until hot but not smoking and sauté chicken, stirring, until golden, about 3 minutes. Add polenta and cook, stirring occasionally, 1 minute.

Stir in cooked vegetables, tomatoes, thyme, and parsley and simmer, stirring, until heated through, about 2 minutes. Season ragout with salt and pepper. Serves 2.

MU SHU CHICKEN WITH JÍCAMA ◐

½ pound boneless skinless chicken thighs
1 teaspoon cornstarch
2 tablespoons plus ½ teaspoon soy sauce
2½ tablespoons medium-dry Sherry
2 large eggs
¼ teaspoon salt
a ½-pound piece *jícama*
3 scallions
4 flour tortillas
5 tablespoons vegetable oil

Cut chicken into ¼-inch-thick strips and in a shallow baking dish stir together cornstarch, 1 tablespoon soy sauce, and 1 tablespoon Sherry until combined well. Add chicken to marinade and toss to coat well. Marinate chicken, covered, at room temperature 15 minutes.

Preheat oven to 350° F.

In a bowl whisk together eggs, ½ teaspoon soy sauce, and salt. Peel *jícama* and cut into sticks about 3 inches long and ¼ inch thick. Cut scallions into 1½-inch pieces and halve white pieces lengthwise.

Wrap tortillas in a sheet of foil and heat in oven until hot, about 8 minutes.

While tortillas are heating, heat a wok or an 8- to 10-inch heavy skillet (preferably cast iron) over moderately high heat until a bead of water dropped on cooking surface evaporates immediately. Add 1½ tablespoons oil, swirling wok or skillet to coat evenly, and heat until hot but not smoking. Stir-fry eggs until just cooked through but not browned, about 10 seconds. Transfer eggs to a bowl and break up into bite-size pieces.

Carefully wipe out wok or skillet with paper towels. In wok or skillet heat 1½ tablespoons oil until hot but not smoking. Stir-fry *jícama* 30 seconds and add 1 tablespoon Sherry. Add scallions and stir-fry 10 seconds, or until *jícama* is crisp-tender. Add vegetables to eggs. Add remaining 2 tablespoons oil to wok or skillet and heat until hot but not smoking. Stir-fry chicken with marinade 1 minute, or until just cooked through. Add vegetable mixture with remaining tablespoon soy sauce and remaining ½ tablespoon Sherry and stir-fry until heated through.

Divide chicken mixture between 2 plates and serve with tortillas for wrapping. Serves 2.

GRILLED LEMON GARLIC CHICKEN THIGHS
ON ARUGULA SALAD

For marinade
⅓ cup fresh rosemary leaves (about 3 bunches)
24 garlic cloves (about 3 heads)
3 lemons
¼ cup plus 2 tablespoons honey
¾ cup extra-virgin olive oil
1½ tablespoons coarsely ground black pepper
kosher salt to taste

24 chicken thighs (about 7½ pounds)
1 cup mesquite wood chips* (optional)
3 tablespoons fresh lemon juice
½ cup extra-virgin olive oil
½ tablespoon coarsely ground black pepper
6 apples (preferably Fuji or Gala)
3 cups seedless red grapes
1 bunch fresh chives
4 bunches arugula (about 1 pound)

*available at some hardware stores and by mail
   order from Weber, (800) 446-1071

Make marinade:
Chop rosemary and thinly slice garlic. Cut lemons
into ¼-inch-thick slices. Divide all marinade ingredients between 2 shallow glass dishes (about 13 by 9
inches) and stir to combine well.

Pat chicken dry and add 12 thighs to each dish of
marinade, turning them to coat. *Marinate chicken,
covered and chilled, turning it occasionally, at least
8 hours and up to 12.*
Soak wood chips in 1 cup water 2 hours.
Prepare grill.
Transfer chicken to a large plate and discard
marinade. Drain wood chips well, shaking off excess
water. As soon as briquettes are lightly coated with
gray ash, in about 30 minutes, spread wood chips
evenly on top. When chips begin to smoke, in about
2 minutes, grill is ready. Grill chicken, skin sides
down, covered, on an oiled rack set 5 to 6 inches
over coals (or low to moderate heat if using a gas
grill) 7 minutes and with tongs turn chicken over.
Grill chicken, covered, 8 minutes more, or until
cooked through. (Alternatively, roast chicken, skin
sides up, on a rack in a large shallow baking pan in

middle of a 450° F. oven about 40 minutes, or until
just cooked through.) Transfer chicken to a platter
and keep warm, loosely covered with foil.

In a large bowl whisk together lemon juice, oil,
pepper, and salt to taste. Peel apples and core. Cut
each apple into 16 wedges and add to dressing,
tossing to combine. Halve grapes and finely chop
chives. Discard coarse stems from arugula.

Add grapes, chives, and arugula to apple mixture,
tossing until just combined.

Serve chicken on top of salad. Serves 12 as part of
a buffet.

PHOTO ON PAGE 38

SPICY-SWEET GLAZED CHICKEN WINGS ◐

3 quarts vegetable oil for deep-frying
2½ pounds chicken wings (about 12)
2 teaspoons minced garlic
⅔ cup apricot preserves
⅓ cup soy sauce
⅓ cup ketchup
1 teaspoon Tabasco, or to taste

In a 6-quart kettle heat oil over moderate heat
until a deep-fat thermometer registers 375° F.

While oil is heating, cut off wing tips, reserving
them for another use (such as chicken stock, page
115), and halve chicken wings at joint. In a saucepan
simmer remaining ingredients, stirring, until glaze is
slightly thickened, about 3 minutes, and keep warm
over very low heat.

Preheat oven to 200° F.

Pat chicken wings dry. Working in batches of 8,
fry chicken wings in oil until crisp and golden, about
7 minutes. Return oil to 375° F. between batches.
With a slotted spoon transfer wings as fried to a rack
set in a shallow baking pan and keep warm in oven.

In a large bowl toss chicken wings with glaze to
coat. Serves 2 generously.

SPICED GRILLED CORNISH HEN

2 tablespoons unsalted butter
1 tablespoon honey
2 teaspoons chili powder
¼ teaspoon cayenne
1 teaspoon fresh orange juice
a 1¼-pound Cornish hen, halved lengthwise*

*available by request from butcher

Prepare grill.

In a small saucepan melt butter with honey, chili powder, and cayenne. Remove pan from heat and stir in juice and salt and pepper to taste.

Rinse and pat hen halves dry and season with salt. Grill hen halves, skin sides down, on an oiled rack set 5 to 6 inches over glowing coals 5 minutes. Turn halves over with metal tongs and grill, basting with spice mixture, 20 minutes more. Grill halves, without basting, until cooked through, about 10 minutes more. (Alternatively, grill hen halves in a hot oiled well-seasoned ridged grill pan over moderately high heat.) Serves 2.

CRISP DUCK BREAST WITH PINK PEPPERCORN SAUCE

2 whole boneless duck breasts with skin* such as
    Long Island (also known as Pekin; each about
    1½ pounds)
a 6½-ounce container duck-and-veal *demiglace**
1 tablespoon balsamic vinegar
½ teaspoon sugar
½ teaspoon coarsely crushed peppercorns
    (preferably pink)

*available from many butchers and by mail order
    from D'Artagnan, (800) 327-8246

Halve duck breasts and trim excess fat. Pat duck dry. Pierce skin of duck all over with a fork and score with a knife to allow fat to drain and help skin become crisp. Season duck with salt. Heat a large heavy skillet (preferably cast iron) over high heat until very hot. Put duck, skin sides down, in skillet and immediately reduce heat to moderately low. Cook duck 20 minutes, or until skin is mahogany-colored and most of fat is rendered. Remove fat from skillet with a metal bulb baster or by very carefully pouring it off. (Reserve 1 tablespoon rendered fat if sautéing kohlrabi, as part of the Fireside Dinner menu.) Turn duck over and cook 2 minutes more. Transfer duck to a cutting board and let stand 5 minutes. (Duck will continue to cook as it stands until it reaches medium.)

While duck is standing, in a small saucepan boil *demiglace* until reduced to about ¾ cup and add vinegar, sugar, and peppercorns. Remove pan from heat and keep sauce warm, covered.

Diagonally cut duck breast halves and serve with sauce. Serves 4.

PHOTO ON PAGE 14

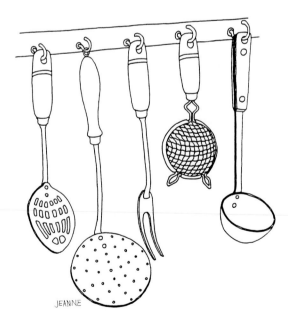

JEANNE

Sautéed Quail with Paprika Sauce and Moroccan-Spiced Vegetables

6 whole jumbo quail* (6 to
   8 ounces each)
For paprika sauce
1 small garlic clove
¼ teaspoon salt
1 tablespoon paprika (preferably
   sweet Hungarian)
1 tablespoon extra-virgin olive oil
2 tablespoons fresh lime juice
⅛ teaspoon cayenne, or to taste

freshly ground black pepper
2 tablespoons corn or canola oil
2 tablespoons unsalted butter

Accompaniments:
Moroccan-spiced vegetables
   (recipe follows)
bulgur pilaf or couscous

*available by mail order from D'Artagnan,
   (800) 327-8246

With poultry shears or a sharp knife cut off necks, feet, and first 2 wing joints of each quail and discard. Cut out and discard backbones and halve each quail lengthwise through breast.
Make sauce:
Mince garlic and mash to a paste with salt. In a small heavy skillet heat garlic paste and paprika in olive oil over moderate heat, stirring, until fragrant, about 1 minute. Remove skillet from heat and stir in lime juice and cayenne.

Pat quail dry and season with pepper and salt. Divide corn or canola oil and butter between two 12-inch heavy skillets and heat over moderately high heat until hot but not smoking. Add quail and sauté, skin sides down, until skin is golden, about 2 minutes. Turn quail over and sauté 2 minutes more. Turn quail skin sides down and sauté 1 minute more, or until skin is golden brown but meat is barely pink for medium.

Serve quail with Moroccan vegetables and bulgur pilaf or couscous. Drizzle paprika sauce over and around vegetables and quail. Serves 4.

Moroccan-Spiced Vegetables

1 large onion
1 garlic clove
1 medium fennel bulb (sometimes
   called anise; about ½ pound)
1 large zucchini
2 small carrots
1 large vine-ripened tomato
2 tablespoons extra-virgin olive oil
1 teaspoon turmeric
½ teaspoon ground cumin
¼ teaspoon ground ginger
freshly ground black pepper

Cut enough onion into ¼-inch dice to measure 1 cup and thinly slice garlic. Trim fennel stalks flush with bulb, discarding stalks. Halve bulb and core. Cut enough fennel bulb into ¼-inch dice to measure 1½ cups. Cut enough zucchini into ¼-inch dice to measure 1½ cups. Cut enough carrot into ¼-inch dice to measure ⅔ cup.

Peel tomato (procedure follows), reserving boiling water and ice water, and seed. Cut enough tomato into ¼-inch dice to measure ¾ cup. Add carrot to boiling water and cook 1 minute. Drain carrot in a colander. Transfer carrot to ice water to stop cooking and drain.

In a large heavy skillet cook onion and garlic in oil over moderately low heat, stirring, until softened. Add fennel, zucchini, and carrot and cook, stirring, until slightly softened, about 5 minutes. Add spices and cook, stirring, 1 minute. Stir in tomato and pepper and salt to taste and cook, covered, over low heat, stirring occasionally, until fennel and carrot are just tender, 10 to 12 minutes. Keep vegetables warm, partially covered. *Vegetables may be prepared 1 day ahead and chilled, covered. Reheat vegetables with 1 to 2 tablespoons water.* Serves 4.

To Peel Tomatoes

Have ready a bowl of ice and cold water. Cut an X in blossom end of each tomato. In a saucepan of boiling water blanch tomatoes 10 seconds. Transfer tomatoes with a slotted spoon to ice water to stop cooking. Peel tomatoes.

GRILL-ROASTED BRINED TURKEY WITH ANAHEIM CHILE SALSA VERDE

We cooked this turkey on a gas grill, but a 22½-inch charcoal kettle grill will also work. Cooking times and results may vary according to the weather and type of grill. The gas grill we used had a thermometer, and at the lowest settings, the grill (with lid closed) maintained temperatures between 350° F. and 400° F. We did not stuff the bird because when cooking on a grill it is difficult to maintain a steady temperature to adequately cook the stuffing. Brining the meat adds exceptional flavor and moistness, but feel free to omit this step. Simply season the bird with salt, then cook as directed.

a 12- to 14-pound turkey
8 quarts cold water
2 cups kosher salt
½ cup packed brown sugar
1 tablespoon chili powder
kitchen string

Garnish: fresh Anaheim chiles, small heads of
   garlic, and tomatillos
Accompaniment: Anaheim chile *salsa verde*
   (page 148)

Rinse turkey inside and out and reserve neck, giblets, and liver for another use. In a container large enough to hold turkey and 8 quarts water (we used a 5-gallon bucket lined with a large heavy-duty plastic bag) stir together water, salt, and brown sugar until solids are dissolved. *Soak turkey in brine, covered and chilled, 10 hours.*

Remove turkey from brine and pat dry inside and out. Fold neck skin under body and fasten with a small skewer. If desired, secure wings to body with small skewers. Set an oiled metal rack in a roasting pan that will fit in covered grill. Transfer turkey to rack in pan and sprinkle with chili powder. Loosely tie drumsticks together with kitchen string. *Turkey may be prepared up to this point 1 day ahead and chilled, covered.*

Prepare grill:

Preheat gas grill. (If using a charcoal grill, open vents in lid and bottom of grill and divide 50 briquettes between 2 opposite sides of bottom, leaving middle clear. Position grill rack with wider openings over briquettes and light briquettes. They will be ready for cooking as soon as they are lightly coated with gray ash, 20 to 30 minutes.)

Put turkey in roasting pan on grill and cover grill. Turn all gas settings to low. Grill-roast turkey, basting with pan juices and rotating pan 180 degrees every hour, 3 hours. (If using charcoal grill, add 10 more briquettes to each mound of coals every hour to maintain even temperature.)

After 3 hours insert an instant-read thermometer in fleshy part of an inner thigh. If thermometer registers 175° F. and juices run clear when thigh is pierced, turkey is done. If turkey is not done, continue to cook (if using charcoal grill, add 10 more briquettes to each mound of coals), checking for doneness every 20 minutes. Transfer turkey to a heated platter and discard string. Loosely cover turkey with aluminum foil and let stand 20 minutes before carving.

Garnish turkey with chiles, garlic, and tomatillos and serve with *salsa verde.* Serves 6 to 8.

PHOTO ON PAGE 68

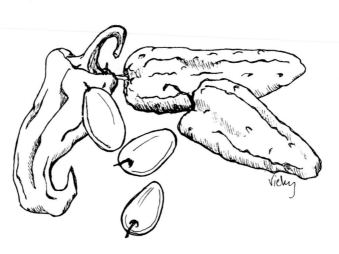

ANAHEIM CHILE SALSA VERDE

This beautiful, mild-flavored green salsa may be served either heated or at room temperature. For the brightest green color possible, add the fresh cilantro sprigs just before serving.

6 fresh green Anaheim chiles*
   (about ¾ pound)
¾ pound fresh tomatillos or 1¼ cups
   drained canned tomatillos** (about
   half of a 28-ounce can)
1 cup chicken broth
2 garlic cloves
1 cup packed fresh cilantro sprigs

*available at Latino and specialty produce
   markets and some supermarkets
**available by mail order from Kitchen Market,
   (888) 468-4433

Preheat broiler.

Arrange chiles on rack of a broiler pan and broil about 2 inches from heat, turning them frequently, until skins are blistered and charred, 8 to 12 minutes. (Alternatively, if using a gas stove, lay chiles on their sides on racks of burners and turn flames on high. Char chiles, turning them with tongs, until skins are blackened, 3 to 6 minutes.) Transfer chiles to a bowl and let stand, covered, until cool enough to handle. Wearing rubber gloves, peel chiles. Cut off tops and discard seeds and ribs.

Remove husks from fresh tomatillos and rinse tomatillos under warm water to remove stickiness. In a saucepan simmer tomatillos, chicken broth, and garlic cloves until tomatillos are tender, about 10 minutes if using fresh tomatillos and about 5 minutes if using canned. Add chiles to tomatillo mixture. Cool salsa slightly and in a blender pulse until coarsely chopped (use caution when blending hot liquids). *Salsa may be made up to this point 2 days ahead and cooled, uncovered, before being chilled, covered. Bring salsa to room temperature or reheat before proceeding.*

Just before serving, in blender pulse salsa with cilantro until cilantro is finely chopped (use caution when blending if salsa is heated) and season with salt. Makes about 3 cups.

CHORIZO, ROASTED CORN, AND CURRANT DRESSING

1 loaf firm white sandwich bread (about 1 pound)
2 tablespoons olive oil
2 ears corn
½ pound Spanish *chorizo** (spicy cured pork
   sausage; about 3 links)
1 large onion
6 celery ribs
½ stick (¼ cup) unsalted butter
1½ cups coarsely crumbled salted tortilla chips
½ cup dried currants
3 tablespoons chopped fresh flat-leafed parsley
   leaves
½ teaspoon dried rubbed sage
2½ cups water

*available at Latino markets and specialty foods
   shops and by mail order from D'Artagnan,
   (800) 327-8246

Preheat oven to 350° F.

Cut bread into ½-inch pieces and spread evenly in a shallow baking pan. Toast bread in middle of oven, stirring occasionally, until golden, 10 to 15 minutes, and transfer croutons to a large bowl.

Increase temperature to 400° F.

In shallow baking pan put 1 tablespoon oil and add corn, turning to coat. Season corn with salt and roast in middle of oven, turning once halfway through roasting, about 30 minutes. Cool corn to room temperature. Cut corn kernels from cobs and transfer to a bowl.

Cut *chorizo* into ½-inch cubes. Coarsely chop onion and celery and in a large skillet cook in butter over moderate heat, stirring occasionally, until tender, about 10 minutes. Add vegetables and any butter remaining in skillet to corn. In skillet cook *chorizo* in remaining tablespoon oil over moderate heat, stirring occasionally, until browned and with a slotted spoon transfer to paper towels to drain.

Preheat oven to 350° F.

To croutons add corn mixture, *chorizo*, and all remaining ingredients except water, tossing to combine well, and season with salt and pepper. Drizzle water over dressing and toss to evenly distribute. Transfer dressing to a 4-quart shallow casserole dish.

Dressing may be made up to this point 1 day ahead and chilled, covered.

Bake dressing, covered, in middle of oven until heated through, about 30 minutes. Uncover dressing and bake until top is crisp, about 15 minutes more. Makes about 12 cups, serving 6 generously.

RED CURRANT—GLAZED TURKEY WITH SAGE AND RED CURRANT GRAVY

a 12- to 14-pound turkey (reserving neck and
    giblets for making stock, but excluding liver)
kitchen string
½ cup red currant jelly
For gravy
pan juices reserved from turkey
4 cups turkey giblet stock (recipe follows) plus
    additional for thinning gravy
¼ cup red currant jelly
3 tablespoons chopped fresh sage leaves
3 tablespoons water
3 tablespoons cornstarch

Garnish: fresh sage leaves

Preheat oven to 350° F.

Rinse turkey inside and out and pat dry. Fold neck skin under body and fasten with a small skewer. If desired, secure wings to body with small skewers. Transfer turkey to a rack set in a flameproof roasting pan and season with salt and pepper. Loosely tie drumsticks together with kitchen string. Roast turkey in middle of oven 2½ hours.

Brush turkey all over with jelly and roast 45 minutes more, or until a meat thermometer inserted in fleshy part of an inner thigh registers 175° F. and juices run clear when thigh is pierced. Transfer turkey to a heated platter and reserve juices in pan. Remove skewers and discard string. Let turkey stand 30 minutes.

Make gravy while turkey is standing:

Skim fat from reserved juices in pan. Add 4 cups stock and deglaze pan over moderately high heat, scraping up brown bits. Add jelly and bring to a boil, whisking until jelly is dissolved. Season gravy with salt and pepper and pour through a sieve into a saucepan. Stir in sage and bring sauce to a boil.

In a small bowl whisk together water and cornstarch and add to gravy, whisking constantly to prevent lumps. Boil gravy, whisking constantly, 5 minutes. If necessary, whisk in additional stock to thin gravy to desired consistency and season with salt and pepper. Transfer gravy to a sauceboat.

Garnish turkey with sage leaves and serve with gravy. Serves 8.

PHOTO ON PAGE 72

TURKEY GIBLET STOCK

1 celery rib
1 carrot
1 onion
5 cups chicken broth
6 cups water
reserved neck and giblets (excluding liver)
    from a 12- to 14-pound turkey
1 bay leaf
8 sprigs mixed fresh herbs such as thyme,
    sage, rosemary and/or marjoram

Coarsely chop celery and carrot and quarter onion. In a large deep saucepan bring broth and water to a boil with celery, carrot, onion, and neck and giblets, skimming froth. Add bay leaf and fresh herb sprigs and cook, uncovered, at a bare simmer 2 hours, or until liquid is reduced to about 6 cups. Pour stock through a fine sieve into a bowl. *Stock may be made 2 days ahead and cooled completely, uncovered, before being chilled or frozen in an airtight container.* Makes about 6 cups.

WHEAT-BERRY STUFFING WITH PEARL ONIONS

It will take about 45 minutes to peel the pearl onions for this recipe. If you're strapped for time, you can substitute 1½ pounds of thawed frozen pearl onions, which won't need to be blanched.

12 slices country-style white bread
2 cups wheat berries* (preferably organic)
2 pounds pearl onions (see note, above)
1 stick (½ cup) unsalted butter
1 cup packed fresh flat-leafed parsley leaves
1½ cups chicken broth

*available at natural foods stores and by mail order from Walnut Acres, (800) 433-3998

Preheat oven to 350° F.

Cut bread into ½-inch pieces and in a large shallow baking pan toast in one layer in middle of oven until just dry, about 15 minutes. *Croutons may be made 1 day ahead and kept, covered, at room temperature.*

In a 4-quart kettle three fourths full of boiling water (do not salt water) cook wheat berries, uncovered, until tender, about 1 hour, and drain in a large sieve. Transfer wheat berries to a large shallow baking dish.

While wheat berries are cooking, in a large saucepan of boiling water blanch onions 3 minutes. Drain onions and, when cool enough to handle, peel. In a large skillet melt butter over moderately high heat and sauté onions, stirring occasionally, until golden, 15 to 20 minutes. Chop parsley and add with onions to wheat berries. *Wheat-berry mixture may be made 1 day ahead and chilled, covered. Bring mixture to room temperature before proceeding.*

Add croutons and broth to wheat-berry mixture and toss to combine well. Bake stuffing in middle of oven, uncovered, 30 minutes, or until top is slightly crisp. Makes about 12 cups, serving 8 generously.

TURKEY B'STILLA
MOROCCAN TURKEY PIE

Traditionally, the Moroccan dish called b'stilla is a pie made with minced squab.

For almond sugar
⅛ cup blanched almonds
1 tablespoon granulated sugar
½ teaspoon cinnamon
For filling
4 garlic cloves
1 cup packed fresh cilantro sprigs
¼ cup packed fresh mint leaves
1 large onion
1¾ cups chicken broth (14 fluid ounces)
¼ teaspoon crumbled saffron threads
1 pound lean ground turkey
5 large egg whites
½ teaspoon vegetable oil
1 tablespoon *ras el hanout* (Moroccan spice blend; recipe follows)
1 tablespoon all-purpose flour
2 teaspoons finely grated peeled fresh gingerroot
¾ cup golden raisins
2 tablespoons fresh lemon juice

four 17- by 12-inch *phyllo* sheets
3 tablespoons fine dry bread crumbs

Garnish: 1 teaspoon each confectioners' sugar and cinnamon for dusting

Make almond sugar:

In a food processor finely grind almonds with sugar and cinnamon.

Make filling:

Mince garlic cloves. Chop cilantro and mint. Chop enough onion to measure 1½ cups.

In a large saucepan bring broth to a boil and remove pan from heat. Stir in saffron and steep 10 minutes. Add turkey and simmer mixture, stirring and breaking up lumps, 2 minutes, or until meat is just cooked through. In a large sieve set over a bowl drain turkey mixture and return drained cooking liquid to pan. Transfer turkey mixture to a large bowl. Boil cooking liquid until reduced to about ¾ cup, about 10 minutes. Transfer ¼ cup liquid to a small bowl and reserve. Reduce heat to moderate and add whites in a stream to liquid remaining in pan, whisking. Cook mixture, whisking, until whites are opaque, about 2 minutes. Add egg mixture to turkey mixture and stir until combined.

In a nonstick skillet heat oil over moderate heat until hot but not smoking and cook onion, stirring, until golden. Add *ras el hanout*, flour, gingerroot, and garlic and cook, stirring constantly, 1 minute. Add reserved cooking liquid and boil, stirring and scraping up brown bits, 1 minute. Add mixture to turkey with golden raisins, lemon juice, cilantro, and mint, stirring until combined well. Cool filling completely. *Filling may be made 1 day ahead and chilled, covered.*

Preheat oven to 350° F.

Stack *phyllo* sheets on a work surface and cover stack with overlapping sheets of plastic wrap and then a dampened kitchen towel. Working quickly (*phyllo* dries out easily), arrange 1 *phyllo* sheet in a 9-inch glass pie plate, letting edges hang over. Sprinkle bottom with 2 teaspoons almond sugar and 1 tablespoon bread crumbs. Repeat layering 2 more times, arranging each *phyllo* sheet in a different position to create an even overhang all around. Top with remaining *phyllo* sheet and spoon filling evenly into shell. Sprinkle filling with 2 teaspoons almond sugar and carefully fold overhanging *phyllo* over top

of filling to enclose it completely (*phyllo* will be very brittle; don't worry if it breaks). Sprinkle remaining almond sugar over top.

Bake pie in lower third of oven 25 minutes (top will be golden brown in places).

Dust pie with confectioners' sugar and cinnamon and serve immediately. Serves 4 as a main course.

☞ each serving about 402 calories and 12.4 grams fat

Ras El Hanout ◗
Moroccan Spice Blend

1 teaspoon ground cumin
1 teaspoon ground ginger
1 teaspoon salt
¾ teaspoon freshly ground black pepper
½ teaspoon ground cinnamon
½ teaspoon ground coriander seeds
½ teaspoon cayenne
½ teaspoon ground allspice
¼ teaspoon ground cloves

In a small bowl whisk together all ingredients until combined well. *Spice blend keeps in an airtight container at cool room temperature 1 month.* Makes about 2 tablespoons.

CHINESE TURKEY IN JADE ◐

Here we've adapted the classic Chinese dish "squab in jade," in which the meat is minced, stir-fried, and served in "cups" of lettuce.

an 8-ounce can water chestnuts
½ cup snow peas
4 scallions
3 heads Bibb lettuce
1 pound lean ground turkey
2 teaspoons honey
4 tablespoons soy sauce
3 tablespoons seasoned rice vinegar
2 tablespoons minced garlic
3 tablespoons finely grated peeled fresh
    gingerroot
1 tablespoon Worcestershire sauce
½ cup water
1½ tablespoons sugar
2 teaspoons cornstarch
2 teaspoons vegetable oil
½ teaspoon Asian sesame oil

Accompaniments:
1 cup packed fresh mint sprigs
1 cup packed fresh cilantro sprigs
2 cups cooked white rice

Rinse and drain water chestnuts and coarsely chop. Diagonally cut snow peas into ½-inch-wide pieces and chop scallions. Separate lettuce leaves.

In a bowl with your hands mix turkey, 1 teaspoon honey, 1 tablespoon each soy sauce, vinegar, and garlic, and 2 tablespoons gingerroot until just combined. Marinate turkey mixture 15 minutes.

In a small bowl whisk together Worcestershire sauce, water, sugar, cornstarch, and remaining teaspoon honey, 3 tablespoons soy sauce, and 2 tablespoons vinegar.

In a wok or large nonstick skillet heat vegetable oil over moderately high heat until hot but not smoking and sauté turkey mixture, stirring and breaking up lumps, until just cooked through, about 3 minutes. With a slotted spoon transfer turkey mixture to clean bowl. In wok or skillet stir-fry remaining tablespoon each garlic and gingerroot 15 seconds. Add water chestnuts and stir-fry 15

seconds. Add turkey mixture, soy-sauce mixture, snow peas, and scallions and stir-fry until sauce is thickened and snow peas are tender, about 3 minutes. Remove wok or skillet from heat and stir in sesame oil and salt and pepper to taste.

Serve turkey mixture with mint and cilantro sprigs on lettuce accompanied by rice. Serves 4 as a main course.

☞ each serving, including rice, about 425 calories
and 11.7 grams fat

TURKEY RAGÙ WITH PASTA

1 medium onion
2 carrots
1 celery rib
1 red bell pepper
3 garlic cloves
1 teaspoon unsalted butter
1 teaspoon olive oil
1 pound lean ground turkey
1 teaspoon dried rosemary, crumbled
¼ teaspoon dried oregano, crumbled
½ cup dry red wine
two 14-ounce cans crushed tomatoes
    in thick purée
1 tablespoon tomato paste
1¾ cups beef broth (14 fluid ounces)
2 pinches cinnamon, or to taste
1 pound dried spiral-shaped pasta such as *fusilli*

Finely chop onion, carrots, celery, and bell pepper. Mince garlic.

In a large heavy nonstick skillet melt butter with oil over moderate heat until foam subsides and cook turkey, stirring and breaking up lumps, until just cooked through, about 3 minutes. With a slotted spoon transfer turkey to a bowl and in fat remaining in skillet cook chopped vegetables, garlic, rosemary, oregano, and salt and pepper to taste over moderate heat, stirring occasionally, until vegetables are just softened, about 4 minutes. Add wine and cook until most of liquid is evaporated. Stir in 1 can tomatoes with purée, tomato paste, broth, and cinnamon and simmer 15 minutes. Add turkey with any juices in bowl and remaining can tomatoes with purée and simmer, stirring, 15 minutes. Season sauce with salt and pepper and keep warm, covered. *Sauce may be made 1 day ahead and cooled, uncovered, before being chilled, covered. Reheat sauce over low heat.*

Fill a 6-quart kettle three fourths full with salted water and bring to a boil for pasta. Cook pasta in boiling water until *al dente*. Drain pasta in a colander and in a serving bowl toss pasta with sauce. Serves 6 as a main course.

☛ each serving about 496 calories and 8 grams fat

SOUTHEAST ASIAN—STYLE TURKEY BURGERS WITH PICKLED CUCUMBERS ◐+

For pickled cucumbers
⅓ cup seasoned rice vinegar
1 tablespoon sugar
¼ cup pickled ginger (optional)
1 English cucumber
For burgers
1 large garlic clove
2 slices firm white sandwich bread
1 pound lean ground turkey
¼ cup chopped fresh cilantro sprigs
¼ cup chopped fresh basil leaves
¼ cup chopped fresh mint leaves

2 tablespoons fresh lime juice
2 teaspoons sugar
¼ teaspoon Tabasco

4 light hamburger buns

Make pickled cucumbers:
In a bowl stir together vinegar and sugar until sugar is dissolved. If using ginger, chop. Slice enough cucumber crosswise into ⅛-inch-thick slices to measure 1½ cups and add to vinegar with ginger, tossing well. *Marinate mixture at least 30 minutes and up to 4 hours.*
Make burgers:
Prepare grill.
Mince garlic. Into a blender tear bread slices and grind into fine crumbs. In a bowl with your hands mix garlic with bread crumbs and remaining burger ingredients until just combined (do not overmix) and form into four 1-inch-thick patties. Season burgers with salt and pepper and grill on a lightly oiled rack set 5 to 6 inches over glowing coals about 5 minutes on each side, or until just cooked through. Transfer burgers to buns and top with drained cucumbers. Serves 4.

☛ each serving, including cucumbers, about 375 calories and 10 grams fat

BREAKFAST, BRUNCH, AND CHEESE DISHES

MIXED GREENS, ASPARAGUS, AND
MORELS TOPPED WITH POACHED EGGS
AND HOLLANDAISE

Very fresh eggs are the key to success when poaching eggs
free form, as we do in this recipe. An egg poacher makes
the classic egg preparation almost foolproof.

1½ cups boiling water
1½ ounces dried morel mushrooms*
2 tablespoons cold unsalted butter
48 thin asparagus stalks (about 1½ pounds)
2 tablespoons distilled white vinegar
6 whole large eggs**
2 teaspoons olive oil
1 teaspoon balsamic vinegar
6 ounces *mesclun*** (mixed baby greens;
    about 6 cups)

Accompaniment: hollandaise (recipe follows)
Garnish: diced seeded peeled tomato and
    chopped chives

*available at specialty foods shops and by mail
    order from Marché aux Delices, (888) 547-5471
**the eggs will not be fully cooked, which may be
    of concern if there is a problem with salmonella
    in your area
***available at specialty produce markets and
    many supermarkets

In a small bowl pour boiling water over dried
mushrooms and soak 30 minutes. Remove mushrooms from water, squeezing out excess liquid, and
reserve soaking liquid. Rinse mushrooms to remove
any grit and transfer to a small saucepan. Line a sieve
set over pan with a dampened paper towel or coffee
filter and strain reserved soaking liquid into pan. Boil
mixture until liquid is reduced to about ½ cup. Swirl
in butter until incorporated and add salt and pepper to
taste. Keep mushroom sauce warm, covered.

Trim asparagus to 6-inch lengths. In a steamer
steam asparagus over boiling water, covered, until
crisp-tender, about 1 minute, and transfer to a bowl.

Have ready a skillet filled with 1 inch warm water.
Fill a 4-quart saucepan half full with water and stir in
distilled vinegar. Bring water and vinegar mixture to
a bare simmer. Break 1 egg into a saucer and slide it
into simmering mixture. Immediately push white
around yolk with a slotted spoon, moving egg gently.
(Egg will become oval, with yolk completely covered
by egg white.) Add 2 more eggs and form in same
manner. Simmer eggs about 1½ minutes for runny
yolks to about 3 minutes for hard yolks and immediately transfer to skillet of warm water. Repeat
procedure with remaining 3 eggs.

In a large bowl whisk together oil and balsamic
vinegar until emulsified and season with salt and
pepper. Add *mesclun* and toss to coat.

Mound *mesclun* in centers of 6 large plates.
Decoratively arrange asparagus around *mesclun* and
spoon mushroom sauce around edge of plate. Transfer
eggs with slotted spoon to paper towels to drain
and trim any ragged edges of whites. Top *mesclun*
with eggs.

Drizzle eggs with some hollandaise and garnish
with tomato and chives. Serve remaining hollandaise
on the side. Serves 6.

PHOTO ON PAGE 19

HOLLANDAISE

3 tablespoons white-wine vinegar
7 black peppercorns
1 bay leaf
4 large egg yolks*
1 cup warm clarified butter (from 2½ sticks;
    procedure on page 91)
1 tablespoon fresh lemon juice
1 teaspoon finely chopped fresh tarragon
    leaves

*the eggs will not be fully cooked, which may be of concern if there is a problem with salmonella in your area

Have ready a medium saucepan of simmering water. In a small saucepan simmer vinegar with peppercorns and bay leaf until vinegar is reduced to about 1 tablespoon. Pour vinegar through a sieve into a metal bowl and whisk in yolks. Set bowl over simmering water and cook mixture, whisking constantly, until it begins to thicken, about 1 minute. Remove pan from heat. Remove bowl from pan, reserving hot water, and add clarified butter to yolks in a slow stream, whisking constantly until sauce begins to thicken. Whisk in lemon juice, tarragon, and salt to taste. (If hollandaise becomes too thick, add a few drops of cold water.) Keep hollandaise warm in bowl set over pan of reserved hot water. Makes about 1½ cups.

CORN AND BASIL EGG ROULADE WITH YELLOW TOMATO COULIS

This recipe is an adaptation of a rolled omelet from Gostilna Devetak, a trattoria in Friuli, Italy.

parchment paper
1 bunch scallions
1 cup packed fresh basil leaves
6 large eggs
2 cups heavy cream
½ teaspoon salt
2 tablespoons unsalted butter
¼ cup (2 ounces) cream cheese
2 cups fresh or thawed frozen white corn kernels

Accompaniments:
yellow tomato *coulis* (recipe follows)
sliced Black Forest ham

Preheat oven to 325° F.
Butter a 15½- by 11- by 1-inch jelly-roll pan and line bottom and sides with parchment paper. Evenly butter parchment paper.
Chop enough scallions to measure ¾ cup. Chop basil. In a large bowl whisk together eggs, heavy cream, and salt until combined well. Pour custard into jelly-roll pan and bake in middle of oven 8 minutes. Rotate jelly-roll pan and continue to bake custard until set, 8 to 10 minutes more.

While custard is baking, in a heavy skillet melt butter over moderately low heat and cook scallions, stirring occasionally, until softened, 2 to 3 minutes. Cut cream cheese into small pieces and add to scallions with corn and salt and pepper to taste. Cook mixture, stirring, until corn is heated through and cream cheese is melted, 2 to 3 minutes.

Spread corn mixture evenly on top of hot egg sheet, leaving a 1-inch border on all sides. Sprinkle basil over corn mixture. With a long side facing you and using parchment as an aid, roll up egg sheet jelly-roll fashion and carefully transfer to a platter.

Carefully cut *roulade* into 16 slices (each about ¾ inch thick) and serve warm or at room temperature with yellow tomato *coulis* and Black Forest ham slices. Serves 8.

PHOTO ON PAGE 55

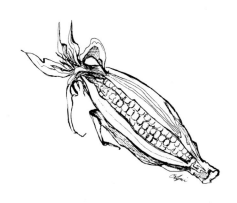

YELLOW TOMATO COULIS

1 pound yellow pear or cherry tomatoes
   (about 2⅔ cups)
2 teaspoons white-wine vinegar
¾ teaspoon salt
1 tablespoon olive oil

Garnish: halved yellow pear or cherry tomatoes

In a blender purée tomatoes, white-wine vinegar, salt, and olive oil until smooth. Pour tomato mixture through a sieve into a bowl, pressing on solids. *Coulis keeps, covered and chilled, 2 days.*
Serve yellow tomato *coulis* garnished with halved tomatoes. Makes about 2 cups.

155

BACON AND EGG EMPANADAS

2 frozen turnover dough (*empanada*) wrappers*,
 thawed
2 ounces sharp Cheddar
3 large eggs
3 scallions
1 tablespoon unsalted butter
2 slices Canadian bacon

*available at Latino markets and many
 supermarkets

Preheat oven to 425° F. and butter a baking pan.

On a lightly floured surface with a rolling pin roll
out each *empanada* wrapper into a 7-inch round.
Finely grate Cheddar and in a bowl whisk together
with eggs and salt and pepper to taste. Chop scallions. In a nonstick skillet heat 1 teaspoon butter
over moderately high heat until foam subsides and
sauté bacon until golden, about 1 minute on each
side. Transfer bacon to a plate and add remaining 2
teaspoons butter to skillet. Heat butter until foam
subsides and sauté scallions 15 seconds. Add egg
mixture and cook, stirring constantly, until eggs
just begin to set but are still very loose, about 30
seconds. Arrange 1 piece bacon ¼ inch from edge of
1 *empanada* wrapper and spoon half of egg mixture
on top of bacon. Fold *empanada* wrapper over filling
to create a half-moon shape and seal by pressing
edges together firmly with a fork. Make another
empanada in same manner.

Transfer *empanadas* to baking pan and cut a few
small slits in top of each *empanada* to create steam
vents. Bake *empanadas* in middle of oven until
golden, about 10 minutes. Serves 2.

EGG, CANADIAN BACON, AND CHEDDAR SANDWICHES

2 English muffins
3 tablespoons unsalted butter, softened
¾ cup coarsely grated Cheddar (about 3 ounces)
8 thin slices Canadian bacon
4 large eggs

Preheat broiler.

Split muffins and spread cut sides with 2 tablespoons butter. On a baking sheet broil muffins, cut
sides up, about 4 inches from heat until lightly
toasted. Divide cheese between bottom halves of
muffins and broil until cheese is just melted.

In a 10-inch nonstick skillet heat ½ tablespoon
butter over moderate heat until foam subsides and
cook bacon, turning once, until heated through and
just golden. Arrange bacon on cheese.

In same skillet heat remaining ½ tablespoon butter
over moderate heat until foam subsides and break
eggs into skillet. Season eggs with salt and pepper
and cook 2 minutes, or until whites are set on bottom
but still runny on top. With a spatula gently turn
each egg over and cook 2 minutes more, or until
yolks are just set. With spatula gently transfer 2 eggs
to each bottom half and top with remaining muffin
halves. Serves 2.

CREAMY EGGS WITH SMOKED SALMON ON BRIOCHE

1½ tablespoons unsalted butter
four 1-inch-thick slices brioche loaf or challah
8 large eggs
¾ cup heavy cream
1 teaspoon salt
3 tablespoons chopped fresh chives
freshly ground black pepper to taste
4 ounces sliced smoked salmon

Preheat oven to 350° F.

Melt butter. With a 3-inch round cutter cut out 1
round from each bread slice. Brush both sides of
rounds with melted butter and season with salt. On a
baking sheet bake rounds in middle of oven until
golden and crisp.

In a blender blend eggs, cream, and salt until just combined and stir in 2 tablespoons chives. In a double boiler or a metal bowl set over a saucepan of barely simmering water cook egg mixture, stirring, until creamy and just cooked through, about 4 minutes, and season with pepper.

Put 1 bread round onto each of 4 plates and divide egg mixture among rounds. Top egg with salmon and garnish plates with remaining tablespoon chives. Serves 4 as a light main course.

POPOVER PUDDING WITH IRISH BACON

If desired, you may substitute Canadian bacon for the Irish bacon called for below. You will need to sauté the Canadian bacon in ¼ cup additional vegetable oil because it does not contain the same amount of fat as Irish bacon.

2 cups whole milk
4 large eggs
1¾ cups all-purpose flour
1½ teaspoons salt
1 large bunch fresh chives
1 pound sliced Irish bacon*
about ½ cup vegetable oil

*available at many supermarkets and by mail order from DPI Skandia Foods, (800) 729-4735

In a blender blend milk, eggs, flour, and salt until just smooth. Transfer batter to a bowl. Finely chop enough chives to measure ½ cup and whisk into batter. *Chill batter, covered, at least 1 hour and up to 1 day.*

Preheat oven to 400° F.

Trim fat from bacon. In a large nonstick skillet cook fat over low heat, stirring occasionally, until most of fat is rendered and solids are golden brown. Discard solids and increase heat to moderately high. Heat rendered fat until hot but not smoking and sauté bacon in batches until just golden, about 1 minute on each side. Transfer bacon as cooked to paper towels to drain. Pour rendered fat into a measuring cup and add enough oil to measure ½ cup total.

In a 12- by 2-inch enameled cast-iron casserole (3½-quart) or a 13- by 9- by 2-inch glass baking dish heat oil mixture in middle of oven 5 minutes. Quickly arrange bacon evenly in skillet or baking dish and pour batter over it. Bake pudding in middle of oven until puffed and golden brown, about 50 minutes. Serves 8.

PHOTO ON PAGE 80

TOMATO AND MOZZARELLA BREAD-BOWL SOUFFLÉS

½ cup dried tomatoes (about 3 ounces)
3 plum tomatoes
4 ounces fresh mozzarella
6 round whole-wheat rolls (about 3 to
  4 inches in diameter)
½ stick (¼ cup) unsalted butter
3 tablespoons all-purpose flour
½ cup whole milk
¼ cup heavy cream
2 tablespoons fresh flat-leafed parsley leaves
4 large eggs

Preheat oven to 375° F.

In a small bowl cover dried tomatoes with boiling water by 1 inch. *Soak dried tomatoes 30 minutes.* Drain tomatoes in a sieve and pat very dry.

Quarter and seed plum tomatoes. Cut tomatoes into ¼-inch dice and drain on paper towels. Pat tomatoes dry. Cut mozzarella into ¼-inch dice.

Cut off and discard top thirds of rolls. Hollow out centers of rolls, leaving a ⅓-inch-thick shell. Melt 2 tablespoons butter and brush insides of shells. Season shells with salt and pepper and arrange on a baking sheet.

In a saucepan melt remaining 2 tablespoons butter over moderately low heat and whisk in flour. Cook *roux*, stirring, 3 minutes and whisk in milk and cream. Bring mixture to a boil, whisking constantly, and simmer, whisking occasionally, 3 minutes. In a food processor purée together milk mixture, dried tomatoes, parsley, and salt and pepper to taste until smooth.

Separate eggs. Transfer purée to a bowl and stir in yolks, plum tomatoes, and mozzarella. Cool mixture completely. *Bread shells, whites, and tomato mixture may be chilled, covered, up to 6 hours.*

In a large bowl with an electric mixer beat whites with a pinch salt until they just hold stiff peaks. Stir one fourth whites into tomato mixture to lighten and fold in remaining whites gently but thoroughly.

Divide soufflé mixture among shells and run tip of a knife around edges of soufflés to aid rising. Bake soufflés in lower third of oven until puffed and golden brown, 18 to 20 minutes. Serves 6 as a light main course.

SMOKED TROUT SOUFFLÉ IN A PHYLLO CRUST

eight 17- by 12-inch *phyllo* sheets
5½ tablespoons unsalted butter
1½ tablespoons all-purpose flour
½ cup whole milk
½ cup heavy cream
2 smoked trout fillets* (about ½ pound total)
6 large eggs
1½ teaspoons drained bottled horseradish
2 tablespoons fresh dill leaves

*available at fish markets, the deli counter of
  many supermarkets, and by mail order from
  Ducktrap River Fish Farm, (800) 828-3825

Cover *phyllo* stack with overlapping sheets of plastic wrap and then a damp kitchen towel.

Melt 4 tablespoons butter. Arrange 1 *phyllo* sheet on a work surface and brush with some melted butter. Arrange another sheet to overlap the first and form a 17-inch square and brush with butter. Continue layering with remaining 6 sheets and butter. Drape *phyllo* stack over a 10-inch tart pan with a removable bottom and fit *phyllo* into pan. Crumple overhang against inside edge of rim to create a ragged edge that stands about 1 inch above rim. *Chill shell, loosely covered, until firm, at least 3 hours.*

Preheat oven to 375° F.

Prick bottom of shell all over with a fork and bake in middle of oven until golden, about 15 minutes. Cool shell in pan on a rack. *Shell may be made 1 day ahead and kept, covered, at cool room temperature.*

In a saucepan melt remaining 1½ tablespoons butter over moderately low heat and whisk in flour. Cook *roux*, stirring, 3 minutes and whisk in milk and cream. Bring mixture to a boil, whisking constantly, and simmer, whisking occasionally, 3 minutes. Season mixture with salt and pepper and cool.

Discard skin and bones from trout. Break fish into small pieces. Separate eggs. In a food processor pulse milk mixture, trout, yolks, horseradish, and dill until smooth and transfer to a large bowl.

In another large bowl with an electric mixer beat whites with a pinch salt until they just hold stiff peaks. Stir one fourth whites into trout mixture to lighten and fold in remaining whites gently but thoroughly.

Pour soufflé mixture into shell and run tip of a knife around edge of soufflé to aid rising. Bake soufflé on a baking sheet in lower third of oven until puffed and golden brown, about 25 minutes. Serve soufflé immediately. Serves 6 as a main course.

BANANA, RASPBERRY, AND GRANOLA YOGURT

1½ firm-ripe bananas
an 8-ounce container plain yogurt
1 cup raspberries
½ cup plus 2 tablespoons granola
¼ cup sour cream
1 teaspoon packed dark brown sugar

Coarsely grate bananas. In a bowl gently stir together banana, yogurt, ⅔ cup raspberries, ½ cup granola, sour cream, and sugar until combined.

Divide mixture between 2 bowls. Sprinkle yogurt with remaining 2 tablespoons granola and garnish with remaining ⅓ cup raspberries. Serves 2.

BLUEBERRIES WITH YOGURT AND MAPLE-BLUEBERRY SYRUP

6 tablespoons pure maple syrup
¼ cup water
8 cups blueberries (about 3 pounds)
2 to 3 teaspoons fresh lemon juice
2 cups plain yogurt

In a small heavy saucepan combine maple syrup, water, and 1½ cups blueberries and simmer mixture, covered, 5 minutes. Pour mixture through a sieve into a bowl, pressing on solids, and stir in lemon juice to taste. *Syrup keeps, covered and chilled, 2 days. Reheat syrup or bring to room temperature before serving.*

Serve remaining 6½ cups blueberries topped with yogurt and maple-blueberry syrup. Serves 8.

PHOTO ON PAGE 6

GRILLED CHEESE WITH SMOKED TURKEY AND AVOCADO

3 ounces whole-milk mozzarella
½ firm-ripe California avocado
2 tablespoons unsalted butter, softened
4 slices firm pumpernickel
1 tablespoon Dijon mustard
6 ounces thinly sliced smoked turkey

Accompaniment: cucumber, radish, and red onion salad (page 190)

Thinly slice mozzarella. Pit, peel, and thinly slice ripe avocado. Spread softened butter on one side of each bread slice and turn slices over. Spread mustard on bread slices and top 2 slices with mozzarella, avocado, and turkey. Season turkey with salt and pepper and top with remaining 2 pumpernickel slices, buttered sides up.

Heat a heavy skillet over moderate heat until hot but not smoking and cook sandwiches until bread is crisp and cheese is melted, about 1½ minutes on each side.

Serve sandwiches with cucumber salad. Makes 2 sandwiches.

SPINACH, FETA, AND PINE-NUT PHYLLO TART

In this recipe we call for a 10½- by 7½- by 1-inch rectangular tart pan. The tart could also be made using a baking sheet or a jelly-roll pan, as the filling is dense enough to hold its shape on its own.

For filling
½ cup pine nuts (about 3 ounces)
1 medium onion
⅓ cup olive oil
two 10-ounce packages frozen chopped spinach, thawed
½ teaspoon salt
2 large eggs
½ cup crumbled feta (about 3 ounces)
1 tablespoon fine dry bread crumbs

seven 17- by 12-inch *phyllo* sheets
5 tablespoons unsalted butter
6 tablespoons plus ¼ cup freshly grated Parmesan

Preheat oven to 375° F.
Make filling:
In a shallow baking pan toast pine nuts in middle of oven until golden, about 4 minutes, and cool. Finely chop onion and in a large heavy skillet cook in oil over moderately low heat, stirring, until softened. Squeeze spinach to remove as much liquid as possible and stir with salt into onion. Cook spinach mixture over moderate heat, stirring occasionally, until any liquid is evaporated, 1 to 2 minutes, and cool slightly. In a large bowl whisk eggs until combined and stir in spinach mixture, pine nuts, feta, and bread crumbs until combined well. *Filling may be made 1 day ahead and chilled, covered. Bring filling to room temperature before proceeding.*

Stack *phyllo* sheets and cover with 2 overlapping sheets plastic wrap and then a dampened kitchen towel. In a small saucepan melt butter and cool slightly. Lightly brush a 10½- by 7½- by 1-inch rectangular tart pan with a removable fluted rim with butter.

On a work surface lightly brush 1 *phyllo* sheet with butter. Sprinkle 1 tablespoon Parmesan evenly over buttered *phyllo* and repeat layering with 5 more *phyllo* sheets, butter, and 5 tablespoons Parmesan. Arrange last *phyllo* sheet on stack and lightly brush with butter. Transfer *phyllo* to tart pan, letting excess hang over edge, and spoon filling onto *phyllo*, spreading evenly. Fold edges of pastry over filling, leaving center uncovered, and lightly brush top of *phyllo* with butter. Sprinkle remaining ¼ cup Parmesan over exposed filling and bake tart in middle of oven until golden, 25 to 30 minutes. Serve tart warm or at room temperature. Serves 6 as a main course.

PASTA AND GRAINS

GRILLED ZUCCHINI AND
BELL PEPPER COUSCOUS

1 pound zucchini (about
   3 medium)
1 small red bell pepper
1 teaspoon olive oil
2 small garlic cloves
½ teaspoon salt
½ teaspoon cumin seeds
½ cup chicken broth
¾ cup water
¾ cup couscous

Prepare grill.

Trim zucchini and cut each lengthwise into ¼-inch-thick slices. Quarter red bell pepper lengthwise, discarding seeds, stem, and ribs. Brush zucchini with olive oil and grill with pepper on a lightly oiled rack set 5 to 6 inches over glowing coals until zucchini is just tender and pepper is crisp-tender, about 5 minutes on each side. (Alternatively, zucchini and bell pepper may be grilled in a hot well-seasoned ridged grill pan over moderately high heat.) Cut zucchini into 1-inch-wide pieces and cut bell pepper into ¼-inch-wide strips.

Mince garlic and mash to a paste with salt. In a dry 1½-quart heavy saucepan toast cumin seeds over moderately low heat, swirling pan occasionally, until fragrant, about 1 minute. Add broth and water and bring to a boil. Add couscous and immediately cover pan. Remove saucepan from heat and let couscous stand 5 minutes.

Fluff couscous with a fork and in a bowl toss with vegetables, garlic paste, and salt to taste. Serves 4.

PHOTO ON PAGE 83

🍃 each serving about 165 calories and 2 grams fat

CUMIN COUSCOUS WITH FRIED SHALLOTS ◗

3 large shallots
1 cup water
1 tablespoon extra-virgin olive oil
½ teaspoon ground cumin
freshly ground pepper to taste
⅔ cup couscous
about 2 cups vegetable oil for frying

Thinly slice shallots crosswise and separate into rings. In a small saucepan bring water to a boil with olive oil, cumin, pepper, and salt to taste. Stir in couscous and cover. Immediately remove pan from heat and let couscous stand, covered, 5 minutes.

While couscous is standing, in a deep 8- to 10-inch heavy skillet heat about ½ inch vegetable oil over moderately high heat until hot but not smoking and fry shallots, stirring occasionally, until golden, 1 to 2 minutes. Transfer shallots with a slotted spoon to paper towels to drain and season with salt.

Fluff couscous with a fork. Serve couscous topped with shallots. Serves 2 generously.

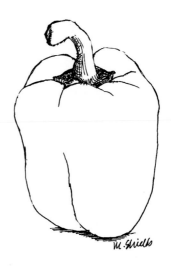

PASTA WITH CAPERS, GARLIC, AND BREAD CRUMBS ◐

¾ pound *gigli di semola* or short spiral pasta
a 6-inch piece stale baguette
6 tablespoons drained capers
4 garlic cloves
½ cup extra-virgin olive oil
¼ cup chopped fresh parsley leaves
freshly grated Parmesan (optional)

Fill a 6-quart kettle three fourths full with salted water and bring to a boil for pasta. Cut crust from bread and, using large holes of a hand grater, grate enough bread to measure ⅔ cup. Finely chop separately capers and garlic.

Boil pasta until *al dente*.

While pasta is cooking, in a large heavy skillet cook garlic in oil over moderate heat, stirring, just until pale golden, about 2 minutes. Stir in capers, parsley, and bread crumbs and cook, stirring, until bread crumbs and garlic are golden, 1 to 2 minutes.

Drain pasta in a colander and transfer to a heated large bowl. Pour sauce over pasta and toss to combine well.

Serve pasta with Parmesan. Serves 4 as a main course.

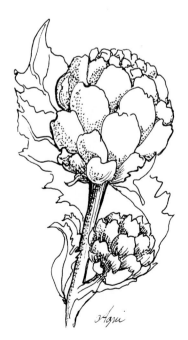

ARTICHOKE AND PANCETTA FETTUCCINE

Egg fettuccine, which is thinner than regular fettuccine, makes this dish much lighter.

6 medium artichokes (about 3 pounds total)
½ lemon
3 ounces sliced *pancetta** (Italian unsmoked cured bacon)
1 large garlic clove
2 tablespoons salt
about 9 ounces dried thin egg fettuccine such as De Cecco or Cipriani* or 12 ounces regular dried fettuccine
1 tablespoon olive oil
2 tablespoons unsalted butter
¼ cup dry white wine
½ cup freshly grated Parmesan
2 tablespoons chopped fresh flat-leafed parsley leaves
1 tablespoon fresh lemon juice

*available at Italian markets, specialty foods shops, and some supermarkets

Trim artichokes Italian style (procedure follows). Fill a 4-quart saucepan three fourths full with water and bring to a boil with lemon. Quarter 1 artichoke lengthwise through stem and with a stainless-steel paring knife cut out choke. Trim any spiky purple-tipped leaves. Halve quarters lengthwise and return to bowl. Prepare remaining artichokes in same manner. Simmer artichoke pieces in boiling water 5 minutes, or until almost tender, and drain in a colander. *Artichokes may be prepared up to this point 1 day ahead, cooled completely, and chilled, rolled in dampened paper towels in a sealable plastic bag.*

Chop *pancetta* and mince garlic. Fill a 6-quart kettle three fourths full with water and bring to a boil with salt for fettuccine.

In a deep 12-inch heavy skillet cook *pancetta* in oil over moderate heat, stirring occasionally, until crisp and with a slotted spoon transfer to a bowl. Discard fat from skillet.

In skillet heat butter over moderate heat until foam subsides and cook artichokes, stirring occasionally, until golden, about 5 minutes. Add garlic and cook, stirring, 1 minute. Add wine and simmer, stirring and scraping up brown bits, 1 minute.

Cook fettuccine in boiling water until *al dente*. Reserve 1 cup pasta cooking liquid and drain pasta in colander. Add reserved pasta cooking liquid to artichoke mixture and bring to a boil. Add pasta, *pancetta*, Parmesan, parsley, and lemon juice, tossing to combine well. Serves 6 as a first course.

PHOTO ON PAGE 26

To Trim Artichokes Italian Style ☺

1 lemon
artichokes (preferably with long stems)

Halve lemon and into a large bowl of cold water squeeze juice from 1 half, dropping squeezed half into water.

Do not cut off stems of artichokes. Working with 1 artichoke at a time, bend back outer leaves until they snap off close to base and discard several more layers of leaves in same manner until exposed leaves are pale green at top and pale yellow at base.

With a sharp stainless-steel knife cut off tops of leaves about 1 to 1¼ inches from top of artichoke. Trim fibrous parts from base of artichoke, being careful not to break off stem.

Cut a thin slice from end of stem to expose a fresh cross section. Trim outer green fibrous part from stem, leaving pale core intact. Rub artichoke all over with cut side of remaining lemon half and put artichoke in bowl of lemon water.

Gemelli Alfredo with Prosciutto ☺

½ pound *gemelli* (short pasta twists)
    or short spiral pasta
2 ounces thinly sliced prosciutto
½ tablespoon olive oil
¾ cup heavy cream
3 tablespoons unsalted butter
½ cup freshly grated Parmesan
1 tablespoon chopped fresh parsley
    leaves
freshly ground black pepper
    to taste

Fill a 4-quart kettle three fourths full with salted water and bring to a boil for pasta.

Chop prosciutto. In a skillet heat oil over moderately high heat until hot but not smoking and sauté prosciutto, stirring, until it begins to brown, about 2 minutes. With a slotted spoon transfer prosciutto to paper towels to drain.

Boil pasta until *al dente* and drain in a colander. Return pasta to kettle and add remaining ingredients except prosciutto and salt to taste. Cook pasta over low heat, stirring, until butter is melted and sauce coats pasta.

Serve pasta sprinkled with prosciutto. Serves 2.

Orzo with Feta, Green Beans, and Tomatoes ☺

10 ounces *haricots verts* (thin French green
    beans) or green beans
1 cup *orzo* (rice-shaped pasta)
1 medium onion
2 garlic cloves
3 medium vine-ripened tomatoes
2 tablespoons olive oil
1 tablespoon white-wine vinegar
1 tablespoon chopped fresh flat-leafed
    parsley leaves
1 cup crumbled feta (about 6 ounces)

Fill a 4-quart kettle three fourths full with salted water and bring to a boil for beans and *orzo*.

Chop onion and mince garlic. Quarter and seed tomatoes. Cut quarters lengthwise into ¼-inch-thick slices. Trim beans and cut into 1-inch pieces. In a large skillet cook onion and garlic in oil over moderate heat until onion is softened. Add tomatoes and cook, stirring, until tomatoes are softened, about 2 minutes. Remove skillet from heat.

Have ready a bowl of ice and cold water. In boiling salted water blanch beans 1 minute. With a slotted spoon transfer beans to ice water to stop cooking. Drain beans well in a colander and pat dry. Add beans to tomato mixture and return water in kettle to a boil. Boil *orzo* until *al dente* and drain in colander. Add *orzo* to bean mixture with vinegar, parsley, feta, and salt and pepper to taste, tossing to combine well. Serves 2.

PASTA WITH PEAS, RICOTTA SALATA, AND LEMON ☺

6 ounces dried pasta such as *farfalle*
1 cup frozen peas
¼ cup packed fresh basil leaves
3 ounces *ricotta salata* cheese*
1 lemon
1½ tablespoons extra-virgin olive oil
1 tablespoon finely chopped fresh
   tarragon leaves

*available at specialty foods shops and many
   supermarkets

Fill a 4-quart kettle three fourths full with salted water and bring to a boil for pasta and peas.

Tear basil into bite-size pieces and break *ricotta salata* into about ½-inch-thick pieces. Into a large bowl finely grate zest from lemon and squeeze enough juice to measure 1 tablespoon. Add basil, cheese, and oil.

Cook pasta in boiling water until almost *al dente*. Stir in peas and continue to cook until pasta is *al dente* and peas are tender. Drain pasta and peas well. Add pasta and peas to bowl and toss to combine. Season pasta with salt and pepper and sprinkle with tarragon. Serves 2 as a main course.

MACARONI AND CHEESE

For those who prefer a greater ratio of crunchy topping to creamy center, we suggest dividing the macaroni and cheese between two 3-quart shallow baking dishes and doubling the topping.

¾ pound elbow macaroni
For topping
2 tablespoons unsalted butter
2 cups *panko** (Japanese bread crumbs) or
   coarse dry bread crumbs
1 cup coarsely grated extra-sharp Cheddar
   (about 4 ounces)
For cheese sauce
3 tablespoons unsalted butter
3 tablespoons all-purpose flour
½ teaspoon dried hot red pepper flakes

2¾ cups whole milk
¾ cup heavy cream
4 cups coarsely grated extra-sharp Cheddar
   (about 1 pound)
2 teaspoons Dijon mustard
1½ teaspoons salt
¼ teaspoon freshly ground black pepper

*available at Asian markets, some specialty foods
   shops and supermarkets, and by mail order
   from Uwajimaya, (800) 889-1928

Preheat oven to 400° F. and butter a 3-quart shallow baking dish. Fill a 6-quart kettle three fourths full with salted water and bring to a boil for macaroni.

Make topping:
Melt butter and in a bowl stir together with crumbs and Cheddar until combined well. *Topping may be made 1 day ahead and chilled, covered.*

Make cheese sauce:
In a 5-quart heavy saucepan melt butter over moderately low heat and stir in flour and red pepper flakes. Cook *roux*, stirring, 3 minutes and whisk in milk. Bring sauce to a boil, whisking constantly, and simmer, whisking occasionally, 3 minutes. Stir in cream, Cheddar, mustard, salt, and pepper. Remove pan from heat and cover surface of cheese sauce with wax paper.

Cook macaroni in boiling water until *al dente*. Reserve 1 cup cooking water and drain macaroni in a colander. In a large bowl stir together macaroni, reserved cooking water, and cheese sauce. Transfer mixture to baking dish.

Sprinkle topping evenly over macaroni and bake in middle of oven 20 to 25 minutes, or until golden and bubbling. Serves 6 as a main course.

BAKED ZITI WITH MUSHROOMS, PEPPERS, AND PARMESAN

3 large yellow bell peppers
1 large onion
3 garlic cloves
3 tablespoons olive oil
1½ cups heavy cream
1½ pounds mushrooms
2 medium red bell peppers
2 medium orange bell peppers
1 pound ziti
8 scallions (green part only)
2 cups freshly grated Parmesan
    (about 6 ounces)

Chop yellow bell peppers and onion and mince garlic. In a 3- to 4-quart heavy saucepan cook yellow peppers, onion, and garlic in 1 tablespoon oil, covered, over moderately low heat, stirring occasionally, until peppers are soft, about 30 minutes. Stir in heavy cream. In a blender purée mixture in batches (use caution when blending hot liquids), transferring to a large bowl, and season with salt and pepper. *Sauce may be made 2 days ahead and chilled, covered. Bring sauce to room temperature before proceeding.*

Thinly slice mushrooms lengthwise and cut red and orange bell peppers into ¼-inch-wide strips. In a deep large heavy skillet cook mushrooms and peppers in remaining 2 tablespoons oil over moderately high heat, stirring occasionally, until peppers are softened and most of liquid is evaporated, about 8 minutes, and season with salt and pepper.

Preheat oven to 375° F.

Fill a 6- to 7-quart kettle three fourths full with salted water and bring to a boil. Stir in ziti and cook until just tender, about 10 minutes. Reserve 1 cup pasta cooking water and drain ziti well in a colander. Rinse ziti and drain well. Thinly slice scallion greens. Into sauce stir ziti, mushroom mixture, scallion greens, 1½ cups Parmesan, reserved cooking water, and salt and pepper to taste. Spoon mixture into a 3-quart shallow baking dish and sprinkle with remaining ½ cup Parmesan.

Bake ziti in middle of oven until hot and pasta begins to brown, about 20 minutes. Serves 8 to 10.

PHOTO ON PAGE 16

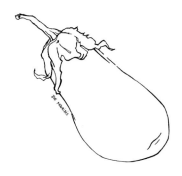

RIGATONI WITH EGGPLANT, TOMATO, AND RICOTTA ◉

½ pound rigatoni or other large tubular pasta
1 onion
1 small eggplant (about 1 pound)
1 large garlic clove
2 tablespoons olive oil
½ teaspoon salt
½ to 1 cup water
a 16-ounce can whole tomatoes including juice
2 tablespoons chopped fresh basil leaves
¼ cup ricotta

Fill a 5-quart kettle three fourths full with salted water and bring to a boil for pasta.

Chop onion and cut eggplant into 1-inch cubes. Mince garlic. In a large deep heavy skillet heat oil over moderately high heat until hot but not smoking and sauté onion, stirring occasionally, until softened. Add eggplant and salt and sauté, stirring frequently, until eggplant is lightly browned.

Add ½ cup water to eggplant mixture and cook, covered, over moderate heat, stirring occasionally, adding more water, ¼ cup at a time, if mixture becomes dry, until eggplant is tender, about 10 minutes. Add tomatoes with juice and simmer, stirring vigorously to break up tomatoes, 5 minutes, or until mixture has a sauce-like consistency. Stir in garlic and basil and season with salt.

While sauce is simmering, cook pasta in boiling water until al dente and drain well in a colander. Add pasta to sauce and toss to coat.

Divide pasta between 2 bowls and serve with dollops of ricotta on top. Serves 2.

LEMON AND SALMON ROE PASTA ☺

1 pound fresh *pappardelle* (wide pasta
    ribbons) or fettuccine
¾ stick (6 tablespoons) unsalted butter
1¼ cups heavy cream
1½ tablespoons freshly grated lemon
    zest
½ cup fresh lemon juice
6 ounces salmon roe
3 tablespoons chopped fresh dill sprigs

Fill a 6-quart kettle three fourths full with salted
water and bring to a boil for pasta.

In a deep 12-inch skillet heat butter and cream
over moderately low heat until butter is melted. Stir
in zest, lemon juice, and pepper to taste. Remove
skillet from heat and cover to keep sauce warm.

Cook pasta in boiling water, stirring occasionally,
until *al dente*. Ladle ¼ cup pasta water into sauce
and drain pasta in a colander. Add pasta, roe, dill,
and salt to taste to sauce and cook over moderate
heat, tossing, 1 minute, or until just heated through.
Serves 6 as a first course.

GRAINS

RAW BEET AND APPLE TABBOULEH ☺

1 cup bulgur
1⅓ cups boiling-hot water
2 small red beets
1 Granny Smith apple
1 cup packed fresh basil leaves
¼ cup extra-virgin olive oil
1½ tablespoons fresh lemon juice

In a large bowl stir together bulgur and boiling-
hot water. *Let mixture stand, covered, 30 minutes.*

While bulgur is standing, trim beets (reserve
greens for another use) and peel. Using a *mandoline*
or very sharp knife separately cut beets and apple
into ⅛-inch-thick slices. Separately cut beet and
apple slices into 1-inch-long julienne strips. In a
blender or food processor purée basil with oil, lemon
juice, and salt and pepper to taste until smooth.

Fluff bulgur with a fork. Add beets, apple, and
about ¼ cup dressing, tossing to combine.

Serve *tabbouleh* with remaining dressing on the
side. Serves 4 as a first course.

CHICKEN FRIED RICE WITH
FERMENTED BLACK BEANS

*This dish is equally delicious prepared with turkey, seafood,
beef, or pork.*

For marinade
3 tablespoons soy sauce
2 tablespoons minced garlic
1 teaspoon Asian sesame oil*

2 skinless boneless chicken breast halves
1 red onion
1 large red bell pepper
½ pound snow peas
3 tablespoons fermented black beans*
2½ tablespoons corn or safflower oil
For seasoning liquid
1 tablespoon chicken broth
3 tablespoons soy sauce
1½ tablespoons Chinese rice wine or *sake*
1½ teaspoons sugar

5 cups chilled Chinese-style white or brown rice
    (recipe follows)
2 tablespoons minced garlic
2 tablespoons minced peeled fresh gingerroot

*available at Asian markets, some specialty foods
    shops and supermarkets, and by mail order
    from Adriana's Caravan, (800) 316-0820

Make marinade:
In a small bowl stir together marinade ingredients.

Add chicken to marinade, turning it to coat.
Marinate chicken breast halves at room temperature
while preparing vegetables.

Cut onion and bell pepper into ¼-inch dice. Trim
snow peas and cut crosswise into ¼-inch slices.
Rinse black beans and mince.

Remove chicken from marinade and pat dry.
Discard marinade. In a heavy nonstick skillet heat

½ tablespoon corn or safflower oil over moderately high heat until hot but not smoking and sauté chicken until browned on bottom, about 4 minutes. Turn chicken over and cook over moderate heat 6 minutes more, or until just cooked through. Transfer chicken to a plate and cool completely. *Recipe may be prepared up to this point 1 day ahead and ingredients chilled separately in sealable plastic bags.*

Cut chicken into ½-inch cubes.

Make seasoning liquid:

In a small bowl stir together all seasoning liquid ingredients.

Spread rice in a shallow baking pan and separate grains with a fork.

In a deep 12-inch heavy nonstick skillet heat remaining 2 tablespoons corn or safflower oil over moderately high heat until hot but not smoking and stir-fry black beans, garlic, and gingerroot 20 seconds, or until fragrant. Add onion and bell pepper and stir-fry 2 minutes. Add snow peas, chicken, and rice and cook, stirring frequently, 2 to 3 minutes, or until heated through. Stir seasoning liquid and add to chicken fried rice, tossing to coat evenly. Serves 4 as a main course.

CHINESE-STYLE RICE ○+

The secret to properly cooked Chinese-style rice, whether white or brown, is to first rinse the rice and then to avoid cooking it in too much water. For fried rice, the rice should be cooked until just tender to the bite.

2¾ cups long-grain white rice (not converted) or brown rice
4 or 5 cups water

Put rice in a 3- to 4-quart heavy saucepan and, using your fingers as a rake, rinse under cold running water. Drain rice in a colander.

In pan bring water (4 cups for white rice and 5 cups for brown) to a boil with rice. Simmer rice, covered, over moderately low to low heat until steam holes appear on surface and water is absorbed, about 16 minutes for white rice and 35 to 40 minutes for brown rice.

With a fork fluff rice and spread in a shallow baking pan. Cool rice completely. *Chill rice, covered with plastic wrap, at least 12 hours. Rice may be made 2 days ahead and chilled in a sealable plastic bag.* Makes about 10 cups.

SHRIMP FRIED RICE

2 bunches scallions
¾ pound cooked and shelled shrimp
   (about 18 large)
5 cups chilled Chinese-style white rice
   (page 167)
2 large eggs
For seasoning liquid
2 tablespoons chicken broth
2 tablespoons Chinese rice wine or *sake*
1 tablespoon soy sauce
1 teaspoon salt
1 teaspoon Asian sesame oil
¼ teaspoon freshly ground black pepper

2 tablespoons corn or safflower oil
1 tablespoon minced peeled fresh gingerroot
a thawed 10-ounce package frozen peas

Finely chop enough scallions to measure about 2 cups and halve shrimp lengthwise. Spread rice in a shallow baking pan and separate grains with a fork. In a small bowl lightly beat eggs.

Make seasoning liquid:

In a small bowl stir together all seasoning liquid ingredients.

In a deep 12-inch heavy nonstick skillet heat corn or safflower oil over moderately high heat until hot but not smoking and stir-fry eggs until scrambled, about 30 seconds. Add scallions and gingerroot and stir-fry 1 minute. Add shrimp and peas and stir-fry until heated through. Add rice and cook, stirring frequently, 2 to 3 minutes, or until heated through. Stir seasoning liquid and add to fried rice, tossing to coat evenly. Serves 4 as a main course.

VIETNAMESE FRIED RICE

2 bunches scallions
3 large carrots
2 cups fresh bean sprouts
2 large eggs
For seasoning liquid
2 tablespoons Asian fish sauce*
1½ tablespoons rice vinegar
2 tablespoons sugar

5 cups chilled Chinese-style white rice
   (page 167)
2½ tablespoons corn or
   safflower oil
2 tablespoons minced garlic
1 teaspoon dried hot red pepper flakes
¼ cup chopped fresh cilantro or
   mint leaves
¼ cup chopped dry-roasted peanuts

*available at Asian markets, some specialty foods shops and supermarkets, and by mail order from Adriana's Caravan, (800) 316-0820, or Uwajimaya, (800) 889-1928

Finely chop enough scallions to measure about 2 cups and coarsely shred enough carrots to measure about 2 cups. Rinse bean sprouts and trim stringy root ends. In a small bowl lightly beat eggs.

Make seasoning liquid:

In a small bowl stir together all seasoning liquid ingredients.

Spread rice in a shallow baking pan and separate grains with a fork.

In a deep 12-inch heavy nonstick skillet heat oil over moderately high heat until hot but not smoking and stir-fry eggs until scrambled, about 30 seconds. Add scallions, garlic, and red pepper flakes and stir-fry about 15 seconds, or until fragrant. Add carrots and bean sprouts and stir-fry until carrots begin to soften, about 1 minute. Add rice and cook, stirring frequently, 2 to 3 minutes, or until heated through. Stir seasoning liquid and add to fried rice, tossing to coat evenly.

Serve Vietnamese fried rice sprinkled with cilantro or mint leaves and dry-roasted peanuts. Serves 4 as a main course.

RICE WITH PINE NUTS AND CILANTRO ◔

2 tablespoons pine nuts
3 cups packed fresh cilantro sprigs
1 garlic clove
¾ cup long-grain white rice
1½ tablespoons olive oil
1½ cups water
½ teaspoon salt

In a dry small heavy saucepan toast pine nuts over moderate heat, stirring, until golden, about 5 minutes, and transfer to a small bowl. Finely chop cilantro and reserve ¼ cup for garnish. Mince garlic. In pan cook rice in oil with garlic and remaining cilantro over moderate heat, stirring, 3 minutes and add water and salt. Bring mixture to a boil and cook, covered, over low heat 15 minutes, or until water is absorbed and rice is tender. Remove pan from heat and let rice stand, covered, 5 minutes.

Serve rice sprinkled with pine nuts and reserved cilantro. Serves 2.

BEET AND BEET GREEN RISOTTO WITH HORSERADISH

1 small onion
1 pound red beets with greens (about 3 medium)
4 cups water
½ stick (¼ cup) unsalted butter
1 cup Arborio or long-grain rice
½ cup freshly grated Parmesan (about 1½ ounces)
1 tablespoon bottled horseradish

Finely chop onion and trim stems close to tops of red beets. Cut greens into ¼-inch-wide slices and chop stems. Peel beets and cut into fine dice. In a small saucepan bring water to a simmer and keep at a bare simmer.

In a 3-quart heavy saucepan cook onion in butter over moderate heat until softened. Add beets and stems and cook, stirring occasionally, 5 minutes. Stir in rice and cook, stirring constantly, 1 minute. Stir in 1 cup simmering water and cook, stirring constantly

and keeping at a strong simmer, until absorbed. Continue cooking at a strong simmer and adding water, about ½ cup at a time, stirring constantly and letting each addition be absorbed before adding next.

After 10 minutes, stir in greens and continue cooking and adding water, about ½ cup at a time, in same manner until rice is tender and creamy-looking but still *al dente*, about 8 minutes more. (There may be water left over.) Remove saucepan from heat and stir in Parmesan.

Serve risotto topped with horseradish. Serves 4.

RISOTTO WITH TURNIPS AND BACON ◔

3 bacon slices
1 small onion
2 medium turnips (preferably with greens; about ½ pound total)
3½ cups chicken broth
¾ cup Arborio rice

Garnish: freshly grated Parmesan

In a 3-quart heavy saucepan cook bacon over moderate heat until crisp and golden and transfer with a slotted spoon to paper towels to drain. Reserve 1 tablespoon fat in pan. Chop onion. Peel turnips and cut into ¼-inch dice (if using greens, cut into ¼-inch slices and chop stems). In a saucepan bring broth to a simmer and keep at a bare simmer.

Heat reserved fat over moderately high heat until hot but not smoking and sauté onion, stirring, until just beginning to soften. Stir in turnips (and greens if using) and rice and sauté, stirring constantly, 1 minute. Stir in 1 cup simmering broth and cook, stirring constantly and keeping at a strong simmer, until absorbed. Continue simmering and adding broth, about ½ cup at a time, stirring constantly and letting each addition be absorbed before adding next, until rice is tender and creamy-looking but still *al dente*, about 18 minutes total.

Crumble bacon. Serve risotto sprinkled with bacon and garnished with Parmesan. Serves 2 as a main course.

VEGETABLES AND BEANS

CREAMY CABBAGE, PARSNIP, AND POTATO CASSEROLE WITH ROBIOLA

The broth that accumulates at the bottom of this casserole is delicious spooned over the vegetables. Robiola, a fresh, rindless cheese from Italy's Piedmont, has a tangy richness that makes the dish particularly distinctive.

a 2½-pound cabbage (preferably with dark-green
    outer leaves intact)
1 pound parsnips (about 3 large)
1 onion (about ½ pound)
1 pound russet (baking) potatoes (about
    2 medium)
3½ tablespoons unsalted butter
2 teaspoons salt
freshly grated nutmeg to taste
5 ounces fresh Robiola cheese* (about 150 grams)
    or *mascarpone* cheese* (about ⅔ cup)

*available at specialty foods shops and by
    mail order from Zabar's, (800) 697-6301
    or (212) 787-2000

Keeping cabbage whole, cut out and discard core and any discolored outer leaves. Beginning at top of head and working with 1 leaf at a time, remove 6 outer leaves, rolling each one back on itself until it can be loosened intact from head, and reserve. Cut remaining cabbage head into 8 wedges and cut each wedge crosswise into 3 pieces. Separate layers of cabbage pieces. Peel parsnips and diagonally cut into ⅛-inch-thick slices. Chop onion. Peel potatoes and cut crosswise into ⅛-inch-thick slices.

Bring a large kettle of salted water to a boil and cook reserved cabbage leaves until just tender, 3 to 5 minutes. With a slotted spoon transfer cabbage leaves to a kitchen towel to drain. Add cabbage pieces to boiling water and cook until crisp-tender, about 3 minutes. With slotted spoon transfer pieces to a colander to drain and transfer to a bowl. Add potatoes to boiling water and cook until just tender, about 4 minutes. With slotted spoon transfer potatoes to colander to drain and transfer to another bowl. Add parsnips to boiling water and cook until tender, 3 minutes. Drain parsnips in colander.

In a 12-inch heavy skillet cook onion in 3 tablespoons butter over moderately low heat, stirring, until softened. Add cabbage pieces, salt, nutmeg, and pepper to taste and cook mixture over moderate heat, stirring occasionally, until cabbage is tender, about 10 minutes. If any liquid remains in skillet, cook mixture over high heat until liquid is evaporated, about 1 minute.

If using Robiola, cut into pieces. Stir Robiola or *mascarpone* into cabbage mixture and cook over moderate heat, stirring, until cheese is melted.

Preheat oven to 375° F.

Butter a 2-quart ovenproof round serving dish (about 8½ to 9 inches across and 2½ inches deep) and line with cabbage leaves, letting leaves overhang 1 to 2 inches. Arrange half of potatoes in serving dish and season with salt and pepper. Top potatoes in dish with half of cabbage mixture and arrange half of parsnips over cabbage. Repeat layering with remaining potatoes, cabbage mixture, and parsnips, arranging last layer of parsnips decoratively around edge of casserole and leaving cabbage exposed in center. Dot parsnips with remaining ½ tablespoon butter. Fold cabbage leaves over parsnips and cover tightly with a double layer of foil. *Casserole may be prepared up to this point 1 day ahead and chilled. Bring casserole to room temperature before proceeding.* Bake casserole until heated through and bubbling, about 1 hour. (If baking casserole simultaneously with another dish, baking time increases.)

Let casserole stand 10 minutes before serving. Serves 8.

PHOTO ON PAGE 75

BROCCOLI RABE AND BUTTERNUT SQUASH ◐

½ small butternut squash (about 1½ pounds)
1 medium red onion
6 ounces broccoli rabe (about ½ bunch)
2 tablespoons olive oil
¼ cup water

With a vegetable peeler or paring knife peel squash. Cut squash and onion into ¼-inch dice and cut broccoli rabe into ½-inch pieces.

In a 12-inch nonstick skillet heat oil over moderately high heat until hot but not smoking and add vegetables and salt to taste, stirring to coat with oil. Add ¼ cup water and cook vegetables, covered, over moderate heat 5 minutes, or until tender. Remove lid and cook vegetables over moderately high heat, stirring occasionally, until liquid is evaporated and vegetables begin to brown, about 3 minutes more. Serves 2.

WILTED RED CABBAGE WITH BALSAMIC VINEGAR ◐

10 red cabbage leaves
1 small onion
2 tablespoons water
2½ teaspoons balsamic vinegar
½ teaspoon sugar
2 teaspoons olive oil
freshly ground black pepper to taste

Thinly slice cabbage and onion separately. In a small bowl stir together water, vinegar, and sugar until sugar is dissolved. In a 10- to 12-inch heavy skillet cook onion in oil over moderately low heat, stirring occasionally, until softened. Add cabbage and sauté over moderately high heat, stirring, until crisp-tender, about 5 minutes. Stir in vinegar mixture and pepper until combined well. Serves 2.

BABY CARROTS AND ASPARAGUS ◐

2 pounds baby carrots with tops (about 5 bunches)
1½ pounds thin asparagus
1½ tablespoons unsalted butter, softened

Trim carrot tops to ¾ inch and diagonally cut asparagus into 4-inch lengths. In a large saucepan of boiling salted water cook carrots until crisp-tender, about 4 minutes, and transfer with a slotted spoon to a colander to drain. Return water to a boil and cook asparagus until crisp-tender, about 2 minutes. Drain asparagus in colander with carrots and in a bowl toss vegetables with butter and salt and pepper to taste. Serves 6.

PHOTO ON PAGE 34

MASHED JERUSALEM ARTICHOKES

3½ pounds Jerusalem artichokes*
1 pound boiling potatoes
1 tablespoon salt
3 cups milk
3 tablespoons unsalted butter, softened

*available at specialty produce markets and many supermarkets

Peel Jerusalem artichokes and cut into 2-inch pieces. Peel potatoes and cut into ¾-inch pieces. In a 5-quart kettle combine artichokes, potatoes, salt, and milk with enough water to cover vegetables by 2 inches and simmer until vegetables are tender, about 25 minutes. Drain vegetables in a colander and return to kettle. With a potato masher mash vegetables with butter and salt and pepper to taste until smooth. *Vegetables may be made 3 days ahead and chilled, covered. Bring vegetables to room temperature before reheating, covered.* Serves 6.

ROASTED BEETS WITH PARSLEY

3 pounds beets (10 to 15 medium)
¼ cup packed fresh flat-leafed parsley leaves
2 tablespoons unsalted butter

Preheat oven to 475° F.

Trim beets, leaving about 1 inch of stems attached. Wrap beets tightly in double layers of foil to make 3 packages and roast until tender, about 1 hour.

When beets are cool enough to handle, slip off skins and stems and cut each beet into about 6 wedges. *Beets may be prepared up to this point 1 day ahead and chilled, covered.* Transfer beets to a baking dish and cover with foil.

Reduce temperature to 375° F. and reheat beets until heated through, about 20 minutes.

While beets are reheating, put parsley in a small bowl and with kitchen shears very coarsely snip.

Toss beets with butter, parsley, and salt and pepper to taste. Serves 8.

PHOTO ON PAGE 75

ARTICHOKES WITH
TOMATO-BACON VINAIGRETTE ◖

2 medium artichokes
4 bacon slices
2 vine-ripened tomatoes
1 shallot
3 tablespoons drained capers
2 tablespoons fresh lemon juice
⅓ cup olive oil

With a serrated knife cut artichoke stems flush with bottoms. Cut off and discard top inch from artichokes. In a saucepan cover artichokes with salted water and bring to a boil. Simmer artichokes, covered, until just tender, 20 to 25 minutes.

While artichokes are cooking, coarsely chop bacon and in a skillet cook over moderate heat, stirring, until golden. With a slotted spoon transfer bacon to paper towels. Halve and seed tomatoes and cut into ¼-inch dice. Finely chop shallot and capers. In a bowl combine lemon juice and salt and pepper to taste. Whisk in oil in a slow stream until emulsified and add bacon, tomatoes, shallot, and capers.

Drain artichokes upside down on a rack and arrange each on a plate. Separating leaves slightly, drizzle vinaigrette between leaves and onto plates. Serves 2.

SAUTÉED KOHLRABI AND WATERCRESS ◖

1 pound small kohlrabi bulbs* (about
    1 bunch)
1 bunch watercress
1 tablespoon unsalted butter
1 tablespoon reserved rendered duck fat from
    crisp duck breast (page 145) or 1 tablespoon
    additional unsalted butter
2 tablespoons fresh lemon juice

*available at specialty produce markets and
    some supermarkets

Peel kohlrabi with a vegetable peeler and cut into 2-inch-long julienne strips. Discard coarse stems from watercress. In a large heavy skillet heat butter and reserved duck fat or additional butter over moderately high heat until foam subsides and sauté kohlrabi, stirring, until crisp-tender, 5 to 10 minutes. Add lemon juice and sauté kohlrabi, stirring, 1 minute more. Remove skillet from heat and immediately stir in watercress. Season vegetables with salt and pepper. Serves 4.

PHOTO ON PAGE 14

CREAMED CHAYOTE WITH CHIVES ⊙

4 chayotes* (also called mirlitons or
    christophenes; about 2½ pounds)
2 tablespoons vegetable oil
1 cup heavy cream
3 tablespoons chopped fresh chives

*available at Latino and specialty produce
    markets and many supermarkets

Cut each chayote lengthwise into ½-inch wedges and discard seed if necessary. In a 12-inch heavy skillet heat oil over moderate heat until hot but not smoking and cook chayotes, stirring occasionally, until crisp-tender, about 5 minutes. Add cream and simmer until chayotes are tender and cream is slightly thickened, about 3 minutes. Add chives and season with salt. Serves 6.

PHOTO ON PAGE 66

STEAMED SAVOY CABBAGE AND MUSTARD GREENS WITH BACON ⊙

¾ pound sliced bacon
1 large head Savoy cabbage (about 2 pounds)
2 bunches mustard greens (about 2½
    pounds total)
6 large garlic cloves
3 tablespoons unsalted butter
3 tablespoons extra-virgin olive oil

Cut bacon into ½-inch pieces and in a large heavy skillet cook over moderate heat, stirring, until crisp and golden. With a slotted spoon transfer bacon to paper towels to drain.

Thinly slice cabbage and discard coarse stems from mustard greens. In a large steamer rack set over boiling water steam sliced cabbage, covered, until crisp-tender, about 10 minutes. Transfer cabbage to a large bowl and keep warm, covered. In steamer rack set over boiling water steam mustard greens until tender, 10 to 15 minutes. Add mustard greens to cabbage and keep warm, covered.

Mince garlic. In a small saucepan heat garlic, butter, and oil until butter is just melted. Drizzle butter mixture over vegetables, tossing to distribute evenly, and season with salt and pepper.

Transfer vegetables to a serving dish and serve topped with bacon. Serves 8.

PHOTO ON PAGE 72

GRILLED CORN WITH CUMIN SCALLION BUTTER

1 tablespoon cumin seeds
½ teaspoon kosher salt
3 scallions
1½ sticks (¾ cup) unsalted butter
1 teaspoon fresh lemon juice
12 ears corn in husks

In a dry small heavy skillet toast seeds over moderate heat, shaking skillet, until fragrant, about 1 minute, and cool. In an electric coffee/spice grinder finely grind seeds and salt. Finely chop enough scallion greens to measure ⅓ cup. In a saucepan melt butter with cumin salt, stirring, and stir in scallion greens and lemon juice. Cool butter.

While butter is cooling, peel back husks from corn, leaving them attached at base of ears, and discard silk. Brush kernels with some butter and reassemble husks over ears. Chill remaining butter, covered. Peel off a few layers of husks and tear lengthwise into strips. Tie ends of reassembled ears with strips of husks. *Corn may be prepared 1 day ahead and chilled, covered.*

Prepare grill.

Grill corn on a rack set 5 to 6 inches over glowing coals, turning it occasionally, 20 minutes. (Alternatively, in a shallow baking pan roast corn in middle of a preheated 450° F. oven, turning it occasionally, 35 minutes.) Reheat remaining cumin scallion butter.

Serve corn with melted butter. Serves 8.

PHOTO ON PAGE 57

CORIANDER AND CUMIN BROILED EGGPLANT ◔

½ large eggplant
¼ cup packed fresh cilantro sprigs
2 tablespoons extra-virgin olive oil
1 tablespoon fresh lemon juice
1 teaspoon ground cumin
½ teaspoon ground coriander seeds
a pinch cinnamon

Preheat broiler and lightly oil a baking pan.

Cut eggplant into ¼-inch-thick slices. Chop cilantro and in a bowl stir together with remaining ingredients and salt and pepper to taste. Brush cilantro mixture on both sides of eggplant slices and transfer to baking pan. Broil eggplant 5 to 6 inches from heat until golden and cooked through, about 10 minutes. Serves 2 as a side dish.

SPICY EGGPLANT

1½ pounds Asian or other small eggplants
   (each about 1½ inches in diameter)
4 tablespoons vegetable oil
3 cups water
1½ tablespoons sugar
3 tablespoons soy sauce (preferably Kikkoman)
3 tablespoons *mirin** (sweet rice wine)
1½ teaspoons instant *dashi* (seasoned stock)
   granules*
¼ to ½ teaspoon dried hot red pepper flakes

Garnish: julienne strips of peeled fresh
   gingerroot, chopped fresh cilantro leaves,
   and radish sprouts

*available at Japanese markets and by mail order
   from Uwajimaya, (800) 889-1928

Cut eggplants crosswise into 1-inch-thick rounds. In a 5-quart heavy kettle heat 2 tablespoons oil over moderately high heat until hot but not smoking and brown cut sides of eggplant in 2 batches (adding remaining 2 tablespoons oil before second batch), turning eggplant occasionally with tongs.

In kettle combine eggplant and remaining ingredients. Simmer mixture, uncovered, stirring occasionally, until eggplant is very tender but not falling apart, about 15 minutes. With a slotted spoon carefully transfer eggplant to a bowl. Boil liquid remaining in kettle, skimming froth, until reduced to about ½ cup and add sauce to eggplant.

Serve eggplant warm or at room temperature with some sauce and garnish with gingerroot, cilantro, and sprouts. Serves 6.

PHOTO ON PAGE 60

PEAS WITH MINT AND BLACK PEPPER ◔

½ cup packed fresh mint leaves
a 10-ounce package frozen peas
¼ cup cold water
1 teaspoon sugar
1 tablespoon unsalted butter
½ teaspoon freshly ground black pepper

Chop mint. In a small saucepan cook peas with water and sugar, covered, over moderately high heat until tender, 4 to 5 minutes. In a sieve drain peas and in a bowl toss with mint, butter, pepper, and salt to taste. Serves 2.

FRIED "CHRYSANTHEMUM" ONIONS ◔

2 medium onions
2 quarts vegetable oil for deep-frying
⅓ cup milk
¼ cup all-purpose flour
½ cup fine dry bread crumbs
1 large egg

Trim root end of 1 onion flush and cut a ½-inch slice from opposite end. Repeat procedure with remaining onion. Stand 1 onion on cutting board, root end up, and with tip of a paring knife inserted just outside of root base, make vertical cuts through onion at ¼-inch intervals, rotating onion as you go and leaving root end intact. Repeat procedure with remaining onion. Turn onions root end down and gently open cuts to form chrysanthemum shape.

In a 4-quart heavy saucepan heat vegetable oil over moderate heat until a deep-fat thermometer registers 375° F.

Put milk and flour in 2 separate small bowls and season flour with salt. Put bread crumbs in a bowl. Working with 1 onion at a time, dip onions into milk, spooning milk over centers to moisten and letting excess drip off. Dip onions into flour, spooning flour into centers to coat and gently shaking off excess.

To remaining milk in bowl add egg, beating with a fork until combined well. Working with 1 onion at a time, dip onions into egg mixture, spooning egg mixture into centers to coat. Roll onions in bread crumbs, sprinkling bread crumbs into centers and gently shaking off excess.

Fry onions, 1 at a time, in oil until golden brown, about 5 minutes, returning oil to 375° F. between onions. Transfer onions as fried to brown paper to drain. Serves 2.

MASHED-POTATO CAKES

1 pound boiling potatoes (preferably
    yellow-fleshed such as Yukon Gold;
    about 2 medium)
½ stick (¼ cup) unsalted butter, softened
½ cup packed fresh flat-leafed parsley leaves
1½ teaspoons minced garlic
1 large egg
2 teaspoons vegetable oil

In a 4-quart kettle cover potatoes with cold water by 2 inches and simmer until tender, 35 to 40 minutes. Drain potatoes in a colander. Cool potatoes just until they can be handled and peel. While potatoes are still warm, in a bowl mash with a potato masher or fork and stir in 3 tablespoons butter. Chop parsley and add to potatoes with garlic and egg, stirring to combine well. Chill mashed potatoes until cold. *Mashed potatoes may be made 1 day ahead and chilled, covered.*

Form ½ cupfuls mashed potatoes into four 4-inch cakes. In a 12-inch nonstick skillet heat remaining tablespoon butter and oil over moderately low heat until foam subsides and cook cakes 5 minutes on each side, or until golden. *Potato cakes may be made 1 hour ahead and reheated in a 400° F. oven.* Makes 4 cakes.

PHOTO ON PAGE 14

TWICE-BAKED POTATOES WITH BASIL AND SOUR CREAM

8 medium Yukon Gold or other yellow-fleshed
    potatoes (about 2¾ pounds)
5 tablespoons unsalted butter, softened
½ cup milk
1 cup packed fresh basil leaves
½ cup sour cream

Preheat oven to 400° F.

With a fork prick potatoes and on a baking sheet bake in middle of oven 1 hour, or until tender. Leave oven on. When potatoes are just cool enough to handle, halve lengthwise and scoop flesh into a 3-quart saucepan, leaving ¼-inch-thick shells.

With a potato masher mash potatoes in saucepan with 3 tablespoons butter. Stir in milk and salt and pepper to taste. Transfer shells to baking sheet and brush insides with remaining 2 tablespoons butter. Season shells with salt and pepper. *Mashed potatoes and shells may be prepared up to this point 1 day ahead and chilled, covered. Reheat mashed potatoes before proceeding.*

Bake potato shells in middle of oven until golden, about 20 minutes. While shells are baking, cut basil into thin strips and stir about three fourths into warm mashed potatoes. Spoon mashed potatoes into shells and bake until heated through, about 10 minutes. Serve each potato half topped with ½ tablespoon sour cream and some remaining basil. Serves 8.

PHOTO ON PAGE 48

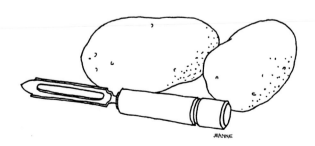

SPICY FRENCH FRIES ◐

¾ teaspoon coarse kosher salt
⅛ teaspoon cayenne
⅛ teaspoon paprika
⅛ teaspoon ground coriander seeds
4 cups vegetable oil
2 medium russet (baking) potatoes
    (about 12 ounces total)

In a large bowl stir together salt, cayenne, paprika, and coriander. In a 4-quart heavy kettle heat oil over moderate heat until a deep-fat thermometer registers 325° F.

While oil is heating, cut potatoes lengthwise into ¼-inch-thick sticks. Fry potatoes in oil 1½ minutes (they will not be golden) and with a slotted spoon transfer to brown paper or paper towels to drain.

Heat oil to 350° F. Return potatoes to oil and fry until golden and crisp, about 5 minutes. Transfer fries with slotted spoon to clean brown paper or paper towels to drain and toss fries in spice mixture. Serves 2.

PORCINI MUSHROOM MASHED POTATOES

2 cups boiling water
1½ ounces dried porcini mushrooms*
    (about 1½ cups)
½ pound fresh white mushrooms
2 teaspoons olive oil
3 pounds yellow-fleshed potatoes such
    as Yukon Gold

Garnish: chopped fresh chives

*available at specialty foods shops and some
    supermarkets and by mail order from Marché
    aux Delices, (888) 547-5471

In a heatproof bowl pour boiling water over *porcini. Soak porcini 30 minutes.* Lift out *porcini,* squeezing out excess liquid, and reserve soaking liquid. In a sieve rinse *porcini* to remove any grit and pat dry. Chop *porcini.* Pour reserved soaking liquid through a sieve lined with a dampened paper towel or coffee filter into another bowl.

Thinly slice white mushrooms. In a skillet heat oil over moderately high heat until hot but not smoking and sauté white mushrooms until liquid mushrooms give off is evaporated and they begin to brown. Stir in *porcini* and salt and pepper to taste and sauté, stirring, 2 minutes.

Peel and quarter potatoes. In a kettle cover potatoes with salted cold water by 2 inches and simmer until very tender, about 30 minutes. Drain potatoes in a colander and transfer to a large bowl. With a potato masher mash potatoes.

Stir mushrooms and ½ cup soaking liquid, or to taste, into potatoes until combined well and season with salt and pepper. *Potatoes may be made 1 day ahead and chilled, covered. Reheat potatoes, covered, in a 350° F. oven about 30 minutes.*

Garnish potatoes with chives. Serves 6.

☞ each serving about 178 calories and 2 grams fat

LEEK AND CABBAGE MASHED POTATOES

2½ pounds Yukon Gold potatoes
1 medium head cabbage (about
    2 pounds)
3 large leeks (white and pale green
    parts only)
1 cup chicken broth

Peel potatoes and quarter. Cut cabbage into 1-inch squares. In a 5- to 6-quart kettle cover potatoes and cabbage with salted cold water by 2 inches and simmer until very tender, about 30 minutes.

While vegetables are simmering, cut leeks into ½-inch pieces and in a bowl of cold water wash leeks well. Lift leeks from water into a colander to drain. In a saucepan simmer leeks in broth, covered, until very tender, about 20 minutes. Drain leeks in a sieve set over a bowl and reserve cooking liquid.

Drain potatoes and cabbage in colander and transfer to a bowl. With a potato masher mash mixture. Stir in leeks, adding some of reserved cooking liquid to thin potatoes if desired. Season potatoes with salt and pepper. *Mashed potatoes may be made 1 day ahead and chilled, covered. Reheat potatoes, covered, in a 350° F. oven about 30 minutes.* Serves 6.

☞ each serving about 190 calories and less than 1 gram fat

Preheat oven to 400° F. and butter a 3-quart gratin dish (about 15 by 10 by 2 inches).

Mince garlic and chop parsley. In a nonstick skillet heat remaining 2 tablespoons butter over moderate heat until foam subsides and cook garlic, stirring, until fragrant, about 1 minute. Add bread crumbs and cook, stirring, until golden. Transfer mixture to a bowl and cool. Stir in parsley and Parmesan and season with salt and pepper.

Cut tomatoes into ¼-inch-thick slices. Spread potatoes in gratin dish and top with tomatoes, overlapping them to completely cover potatoes. Sprinkle crumb mixture over tomatoes and bake gratin in middle of oven until top is golden brown and tomatoes are tender, about 25 minutes. *Gratin may be made 1 day ahead and cooled completely, uncovered, before being chilled, covered. Reheat gratin, uncovered.* Serves 6 to 8 as a side dish.

SMASHED-POTATO TOMATO GRATIN

3 pounds yellow-fleshed potatoes such as
   Yukon Gold
½ cup milk
1 stick (½ cup) unsalted butter
1 cup Kalamata olives
4 scallions
1 garlic clove
½ cup fresh parsley leaves
3 cups fresh bread crumbs
½ cup freshly grated Parmesan
3 pounds vine-ripened red or yellow tomatoes
   (about 7 medium)

In a 4-quart heavy kettle cover potatoes with salted cold water by 2 inches and simmer until tender, about 30 minutes. While potatoes are simmering, in a small saucepan heat milk with 6 tablespoons butter over moderate heat until butter is melted. Remove pan from heat and keep mixture warm, covered. Pit olives and separately chop olives and scallions. In a colander drain potatoes and when just cool enough to handle, peel them. Coarsely smash potatoes with a potato masher and gently fold in milk mixture, olives, scallions, and salt and pepper to taste.

OLIVE OIL AND GARLIC WHIPPED POTATOES

1 large head of garlic
3 pounds yellow-fleshed potatoes
   such as Yukon Gold
1 cup extra-virgin olive oil
½ cup whole milk
1½ teaspoons salt
¼ teaspoon freshly grated nutmeg
¼ teaspoon freshly ground black pepper

Preheat oven to 400° F.

Separate garlic head into cloves, discarding loose papery outer skin but keeping skin intact on cloves, and wrap tightly in foil. Roast garlic in middle of oven 30 minutes, or until soft. Unwrap garlic and cool slightly. Peel skins from each clove and on a plate with a fork mash garlic pulp until smooth.

While garlic is roasting, peel potatoes and cut into 2-inch pieces. In a 4-quart kettle cover potatoes with cold salted water by 2 inches and simmer until potatoes are very tender, about 30 minutes. Drain potatoes in a colander and transfer to a large bowl. With a potato masher mash potatoes. Add garlic pulp, ¾ cup oil, milk, salt, nutmeg, and pepper and with an electric mixer beat until smooth.

Serve potatoes drizzled with remaining ¼ cup oil. Serves 6 to 8.

GOAT CHEESE MASHED POTATOES

¾ pound small red potatoes
2½ ounces soft mild goat cheese
   (about ¼ cup)
1 tablespoon unsalted butter
¼ teaspoon fresh lemon juice, or to taste
¾ teaspoon chopped fresh thyme leaves

In a saucepan cover potatoes with salted cold water by 1 inch and simmer, covered, until tender, 15 to 20 minutes. Reserve ¼ cup cooking liquid and drain potatoes. Return potatoes to pan and with a fork mash together with reserved liquid, remaining ingredients, and salt and pepper to taste. Serves 2.

POTATO, TOMATO, AND ROSEMARY GRATIN

1 medium onion
1 large garlic clove
a 16-ounce can whole tomatoes
2 pounds boiling potatoes
5 tablespoons olive oil
1 teaspoon minced fresh rosemary leaves
⅓ cup water
¼ cup freshly grated Parmesan

Cut onion crosswise into ½-inch-thick slices and mince garlic clove. Drain tomatoes well and coarsely chop. Peel potatoes and cut crosswise into ¼-inch-thick slices.
Preheat oven to 350° F.
In a 12-inch heavy skillet heat 1 tablespoon oil over moderately high heat until hot but not smoking and sauté potatoes in 3 batches, turning them, until golden on both sides, adding 1 tablespoon oil for each batch. Transfer potatoes to a bowl as sautéed.
In skillet cook onion in 1 tablespoon oil over moderate heat, stirring occasionally, until softened. Add onion to potatoes with tomatoes, garlic, rosemary, and salt and pepper to taste and toss to combine well. Transfer potato mixture to a 2-quart gratin dish or other shallow baking dish and drizzle with water and remaining tablespoon oil. Sprinkle Parmesan over potatoes. *Gratin may be made up to this point 2 hours ahead and kept, covered, at cool room temperature.*

Bake gratin 30 minutes, or until potatoes are tender and beginning to brown. Serves 6.

PHOTO ON PAGE 27

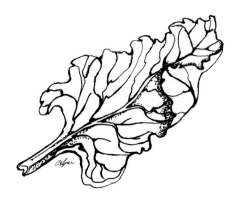

ROASTED ACORN SQUASH AND CHESTNUTS

4 small acorn squash
½ stick (¼ cup) unsalted butter
½ cup packed brown sugar
½ teaspoon freshly grated nutmeg
½ teaspoon ground cloves
2 cups vacuum-packed whole chestnuts*
   (not canned; about ¾ pound)

*available at specialty foods shops and some
   supermarkets

Preheat oven to 450° F.
Halve squash lengthwise and discard seeds and strings. Cut each half lengthwise into 3 wedges and arrange wedges, skin sides down, in a shallow baking pan. In a small saucepan melt butter with brown sugar over moderate heat, stirring occasionally until sugar is dissolved. Stir in nutmeg and cloves and remove pan from heat. Spoon butter mixture over squash and cover baking pan with foil.
Bake squash in middle of oven 30 minutes. Remove baking pan from oven and scatter chestnuts over squash. Re-cover pan with foil and roast squash and chestnuts 30 minutes, or until squash is tender. *Acorn squash and chestnuts may be made up to this point 6 hours ahead and kept, covered, at room temperature.*

Remove foil from baking pan and bake squash and chestnuts 20 minutes more. With a slotted spoon transfer squash and chestnuts to a serving dish. Stir sauce, scraping up brown-sugar drippings, and spoon over squash and chestnuts. Serves 8.

PHOTO ON PAGE 73

SESAME SPINACH AND BROCCOLI ☺

½ bunch broccoli (about ½ pound)
1 garlic clove
1 tablespoon sesame seeds
1 teaspoon vegetable oil
¼ teaspoon dried hot red pepper flakes
1 bunch spinach (about
   1 pound)
2 teaspoons Asian sesame oil

Cut broccoli into 1-inch flowerets and cut stems lengthwise into 2- by ¼-inch sticks. Mince garlic. In a dry 10-inch heavy skillet toast sesame seeds over moderate heat, stirring, until golden and transfer to a small bowl. In skillet heat vegetable oil over moderate heat until hot but not smoking and cook broccoli, garlic, and red pepper flakes, stirring occasionally, until broccoli is crisp-tender, about 7 minutes. Add spinach and cook, stirring, until wilted, about 2 minutes. Remove skillet from heat and toss vegetables with sesame oil, seeds, and salt to taste. Serves 2.

BALSAMIC MASHED SWEET POTATOES

3 pounds sweet potatoes
2 tablespoons fine-quality balsamic vinegar
½ teaspoon ground cinnamon
¼ cup nonfat sour cream

Preheat oven to 425° F.
With a fork prick sweet potatoes in several places and on a baking sheet bake in middle of oven until very tender, about 1¼ hours. When potatoes are cool enough to handle, remove skins and discard. In a food processor blend potatoes with vinegar and ¼ teaspoon cinnamon until smooth. Transfer potatoes to a bowl and stir in sour cream until combined well.

Season potatoes with salt and pepper. *Sweet potatoes may be made 1 day ahead and chilled, covered. Reheat sweet potatoes, covered, in a 350° F. oven about 30 minutes.*

Serve sweet potatoes sprinkled with remaining ¼ teaspoon cinnamon. Serves 6.

☛ each serving about 189 calories and less than 1 gram fat

CREAMED SPINACH ☺

1¼ pounds spinach (about 2 bunches)
1 tablespoon unsalted butter
1 tablespoon all-purpose flour
⅔ cup heavy cream

Discard stems from spinach and coarsely chop leaves. In a steamer set over boiling water steam spinach, covered, 1 minute, or until just wilted. Drain spinach well.
In a saucepan melt butter. Add flour and cook over moderate heat, stirring, 1 minute. Stir in cream and simmer, stirring constantly, 2 minutes (mixture will be thick). Stir spinach into sauce and season with salt and pepper. Serves 2.

SWISS CHARD WITH GARLIC ☺

3 pounds Swiss chard (about 2 large bunches)
1 large garlic clove
1 tablespoon olive oil

Tear Swiss chard leaves from thick white stalks and coarsely chop leaves, reserving stalks. In a large saucepan or kettle of boiling salted water simmer stalks until tender, 5 to 10 minutes, and drain in a colander. *Chard may be prepared up to this point 1 day ahead, stalks cooled completely and leaves and stalks chilled separately in sealable plastic bags.*
Mince garlic. In a large skillet heat oil over moderate heat until hot but not smoking and cook garlic, stirring, 30 seconds. Add leaves in 2 batches, tossing to coat with oil and stirring after each addition, and cook until leaves are wilted. Add stalks and cook, stirring occasionally, until heated through. Season chard with salt and pepper. Serves 6.

PHOTO ON PAGE 27

ANCHO SWEET-POTATO PURÉE

5 pounds sweet potatoes (about 6 large)
3 or 4 dried ancho chiles* (about 1½ ounces)
¾ cup heavy cream
2 teaspoons salt
2 tablespoons unsalted butter, or to taste

*available at specialty foods shops and by mail order from Chile Today–Hot Tamale, Inc., (800) 468-7377

Preheat oven to 450° F. and line a baking sheet with foil.

Prick sweet potatoes in several places with a fork and bake on baking sheet in middle of oven until tender, about 1 hour. Cool potatoes until they can be handled.

Wearing rubber gloves, stem and seed chiles and tear into 1-inch pieces. In a small saucepan bring chiles and heavy cream to a boil. In a blender purée mixture until smooth (use caution when blending hot liquids).

Scoop flesh from potatoes into a food processor, discarding skins, and purée with cream mixture, salt, and 2 tablespoons butter. *Purée may be made up to this point 1 day ahead and cooled before being chilled, covered.*

Transfer purée to a large saucepan and heat over moderate heat, stirring, until hot, stirring in more salt and butter if desired. Serves 6.

PHOTO ON PAGE 66

BEANS

HOPPIN' JOHN

BLACK-EYED PEAS WITH KIELBASA

1 cup dried black-eyed peas
6 ounces smoked *kielbasa* sausage
1 medium onion
2 garlic cloves
2 celery ribs
½ fresh jalapeño chile
1 bay leaf
1½ tablespoons vegetable oil
1¾ cups chicken broth
3 tablespoons chopped fresh cilantro leaves

Accompaniment: cooked rice

Quick-soak peas (procedure on page 109).
Quarter *kielbasa* lengthwise and cut quarters crosswise into ½-inch pieces. Chop onion and mince garlic. Cut celery crosswise into ½-inch-thick slices. Wearing rubber gloves, seed and mince jalapeño.

In a 3-quart heavy kettle cook *kielbasa*, onion, garlic, celery, jalapeño, and bay leaf in oil over moderate heat, stirring, until onion is softened. Add peas and broth and simmer, covered, 20 minutes, or until peas are tender. Discard bay leaf and stir in cilantro and salt and pepper to taste.

Serve Hoppin' John spooned over rice. Serves 4.

PICKLED BLACK-EYED PEAS

1 cup dried black-eyed peas
1 yellow bell pepper
½ red bell pepper
½ fresh jalapeño chile
¼ cup extra-virgin olive oil
¼ cup white-wine vinegar
¼ cup minced fresh chives
2 tablespoons minced red onion
1 teaspoon minced garlic

Accompaniment: toasts or grilled or roasted meats

Quick-soak black-eyed peas (procedure on page 109). In a saucepan simmer peas in water to cover until tender, about 20 minutes, and drain in a sieve.

Cut bell peppers into ¼-inch dice. Wearing rubber gloves, seed and mince jalapeño. In a bowl stir together all ingredients and salt and pepper to taste. *Chill pickled peas, covered, at least 4 hours and up to 2 days.*

Serve peas chilled or at room temperature on toasts or with grilled or roasted meats. Makes about 3 cups.

SALADS

Grilled Chicken and Chick-Pea Salad with Carrot-Cumin Dressing

For dressing
2 cups fresh carrot juice*
2 tablespoons fresh lemon juice
1 tablespoon extra-virgin olive oil
1½ teaspoons ground cumin

2 hearts of romaine (about 1 pound total)
1 bunch spinach
1 pound carrots
1¼ pounds vine-ripened tomatoes
2 cups drained canned chick-peas
10 ounces skinless boneless chicken breast
   halves (about 2)

*available at natural foods stores, juice bars, and
   some specialty foods shops

Prepare grill.
Make dressing:
In a saucepan boil carrot juice until reduced to
about ¾ cup, about 10 minutes, and cool. In a bowl
whisk together carrot juice, lemon juice, oil, and
cumin and season with salt and pepper. *Dressing may
be made 1 day ahead and chilled, covered.*

Cut romaine and spinach crosswise into ¼-inch-
wide strips and, using side of a grater with largest
holes, grate carrots. Cut tomatoes into ¼-inch dice.
Rinse chick-peas and slip off skins. *Vegetables may
be prepared up to this point 4 hours ahead and
chilled separately, covered.*

Pat chicken dry and season with salt and pepper.
Grill chicken on a lightly oiled rack set 5 to 6 inches
over glowing coals 7 minutes on each side, or until
cooked through. (Alternatively, grill chicken in a hot
lightly oiled well-seasoned ridged grill pan over

moderately high heat.) Let chicken stand 2 minutes
and slice. In a large bowl toss grilled chicken
with vegetables.

Just before serving, toss salad with dressing.
Serves 4 as a main course.

☙ each serving about 363 calories and 7 grams fat

Smoked Chicken and Stilton Cobb Salad

16 quail eggs or 4 large eggs
½ pound bacon
4 vine-ripened tomatoes
3 scallions
2 heads *radicchio*
2 hearts of romaine
1 firm-ripe California avocado
1 smoked chicken breast half* (about 6 ounces)
6 ounces Stilton or other blue cheese
3 tablespoons extra-virgin olive oil
1½ tablespoons balsamic vinegar

*available at specialty foods shops and many
   supermarkets

In a saucepan cover eggs with cold water by 1 inch
and bring to a boil. Remove pan from heat and let
eggs stand, covered, 7 minutes if using quail eggs and
17 minutes if using large eggs. Peel and halve eggs.

Cut bacon into 1-inch pieces. In a large heavy
skillet cook bacon over moderate heat until crisp and
golden and transfer to paper towels to drain. Quarter
and seed tomatoes and cut into ¼-inch-thick slices.
Thinly slice scallions, *radicchio*, and romaine separately. Halve, pit, and peel avocado. Cut avocado
into ½-inch pieces. Cut chicken crosswise into ¼-
inch-thick slices and crumble cheese.

In a large bowl toss together all ingredients and
season with salt and pepper to taste. Serves 4 as a
main course.

LOBSTER SALAD WITH CORN, SUGAR SNAP PEAS, AND BASIL-MINT OIL

We call for live lobsters in this recipe, but, to save time, you could use 1 pound (about 3 cups) cooked lobster meat from your fish market.

2 bay leaves
6 tablespoons coarse salt (preferably sea salt)
two 2½-pound live lobsters
4 ears corn
¼ pound sugar snap peas
2 bell peppers (preferably yellow)
3 large shallots
2 tablespoons olive oil
2 tablespoons fresh lemon juice, or to taste

Accompaniments:
basil-mint oil (recipe follows)
lemon wedges

In a 10- to 12-quart kettle bring 8 quarts water to a boil with bay leaves and coarse salt. Plunge 1 lobster into water headfirst and simmer, covered, 12 minutes. With tongs immediately transfer lobster to a bowl to cool. Return water to a boil and cook remaining lobster in same manner.

When lobsters are cool enough to handle, break off claws at body of each lobster. Crack claws and remove meat. Reserve some claw meat, covered and chilled, for garnish if desired and cut remainder into bite-size pieces. Twist tails off lobster bodies and discard bodies. With kitchen shears remove thin hard membrane from underside of each tail by cutting just inside outer edge of shell. Remove meat from each tail and cut into bite-size pieces. Transfer claw and tail meat to a large bowl and chill, covered.

Shuck corn and cut kernels from cobs. Trim sugar snap peas and diagonally cut into ¼-inch-thick slices. Cut bell peppers into 1- by ¼-inch strips. Finely chop enough shallots to measure ⅓ cup.

In a large nonstick skillet heat 1 tablespoon oil over moderately high heat until hot but not smoking and sauté peas and bell peppers with salt and pepper to taste, stirring, until crisp-tender, about 2 minutes. Transfer sautéed vegetables to a plate and cool completely. Add remaining tablespoon oil to skillet and sauté corn and shallots with salt and pepper to taste, stirring, until just tender, about 2 minutes. Transfer corn mixture to another plate and cool completely. Add all vegetables with salt and pepper to taste to lobster, tossing to combine. *Chill salad, covered, until cold and up to 1 day.*

Toss salad with lemon juice and serve with basil-mint oil and lemon. Serves 4 as a main course.

PHOTO ON PAGE 44

BASIL-MINT OIL ☾

1 cup packed fresh mint leaves
1 cup packed fresh basil leaves
½ cup extra-virgin olive oil
½ teaspoon sugar
1 tablespoon coarse salt (preferably sea salt)

Have ready a bowl of ice and cold water. In a saucepan of boiling water blanch herbs 5 seconds and with a slotted spoon immediately transfer to ice water to stop cooking. Drain herbs well and pat dry. In a blender purée herbs with remaining ingredients until smooth. Pour oil through a fine sieve into a bowl, pressing on solids, and discard solids. *Basil-mint oil may be made 1 day ahead and chilled, covered. Bring oil to room temperature before using.* Makes about ½ cup.

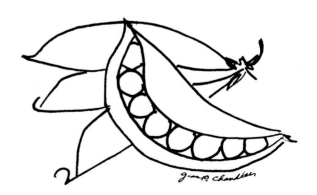

GRILLED PORK, TOMATO, FRISÉE, AND BLACK
BEAN SALAD WITH CHIPOTLE CITRUS DRESSING

For dressing
2 canned *chipotle* chiles in *adobo**
¼ cup bottled Major Grey's
   chutney
¼ cup fresh orange juice
¼ cup fresh lime juice

2 ears corn
1 pound vine-ripened tomatoes
   (about 3 medium)
10 radishes
1 pound pork tenderloin
2 large heads *frisée* (French curly endive;
   about ½ pound total)
1 cup drained canned black beans

*available at Latino markets, some specialty
   foods shops, and by mail order from
   Adriana's Caravan, (800) 316-0820

Prepare grill.
Make dressing:
Mince enough *chipotles* to measure 2 teaspoons.
In a blender purée *chipotles*, chutney, citrus juices,
and salt to taste until dressing is smooth. *Chipotle
citrus dressing may be made 1 day ahead and
chilled, covered.*

Cut enough corn from cobs to measure 1 cup. In a
small saucepan boil corn in water to just cover until
crisp-tender, about 2 minutes. In a colander drain
corn and rinse under cold water to stop cooking. Pat
corn kernels dry and cut tomatoes and radishes into
¼-inch dice. *Corn, tomatoes, and radishes may be
prepared up to this point 4 hours ahead and chilled
separately, covered.*

Pat pork tenderloin dry and season with salt and
pepper. Grill pork on a lightly oiled rack set 5 to 6
inches over glowing coals, turning it, until a meat
thermometer inserted diagonally into center registers
155° F., 15 to 20 minutes. (Alternatively, pork may
be grilled in a hot lightly oiled well-seasoned ridged
grill pan over moderately high heat.) Let pork stand
5 minutes and thinly slice. Chop *frisée* and transfer
with corn, tomatoes, radishes, beans, and pork to a
large bowl.

Just before serving, toss salad with dressing.
Serves 4 as a main course.

☛ each serving about 327 calories and
8 grams fat

SOUTHEAST ASIAN STEAK SALAD ◐

½ head romaine
½ small English cucumber
1 small shallot
1 small fresh jalapeño chile
1 garlic clove
2 tablespoons fresh lime juice
1 tablespoon soy sauce (preferably
   Kikkoman)
2 tablespoons vegetable oil
2 teaspoons Asian fish sauce*
½ teaspoon sugar
a 1¼-inch-thick rib-eye steak (about
   ¾ pound)
¼ cup packed fresh mint leaves

*available at Asian markets and many specialty
   foods shops and supermarkets

Tear romaine into pieces into a bowl. Halve cucumber lengthwise and seed. Thinly slice cucumber
crosswise and add to romaine. Chill romaine mixture, covered. Mince shallot, jalapeño, and garlic
(wear rubber gloves when handling jalapeño) and in
a large bowl stir together with lime juice, soy sauce,
1 tablespoon oil, fish sauce, and sugar until sugar
is dissolved.

Pat steak dry and season with salt. In an 8- to 10-
inch heavy skillet heat remaining tablespoon oil over
moderately high heat until hot but not smoking and
sauté steak 4 minutes on each side for medium-rare.
Transfer steak to a cutting board and let stand about
5 minutes.

While steak is standing, stack mint leaves and
thinly slice. Add mint to romaine mixture with all
but about 2 tablespoons dressing and toss until
combined well.

Divide salad between 2 plates and slice steak.
Toss steak with remaining dressing and arrange on
salads. Serves 2 as a main course.

GRILLED SQUID SALAD

1 bunch celery with leaves
2 cups pitted green olives
½ cup packed fresh flat-leafed parsley leaves
3 tablespoons finely chopped garlic
½ tablespoon dried oregano, crumbled
¾ teaspoon dried hot red pepper flakes
3 tablespoons red-wine vinegar
¾ cup extra-virgin olive oil
3 pounds cleaned squid

Prepare grill.

Remove outer green ribs from celery and thinly slice enough of pale green ribs to measure ¾ cup. Remove celery leaves and coarsely chop enough to measure ⅓ cup. Slice green olives and coarsely chop parsley. In a large bowl toss together sliced celery, celery leaves, olives, parsley, garlic, oregano, red pepper flakes, vinegar, and 6 tablespoons oil.

Pat squid dry. In a bowl toss squid with remaining 6 tablespoons oil and season with salt and pepper. Grill squid on an oiled rack set 5 to 6 inches over glowing coals (or moderate heat if using a gas grill), turning it once, until just cooked through, about 1½ minutes total. (Alternatively, grill squid in batches in a hot well-seasoned ridged grill pan over moderately high heat.) Cut warm squid sacs crosswise into ½-inch rings and leave tentacles whole. Immediately add warm squid to celery mixture, tossing to combine. *Chill salad, covered, at least 1 hour and up to 8. Bring salad to room temperature before serving.* Serves 12 as part of a buffet.

PHOTO ON PAGE 37

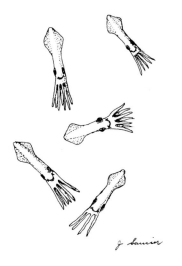

ARUGULA AND RADICCHIO SALAD WITH SESAME-SCALLION VINAIGRETTE

2 tablespoons olive oil
1 tablespoon sesame seeds
1 scallion
2 teaspoons balsamic vinegar
½ teaspoon Dijon mustard
½ head *radicchio*
1 bunch arugula

In a small skillet heat 1 tablespoon oil over moderate heat until hot but not smoking and cook sesame seeds, stirring, until pale golden, about 1 minute. Mince scallion and in a small bowl whisk together with sesame seeds, remaining tablespoon oil, vinegar, mustard, and salt and pepper to taste until emulsified. Tear *radicchio* into bite-size pieces and in a bowl toss together with arugula and vinaigrette. Serves 2.

FRESH FIG, PROSCIUTTO, AND ARUGULA SALAD WITH PARMESAN SHAVINGS

For vinaigrette
2 tablespoons balsamic vinegar
½ teaspoon Dijon mustard
freshly ground black pepper to taste
6 tablespoons extra-virgin olive oil

2 large bunches arugula (about ½ pound total)
6 firm-ripe green or purple figs (about ½ pound)
6 to 8 large thin prosciutto slices (preferably San Daniele; about 6 ounces total)
a piece Parmigiano-Reggiano (about ⅓ pound)

Make vinaigrette:
In a small bowl whisk together vinegar, mustard, pepper, and salt to taste. In a slow stream whisk in oil until emulsified.

Discard stems from arugula and transfer leaves to a large bowl. Trim tough stem ends from figs and cut each fig into 8 wedges. Trim some of fat from prosciutto if desired. Halve 6 prosciutto slices lengthwise. Overlap narrow ends of 2 halves by 1 to 2 inches, pressing together gently, to form 6 pieces about 13 inches long (use remaining 2 prosciutto slices if necessary). Transfer long prosciutto pieces as prepared to a tray lined with plastic wrap. With a vegetable peeler shave about 36 thin slices from Parmigiano-Reggiano.

Toss arugula with about 3 tablespoons vinaigrette and mound in center of each of 6 plates. Arrange long prosciutto pieces in a ring around each mound of arugula, overlapping ends to secure. Arrange figs and Parmigiano-Reggiano shavings on and around salad and drizzle salads with remaining vinaigrette. Serves 6.

PHOTO ON PAGE 50

Frisée and Watercress Salad with Balsamic Thyme Vinaigrette and Artichoke Ragout

For artichoke ragout
8 medium artichokes (about 4 pounds)
1 large carrot
1 large celery rib
2 medium shallots
4 plum tomatoes (about ¾ pound)
8 fresh thyme sprigs
¼ cup olive oil
1 cup dry white wine

2 bunches watercress
1 head *frisée** (French curly endive)
1 small Belgian endive (preferably red)
¼ cup balsamic thyme vinaigrette
    (page 186)

Garnish: blanched artichoke leaves

Make ragout:
Trim artichokes into bottoms (procedure follows). Cut carrot and celery into 2½- by ¼-inch sticks. Finely chop shallots. Peel plum tomatoes (page 146) and halve lengthwise. Seed tomatoes. Tie thyme sprigs together with kitchen string.

Pat artichoke bottoms dry. In a 10- to 12-inch heavy skillet heat oil over moderately high heat until hot but not smoking and sauté artichoke bottoms, carrot, and celery, stirring occasionally (do not break

up vegetables), until carrot and celery are golden, about 5 minutes. Add shallots and sauté, stirring, until softened, about 1 minute.

Add tomato halves and thyme sprigs and cook over moderate heat, gently stirring once or twice, 10 minutes. Add wine and simmer until artichokes are tender and most liquid is evaporated, about 15 minutes. Season ragout with salt and cool to room temperature. *Ragout may be made 2 days ahead and chilled, covered. Bring ragout to room temperature before proceeding.*

Discard tough stems from watercress and tear watercress and *frisée* into bite-size pieces. Separate endive leaves and halve large leaves lengthwise.

Remove artichoke bottoms from ragout and on each arrange a tomato half and some carrot and celery. In a large bowl toss greens with vinaigrette and season with salt and pepper.

Arrange greens and artichoke bottoms on 8 plates. Serves 8.

PHOTO ON PAGE 42

To Trim Artichokes into Bottoms

When trimming artichokes in the following manner, make sure you scrape out every bit of the choke, as this will help prevent the artichoke bottoms from turning brown.

1 lemon
artichokes

Halve lemon and into a large bowl of cold water squeeze juice from 1 half, dropping squeezed half into water.

Cut off artichoke stems and discard. Working with 1 artichoke at a time, bend back outer leaves until they snap off close to base and discard several more layers of leaves in same manner until exposed leaves are pale green at top and pale yellow at base.

With a very sharp stainless-steel knife cut across artichoke 1½ inches above stem end and with a spoon scrape out all of choke. Trim dark green fibrous parts from base and sides of artichoke bottom and trim any remaining leaves. Rub artichoke bottom all over with cut side of remaining lemon half and put artichoke in a bowl of lemon water. Trim remaining artichokes in same manner.

BALSAMIC THYME VINAIGRETTE ◎

¼ cup balsamic vinegar
1 tablespoon honey
1 tablespoon fresh thyme leaves
1 teaspoon Dijon mustard
¼ teaspoon salt
¼ teaspoon freshly ground black pepper
¼ cup olive oil

In a blender blend all ingredients except oil. With motor running, add oil in a slow stream and blend until emulsified. *Vinaigrette keeps, covered and chilled, 1 week.* Makes about ½ cup.

ARUGULA, ENDIVE, AND RADICCHIO SALAD ◎

⅓ cup extra-virgin olive oil
2 tablespoons white-wine vinegar
2 bunches arugula (about
    1 pound)
1 small head *radicchio*
2 large Belgian endives

In a bowl whisk together oil and vinegar and season with salt and pepper.

Discard coarse stems from arugula. Thinly slice *radicchio* and cut endives crosswise into ½-inch pieces. In a large bowl toss greens with vinaigrette until coated well. Serves 8.

PHOTO ON PAGE 79

ASPARAGUS, BACON, AND FRISÉE SALAD ◎

5 slices bacon (about ¼ pound)
½ pound asparagus
1½ tablespoons balsamic vinegar
½ teaspoon Dijon mustard
3 tablespoons extra-virgin olive oil
½ head *frisée* (French curly endive) or
    ¼ head chicory (curly endive)

In a skillet cook bacon over moderate heat until crisp. Drain bacon on paper towels and crumble. Trim asparagus and in a saucepan of boiling salted water cook until crisp-tender, about 4 minutes. In a colander drain asparagus and refresh under cold water. Cut asparagus into ½-inch-thick pieces, leaving about 2 inches of tops intact.

In a large bowl whisk together vinegar, mustard, and salt and pepper to taste and add oil in a stream, whisking until emulsified. Tear *frisée* or chicory into bite-size pieces and add to dressing with asparagus and bacon. Toss salad to combine. Serves 2.

MESCLUN AND RADICCHIO SALAD WITH SHALLOT VINAIGRETTE ◎

¼ cup balsamic vinegar
1 tablespoon chopped shallot
2 teaspoons honey
½ teaspoon Dijon mustard
¼ cup extra-virgin olive oil
2 heads *radicchio* (about 1¼ pounds)
1 pound *mesclun** (mixed baby lettuces;
    about 4 quarts loosely packed)
1 cup packed fresh flat-leafed parsley leaves

*available at specialty produce markets and
    many supermarkets

In a small bowl whisk together vinegar, shallot, honey, mustard, and salt and pepper to taste. Add oil in a slow stream, whisking until emulsified. *Vinaigrette may be made 1 week ahead and chilled, covered. Bring vinaigrette to room temperature before using.*

Trim *radicchio* and tear into bite-size pieces. In a large bowl toss together *radicchio, mesclun,* and parsley leaves.

Just before serving, drizzle vinaigrette over salad and toss well with salt and pepper to taste. Serves 12 as part of a buffet.

PHOTO ON PAGE 30

SAVOY CABBAGE AND ARUGULA SALAD ◎

half a 2-pound head Savoy cabbage
3 cups packed arugula leaves
¼ cup extra-virgin olive oil
1½ tablespoons red-wine vinegar
¾ teaspoon sugar

With a knife cut cabbage into very thin slices and coarsely chop arugula. In a large bowl toss together all ingredients with salt and pepper to taste until greens are coated. Serves 6.

PHOTO ON PAGE 25

MAKE-YOUR-OWN SALAD WITH LEMON GARLIC DRESSING

For dressing
1 garlic clove
1 teaspoon salt
4 tablespoons fresh lemon juice
2 tablespoons white-wine vinegar
½ teaspoon freshly grated lemon zest
freshly ground black pepper to taste
¾ cup extra-virgin olive oil

1 bunch broccoli
3 hearts of romaine
4 carrots
1 red onion
1 can anchovy fillets

Make dressing:
Mince garlic and mash to a paste with salt. In a bowl whisk together garlic paste, lemon juice, vinegar, zest, and pepper and whisk in oil until emulsified. *Dressing may be made 1 day ahead and chilled, covered. Bring dressing to room temperature before serving.*

Cut 1-inch flowerets from broccoli, reserving remainder for another use. Separate romaine into leaves. *Broccoli and romaine may be prepared 1 day ahead and chilled in airtight containers.*

Have ready a large bowl of ice and cold water. In a large saucepan of boiling salted water cook broccoli until crisp-tender, about 3 minutes, and drain in a colander. Plunge broccoli into ice water to stop cooking and drain well.

Peel carrots and with a *mandoline* or other manual slicer or in a food processor finely shred. Halve onion lengthwise and slice very thin crosswise.

Arrange vegetables and anchovies decoratively on platters and in serving bowls and pour dressing into a cruet. Serves 8 to 10 as part of a buffet.

PHOTO ON PAGE 16

SPINACH AND ENDIVE SALAD WITH LEMON-GINGER DRESSING AND CRISP WON TON STRIPS ◐

For dressing
1½ tablespoons fresh lemon juice
1 tablespoon finely grated peeled fresh gingerroot
1 teaspoon sugar
1 tablespoon water
¾ teaspoon Asian sesame oil

2 Belgian endives
1½ cups lightly packed small spinach leaves
1½ cups lightly packed tender watercress sprigs

Accompaniment: crisp won ton strips
  (page 188)

Make dressing:
In a bowl whisk together dressing ingredients and salt and pepper to taste.

Cut enough endive crosswise into ½-inch pieces to measure 2 cups. In a large bowl toss together endive, spinach, watercress, dressing, and salt and pepper to taste.

Serve salad topped with won ton strips. Serves 4.

PHOTO ON PAGE 84

◢ each serving, with won ton strips, about 76 calories and 1 gram fat

CRISP WON TON STRIPS ◐

8 won ton wrappers*

*available at Asian markets and some specialty
   foods shops and supermarkets

Preheat oven to 475° F.

Stack won ton wrappers and cut into ¼-inch-wide
strips. In a small bowl toss won ton strips with salt
and pepper to taste and arrange, overlapping slightly,
on a nonstick baking sheet. Bake won ton strips in
middle of oven, stirring strips and breaking them up
into large clusters halfway through baking, until
golden brown and slightly crisp, about 6 minutes.

Transfer strips to a plate to cool and season with
salt (strips will continue to crisp as they cool). *Strips
may be made 2 days ahead, cooled completely, and
kept in an airtight container at room temperature.*
Makes about 1½ cups.

SPINACH AND SPROUT SALAD ◐

1 red onion
For dressing
3 tablespoons cider vinegar
1½ teaspoons sugar
1 teaspoon powdered mustard or 2 teaspoons
   Dijon mustard
½ cup extra-virgin olive oil

1 pint vine-ripened cherry tomatoes
4 cups mixed crunchy sprouts* such as pea
   and lentil
¾ pound baby spinach

*available at specialty produce markets and some
   natural foods stores and supermarkets

Halve red onion lengthwise and very thinly slice
crosswise. In a bowl cover onion with cold water.
Chill onion in water 30 minutes.
   Make dressing while onion is chilling:
In a bowl whisk together vinegar, sugar, mustard,
and salt and pepper to taste and add oil in a slow
stream, whisking until emulsified. *Dressing may be
made 2 days ahead and chilled, covered.*

Drain red onion well in a colander and pat dry.
Quarter tomatoes and in a large bowl toss with
onion, sprouts, spinach, and dressing. Serves 8.

PHOTO ON PAGE 48

WATERCRESS SESAME SALAD ◐

1 bunch watercress
1 tablespoon sesame seeds
1½ teaspoons white-wine vinegar
1½ tablespoons vegetable oil
¼ teaspoon Asian sesame oil

Discard coarse stems from watercress. Lightly
toast sesame seeds. In a small bowl whisk together
vinegar, oils, and salt and pepper to taste until combined well. In a bowl toss watercress with dressing
and 2 teaspoons sesame seeds.

Serve salad sprinkled with remaining teaspoon
sesame seeds. Serves 2.

VEGETABLE SALADS AND SLAWS

AVOCADO, ORANGE, AND JÍCAMA SALAD ◐

3 navel oranges
½ teaspoon curry powder
½ teaspoon salt
¼ teaspoon ground cumin
¼ teaspoon sugar
2 tablespoons white-wine vinegar
2 tablespoons olive oil
1 medium *jícama* (about ¾ pound)
2 firm-ripe California avocados

With a sharp knife cut peel and pith from oranges.
Working over a bowl, cut sections free from membranes and squeeze enough juice from membranes to
measure ¼ cup. In a bowl whisk together orange
juice, curry powder, salt, cumin, sugar, and vinegar.
Add oil in a stream, whisking until emulsified.

Peel *jícama* and halve lengthwise. Thinly slice
jícama crosswise and add to vinaigrette, tossing to
combine. Halve, pit, and peel avocados and thinly
slice crosswise.

Lift *jícama* from vinaigrette and arrange on 4 plates with oranges and avocados. Pour remaining vinaigrette over and around salads. Serves 4.

PICKLED RED CABBAGE WITH TOASTED SESAME SEEDS ◐+

a 3½-pound red cabbage (about 1 medium head)
4¾ cups sugar
8 cups white-wine vinegar
1 tablespoon chopped garlic
1 teaspoon fresh thyme leaves
3 tablespoons chopped shallot (about 2 large)
¼ cup sesame seeds

Core cabbage and halve. With a manual slicer or sharp knife cut cabbage into ¼-inch-thick slices.

In a heavy kettle (about 5 quarts) stir together sugar, vinegar, garlic, thyme, and shallot and simmer, stirring, until sugar is dissolved, about 5 minutes. Bring mixture to a boil and stir in cabbage. Cook cabbage, covered, stirring occasionally, 3 minutes. Cool cabbage in kettle on a rack until warm and season with salt and pepper. *Chill cabbage, covered, at least 8 hours and up to 2 weeks.*

In a dry heavy skillet toast sesame seeds over moderate heat until golden, about 3 minutes.

Transfer cabbage with tongs to a serving dish and drizzle with some pickling liquid. Sprinkle cabbage with sesame seeds. Serves 8 to 10.

PHOTO ON PAGE 20

CUMIN COLESLAW ◐

2 tablespoons mayonnaise
1 tablespoon milk
½ teaspoon minced fresh jalapeño chile
    (wear rubber gloves)
1 tablespoon chopped fresh cilantro leaves
½ teaspoon ground cumin
a 6-ounce piece cabbage (about ¼ head)
1 large carrot
1 scallion

In a large bowl stir together mayonnaise, milk, jalapeño, cilantro, and cumin. Thinly slice cabbage

and cut carrot into julienne strips. Diagonally cut scallion into thin slices.

Stir cabbage, carrot, and scallion into dressing and season with salt and pepper. Serves 2.

CELERY ROOT AND APPLE SALAD WITH CREAMY MUSTARD DRESSING

For dressing
3 tablespoons mayonnaise
2 tablespoons Champagne vinegar
1 tablespoon coarse-grained mustard
2 tablespoons chopped fresh parsley leaves
⅔ cup olive oil
1 tablespoon water

2 pounds celery root (about 2 medium)
2 Granny Smith apples
2 tablespoons fresh lemon juice

Make dressing:
In a bowl whisk together mayonnaise, vinegar, mustard, parsley, and salt and pepper to taste. Whisk in oil and water in a stream until emulsified.

With a sharp knife cut off ends of celery root and arrange, a cut side down, on a cutting board. Cutting from top to bottom, remove skin. Halve celery root lengthwise and cut crosswise into ¼-inch-thick slices. Cut slices into 1-inch matchsticks.

Have ready a bowl of ice and cold water. In a kettle (about 4 quarts) of boiling salted water blanch celery root 1 minute. Immediately drain celery root in a colander and transfer to ice water to stop cooking. Drain celery root and transfer to a large bowl. Pat celery root dry with paper towels.

Cut apples into 1- by ¼-inch sticks and in a small bowl toss with lemon juice. Gently stir apples and dressing into celery root and season with salt and pepper. *Salad may be made 4 hours ahead and chilled, covered.* Serves 8 to 10.

HEARTS OF PALM SALAD ◐

¼ cup mayonnaise
½ tablespoon red-wine vinegar
1 tangerine
a 14.8-ounce jar or can hearts of palm
1 firm-ripe California avocado
2 cups packed trimmed arugula

In a bowl whisk together mayonnaise and vinegar until smooth. Cut peel and pith from tangerine and, holding fruit over a small bowl (to catch juice), cut sections free from membranes, discarding seeds.

Rinse and drain hearts of palm and diagonally cut into ¾-inch-thick slices. Pit and peel avocado and cut into 1-inch pieces. Tear arugula into bite-size pieces and add to dressing with tangerine and juice, hearts of palm, and avocado.

Toss salad to coat with dressing and season with salt and pepper. Serves 2.

FENNEL CONFIT AND TOMATO SALAD

Only a small amount of the fennel cooking liquid is used in this salad. The remainder is delicious mixed into mashed potatoes, drizzled over fish or roasted vegetables, or used as a base for a vinaigrette. (It keeps, covered and chilled, about 2 weeks.)

6 large garlic cloves
6 large shallots
2 pounds fennel bulbs (sometimes called anise; about 2 medium)
4 cups olive oil
2 cups dry white wine
1 fresh thyme sprig
6 whole star anise*
2 pounds plum tomatoes (about 8)
1 cup packed fresh basil leaves
1 cup packed fresh flat-leafed parsley leaves
1 tablespoon fresh lemon juice, or to taste

*available at specialty foods shops and Asian markets

Cut garlic and shallots lengthwise into very thin slices. Trim all fennel stalks flush with bulbs,

discarding stalks, and discard tough outer layers. Quarter bulbs and remove cores. With a *mandoline* or other manual slicer cut fennel lengthwise into paper-thin slices.

In a 4-quart heavy kettle bring oil and wine to a boil with garlic, shallots, fennel, thyme sprig, and star anise and simmer 1 minute. Cool fennel mixture in kettle on a rack until warm, about 2 hours. *Fennel mixture may be made 2 days ahead and cooled before being chilled, covered. Bring fennel mixture to cool room temperature before proceeding.*

Peel tomatoes and quarter. Seed tomatoes and transfer to a large bowl. Tear basil leaves into pieces and add to tomatoes.

Strain fennel mixture through a large sieve into another large bowl and reserve liquid. Discard thyme sprig and star anise. Add strained fennel mixture (the solids) to tomatoes. Add parsley, lemon juice, ¼ cup reserved liquid (reserve remainder for another use; see headnote), and salt and pepper to taste and toss to combine. Serves 8 to 10.

PHOTO ON PAGE 20

CUCUMBER, RADISH, AND RED ONION SALAD ◐

¾ cucumber
2 radishes
¼ cup thinly sliced red onion
1 teaspoon olive oil
1 teaspoon fresh lemon juice

Peel, halve, and seed cucumber. Diagonally cut cucumber into thin slices and cut radishes into julienne strips. In a bowl toss together all ingredients and season with salt and pepper. Serves 2.

CELERY, FENNEL, AND RED PEAR SALAD ☺

6 celery ribs
2 large fennel bulbs (sometimes called anise; about 1½ pounds)
1 English cucumber
3 firm-ripe pears (preferably red; about 1½ pounds)
2½ tablespoons fresh lemon juice
2 tablespoons extra-virgin olive oil

Diagonally cut celery into ¼-inch-thick slices. Trim fennel stalks flush with bulb, discarding stalks, and halve lengthwise. Cut out and discard cores and cut fennel lengthwise into thin strips. Halve cucumber lengthwise. Seed cucumber and diagonally cut into ¼-inch-thick slices. Quarter pears and core. Slice pears lengthwise into ¼-inch-thick slices.

In a large bowl toss celery, fennel, cucumber, and pears with lemon juice and oil and season with salt and pepper. Serves 12 as part of a buffet.

PHOTO ON PAGE 30

VINEGARED CUCUMBER SALAD ☺

Japanese cucumbers are small, virtually seedless, and quite crunchy. Young English cucumbers make a good alternative.

1 tablespoon sesame seeds
1 pound Japanese or English cucumbers
½ teaspoon salt
⅓ cup seasoned rice vinegar
¼ teaspoon instant *dashi* (seasoned stock) granules*
1 teaspoon Asian sesame oil, or to taste

*available at Japanese markets and by mail order from Uwajimaya, (800) 889-1928

In a dry small heavy skillet toast sesame seeds over moderate heat, shaking skillet, until golden and let cool. With a *mandoline* or other hand-held manual slicer or a sharp knife cut cucumbers into very thin slices. Sprinkle cucumbers with salt and drain in a colander 10 minutes.

In a bowl stir together vinegar and *dashi* granules until granules are dissolved. Add cucumber and oil, tossing to coat. *Salad may be made 1 hour ahead and chilled, covered.*

Serve salad at room temperature or chilled, sprinkled with sesame seeds. Serves 6.

PHOTO ON PAGE 60

CUCUMBER AND CELERY SALAD WITH YOGURT ☺

¼ cup plain yogurt
2 medium celery ribs
½ English cucumber
2 tablespoons chopped fresh flat-leafed parsley or cilantro leaves
2 tablespoons fresh lemon juice
1 teaspoon extra-virgin olive oil

In a cheesecloth-lined sieve or colander set over a bowl drain yogurt, covered and chilled, 20 minutes. Discard liquid.

Diagonally cut celery ribs into thin slices. Seed cucumber and diagonally cut into thin slices. In bowl toss together celery, cucumber, yogurt, parsley or cilantro, lemon juice, oil, and salt and pepper to taste. Serves 2.

CUCUMBER SALAD WITH MUSTARD DRESSING ☺+

2 English cucumbers
2 teaspoons salt
3 tablespoons Dijon mustard
1 teaspoon white-wine vinegar
¼ teaspoon sugar
3 tablespoons chopped fresh dill leaves (optional)

Cut cucumbers into ⅛-inch-thick slices and in a bowl layer slices, sprinkling each layer with salt. *Chill cucumbers, covered, 2 hours.*

In a large colander drain cucumbers and rinse thoroughly. Drain cucumbers well and squeeze dry in handfuls. Pat cucumbers dry on towels. In a bowl stir together mustard, vinegar, and sugar and stir in cucumbers and dill. Serves 4.

POTATO, GREEN BEAN, AND CORN SALAD

4 pounds small white boiling potatoes
   (about 2 inches in diameter)
5 tablespoons cider vinegar
3 tablespoons coarse-grained mustard
¼ cup plus 2 tablespoons olive oil, or to taste
1 pound *haricots verts* (thin French green
   beans) or regular green beans
6 ears corn

In a kettle cover potatoes with salted cold water by 2 inches and simmer until just tender, about 25 minutes. Drain potatoes in a colander. When potatoes are just cool enough to handle, halve larger ones and in a large bowl toss potatoes with 2 tablespoons vinegar.

In a small bowl whisk together mustard, remaining 3 tablespoons cider vinegar, and salt and pepper to taste. Add oil in a slow stream, whisking until emulsified. *Dressing may be made 1 day ahead and chilled, covered. Bring dressing to room temperature before using.*

Trim beans and, working over a bowl, cut corn kernels from cobs. Have ready a bowl of ice and cold water. In a large saucepan of boiling salted water cook beans until crisp-tender, about 1 minute for *haricots verts* and about 5 minutes for regular green beans, and transfer with a slotted spoon to ice water to stop cooking. Drain beans well and add to potatoes. Return water in pan to a boil and blanch corn 30 seconds, or until crisp-tender. Drain corn in a sieve and rinse under cold water to stop cooking. Drain corn well and add to salad. *Salad may be prepared up to this point 1 day ahead and chilled, covered. Bring salad to room temperature before proceeding.* Gently toss salad with dressing and salt and pepper to taste until combined well. Serves 12.

PHOTO ON PAGE 63

SICILIAN OLIVE SALAD ◐+

2½ cups large green olives (about 1 pound)
3 celery ribs
1 carrot
1 small red onion
1 garlic clove
½ cup drained caperberries

1 tablespoon chopped fresh oregano leaves or
   1½ teaspoons crumbled dried oregano
½ teaspoon freshly ground black pepper
½ cup extra-virgin olive oil

In a large sieve rinse olives and drain well. Thinly slice celery, carrot, onion, and garlic and in a bowl stir together with remaining ingredients. *Marinate salad, covered and chilled, at least 1 day and up to 3 days. Bring salad to room temperature before serving.* Serves 6 to 8 as an antipasto.

WARM POTATO SALAD WITH CAVIAR DRESSING ◐+

It's important to use beluga or osetra caviar for this dressing. A lesser grade, with its higher percentage of broken eggs, is likely to turn this potato salad an unappetizing grayish color.

2 pounds small red potatoes (about 1½ inches
   in diameter)
⅓ cup olive oil
3 tablespoons finely chopped fresh chives
1 tablespoon finely grated fresh lemon zest
1 teaspoon freshly ground white pepper
1.75 ounces beluga or osetra caviar*
2 shallots
1½ tablespoons unsalted butter
¼ cup rice vinegar

*available at specialty foods shops (Restaurant
   Daniel Private Stock Caviar is available
   by mail order from Browne Trading,
   (800) 944-7848)

In a saucepan cover potatoes with salted cold water by 2 inches and simmer until tender, about 15 minutes. Drain potatoes in a colander. *Potatoes may be cooked 1 day ahead and cooled completely before being chilled in a sealable plastic bag. Bring potatoes to room temperature before proceeding.*

Quarter potatoes. In a small bowl gently stir together oil, chives, zest, white pepper, and caviar. Mince shallots. In a large skillet heat butter over moderate heat until foam subsides and cook shallots until softened, about 5 minutes. Add vinegar and simmer until most liquid is evaporated. Add potatoes and cook, tossing gently, until heated through. Transfer potato mixture to a bowl.

Add dressing to warm potatoes and gently toss to coat. Serves 8.

PHOTO ON PAGE 41

GRILLED RED POTATO AND SMOKED HAM SALAD WITH TOMATO DRESSING

For tomato dressing
3 vine-ripened tomatoes (about ¾ pound total)
½ tablespoon chopped garlic
¼ cup white-wine vinegar
1 cup corn oil
kosher salt to taste
freshly ground black pepper to taste
For salad
22 medium red potatoes (about 6 pounds)
3 tablespoons olive oil
kosher salt to taste
freshly ground black pepper to taste
1 pound ⅛-inch-thick slices smoked ham
1 bunch scallions
1½ celery ribs
1½ tablespoons cumin seeds
1½ cups cooked corn
1½ tablespoons minced garlic
1½ tablespoons minced fresh cilantro sprigs

Make dressing:
Preheat oven to 500° F. and line a baking sheet with foil.

Roast tomatoes on baking sheet in middle of oven 20 minutes. Cool tomatoes and peel. In a blender purée tomatoes and garlic with vinegar until smooth. With motor running, add oil in a stream and blend until emulsified. Season dressing with salt and pepper. *Dressing may be made 1 day ahead and chilled, covered.*

Make salad:
Prepare grill.

Working in batches, cut potatoes into ⅛-inch-thick rounds and in a large bowl toss with oil and salt and pepper. Grill potato rounds in batches on a rack set 5 to 6 inches over glowing coals (or moderate heat if using a gas grill), turning them occasionally, until

tender, about 10 minutes, and transfer to another large bowl. (Alternatively, roast potatoes in a 450° F. oven: Arrange half of oiled potatoes, slightly overlapping, in 2 large shallow baking pans and roast in upper and lower thirds of oven, turning them occasionally, until golden and tender, about 15 minutes. Roast remaining potatoes in same manner.)

Cut ham into 1- by ⅛-inch strips. Chop scallions and celery. In a dry small heavy skillet toast cumin seeds over moderate heat, stirring, until fragrant, about 30 seconds, and cool. In an electric coffee/spice grinder finely grind cumin seeds. To potatoes add cumin, ham, scallions, celery, and remaining salad ingredients.

Add dressing to salad and toss to coat. *Chill salad at least 4 hours and up to 1 day.* Serves 12 as part of a buffet.

PHOTO ON PAGE 38

LEMONY POTATO AVOCADO SALAD ◯

¾ pound small red potatoes (about 6)
2 tablespoons extra-virgin olive oil
2 tablespoons fresh lemon juice
1 teaspoon finely grated fresh lemon zest
3 tablespoons minced fresh chives
1 firm-ripe California avocado

In a saucepan cover potatoes with salted cold water by 1 inch and simmer, covered, until tender, 15 to 20 minutes. Drain potatoes in a colander and quarter. In a bowl stir together warm potatoes, oil, lemon juice, zest, chives, and salt and pepper to taste. Pit and peel avocado and cut into ¾-inch pieces. Add avocado to potato mixture, gently tossing to combine. Serves 2.

MUSTARD SCALLION POTATO SALAD ☺

1 pound small boiling potatoes (about
     1½ inches each)
1 teaspoon cider vinegar, or to taste
2 teaspoons olive oil
1 teaspoon Dijon mustard, or to taste
¼ cup sliced scallion greens

In a saucepan cover potatoes with salted cold
water by 1 inch and simmer, covered, until just
tender, about 15 minutes. Drain potatoes well in a
colander and, when just cool enough to handle,
halve. Transfer hot potatoes to a bowl and immediately toss with vinegar. Add remaining ingredients
and salt and pepper to taste and gently toss until
combined well. Serve potato salad warm or at room
temperature. Serves 2.

JÍCAMA, CARROT, AND RED CABBAGE SLAW
WITH ANISE AND LIME

1 tablespoon anise seeds
a 2-pound piece *jícama*
½ pound carrots (about 2 large)
a ¾-pound piece red cabbage
½ cup packed fresh flat-leafed parsley leaves
⅓ cup vegetable oil
2 tablespoons fresh lime juice
½ teaspoon Dijon mustard
½ teaspoon salt

In a dry heavy skillet toast anise seeds over
moderate heat, shaking skillet occasionally, until
fragrant, about 1 minute. Cool seeds and coarsely
grind with a mortar and pestle or a cleaned electric
coffee/spice grinder.

Peel *jícama* and carrots and quarter *jícama*. Using
a *mandoline* or other manual slicer, cut *jícama* and
carrots into very thin slices, about ¹⁄₁₆ inch. Stack
slices and cut into julienne strips. With a knife cut
cabbage into very thin shreds. *Vegetables may be
prepared 1 day ahead and chilled separately in
sealable plastic bags.*

Coarsely chop parsley. In a bowl stir together
anise, oil, lime juice, mustard, and salt. Add vegetables and parsley, tossing to coat, and season with
salt and pepper. *Slaw may be made 2 hours ahead
and chilled, covered.* Serves 6.

PHOTO ON PAGE 66

GINGERED WATERMELON AND
YELLOW TOMATO SALAD

a 4-pound piece watermelon (preferably
     seedless)
2 pounds vine-ripened tomatoes (about
     6 medium; preferably yellow)
1 teaspoon coarse salt (preferably sea salt)
½ small red onion
2 tablespoons fresh lime juice, or to taste
1 teaspoon finely grated peeled fresh gingerroot,
     or to taste
½ teaspoon sugar, or to taste

Remove rind and any seeds from watermelon. Cut
fruit into 1½-inch pieces and put in a large bowl. Cut
tomatoes into 1½-inch pieces. Add tomatoes and salt
to watermelon, tossing to combine. *Let mixture stand
at cool room temperature 3 hours.*

In a colander set over a small saucepan drain
mixture and transfer to a bowl. Simmer liquid until
reduced to about 2 tablespoons and cool completely.
Halve onion and thinly slice enough to measure ¼
cup. Add onion to watermelon mixture. (For best
results do not chill salad, as it will lose flavor.) In a
small bowl stir together reduced watermelon-tomato
juice, lime juice, gingerroot, and sugar.

Just before serving, toss salad with juice mixture.
Serves 4.

PHOTO ON PAGE 44

GRAIN SALADS

BARLEY, FETA, AND PEAR SALAD ◐

⅓ cup pearl barley
3 tablespoons walnuts
½ cup packed fresh flat-leafed parsley leaves
1 celery rib
½ small head radicchio (about 1½ ounces)
½ firm-ripe pear
¼ cup crumbled feta
2 tablespoons fresh lemon juice
1½ tablespoons extra-virgin olive oil

Preheat oven to 375° F.

In a 2-quart saucepan three fourths full with boiling water boil barley, partially covered, until tender, about 30 minutes.

While barley is cooking, in a baking pan toast walnuts in middle of oven until golden, about 7 minutes. Chop parsley and cut celery and radicchio into ¼-inch dice. Peel and core pear and cut into ¼-inch dice.

Drain barley in a sieve and transfer to a bowl. Add feta to barley and add nuts, parsley, celery, radicchio, pear, lemon juice, oil, and salt and pepper to taste. Toss salad until combined. Serves 2.

RICE, BEAN, AND CORN SALAD ◐

1 garlic clove
1 onion
1 ear corn
¾ cup water
1 teaspoon ground cumin
½ teaspoon ground coriander seeds
¼ teaspoon salt
⅓ cup long-grain rice (not converted)
¾ cup drained canned black beans
3 tablespoons chopped fresh cilantro leaves
1 tablespoon fresh lime juice

Mince garlic and finely chop enough onion to measure ½ cup. Cut enough kernels from cob to measure ¾ cup.

In a small heavy saucepan with a tight-fitting lid bring water to a boil with garlic, onion, cumin, coriander, and salt. Stir in rice and cook, covered, over low heat 15 minutes. Stir in corn and cook, covered, 3 minutes, or until water is absorbed and rice is just tender. Fluff mixture with a fork and transfer to a large bowl to cool completely.

Rinse and drain black beans. Stir cilantro into rice with beans, lime juice, and salt and pepper to taste. Serves 4.

PHOTO ON PAGE 87

☛ each ¾-cup serving about 136 calories and less than 1 gram fat

BULGUR, PARSLEY, AND MINT SALAD

1¼ cups fine or medium bulgur*
1¼ cups water
1 red onion
1¼ teaspoons salt
¼ teaspoon ground allspice
¼ teaspoon cinnamon
5 cups packed fresh flat-leafed parsley leaves
1½ cups packed fresh mint leaves
   (about 1 large bunch)
1 bunch scallions
½ small English cucumber
½ pound vine-ripened tomatoes
⅓ cup fresh lemon juice
⅓ cup olive oil

*available at natural foods stores and
   many supermarkets

In a bowl stir together bulgur and water. *Let bulgur stand 1 hour and 15 minutes. Bulgur may be prepared 1 day ahead and chilled, covered.*

Mince enough onion to measure 1 cup and in a bowl stir together with salt, allspice, and cinnamon. *Let onion-spice mixture stand 30 minutes.* Finely chop parsley and mint. Finely chop enough scallion greens to measure ⅔ cup. Quarter and seed cucumber and tomatoes and thinly slice. In a bowl toss together all salad ingredients with salt and pepper to taste. *Salad may be made 1 hour ahead and chilled, covered.* Serves 8.

PHOTO ON PAGE 56

Umeboshi and Rice Salad with Pickled Ginger and Sugar Snap Peas

Umeboshi, or pickled plums, are not technically plums at all, but apricots. They are mixed with rice to make a popular summer dish in Japan. We've enlivened this salad with pickled ginger and sugar snap peas.

2 cups Japanese rice* or other short-grain
  rice such as Arborio
3 cups water
3 tablespoons seasoned rice vinegar
⅓ cup *umeboshi** (pickled plums)
¼ cup drained pickled ginger* (preferably
  amazu shōga)
¼ pound sugar snap peas or
  snow peas

*available at Japanese markets and by mail order
  from Uwajimaya, (800) 889-1928

In a bowl rinse rice in several changes of cold water until water is almost clear and drain in a colander. *Let rice stand, uncovered, in colander at least 30 minutes and up to 1 hour.*

In a 3-quart saucepan bring water to a boil with rice over high heat and boil, covered, 2 minutes. Reduce heat to moderate and boil rice, covered, 5 minutes more. Reduce heat to low and cook rice, covered, until liquid is absorbed, 10 to 15 minutes. Let rice stand, covered, 10 minutes and spread in a large shallow baking pan. Sprinkle rice with vinegar and toss with a wooden spoon to cool slightly.

Pit *umeboshi* and coarsely chop *umeboshi* and ginger. In a bowl stir together rice, *umeboshi*, and ginger and cool to room temperature. *Salad may be prepared up to this point 4 hours ahead and kept, covered, at cool room temperature.*

Have ready a bowl of ice and cold water. In a saucepan of boiling water cook peas until bright green, about 30 seconds, and transfer to ice water to stop cooking. Drain peas and cut crosswise into thin strips. *Peas may be cooked 1 day ahead and chilled in a sealable plastic bag.*

Just before serving, stir peas into salad and season with salt. Serves 6.

PHOTO ON PAGE 60

Gingered Bulgur Salad with Grapes

½ cup bulgur*
¾ teaspoon salt
⅔ cup boiling-hot water
½ cup seedless green grapes
⅓ cup packed fresh cilantro leaves
1 garlic clove
1 teaspoon grated peeled fresh gingerroot
2 tablespoons fresh lemon juice
2 tablespoons olive oil

*available at natural foods stores and most
  supermarkets; or use Near East *tabbouleh* mix
  (bulgur) without the seasoning pouch

In a bowl stir together bulgur and salt and stir in water. *Let bulgur stand, covered, 30 minutes.*

While bulgur is standing, slice grapes and chop cilantro. Mince garlic. In a small bowl combine grapes, cilantro, garlic, gingerroot, lemon juice, and oil. Fluff bulgur with a fork and stir in grape mixture. Serves 2 as a side dish.

SAUCES AND CONDIMENTS

MUSTARD BUTTER WITH BASIL AND CAPERS ◯+

This butter is excellent on grilled or broiled chicken,
meat, or fish, or tossed with cooked vegetables.

1¼ teaspoons drained capers
1 large garlic clove
½ teaspoon salt
3 tablespoons chopped fresh basil leaves
1 stick (½ cup) unsalted butter,
    softened
1½ tablespoons coarse-grained mustard
3 tablespoons Dijon mustard

Mince capers and garlic and mash with salt. In a bowl stir together garlic-caper paste with remaining ingredients and salt and pepper to taste. Chill mustard butter 10 minutes. Using wax paper as an aid, shape mustard butter into a 6-inch log and wrap. *Chill butter until firm, at least 1 hour, and up to 3 days. Butter may be frozen, wrapped well in plastic wrap, 1 month.* Slice mustard butter as needed. Makes about ¾ cup.

BATTER-FRIED CAPERS

These crisp little bites are great for salads and canapés.

4 tablespoons capers
½ cup all-purpose flour
½ cup beer
¼ teaspoon salt, or to taste
about 2 cups vegetable oil for
    deep-frying

Rinse salted capers, if using, and soak in cold water to cover by 3 inches for 30 minutes (to remove excess salt). In a small bowl whisk together flour, beer, and salt. Let mixture stand 15 minutes. Drain capers and dry well. Stir capers into batter.

In a small saucepan heat 1 inch oil over moderate heat until a deep-fat thermometer registers 375° F. With a slotted spoon remove capers, about 10 at a time, from batter. With fingers carefully drop coated capers into oil and fry until golden, about 1 minute. With another slotted spoon transfer capers as fried to paper towels to drain. *Batter-fried capers will stay crisp, uncovered, at room temperature 1 day.* Makes about ⅓ cup.

CAPER, RAISIN, AND LEMON PESTO ◯

This combination was inspired by a scallop dish served at Jean Georges, a restaurant in New York City. We recommend the pesto with grilled or sautéed scallops, chicken, or fish.

¼ cup salted capers*
1 lemon
¼ cup packed fresh flat-leafed parsley leaves
2 tablespoons golden raisins
1 tablespoon chopped shallot
1 tablespoon water
¼ teaspoon freshly ground black pepper
3 tablespoons extra-virgin olive oil

*available at specialty foods shops

Rinse capers well and soak in cold water to cover by 3 inches for 30 minutes (to remove excess salt). Drain capers well.

With a vegetable peeler remove six 2½- by ½-inch strips zest from lemon and finely chop. Halve lemon and squeeze enough juice to measure 4 teaspoons, or to taste. In a food processor combine capers, zest, juice, parsley, raisins, shallot, water, and pepper. With motor running, add oil in a stream and purée until smooth. Season pesto with salt if necessary. *Pesto keeps, covered and chilled, 1 day.* Makes about ½ cup, serving 4.

PICKLED PLUMS AND RED ONIONS ☺+

2½ pounds assorted plums (about 10)
2 medium red onions
2 cups water
2 cups red-wine vinegar
2¼ cups sugar
3 cinnamon sticks
1½ teaspoons whole allspice
½ teaspoon whole cloves
½ teaspoon salt

Pit plums and cut into ½-inch wedges. Cut onions into ¾-inch pieces and transfer with plums to a 10-cup (2½-quart) heatproof glass jar with a lid.

In a large saucepan bring water and vinegar to a boil with remaining ingredients, stirring until sugar is dissolved, and immediately pour over plums and onions. Cool mixture, uncovered. *Plums and onions may be pickled 1 week ahead and chilled, covered.* Serves 12.

PHOTO ON PAGE 64

PICKLED PEPPERS AND ONIONS ☺+

These pickled peppers are delicious served with Cheddar and other firm/hard cheeses.

3 red bell peppers
3 yellow bell peppers
8 ounces pearl onions
3 garlic cloves
3 cups water
¾ cup rice vinegar (not seasoned)
¾ cup white-wine vinegar
8 whole juniper berries*
½ cup sugar
1 tablespoon salt

*available in spice section of supermarket

Halve bell peppers and discard seeds, ribs, and blossom ends. Cut bell peppers lengthwise into ½-inch-wide irregular pieces and transfer to a large heatproof bowl. Trim and peel onions. Halve garlic cloves. Add onions and garlic to peppers. In a saucepan bring water and vinegars to a boil and add

juniper berries, sugar, and salt. Simmer mixture, stirring occasionally, 3 minutes, or until sugar is dissolved. Pour vinegar mixture over peppers and onions, covering them completely, and cool. *Chill peppers and onions in an airtight container at least 12 hours and up to 5 days.* Makes about 6½ cups.

PHOTO ON PAGE 30

CRANBERRY APRICOT COMPOTE ☺

1 cup dried apricots (about 6 ounces)
two 12-ounce bags fresh or unthawed frozen
    cranberries (about 7 cups total)
1 cup water
1 cup sugar, or to taste
3 large shallots

Quarter apricots and pick over cranberries. In a 3-quart saucepan bring water, sugar, and apricots to a boil and simmer, stirring until sugar is dissolved, 5 minutes. Add cranberries and simmer until berries have burst, about 5 minutes.

Finely chop shallots and stir into compote. Remove pan from heat and cool compote completely. *Compote may be made 2 days ahead and chilled, covered.* Makes about 4 cups.

PHOTO ON PAGE 73

WHITE BEAN, GARLIC, AND TOMATO SALSA

1 head garlic
a 16-ounce can small white beans such as navy
3 medium vine-ripened tomatoes
    (about 1¼ pounds)
1 small sweet onion such as Vidalia
½ cup packed fresh basil leaves
2 tablespoons fresh lemon juice

Preheat oven to 400° F.

Separate garlic head into cloves, discarding loose papery outer skin but keeping skin intact on cloves, and wrap in foil, crimping seams to seal tightly. Roast garlic in middle of oven 30 minutes, or until soft. Unwrap garlic and cool slightly. Peel skins from each clove and in a bowl with a fork mash garlic pulp until smooth.

Rinse and drain enough beans to measure 1 cup, reserving remainder for another use, and add to garlic. Cut 2 tomatoes into ¼-inch dice and add to beans. Quarter remaining tomato and in a blender or food processor purée until smooth. Add purée to bean mixture. Finely chop onion and basil and add to bean mixture with lemon juice, tossing to combine. Season salsa with salt and pepper. *Salsa may be made 1 hour ahead and chilled, covered.* Makes about 4 cups.

☞ each 1-cup serving about 159 calories and less than 1 gram fat

PROVENÇAL OVEN-ROASTED TOMATO SAUCE

olive oil for brushing pans
1 head garlic
4 pounds vine-ripened red tomatoes
   (about 10 medium)
1 tablespoon fresh rosemary leaves
1 tablespoon fresh thyme leaves
3 tablespoons fresh orange juice, or to taste

Preheat oven to 450° F. and lightly brush 2 shallow baking pans with oil.

Separate garlic head into cloves, discarding loose papery outer skin but keeping skin intact on cloves, and wrap in foil, crimping seams to seal tightly. Cut tomatoes into ½-inch-thick slices and arrange in one layer in baking pans. Sprinkle 2 teaspoons each of rosemary and thyme evenly over tomatoes and season with salt and pepper.

Put foil-wrapped garlic in one of baking pans with tomatoes and roast garlic and tomatoes in upper and lower thirds of oven, switching position of pans halfway through roasting, about 35 minutes total, or until garlic is tender and tomatoes are slightly charred. Unwrap garlic and cool slightly. Peel skins from each clove and force pulp with warm tomatoes and herbs through a food mill fitted with small-holed disk into a bowl.

Finely chop remaining teaspoon rosemary and remaining teaspoon thyme and stir into sauce with orange juice. Season sauce with salt and pepper and reheat if necessary. *Sauce keeps, covered and chilled, 4 days or, frozen, 4 months. Reheat sauce over low heat and reseason with orange juice, salt, and pepper.* Makes about 3 cups sauce, enough for 1 pound pasta.

SPICY PINEAPPLE, APRICOT, AND JÍCAMA SALSA ◐

½ small pineapple
a ½-pound piece *jícama**
3 ounces dried apricots (about ⅓ cup)
1 small red onion
½ cup packed fresh cilantro sprigs
½ fresh *habanero* or Scotch bonnet
   chile*

*available at Latino markets and some specialty produce markets and supermarkets

Peel pineapple and cut enough into ¼-inch dice to measure 1¾ cups. Peel *jícama* and cut into ¼-inch dice. Coarsely chop apricots and chop enough onion to measure ¾ cup. Finely chop cilantro and, wearing rubber gloves, finely chop chile with seeds. In a bowl toss together all ingredients and season with salt. *Salsa may be made 6 hours ahead and chilled, covered.* Makes about 4 cups.

☞ each 1-cup serving about 107 calories and less than 1 gram fat

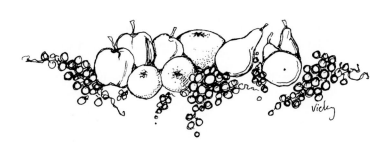

PAPAYA AND RED ONION SALSA ☺

½ firm-ripe papaya
¼ red onion
1 fresh jalapeño chile
1 tablespoon finely chopped fresh
　cilantro
2 teaspoons fresh lime juice
1 teaspoon pure maple syrup

Discard papaya seeds. Peel papaya and chop enough to measure ⅔ cup. Mince enough onion to measure 2 tablespoons and, wearing rubber gloves, mince enough jalapeño (with seeds) to measure ½ tablespoon. In a bowl stir together papaya, onion, jalapeño, and remaining ingredients and season with salt. *Salsa may be made 1 day ahead and chilled, covered.* Serves 4.

PHOTO ON PAGE 83

☛ each serving about 20 calories and less than 1 gram fat

TOMATILLO CELERY SALSA ☺

This refreshing condiment is ideal with lean beef or grilled shrimp.

1 pound fresh tomatillos
4 celery ribs
1 cup packed fresh cilantro
　sprigs
6 radishes
1 tablespoon fresh lemon juice

Remove husks from tomatillos and rinse tomatillos under warm water to remove stickiness. Pat tomatillos dry and cut about three fourths into ¼-inch dice. In a blender or food processor purée remaining tomatillos until smooth. Cut celery into ¼-inch dice and finely chop cilantro. Slice radishes and cut into julienne strips. In a bowl toss together all salsa ingredients and season with salt. *Salsa may be made 1 hour ahead and chilled, covered.* Makes 3 cups.

☛ each ¾-cup serving about 38 calories and less than 1 gram fat

GREEN-OLIVE AND CAPER TAPENADE ☺

Serve this tapenade on bruschetta or as a sandwich spread.

5 tablespoons drained capers
½ cup pimiento-stuffed green olives
　(a 3-ounce jar)
2 flat anchovy fillets
4 garlic cloves
⅓ cup extra-virgin olive oil

In a food processor combine capers, olives, anchovies, and garlic. With motor running, add oil in a stream and purée until mixture forms a coarse paste. *Tapenade keeps, covered and chilled, 1 week.* Makes about ⅔ cup.

CURRIED CORN AND ZUCCHINI SALSA ☺

1 fresh jalapeño chile
3 ears corn
3 large zucchini (about 1¼ pounds total)
1 tablespoon curry powder
¾ cup chicken broth
5 scallions
1 tablespoon fresh lime juice

Wearing rubber gloves, finely chop jalapeño with seeds. With a sharp knife cut enough corn from cobs to measure 1½ cups. Remove peel in ¼-inch-thick strips from 2 zucchini and cut peel into ¼-inch dice. Coarsely chop cores and remaining zucchini.

In a large nonstick skillet cook jalapeño, chopped zucchini (not dice), curry powder, and broth over moderate heat until zucchini is tender, about 5 minutes. In a blender or food processor purée mixture until smooth (use caution when blending hot liquids).

Transfer mixture to skillet and add corn and zucchini dice. Cook salsa over moderate heat, stirring, until corn is just tender, about 5 minutes. Thinly slice scallions and stir into salsa with lime juice, tossing to combine. Season salsa with salt and pepper and serve warm. Makes about 4 cups.

☛ each 1-cup serving about 94 calories and less than 1 gram fat

DESSERTS

CAKES

DARK CHOCOLATE BROWN SUGAR POUND CAKE WITH CHOCOLATE GLAZE

2¼ cups cake flour (not self-rising)
¾ cup unsweetened Dutch-process cocoa powder
½ teaspoon salt
¼ teaspoon baking soda
1 cup sour cream (8½ ounces)
2¼ sticks (1 cup plus 2 tablespoons) unsalted butter, softened
1½ cups granulated sugar
1½ cups packed dark brown sugar
1 tablespoon chocolate extract* (optional)
1 teaspoon vanilla extract
6 large eggs
For glaze
3 ounces fine-quality bittersweet chocolate
2 tablespoons unsalted butter

Accompaniments:
brown sugar sour cream (recipe follows)
strawberries

*available by mail order from Williams-Sonoma, (800) 541-2233

Do not preheat oven. Butter and flour a 12-cup bundt pan, knocking out any excess flour.

Into a small bowl sift together flour, unsweetened cocoa powder, and salt. In another small bowl stir together baking soda and sour cream.

In a large bowl with an electric mixer (preferably a standing electric mixer) beat together butter and sugars until light and fluffy, about 10 minutes. Beat in extracts and add eggs 1 at a time, beating well after each addition. With electric mixer on low speed, add flour mixture and sour cream mixture alternately in batches, beating until just combined.

Pour batter into bundt pan and put in middle of cold oven. Set oven to 350° F. and bake cake 1 hour and 25 minutes, or until a tester comes out clean. Cool cake in pan on a rack 15 minutes and turn out onto rack to cool completely. *Pound cake keeps, wrapped in plastic wrap, at room temperature 1 week. Alternatively, pound cake may be frozen, wrapped well in plastic wrap and foil, 3 months.*

Make glaze:

Chop bittersweet chocolate and in a double boiler or a metal bowl set over a saucepan of barely simmering water melt chocolate with butter, stirring until smooth. Transfer glaze to a pastry bag fitted with a #3 plain tip (slightly smaller than ⅛ inch). (Alternatively, transfer glaze to a small heavy-duty sealable plastic bag and press out excess air. Snip off 1 corner, making a small hole.) Pipe glaze back and forth over top of cake, letting it drip down sides. *Let glaze set at room temperature 30 minutes.*

Serve cake with dollops of sour cream and strawberries. Serves 16 to 20.

BROWN SUGAR SOUR CREAM ◐

1½ cups sour cream
3 tablespoons packed dark brown sugar
¾ teaspoon vanilla extract

In a small bowl stir together all ingredients until smooth. *Sour cream keeps, covered and chilled, 1 week.* Makes about 1⅔ cups.

Buttermilk Cupcakes with Two Frostings

If making these cupcakes for a large crowd, do not double the recipe but make multiple batches.

twenty-four 2½-inch paper muffin cup liners
4 cups cake flour (not self-rising)
2 teaspoons baking powder
2 teaspoons baking soda
1½ teaspoons salt
2 sticks (1 cup) unsalted butter,
    softened
2 cups sugar
2 teaspoons vanilla
4 large eggs
2 cups well-shaken buttermilk
chocolate cream-cheese and lemon
    cream-cheese frostings
    (recipe follows)

Garnish: India Tree brand sparkling sugar
    confetti* or other decorative sprinkles

*available at some specialty foods shops and
    by mail order from Dean & DeLuca,
    (212) 226-6800, ext. 269

Preheat oven to 350° F. Line twenty-four ½-cup muffin cups with paper liners.

Into a bowl sift together flour, baking powder, baking soda, and salt. In a large bowl with an electric mixer beat together butter and sugar until light and fluffy and beat in vanilla. Add eggs 1 at a time, beating well after each addition, and with mixer on low speed beat in buttermilk until just combined. Add flour mixture in 3 batches, beating until just combined after each addition.

Divide batter among muffin cups (batter will fill cups) and bake in upper and lower thirds of oven, switching position of muffin trays halfway through baking, about 22 minutes, or until golden and a tester comes out clean. Cool cupcakes on racks 5 minutes and remove cupcakes from cups. *Cupcakes keep in an airtight container at room temperature 2 days.*

Spread chocolate frosting on half of cupcakes and lemon frosting on remainder and garnish cupcakes with sprinkles. Makes 24 cupcakes.

PHOTO ON PAGE 65

Chocolate Cream-Cheese and Lemon Cream-Cheese Frostings

4 ounces unsweetened chocolate
2½ sticks (1¼ cups) unsalted butter, softened
1¾ cups whipped cream cheese (about 10 ounces)
4 cups confectioners' sugar
3 tablespoons fresh lemon juice

Chop chocolate and in a double boiler or a metal bowl set over a saucepan of barely simmering water melt chocolate, stirring until smooth.

In a bowl with an electric mixer on low speed beat together butter, cream cheese, and confectioners' sugar until light and fluffy. Transfer half of cream-cheese mixture to another bowl and stir in melted chocolate until combined well. Stir lemon juice into plain mixture in other bowl. If frostings are too soft, chill slightly before using. *Frostings may be made 2 days ahead and chilled separately, covered. Bring frostings to cool room temperature and whisk before using.* Makes enough frosting for 24 cupcakes.

Lemon Blueberry Ice-Cream Cake

1½ cups cake flour (not self-rising)
1 teaspoon baking powder
½ teaspoon salt
1 stick (½ cup) unsalted butter,
    softened
1¼ cups sugar
2 large eggs
½ cup whole milk
3 tablespoons finely grated fresh lemon zest
6 tablespoons fresh lemon juice
blueberry filling (recipe follows)
7 cups lemon ice cream (page 203)

Garnish: 2 cups blueberries

Preheat oven to 350° F. Butter a 9-inch round cake pan (2 inches deep) and line bottom with a round of wax paper.

Into a bowl sift together flour, baking powder, and salt. In a large bowl with an electric mixer beat together butter and 1 cup sugar until light and fluffy, about 1 minute. Separate eggs and beat yolks 1 at a time into butter mixture, beating well after each addition. In 3 batches alternately beat in flour mixture and milk, beginning and ending with flour mixture. Add zest and 2 tablespoons lemon juice, beating until just combined (do not overbeat). In a bowl with cleaned beaters beat whites until they hold soft peaks and beat in remaining ¼ cup sugar. Fold whites into batter gently but thoroughly.

Transfer batter to cake pan and bake in middle of oven until a tester comes out clean, 35 to 40 minutes. Cool cake in pan on a rack and invert onto rack. *Cake may be prepared up to this point 1 day ahead and kept in an airtight container at cool room temperature.*

Assemble cake:

With a long serrated knife horizontally halve cake. Put bottom half, cut side up, in a 9-inch springform pan. Brush 2 tablespoons remaining lemon juice over layer. Working quickly, spread half of blueberry filling evenly over layer, leaving a ¼-inch border around edge, and top with one third ice cream, spreading evenly. Put remaining cake half, cut side up, on top of ice cream and brush remaining 2 tablespoons lemon juice over it. Spread remaining blueberry filling evenly over top, leaving a ¼-inch border around edge, and spread half of remaining ice cream evenly over filling. Reserve remaining ice cream for outside of cake. *Freeze cake, covered, until firm, at least 8 hours, and up to 1 day.*

Remove side of springform pan. With a spatula loosen cake from bottom and transfer to a plate. Frost cake with remaining ice cream, spreading evenly around sides and top of cake. *Freeze cake, loosely covered, at least 2 hours and up to 5 days.*

Twenty minutes before serving, garnish top of cake with blueberries and put cake in refrigerator to soften slightly. Serves 8 to 12.

PHOTO ON PAGE 49

BLUEBERRY FILLING ⊙

4½ cups blueberries
¾ cup sugar
¼ cup light corn syrup
1 teaspoon fresh lemon juice

Pick over blueberries. In a 3-quart heavy saucepan combine all ingredients and simmer, stirring, until reduced to about 2 cups, 25 to 30 minutes. Transfer filling to a bowl. *Chill filling, covered, at least 1 hour and up to 2 days.* Makes about 2 cups.

LEMON ICE CREAM ⊙+

We used a 1½-quart ice-cream maker for this recipe. Depending on the capacity of your ice-cream maker, you may have to freeze the cream mixture in batches.

¼ cup finely grated fresh lemon zest
⅔ cup fresh lemon juice
2 cups superfine granulated sugar
3 cups well-chilled heavy cream
1 cup whole milk
¼ teaspoon salt

Have ready an ice-cream maker. In a saucepan whisk together zest, lemon juice, and sugar. Cook mixture over moderate heat, stirring, until sugar is completely dissolved, about 10 minutes, and cool to room temperature.

In a bowl whisk together cream, milk, and salt and stir in lemon syrup. Transfer mixture to ice-cream maker and freeze. Transfer lemon ice cream to an airtight container and put in freezer to harden. *Ice cream may be made 3 days ahead.* Makes about 7 cups.

JEANNE

Ginger Cakes with Molten Chocolate Centers and Ginger Crème Anglaise

We made these little cakes using four 10-ounce mini-bundt pans (not nonstick), available at cookware shops and by mail order from Bridge Kitchenware, (800) 274-3435 or (212) 838-1901. Ten-ounce ramekins would also work.

For ganache
2 ounces fine-quality bittersweet chocolate (not unsweetened)
¼ cup heavy cream
For cakes
1 cup all-purpose flour
2 teaspoons ground ginger
¼ teaspoon baking soda
¼ teaspoon salt
1 stick (½ cup) unsalted butter, softened
¾ cup packed dark brown sugar
2 large eggs
¼ cup sour cream
¼ cup unsulfured molasses

Accompaniment: ginger *crème anglaise* (recipe follows)

Make ganache:
Put a sheet of wax paper on a small baking sheet and put a 3-inch round cutter on it. (Alternatively, line a 3-inch ramekin with plastic wrap, leaving a 2-inch overhang.)

Chop chocolate and transfer to a small bowl. In a small saucepan bring cream to a boil and pour over chocolate. Stir mixture with a rubber spatula until completely smooth and pour into cutter or ramekin. Freeze ganache while preparing cake. *Ganache may be made 1 week ahead and frozen, covered.*

Make cakes:
Preheat oven to 375° F. and generously butter and flour four 10-ounce mini-bundt pans (not nonstick) or ramekins, knocking out excess flour.

Into a bowl sift together flour, ginger, baking soda, and salt. In a large bowl with an electric mixer beat together butter and brown sugar until light and fluffy. Beat in eggs, sour cream, and molasses until combined well. (Mixture will separate but will come together again when flour mixture is added.) Add flour mixture to egg mixture, beating until just combined (do not overbeat).

Spoon about ½ cup batter into each pan or ramekin and bake on a baking sheet in middle of oven 20 minutes. Run a thin knife around side of cutter and remove *ganache*. (Alternatively, lift *ganache* out of ramekin using plastic wrap.) Quarter *ganache* and put 1 piece in center of each cake, pressing down gently (*ganache* will sink into cakes). Bake cakes 15 to 20 minutes more, or until set and a crust is formed on top. Cool cakes in pans or ramekins on a rack 10 minutes. *Cakes may be made 1 day ahead and kept in pans or ramekins, covered, at room temperature. Reheat cakes in a 375° F. oven before serving.*

Invert cakes onto plates and serve warm with *crème anglaise*. Makes 4 individual cakes.

PHOTO ON PAGE 15

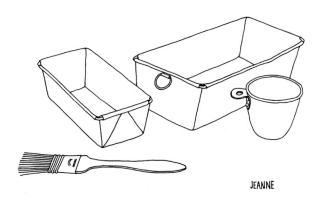

JEANNE

Ginger Crème Anglaise ◑+

a 4-inch piece peeled fresh gingerroot
1 cup half-and-half
3 large egg yolks
2 tablespoons sugar

Cut gingerroot into 4 pieces and smash with flat side of a knife. In a small heavy saucepan bring half-and-half and gingerroot just to a simmer over moderately low heat, about 10 minutes (do not let boil). While mixture is heating, in a bowl whisk together yolks and sugar until smooth. Add hot half-and-half mixture in a slow stream, whisking, and transfer custard to pan. Cook custard over moderately low heat, stirring constantly with a wooden spoon, until a thermometer registers 170° F., about 5 minutes (do not let boil). Pour custard through a fine sieve into a clean bowl and cool. *Crème anglaise may be made 3 days ahead and chilled, covered. Bring crème anglaise to room temperature before serving.* Makes about 1¼ cups.

PINEAPPLE RUM TRIFLE CAKE

For cake layer
parchment paper
¼ cup (1½ ounces) shelled natural pistachios or blanched almonds
¾ cup plus 1 tablespoon all-purpose flour
½ teaspoon salt
5 large eggs
⅔ cup sugar

two 20-ounce cans unsweetened crushed pineapple
rum sabayon (recipe follows)
1 cup well-chilled heavy cream
2 teaspoons sugar

Make cake layer:
Preheat oven to 350° F. Oil bottom and sides of a 15½- by 10½- by 1-inch jelly-roll pan and line bottom and sides with parchment paper.

In a food processor finely grind nuts with flour and salt. In a large bowl with an electric mixer beat together eggs and sugar until thick and pale and mixture forms a ribbon when beaters are lifted (about 10 minutes with a standing mixer and about 15 with a hand-held mixer). Fold flour mixture into egg mixture gently but thoroughly. Spread batter evenly in jelly-roll pan and bake in middle of oven until golden and springs back when lightly touched, 10 to 15 minutes. Cool cake layer in pan on a rack. *Cake layer may be made 3 days ahead and kept wrapped well in plastic wrap at cool room temperature.*

In a food processor pulse undrained pineapple 3 seconds. Drain pineapple in a sieve set over a bowl (you will have about 2 cups) and reserve juice for another use.

Assemble trifle cake:
Invert cake layer onto a work surface and peel off parchment. With a long serrated knife trim layer to form a 14- by 7-inch rectangle, reserving trimmings. Halve rectangle crosswise to form two 7-inch squares and carefully halve squares horizontally (for a total of four 7-inch squares). Horizontally halve reserved trimmings.

Put 1 square on a cake plate. With a spatula spread ½ cup pineapple evenly over square. Top pineapple with ½ cup sabayon, spreading evenly. Make more layers in same manner with remaining 3 squares, pineapple, and sabayon, ending with sabayon. Piece together enough reserved trimmings to form a fifth square over sabayon. *Chill cake, covered, at least 1 hour and up to 2 days.*

In a bowl with an electric mixer beat cream with sugar until it just holds soft peaks and with a spatula spread whipped cream over top and sides of cake. *Cake may be fully assembled 1 day ahead and chilled in a cake keeper or covered with an inverted bowl. Bring cake to room temperature before serving (about 30 minutes).* Serves 6 generously.

PHOTO ON PAGE 35

RUM SABAYON ◔

4 large egg yolks
¼ cup sugar
¼ cup rum (preferably light)
1 cup heavy cream

In a large metal bowl whisk together yolks, sugar, rum, and ¼ cup cream. Set bowl over a saucepan of simmering water and cook mixture, whisking constantly, until frothy and whisk leaves distinct marks. Set bowl in a larger bowl of ice and cold water and cool sauce, stirring gently with a rubber spatula, until cold. In a bowl with an electric mixer beat remaining ¾ cup cream until it just holds stiff peaks and fold into sauce gently but thoroughly. *Sabayon may be made 1 day ahead and chilled, covered.* Makes about 2 cups.

COOKIES AND BARS

CHOCOLATE PEANUT BUTTER CHIP COOKIES

1½ cups all-purpose flour
½ cup unsweetened cocoa powder
   (not Dutch-process)
¾ teaspoon baking soda
¼ teaspoon salt
2 sticks (1 cup) unsalted butter, softened
1 cup granulated sugar
¼ cup packed light brown sugar
1 large egg
1½ teaspoons vanilla
1⅔ cups (a 10-ounce bag) peanut butter chips
1 cup semisweet chocolate chips (about 8 ounces)

Preheat oven to 350° F.

Into a bowl sift together flour, cocoa powder, baking soda, and salt. In a bowl with an electric mixer beat together butter and sugars until light and fluffy and beat in egg and vanilla until combined well. Beat in flour mixture until just combined and stir in chips.

Drop dough by tablespoons about 2 inches apart onto ungreased baking sheets and bake in batches in middle of oven until cookies are just set and begin to crack on top, about 12 minutes. Cool cookies on sheets on racks 1 minute and with a spatula transfer to racks to cool completely. Makes about 55 cookies.

CINNAMON NUTMEG TUILES

½ stick (¼ cup) unsalted butter
¼ cup packed light brown sugar
3 tablespoons light corn syrup
¼ cup all-purpose flour
½ teaspoon cinnamon
1 teaspoon freshly grated nutmeg

Preheat oven to 375° F. Have ready a rolling pin.

In a saucepan melt butter with sugar and syrup over moderate heat, stirring occasionally until sugar is dissolved. Remove pan from heat and stir in flour, cinnamon, nutmeg, and a pinch salt until smooth.

Drop 6 rounded ½-teaspoons batter about 3 inches apart onto an ungreased baking sheet. Bake cookies in middle of oven 6 minutes, or until golden.

Remove 1 cookie from baking sheet with a thin metal spatula and immediately drape over a rolling pin to create a curved shape. Cool cookie completely on rolling pin and transfer to an airtight container. Make more cookies with remaining batter and form into *tuiles* in same manner. (If cookies become too brittle to drape over rolling pin, return baking sheet to oven a few seconds to allow cookies to soften.) *Tuiles keep in an airtight container at cool room temperature 5 days.* Makes about 20 *tuiles*.

PHOTO ON PAGE 71

OATMEAL DATE COOKIES ◔

1¼ cups packed pitted dates (about 10 ounces)
1 stick (½ cup) unsalted butter
¾ cup packed light brown sugar
⅔ cup all-purpose flour
¾ teaspoon baking soda
¾ teaspoon salt
1 large egg
1 teaspoon vanilla
1½ cups quick-cooking rolled oats

Preheat oven to 350° F.

Coarsely chop dates. In a 3-quart saucepan melt butter over low heat and remove pan from heat. Add brown sugar, stirring until smooth, and sift flour, baking soda, and salt over butter mixture. In a cup lightly beat egg and stir into flour mixture with vanilla, oats, and dates until combined well.

Onto 2 large ungreased baking sheets spoon slightly rounded tablespoons dough about 2 inches apart. Roll dough into balls with floured hands, returning to sheets. Bake cookies in upper and lower thirds of oven, switching position of sheets halfway through baking, until golden brown, about 18 minutes total. Transfer cookies to racks to cool. *Cookies keep in an airtight container about 1 week.* Makes about 24 cookies.

CORNMEAL, CHILE, AND PUMPKIN-SEED LACE COOKIES

½ cup sugar
5 tablespoons unsalted butter
3 tablespoons light corn syrup
3 tablespoons all-purpose flour
2 tablespoons cornmeal
1½ teaspoons chili powder
1 tablespoon fresh lemon juice
½ cup hulled green pumpkin
   seeds*

*available at Latino markets, natural foods stores, and some supermarkets and by mail order from Kitchen Market, (888) 468-4433

In a 1- to 1½-quart heavy saucepan bring sugar, butter, and corn syrup to a boil over moderate heat, stirring, and boil 1 minute. Remove pan from heat and stir in remaining ingredients until mixture is smooth. Cool dough to room temperature. *Dough keeps, covered and chilled, 1 month.* Form and bake cookies as directed in following procedure. *Baked cookies keep in an airtight container 1 week.* Makes about 60 cookies.

TO FORM AND BAKE LACE COOKIES

Preheat oven to 350° F. and line 2 large baking sheets with parchment paper.
   Roll level ½-teaspoons dough into balls and arrange 4 inches apart on baking sheets. Bake cookies in batches in upper and lower thirds of oven, switching position of sheets halfway through baking, 10 minutes total, or until cookies are flat and golden.

Transfer parchment with cookies to racks to cool. Cool baking sheets and line with fresh parchment between batches.

GINGER MOLASSES LACE COOKIES

½ cup packed light brown sugar
¾ stick (6 tablespoons) unsalted butter
2 tablespoons unsulfured molasses
1 tablespoon fresh lemon juice
⅓ cup all-purpose flour
1 teaspoon ground ginger

In a 1- to 1½-quart heavy saucepan bring sugar, butter, molasses, and lemon juice to a boil over moderate heat, stirring, and boil 1 minute. Remove pan from heat and stir in flour, ginger, and a pinch salt until mixture is smooth. Cool dough to room temperature. *Dough keeps, covered and chilled, 1 month.* Form and bake cookies as directed in previous procedure. *Baked cookies keep in an airtight container 1 week.* Makes about 60 cookies.

ORANGE ALMOND LACE COOKIES

⅔ cup sliced almonds
½ cup fresh orange juice
½ cup sugar
½ stick (¼ cup) unsalted butter
2 teaspoons freshly grated orange zest
¼ cup all-purpose flour
2 teaspoons cider vinegar

Preheat oven to 350° F. In a baking pan toast almonds in one layer in middle of oven until golden, about 10 minutes.
   In a 1- to 1½-quart heavy saucepan bring orange juice, sugar, and butter to a boil over moderate heat, stirring, and boil about 5 minutes, or until mixture is thick and bubbles are tan-colored. Remove pan from heat and and stir in almonds, zest, flour, vinegar, and a pinch salt until mixture is combined well. Cool dough to room temperature. *Dough keeps, covered and chilled, 1 month.* Form and bake cookies (procedure opposite). *Baked cookies keep in an airtight container 1 week.* Makes about 48 cookies.

PISTACHIO BISCOTTI THINS

For a curved tuile-like shape, these cookies may be draped over a rolling pin after their second baking, while they are still warm. If the cookies become too brittle to form on the rolling pin, return baking sheets to oven for a few seconds.

parchment paper
4 large egg whites
⅔ cup sugar
¾ cup all-purpose flour
⅓ cup (2 ounces) shelled natural pistachios
½ teaspoon vanilla

Preheat oven to 350° F. and line bottom and sides of a 9¼- by 5½- by 2¾-inch metal loaf pan with parchment paper.

In a large bowl with an electric mixer beat whites with a pinch salt until they just hold stiff peaks. Gradually beat in sugar and beat until meringue holds stiff, glossy peaks. Sift flour over meringue and fold in with pistachios and vanilla gently but thoroughly. Spoon meringue into loaf pan, smoothing top, and bake in middle of oven until golden, 25 to 30 minutes. Cool loaf in pan on a rack 15 minutes and turn loaf out onto rack to cool completely.

Reduce temperature to 300° F.

Peel off parchment and with a serrated knife cut loaf crosswise into ⅛-inch-thick slices. Arrange slices about ½ inch apart on 2 baking sheets and bake in upper and lower thirds of oven, switching position of sheets halfway through baking, about 20 minutes total, or until pale golden and crisp. Cool cookies on sheets on racks. *Cookies keep in an airtight container at cool room temperature 1 week.* Makes about 36 cookies.

SESAME HONEY LACE COOKIES

1 cup confectioners' sugar
3 tablespoons unsalted butter
3 tablespoons honey
2 tablespoons water
1 cup sesame seeds
¼ cup all-purpose flour

In a 1- to 1½-quart heavy saucepan bring confectioners' sugar, butter, honey, and water to a boil over moderate heat, stirring, and boil 1 minute. Remove pan from heat and and stir in sesame seeds, flour, and a pinch salt until mixture is combined well. Cool dough to room temperature. *Dough keeps, covered and chilled, 1 month.* Form and bake cookies as directed on page 207. *Cookies keep in an airtight container 1 week.* Makes about 60 cookies.

STAR ANISE LACE COOKIES

2 tablespoons star anise pieces
½ cup sugar
5 tablespoons unsalted butter
2 tablespoons balsamic vinegar
¼ cup all-purpose flour

In an electric coffee/spice grinder finely grind star anise. In a 1- to 1½-quart heavy saucepan bring anise, sugar, butter, and vinegar to a boil over moderate heat, stirring, and boil 1 minute. Remove pan from heat and and stir in flour and a pinch salt until mixture is smooth. Cool dough to room temperature. *Dough keeps, covered and chilled, 1 month.* Form and bake cookies as directed on page 207. *Baked cookies keep in an airtight container 1 week.* Makes about 48 cookies.

PIES, TARTS, AND PASTRIES

APPLE, APRICOT, AND PRUNE TART

The 12½- by 1-inch round tart pan with a removable rim is available at cookware shops and by mail from Bridge Kitchenware, (800) 274-3435 or (212) 838-1901.

frozen-butter pastry dough (page 216)
pie weights or raw rice for weighting shell
5 Granny Smith apples (about 2½ pounds)
1 cup dried apricots
½ cup plus 2 tablespoons sugar
1 cup water
½ cup pitted prunes
½ cup apricot jam

Accompaniment: crème fraîche or whipped cream

On a floured surface with a floured rolling pin roll out dough ¼ inch thick (about a 15-inch round). Fit dough into a 12½- by 1-inch fluted round tart pan with a removable bottom and with a rolling pin roll over top of shell to trim pastry flush with rim. With a fork prick bottom of shell all over. *Chill shell 30 minutes.*

Preheat oven to 425° F.

Line shell with foil and fill with pie weights or raw rice. Bake shell in middle of oven 20 minutes. Carefully remove weights or rice and foil and bake shell until golden, about 10 minutes more. Cool shell in pan on a rack.

Peel, core, and chop 1 apple. In a saucepan cook chopped apple, apricots, ½ cup sugar, and water, covered, over moderately low heat, stirring occasionally, until fruit is tender, about 12 minutes. Cool mixture 20 minutes. In a food processor pulse mixture until smooth and transfer to a small bowl. Chop prunes and stir into purée. Peel remaining 4 apples and quarter. Core apples and cut lengthwise into ⅛-inch-thick slices.

Spoon apricot purée evenly into shell and smooth top. Decoratively arrange apple slices, overlapping them, over purée and sprinkle with remaining 2 tablespoons sugar.

Bake tart in middle of oven until apple slices are slightly browned and crust is golden brown, about 45 minutes. Cool tart slightly in pan on rack. In a small saucepan melt apricot jam over low heat and pour through a fine sieve into a small bowl. Press hard on solids and discard. With a pastry brush, brush glaze over tart, spreading evenly.

Serve tart with *crème fraîche* or whipped cream. Serves 12.

PHOTO ON PAGE 31

BERRY TART WITH MASCARPONE CREAM

sweet pastry dough (page 210)
pie weights or raw rice for
    weighting shell
1 cup *mascarpone** cheese
    (about 8 ounces)
⅓ cup well-chilled heavy cream
¼ cup sugar
1½ cups small strawberries
1 cup raspberries
1 cup blueberries
1 cup blackberries
2 tablespoons sweet orange marmalade
2 tablespoons dark berry liqueur such as
    blueberry, blackberry, or cassis

*available at specialty foods shops and some
    supermarkets

Preheat oven to 375° F.

On a floured surface with a floured rolling pin roll out dough into an 11-inch round (about ⅛ inch thick) and fit into a 9-inch tart pan with a removable fluted rim. Roll rolling pin over top of shell to trim dough flush with rim and with a fork prick bottom of shell all over. *Chill shell 30 minutes, or until firm.*

Line shell with foil and fill with pie weights or raw rice. Bake shell in middle of oven 20 minutes and carefully remove foil and weights or rice. Bake shell until golden, about 10 minutes more, and cool completely in pan on a rack. *Pastry shell may be made 1 day ahead and kept in pan, loosely covered, at room temperature.*

In a bowl with a whisk or an electric mixer beat together *mascarpone*, cream, and sugar until mixture holds stiff peaks. Spoon *mascarpone* mixture into shell, spreading evenly.

Quarter strawberries and in a large bowl combine with remaining berries. In a small saucepan simmer marmalade and liqueur, stirring, until reduced to about 3 tablespoons and pour over berries. With a rubber spatula gently stir berries to coat evenly. Mound berries decoratively on *mascarpone* cream. *Tart may be assembled 2 hours ahead and chilled. Bring tart to room temperature and remove side of pan before serving.* Serves 6 to 8.

PHOTO ON PAGE 53

SWEET PASTRY DOUGH ◐+

1 stick (½ cup) cold unsalted butter
1⅓ cups all-purpose flour
2 tablespoons sugar
¼ teaspoon salt
1 large egg yolk
1½ tablespoons ice water

Cut butter into ½-inch cubes. In a bowl with your fingertips or a pastry blender blend together flour, sugar, salt, and butter cubes until most of mixture resembles coarse meal with remainder in small (roughly pea-size) lumps. In a small bowl or cup stir together yolk and ice water. Drizzle yolk mixture over flour mixture, stirring gently with a fork until incorporated, and gently form mixture into a ball. Turn mixture out onto a floured work surface and divide into 4 portions. With heel of hand smear each portion once in a forward motion to help distribute fat. Gather dough together and form it, rotating on work surface, into a disk. *Chill dough, wrapped in plastic wrap, until firm, at least 1 hour, and up to 1 day.* Makes enough dough for a single-crust 9-inch pie or a 9- to 11-inch tart.

LATTICE-TOPPED APRICOT CROSTATA

For pastry dough
1¾ sticks (¾ cup plus 2 tablespoons) cold
    unsalted butter
1½ cups all-purpose flour
1 cup cake flour (not self-rising)
⅓ cup sugar
¼ teaspoon salt
1 whole large egg
1 large egg yolk
1 teaspoon vanilla
1 teaspoon fresh lemon juice

1½ cups apricot preserves
2 tablespoons sugar
¼ cup sliced almonds

Make pastry dough:
Cut butter into ½-inch pieces. In a bowl whisk together flours, sugar, and salt. With your fingertips or a pastry blender blend in butter until most of mixture resembles coarse meal with remainder in small (roughly pea-size) lumps. In a cup with a fork stir together whole egg and yolk until combined well and stir into flour mixture. Stir in vanilla and lemon juice and with hands gently knead mixture just until it forms a dough.

Preheat oven to 350° F.

Form one third dough (about ½ pound) into a ball and flatten into a thin disk. Chill disk, wrapped in plastic wrap, while working with remaining two thirds dough.

Reserve one fourth remaining dough and crumble remainder into an 11-inch tart pan with a removable bottom. Pat out dough to evenly cover bottom (not side). With lightly floured hands roll reserved piece of dough into several ½-inch-thick ropes. Arrange ropes end-to-end around edge of pastry against rim of pan, pressing gently, to form a shallow side. Spread preserves over bottom.

With a rolling pin roll out chilled dough between 2 sheets plastic wrap into an 11-inch round and transfer in plastic wrap to a baking sheet. Remove top sheet of plastic wrap and with a fluted pastry cutter cut round into 1-inch-wide strips. Freeze dough strips on baking sheet about 10 minutes to firm up dough.

Working quickly, carefully invert dough strips onto baking sheet and remove plastic. Arrange dough strips over tart in an open lattice pattern (do not make a woven lattice), trimming edges to fit inside rim of pan. (Don't worry if strips break while making the lattice. Just lay any broken pieces in place—they will meld together during baking.) Brush lattice with cold water and sprinkle with sugar. Scatter almonds over *crostata* and bake in middle of oven 45 minutes, or until lattice is golden. Cool *crostata* in pan on a rack. *Crostata may be made 2 days ahead and kept, loosely covered, at room temperature.* Serves 8.

PHOTO ON PAGE 25

CHOCOLATE BANANA CREAM PIE

For shell

2½ cups unbleached all-purpose flour

2 tablespoons sugar

1 teaspoon salt

1¼ sticks plus 2 teaspoons (⅔ cup) cold
    unsalted butter

⅓ cup cold vegetable shortening

5 to 7 tablespoons ice water

pie weights or raw rice for weighting shell

For filling

5 ounces fine-quality bittersweet chocolate

4 ounces unsweetened chocolate

½ stick (¼ cup) unsalted butter

2 teaspoons vanilla

6 large egg yolks

1 cup sugar

¼ teaspoon salt

½ cup cornstarch

4½ cups milk

3 ripe large bananas

2 cups well-chilled heavy cream

2 tablespoons sugar

Garnish: chocolate shavings

Make shell:

In a food processor pulse together flour, sugar, and salt until combined. Cut butter and shortening into ½-inch pieces and scatter over flour mixture. Pulse mixture until most of mixture resembles coarse meal with remainder in small (pea-size) lumps. Transfer mixture to a bowl. Sprinkle 5 tablespoons water over mixture and toss to combine. Press mixture together to form a dough. If mixture does not form a dough, add enough remaining water, 1 tablespoon at a time, so that dough just comes together. Form dough into a disk. *Chill dough, wrapped in plastic wrap, 30 minutes.*

On a lightly floured surface with a floured rolling pin roll out dough ⅛ inch thick (about a 16-inch round) and fit into a 10-inch glass pie plate (1½ quarts). Trim dough, leaving a ½-inch overhang, and crimp edge decoratively. With a fork prick bottom of shell all over. *Chill shell, loosely covered, until firm, about 30 minutes.*

Preheat oven to 400° F.

Line shell with foil and fill with pie weights or raw rice. Bake shell in middle of oven 15 minutes. Carefully remove foil and weights or rice and bake shell until golden, about 6 minutes more. Cool shell on a rack.

Make filling:

Finely chop chocolates and cut butter into 1-inch pieces. In a large bowl (at least 3 quarts) combine chocolates, butter, and vanilla.

In a bowl whisk together yolks and sugar until thick and pale, about 1 minute, and whisk in salt. Add cornstarch and slowly whisk until combined well (mixture will be very stiff).

In a 3½- to 4-quart heavy saucepan bring milk just to a boil and remove pan from heat. Slowly add about 1 cup hot milk, about 2 tablespoons at a time, to yolk mixture, whisking until combined after each addition. Whisk yolk mixture into milk remaining in pan. Bring pastry cream to a boil over moderate heat, whisking constantly (to prevent scorching), and gently boil, whisking constantly, 1 minute. Strain pastry cream through a fine sieve into chocolate mixture, whisking until chocolate and butter are melted. Cool chocolate cream, its surface covered with wax paper, to room temperature.

Cut bananas into ¼-inch-thick rounds. Spread about 1½ cups chocolate cream in shell. Arrange half of bananas over chocolate cream in shell and cover with about 1½ cups chocolate cream, spreading evenly. Arrange remaining bananas over chocolate cream in shell and cover with about 1½ cups chocolate cream (you will have about 1 cup chocolate cream left over). *Chill pie, its surface covered with plastic wrap, at least 1 hour and up to 1 day.*

In a bowl with an electric mixer beat cream until it holds soft peaks and beat in sugar until it just holds stiff peaks.

Spread whipped cream decoratively over pie and garnish with chocolate shavings. Serves 12.

PHOTO ON PAGE 39

DRIED-APPLE TART WITH CRISP CRUMBLE TOPPING

For filling
12 ounces dried apples (preferably
    Granny Smith)
½ cup packed light brown sugar
4 cups water
2 cups apple cider
1 tablespoon fresh lemon juice
four 3-inch cinnamon sticks
For topping
¾ stick (6 tablespoons) cold unsalted butter
¾ cup all-purpose flour
½ cup granulated sugar
For pastry dough
1¼ sticks (10 tablespoons) cold unsalted butter
1½ cups all-purpose flour
½ cup confectioners' sugar

Accompaniment: whipped cream or vanilla
    ice cream

Make filling:
In a heavy 5-quart kettle simmer filling ingredients with a pinch salt, covered, until apples are fully plumped, about 15 minutes. Uncover mixture and simmer, stirring occasionally, until thick and any excess liquid is evaporated or absorbed, about 1 hour. (Reduce heat as liquid is evaporated or absorbed and stir apple mixture frequently toward end of cooking to prevent scorching.) Discard cinnamon sticks. *Filling may be made 2 days ahead and cooled before being chilled, covered.*

Make topping:
Cut butter into ½-inch pieces. In a food processor pulse butter, flour, and granulated sugar until crumbly. Transfer topping to a bowl and chill, covered, until ready to use.

Make pastry dough (after filling and topping are completed):
Preheat oven to 375° F.
Cut butter into ½-inch pieces. In cleaned food processor pulse together dough ingredients and a pinch salt until mixture begins to gather together.
Press dough evenly onto bottom and up side of an 11-inch tart pan with a removable fluted rim. Line shell with foil and bake in middle of oven until shell

is set, about 12 minutes. Gently remove foil (if foil sticks to shell, leave it on and bake about 2 minutes more) and bake shell until edge is golden, about 5 minutes (tart shell will not be completely cooked).

Immediately spoon filling into shell and crumble topping evenly over filling. Bake tart in middle of oven 30 minutes, or until topping is golden. Cool tart in pan on a rack. *Tart may be made 1 day ahead and kept, covered and chilled, in pan. Reheat tart, uncovered, if desired or bring to room temperature before serving.* Remove side of pan.

Serve apple tart with whipped cream or ice cream. Serves 8 to 10.

PHOTO ON PAGE 69

CARAMEL NUT TART

all-butter pastry dough (recipe follows)
pie weights or raw rice for weighting shell
1½ cups pecans (about 6 ounces)
1½ cups walnuts (about 6 ounces)
1 stick (½ cup) unsalted butter
1 cup packed light brown sugar
½ cup honey
½ cup heavy cream
2 ounces fine-quality bittersweet chocolate
    (not unsweetened)

Accompaniments:
ginger ice cream (page 221)
cinnamon nutmeg *tuiles* (page 206)

Preheat oven to 400° F.
Between 2 sheets of wax paper roll out dough into a 14-inch round (about ⅛ inch thick). Transfer dough to a baking sheet and chill 10 minutes. Lift top sheet of wax paper from dough and gently replace on top (this will facilitate removal of paper later). Flip dough over, discarding wax paper now on top, and carefully invert dough into an 11-inch tart pan with a removable fluted rim. Lightly press dough up side of rim, using pieces from overhang to patch any holes. *Chill shell, still covered with remaining sheet of wax paper, 30 minutes, or until firm.*

Remove wax paper. Line shell with foil, folding over edge to cover pastry entirely, and fill with pie weights or raw rice. Bake shell on a baking sheet in middle of oven 35 minutes and carefully remove foil and weights or rice. If bottom of crust still has patches of translucent undercooked dough, return shell to oven without foil and weights or rice and bake until pastry is completely cooked and golden, 3 to 5 minutes more. Cool shell in pan on a rack.

Reduce temperature to 350° F.

Coarsely chop nuts. In a 3-quart heavy saucepan melt butter with brown sugar and honey, stirring, and simmer 1 minute. Stir in nuts and cream. Simmer mixture 1 minute and pour into shell. Bake tart on baking sheet in middle of oven 30 minutes, or until filling is a few shades darker. Cool tart in pan on rack.

Chop chocolate and in a double boiler or a metal bowl set over a saucepan of barely simmering water melt chocolate, stirring until smooth. Cool chocolate slightly and transfer to a pastry bag fitted with a #3 plain tip (slightly smaller than ⅛ inch). (Alternatively, transfer chocolate to a small heavy-duty sealable plastic bag. Squeeze chocolate into one corner of bag and with scissors cut a tiny slice off corner to form a small hole.) Pipe thin lines of chocolate over tart in a back and forth motion to form stripes. *Tart may be made 2 days ahead and chilled, covered.*

Serve caramel tart chilled or at room temperature with ice cream and *tuiles.* Serves 8 to 10.

PHOTO ON PAGE 71

ALL-BUTTER PASTRY DOUGH ◌+

1½ sticks (¾ cup) cold unsalted butter
1½ cups all-purpose flour
2 tablespoons sugar
¾ teaspoon salt
1 to 2 tablespoons ice water

Cut butter into ½-inch cubes.
To blend by hand:

In a bowl with your fingertips or a pastry blender blend together flour, sugar, salt, and butter until most of mixture resembles coarse meal with remainder in small (roughly pea-size) lumps. Drizzle 1 tablespoon ice water evenly over mixture and gently stir with a fork until incorporated. Test mixture by gently squeezing a small handful: When it has proper texture it should hold together without crumbling apart. If necessary add enough remaining water, 1 teaspoon at a time, stirring until incorporated and testing, to give mixture proper texture. (If you overwork mixture or add too much water, pastry will be tough.)

To blend in a food processor:

In a food processor pulse together flour, sugar, salt, and butter until most of mixture resembles coarse meal with remainder in small (roughly pea-size) lumps. Add 1 tablespoon ice water and pulse 2 or 3 times, or just until incorporated. Test mixture by gently squeezing a small handful: When it has proper texture it should hold together without crumbling apart. If necessary add enough remaining water, 1 teaspoon at a time, pulsing 2 or 3 times after each addition until incorporated and testing, to give mixture proper texture. (If you overprocess dough mixture or add too much additional water, pastry will be tough.)

To form dough after blending by either method:

Turn mixture out onto a work surface and divide into 4 portions. With heel of your hand smear each portion once in a forward motion to help distribute fat. Gather dough together with a pastry scraper and form it, rotating it on work surface, into a disk. *Chill dough, wrapped in plastic wrap, until firm, at least 1 hour, and up to 1 day.* Makes enough dough for an 11-inch tart or a single-crust 9-inch pie.

DRIED-FRUIT MINCEMEAT PIE

For mincemeat
1½ cups mixed dried fruit such as pears,
    apricots, apples, prunes, peaches, and figs
½ cup pitted dates
½ teaspoon cinnamon
½ teaspoon ground allspice
¼ teaspoon freshly grated nutmeg
⅛ teaspoon salt
⅓ cup sugar
½ cup dried cranberries (about 3 ounces)
2 cups plus 2 tablespoons water
1 tablespoon cornstarch
2 tablespoons brandy

2 recipes pastry dough (page 217)
¾ cup pecans (about 3 ounces)
½ tablespoon water
1 large egg yolk
1 tablespoon sugar

Make mincemeat:

In a food processor coarsely chop mixed dried fruit and dates with spices, salt, and sugar. In a heavy saucepan combine dried-fruit mixture, cranberries, and 2 cups water and cook at a bare simmer, stirring occasionally, 10 minutes, or until fruit is tender (mixture will be very thick). In a small bowl stir together cornstarch and 2 tablespoons water until combined well. Stir cornstarch mixture into dried-fruit mixture and simmer, stirring frequently, 2 minutes. Stir in brandy and cool mincemeat. *Mincemeat may be used immediately but will improve in flavor if kept, covered and chilled, at least 1 day and up to 1 week. Bring mincemeat to room temperature before proceeding.*

Preheat oven to 375° F.

Keeping remaining dough chilled, on a lightly floured surface with a floured rolling pin roll out half of dough into a 13-inch round (about ⅛ inch thick). Fit round into a 9-inch (1-quart) glass pie plate and trim edge, leaving a ½-inch overhang. *Chill shell, covered, 30 minutes, or until firm.*

Coarsely chop pecans and in a shallow baking pan toast in middle of oven until a shade darker, about 4 minutes. Stir pecans into mincemeat and spoon into shell, smoothing top. Roll out remaining dough ⅛

inch thick and arrange over filling. Trim dough, leaving a ¾-inch overhang, and fold overhang under edge of bottom shell, pressing to seal. Crimp edge.

In a small bowl whisk together ½ tablespoon water and yolk and lightly brush crust with egg wash. Sprinkle crust with sugar and with a knife cut several steam vents.

Bake pie in middle of oven until crust is golden, 30 to 35 minutes, and transfer to a rack to cool. *Pie may be made 8 hours ahead and kept at room temperature. Serve pie warm or at room temperature.* Serves 6 to 8.

NECTARINE LIME CURD TART WITH A BROWN-SUGAR CRUST

For curd
1 firm-ripe medium nectarine
5 large egg yolks
⅓ cup granulated sugar
2 tablespoons fresh lime juice
2 tablespoons unsalted butter
⅛ teaspoon vanilla
For crust
¾ stick (6 tablespoons) cold unsalted butter
1 cup all-purpose flour
⅓ cup packed dark brown sugar
¼ teaspoon salt

4 firm-ripe medium nectarines
⅓ cup peach jam

Make curd:

Halve and pit nectarine. Cut halves into pieces and in a blender purée until smooth.

In a heavy saucepan whisk together purée, yolks, granulated sugar, lime juice, butter, and vanilla. Cook mixture over moderately low heat, whisking constantly, until it just reaches a boil, about 7 minutes, and immediately remove pan from heat.

Strain curd through a sieve into a bowl and cool, its surface covered with a buttered round of wax paper. *Chill curd at least 2 hours and up to 2 days.*

Make crust:

Preheat oven to 375° F.

Cut butter into pieces. In a food processor pulse flour, brown sugar, and salt until combined well. Add butter and blend until a dough begins to form (mixture should hold together when squeezed between fingers). Press dough evenly into bottom and up sides of a 13½- by 4- by 1-inch rectangular tart pan (or an 8½- by 1-inch round tart pan) with a removable fluted rim. Bake crust in middle of oven 20 minutes and cool in pan on a rack. *Crust may be made 2 days ahead and kept in pan, covered, at room temperature.*

Halve and pit nectarines. Cut halves into ¼-inch-thick slices. Spoon curd into shell, smoothing top, and arrange nectarine slices decoratively on top. In a small saucepan heat jam over low heat until hot. Pour jam through a sieve into a bowl, pressing hard on solids. Lightly brush fruit with glaze. Chill tart, loosely covered with plastic wrap, until ready to serve. *Tart may be made 1 day ahead and chilled, covered.* Serves 4 generously.

PHOTO ON PAGE 45

PEACH RASPBERRY TOP-CRUST PIES

If making more than 2 pies, do not double this recipe but make multiple batches.

2 recipes frozen-butter pastry dough (page 216)
7 pounds ripe peaches
1¾ cups sugar
⅔ cup cornstarch
3 tablespoons fresh lemon juice
2 teaspoons vanilla
2 cups raspberries (about 8 ounces)
2 large eggs

Divide dough in half. On a lightly floured surface with a lightly floured rolling pin roll out 1 piece of dough ¼ inch thick (about a 15-inch round), keeping remaining piece of dough chilled. Transfer round to a large baking sheet and chill, covered. Roll out and chill remaining dough in same manner and stack it on top of first round. *Chill pastry rounds, loosely covered with plastic wrap, 15 minutes.*

Cut an X in blossom end of each peach. Have ready a large bowl of ice and cold water. Fill a 5-quart kettle three fourths full with water and bring to a boil. Working in batches, blanch peaches 15 seconds and transfer with a slotted spoon to ice water. Slip skins from peaches and, working over a large bowl to catch the juices, cut peaches into ½-inch-thick wedges. Gently toss peaches with sugar, cornstarch, lemon juice, vanilla, and raspberries until combined well.

With a spoon divide filling between two 9-inch (1-quart) glass pie plates, mounding fruit. Juice should reach no higher than ¼ inch below rim of each pie plate. With spoon remove excess juice from pie plates and discard.

In a small bowl whisk eggs and evenly brush onto tops and undersides of pie plate rims. Cover each pie with a pastry round and trim pastry with scissors, leaving a ½-inch overhang and, if desired, reserving scraps for decorations. Brush undersides of overhang with some egg and press overhang onto and under rims of pie plates to seal. *Chill pies until pastry is firm, about 20 minutes.*

Preheat oven to 425° F.

On a lightly floured surface with a floured rolling pin roll out pastry scraps ¼ inch thick and with a sharp small knife cut out 2 decorations, transferring to a plate. *Chill decorations 15 minutes.*

Line 2 jelly-roll pans with foil.

Brush crusts evenly with some egg and arrange decorations in centers, pressing lightly to adhere. With a sharp knife cut three ¾-inch-long slits on top of each pie to form steam vents. Brush decorations with some egg and transfer pies to jelly-roll pans (to catch drips). Bake pies in upper and lower thirds of oven, staggering pans if possible on oven racks and switching position of pans halfway through baking, about 1 to 1¼ hours total, or until pastry is golden brown and cooked through. (If pastry gets too brown too quickly, tent pies with foil).

Let pies stand on racks to set juices at least 1½ hours before serving. *Pies may be made 1 day ahead and kept, loosely covered, at room temperature. If desired, reheat pies, uncovered, in a 350° F. oven.* Makes two 9-inch top-crust pies.

PHOTO ON PAGE 65

FROZEN-BUTTER PASTRY DOUGH

The trick to a successful pastry dough is to handle it as little as possible and to keep it cool. For 2 pies, you will need to make 2 batches of pastry dough (do not double the recipe).

2¼ cups cake flour (not self-rising)
¼ teaspoon salt
2 sticks (1 cup) unsalted butter, frozen
8 to 10 tablespoons ice water

Into a chilled large metal bowl sift together flour and salt. Set a grater in flour bowl and coarsely grate frozen butter into flour, gently lifting and tossing flour to coat butter. *Chill mixture 20 minutes.* Drizzle 6 tablespoons ice water evenly over mixture and gently stir with a fork until just incorporated. Gently squeeze a small handful of mixture to test for proper texture: It should hold together without crumbling apart. If necessary, add additional water, 1 tablespoon at a time and stirring until just incorporated, and test mixture again. (If you overwork or add too much water, pastry will be tough.)

Turn mixture out onto a lightly floured surface and with floured hands mound into 4 portions. With heel of hand smear each portion once in a forward motion to help distribute fat. Gather dough portions together and form dough, rotating it on work surface, into a disk (dough will not be smooth). *Chill dough, wrapped in plastic wrap, at least 2 hours, or until firm, and up to 2 days.* Makes enough dough for one 9- to 10-inch top-crust pie.

FROZEN PISTACHIO HALVAH PIE

5 tablespoons unsalted butter
nine 5- by 2½-inch graham crackers
½ cup shelled natural pistachios
⅓ cup sugar
⅔ cup milk
¼ teaspoon vanilla
⅔ cup crumbled halvah* (ground sesame-seed and honey candy; about 5 ounces)
1 cup well-chilled heavy cream

*available at Middle Eastern markets and some specialty foods shops and by mail order from Kalustyan's, (212) 685-3451

Preheat oven to 350° F.

Melt butter. Into a food processor break crackers and finely grind. With motor running, add butter. Press crumb mixture onto bottom and up side of a 9½-inch (5-cup) pie plate and bake in middle of oven 6 to 8 minutes, or until shell is a shade darker. Cool shell on a rack.

In a shallow baking pan toast pistachios in middle of oven 5 minutes, or until a shade darker. Reserve 1½ tablespoons pistachios for sprinkling on pie and finely chop remainder. In a saucepan dissolve sugar in milk over moderate heat, stirring, and remove pan from heat. In a metal bowl whisk milk mixture and vanilla into halvah until halvah is dissolved. Set bowl with halvah mixture in a larger bowl of ice and cold water and cool mixture, stirring occasionally.

In a bowl beat cream until it just holds stiff peaks. Fold cream and chopped pistachios into halvah mixture and pour into shell. *Freeze pie, uncovered, 1 hour.* Sprinkle reserved pistachios over pie. *Freeze pie, uncovered, until frozen hard, about 4 hours. Pie may be made 2 days ahead and frozen, covered with plastic wrap and foil after 5 hours. Let pie stand at room temperature about 15 minutes to slightly soften (for ease of cutting) before serving.* Serves 8.

PHOTO ON PAGE 57

SPICED PECAN PIE

1½ recipes pastry dough (recipe follows)
½ teaspoon anise seeds
1¼ cups sugar
2½ cups light corn syrup (about 20 ounces)
6 large eggs
¼ teaspoon ground cinnamon
¼ teaspoon ground ginger
a pinch ground cloves
⅛ teaspoon salt
2 cups pecan halves (about 8 ounces)

Accompaniment: superpremium vanilla ice cream such as Häagen-Dazs

On a lightly floured surface with a floured rolling pin roll out pastry dough into a 17-inch round (about

⅛ inch thick). Fit dough into a 10-inch glass pie plate (1½ quarts), and crimp edge decoratively. *Chill shell, covered, at least 1 hour and up to 1 day.*

Preheat oven to 350° F.

In an electric coffee/spice grinder finely grind anise seeds. In a dry heavy saucepan cook ½ cup sugar over moderately low heat, stirring slowly with a fork (to help sugar melt evenly), until melted and pale golden. Cook caramel, without stirring, swirling pan, until deep golden. Add corn syrup and simmer, stirring occasionally, until caramel is dissolved (caramel will harden before dissolving).

In a bowl whisk together remaining ¾ cup sugar, eggs, spices, and salt. Remove pan from heat and cool caramel mixture until it stops bubbling. In a slow stream carefully whisk caramel mixture into egg mixture. Spread pecans in shell and pour in filling, tapping down pecans to coat thoroughly.

Bake pie in middle of oven until crust is pale golden, 40 to 45 minutes (filling will not be set), and transfer to a rack to cool completely (filling will continue to set as pie cools).

Serve pie with ice cream. Serves 8 to 10.

PASTRY DOUGH ◐+

The amount of water necessary to make pastry dough is likely to change slightly from time to time, depending on variables such as humidity and the moisture content of butter and even, believe it or not, flour.

¾ stick (6 tablespoons) cold unsalted butter
1¼ cups all-purpose flour
2 tablespoons cold vegetable shortening
¼ teaspoon salt
2 to 4 tablespoons ice water

Cut butter into ½-inch cubes.
To blend by hand:
In a bowl with your fingertips or a pastry blender blend together flour, butter, shortening, and salt until most of mixture resembles coarse meal with remainder in small (roughly pea-size) lumps. Drizzle 2 tablespoons ice water evenly over mixture and gently stir with a fork until incorporated. Test mixture by gently squeezing a small handful: When it has proper texture it should hold together without crumbling apart. If necessary, add enough remaining water, 1 tablespoon at a time, stirring until incorporated and testing, to give mixture proper texture. (If you overwork mixture or add too much water, pastry will be tough.)

To blend in food processor:
In a food processor pulse together flour, butter, shortening, and salt until most of mixture resembles coarse meal with remainder in small (roughly pea-size) lumps. Add 2 tablespoons ice water and pulse 2 or 3 times, or just until incorporated. Test mixture by gently squeezing a small handful: When it has proper texture it should hold together without crumbling apart. If necessary, add enough remaining water, 1 tablespoon at a time, pulsing 2 or 3 times after each addition until incorporated and testing, to give mixture proper texture. (If you overprocess mixture or add too much water, pastry will be tough.)

To form dough after blending by either method:
Turn mixture out onto a work surface and divide into 4 portions. With heel of hand smear each portion once in a forward motion to help distribute fat. Gather dough together and form it, rotating it on work surface, into a disk. *Chill dough, wrapped in plastic wrap, until firm, at least 1 hour, and up to 1 day.* Makes enough dough for a single-crust 9-inch pie or an 11-inch tart.

ROASTED PINEAPPLE AND MACADAMIA NUT TART

Save the vanilla syrup used in roasting the pineapple to toss with sliced fruit.

For roasted pineapple
½ very ripe pineapple
3 vanilla beans
½ cup granulated sugar
¾ cup unsweetened pineapple juice
For shell
1 stick (½ cup) cold unsalted butter
½ cup confectioners' sugar
1 large egg
1 tablespoon vanilla
2 cups unbleached all-purpose flour
For filling
1¼ sticks (10 tablespoons) unsalted butter
1 cup confectioners' sugar
½ cup unbleached all-purpose flour
½ cup macadamia nuts (about 3 ounces)
2 large eggs

Make roasted pineapple:
Preheat oven to 400° F.

Peel and core pineapple. Cut enough pineapple into ½-inch chunks to measure 1½ cups. Split vanilla beans lengthwise and scrape out seeds, reserving pods and seeds.

In an ovenproof 5-quart heavy kettle (about 10 inches in diameter) cook granulated sugar over moderately low heat, stirring slowly with a fork (to help sugar melt evenly), until melted and pale golden. Cook caramel, without stirring, swirling kettle, until deep golden. Remove kettle from heat and carefully add pineapple juice down side of kettle. (Mixture will steam and harden.) Add reserved vanilla seeds and pods and cook mixture, stirring, until caramel is dissolved. Stir in pineapple and roast in middle of oven, stirring about every 10 minutes, for 30 minutes. Cool pineapple in syrup to room temperature.

Make shell:
Cut butter into ½-inch pieces and in a food processor pulse together with confectioners' sugar until combined well. Add egg and vanilla and pulse until combined (mixture will look curdled). Add

flour and pulse until mixture forms a dough. Form dough into a disk. *Chill dough, wrapped in plastic wrap, 1 hour.*

On a lightly floured surface with a floured rolling pin roll out dough ³⁄₁₆ inch thick (about a 12-inch round) and fit into a fluted 9-inch tart pan with a removable bottom. Roll rolling pin over rim of pan to trim overhang and lightly press dough up side of pan. Chill shell, covered, 15 minutes.

Preheat oven to 350° F.

Make filling:
Cut butter into 1-inch pieces. In a small heavy saucepan heat butter over moderate heat, swirling pan occasionally, until golden brown with a nutlike fragrance. (Bottom of pan will be covered with brown specks.) Remove pan from heat and cool brown butter. In a food processor pulse together confectioners' sugar, flour, and nuts until nuts are finely ground. Add eggs and pulse until just combined. Stir butter, scraping up brown specks, and add to egg mixture, pulsing until just combined.

Pour filling into shell, smoothing top. Drain pineapple in a sieve set over a bowl and reserve syrup (see headnote). Decoratively arrange pineapple over filling. Bake tart in middle of oven until filling is golden brown, about 30 minutes (filling will rise to partially cover pineapple), and transfer to a rack to cool. *Tart may be made 1 day ahead and kept, covered, at cool room temperature.* Serves 12.

PHOTO ON PAGE 39

Strawberry Lime Tart with Spun Sugar

For lime mousse
1½ teaspoons unflavored gelatin
1½ tablespoons cold water
½ cup fresh lime juice
2½ teaspoons finely grated fresh lime zest
¼ cup plus ⅓ cup sugar
1 large egg white
1 cup well-chilled heavy cream

sablé tart shell (recipe follows)
2 pints strawberries (about
    1½ pounds)
spun sugar (optional; page 220)

Make mousse:

In a small bowl sprinkle gelatin over 1½ table-spoons cold water and let soften 1 minute. In a small saucepan heat gelatin mixture, lime juice, zest, and ¼ cup sugar over moderately low heat, stirring, just until sugar and gelatin are dissolved and cool to room temperature.

Set a metal bowl over a saucepan and put enough water in pan so that bottom of bowl just touches the water. Remove bowl from pan and bring water to a boil. In bowl with a metal spoon stir together egg white and remaining ⅓ cup sugar until combined. Remove pan of boiling water from heat and immediately set bowl over pan. Stir egg mixture gently with spoon (keep mixture as froth-free as possible because the froth cooks more quickly) 1 minute (for egg safety).

With an electric mixer beat egg mixture at high speed 5 minutes, or until cool. Reduce speed to medium and beat meringue 3 minutes more, or until it holds tiny peaks. In another bowl beat cream until it holds soft peaks. Gradually stir lime mixture into meringue until combined (mixture will be thin and not completely smooth) and fold in whipped cream gently but thoroughly.

Spoon mousse into tart shell, smoothing top. *Chill tart, uncovered, at least 4 hours, or until mousse is set, and, covered, up to 1 day.*

Trim strawberries and arrange, cut sides down, over tart. Gently gather threads of spun sugar together and arrange over tart. Serves 8.

PHOTO ON PAGE 43

Sablé Tart Shell

We baked the shell in an 8¾- by 1⅝-inch cake ring, available at many cookware shops and by mail order from Bridge Kitchenware, (800) 274-3435 or (212) 838-1901. You can also use a 9- by 1-inch tart pan with a removable bottom, although the mousse layer will not be as thick.

¼ cup whole blanched almonds
1 large egg
1 vanilla bean
5 tablespoons unsalted butter,
    softened
¼ cup confectioners' sugar
⅛ teaspoon salt
1 cup all-purpose flour
pie weights or raw rice for weighting
    shell

In an electric coffee/spice grinder finely grind almonds. In a small bowl lightly beat egg. Split vanilla bean lengthwise and scrape seeds into a bowl. Add butter, confectioners' sugar, and salt and with an electric mixer beat until smooth. Beat in ground almonds and 3 tablespoons beaten egg, beating until smooth, and stir in flour until just combined. Discard remaining egg. Gather dough into a ball and flatten into a disk. *Chill dough, wrapped in plastic wrap, until firm, about 1 hour, and up to 1 day.*

Roll out dough between sheets of plastic wrap into a 12-inch round. Remove top sheet of plastic wrap. Invert dough into an 8¾- by 1⅝-inch cake ring set on a baking sheet or a 9- by 1-inch tart pan with removable bottom and ease dough into ring or pan, pressing to fit. *Chill shell, covered with remaining sheet of plastic wrap, until firm, about 20 minutes.*

Preheat oven to 375° F.

Remove plastic wrap and trim dough flush with edge of ring or pan. Line shell with foil, shiny side down, and fill with pie weights or raw rice. Bake shell in middle of oven 15 minutes. Carefully remove foil and pie weights or rice and bake shell until deep golden, about 15 minutes more. Cool shell in ring on baking sheet on a rack or in pan on a rack. *Shell may be made 1 day ahead and kept, wrapped well in plastic wrap, at room temperature.*

SPUN SUGAR ☺

parchment paper
1 cup sugar
¼ cup water

Cover a work surface with parchment paper. In a small heavy saucepan bring sugar and water to a boil over moderate heat, stirring and washing down any sugar crystals clinging to side of pan with a brush dipped in water, until sugar is dissolved. Boil syrup, without stirring, until very pale golden and remove pan from heat, swirling caramel gently until it stops cooking (caramel will turn a darker golden amber). Cool caramel, without stirring, until thick enough to drizzle in a thin thread, about 8 minutes.

In 1 hand hold 2 forks back to back and dip tines into caramel, letting excess caramel drip back into pan. Rapidly wave forks back and forth over parchment paper to form threads. Repeat procedure. *Spun sugar may be made 1 day ahead and kept in an airtight container at room temperature.*

FROZEN DESSERTS

ARMAGNAC ICE CREAM

½ cup plus 1 tablespoon Armagnac
1 cup heavy cream
1½ cups milk
8 large egg yolks
⅔ cup sugar

Have ready a large bowl of ice and cold water. In a 1½-quart heavy saucepan simmer ½ cup Armagnac (being careful not to let ignite) until reduced by about half. Stir in cream and milk and bring mixture to a simmer. In a bowl whisk together yolks and sugar. Add hot milk mixture to yolk mixture in a slow stream, whisking. Transfer mixture to cleaned saucepan and cook over moderate heat, stirring constantly with a wooden spoon, until slightly thickened and a thermometer registers 170° F. (do not let boil). Pour custard through a fine sieve into a metal bowl set in ice water. Stir in remaining tablespoon Armagnac and cool custard completely.

Freeze custard in an ice-cream maker. Transfer ice cream to an airtight container and put in freezer to harden. *Armagnac ice cream may be made 1 week ahead.* Makes about 1 quart.

BLACK COW ICE-CREAM SODAS ☺

about 16 ounces chilled root beer
2 scoops vanilla ice cream

Fill 2 tall glasses two thirds full with root beer and top each with a scoop of ice cream.

Serve black cows with straws and long-handled spoons. Makes 2 drinks.

WHITE-GRAPE GRANITAS ☺+

1½ cups bottled white grape juice
¼ cup vodka
1 teaspoon grenadine

Pour juice into a shallow metal baking pan. Pour vodka into a small metal bowl. *Freeze both separately, covered, 24 hours (vodka will not freeze solid).*

With tines of a fork scrape frozen juice, crushing lumps. Divide three fourths granita among 4 small bowls or glasses and drizzle grenadine over each serving. Spoon vodka over granita in bowls and top with remaining granita. Serves 4.

PHOTO ON PAGE 82

☞ each serving about 95 calories and less than 1 gram fat

TOMATO BLACK-PEPPER GRANITA

This palate cleanser is a take on the Italian combination of strawberries, black pepper, and balsamic vinegar.

2 pounds vine-ripened tomatoes
¼ cup superfine granulated sugar
2 teaspoons coarsely ground black pepper
1 teaspoon balsamic vinegar

Quarter tomatoes and in a food processor purée with sugar until smooth. Pour purée through a sieve into a shallow metal baking pan, pressing hard on solids. Stir in pepper and vinegar until combined well. *Freeze tomato mixture, covered, stirring and crushing lumps with a fork about every 30 minutes, until no longer slushy but not frozen solid, 2 to 3 hours. Granita may be made 2 days ahead and frozen, covered.*

Just before serving, scrape granita with a fork to lighten and break up ice. Makes about 1 quart.

GINGER ICE CREAM

4 large egg yolks
½ cup sugar
¼ cup coarsely grated peeled fresh gingerroot
2 tablespoons water
2 cups half-and-half
1 cup heavy cream
1 teaspoon vanilla
½ cup crystallized ginger*

*available at some supermarkets and specialty
  foods shops and by mail order from
  Williams-Sonoma, (800) 541-1262

In a large bowl lightly whisk yolks. In a 3-quart heavy saucepan cook sugar, fresh gingerroot, and water over moderate heat, stirring occasionally, 5 minutes. Add half-and-half and bring to a simmer. Add hot half-and-half mixture to yolks in a slow stream, whisking, and pour into pan. Cook custard over moderately low heat, stirring constantly, until a thermometer registers 170° F. (Do not let boil.)

Pour custard through a sieve into cleaned bowl and stir in cream and vanilla. Cool custard. *Chill custard, its surface covered with plastic wrap, until cold, at least 3 hours, and up to 1 day.*

Finely chop crystallized ginger. Freeze custard in an ice-cream maker, adding crystallized ginger three fourths of way through freezing process. Transfer ice cream to an airtight container and put in freezer to harden. *Ice cream may be made 1 week ahead.* Makes about 1 quart.

GINGERSNAP ICE-CREAM SUNDAES WITH RUM SYRUP ◌

2 tablespoons dark rum
1 tablespoon water
1 teaspoon sugar
six 2-inch gingersnap cookies
about ½ pint vanilla ice cream

In a small saucepan simmer dark rum, water, and sugar, stirring until sugar is dissolved, about 1 minute. Pour syrup into a small metal bowl and cool to room temperature. Break cookies into small pieces.

Scoop ice cream into 2 bowls and top with cookie pieces. Drizzle rum syrup over sundaes. Serves 2.

FRESH MINT CHOCOLATE CHIP ICE CREAM

2 cups heavy cream
1 cup whole milk
2 cups packed fresh mint leaves
2 large eggs
¾ cup sugar
3 ounces fine-quality bittersweet chocolate

In a blender blend cream, milk, and mint until mint is finely chopped. In a saucepan bring cream mixture just to a boil and cool 15 minutes. Whisk in eggs and sugar and cook over moderate heat, stirring constantly, until slightly thickened and a thermometer registers 170° F. (Do not let custard boil or it will curdle.) Pour custard through a fine sieve into a bowl. *Chill custard, its surface covered with plastic wrap, until cold, at least 3 hours, and up to 1 day.* Chop chocolate. Freeze custard in an ice-cream maker. Transfer ice cream to an airtight container and stir in chocolate. Put ice cream in freezer to harden. Makes about 1 quart.

MINTED HONEYDEW SORBET

1 small honeydew melon
1 cup minted simple syrup
   (recipe follows)
¼ cup packed fresh mint leaves
1 tablespoon fresh lemon juice

Remove and discard rind and seeds from melon and cut enough fruit into ½-inch cubes to measure 2½ cups. In a blender purée all ingredients until smooth. *Chill purée, covered, until cold, at least 1 hour, and up to 6.* Freeze purée in an ice-cream maker. Transfer sorbet to an airtight container and put in freezer to harden. Makes about 3½ cups.

MINTED SIMPLE SYRUP ☉

1½ cups packed fresh mint leaves
1 cup sugar
1 cup water

Chop mint. In a saucepan bring sugar, water and mint to a boil, stirring until sugar is dissolved. Simmer syrup, undisturbed, 2 minutes. Pour syrup through a fine sieve, pressing hard on solids, and cool. *Syrup keeps, covered and chilled, 2 weeks.* Makes about 1½ cups.

FROZEN PASSION-FRUIT PARFAITS WITH KIWIFRUIT-PINEAPPLE SALSA, STRAWBERRY COULIS, AND COCOA SPIRALS

If you wish to garnish these parfaits with cocoa spirals, you'll need to make the parfaits in conical molds such as short beer glasses; Martini glasses will also work. Otherwise, use any 1-cup molds.

For frozen parfaits
2 pounds fresh passion fruits* (about 25)
   or 1 cup passion-fruit purée, such as
   Goya brand*, thawed if frozen
3 tablespoons fresh lemon juice
1 cup well-chilled heavy cream
1 vanilla bean
3 large egg whites**
½ cup sugar

For strawberry coulis
1 pint strawberries (about ½ pound)
2 tablespoons sugar, or to taste
1 teaspoon fresh lime juice, or to taste
For kiwifruit-pineapple salsa
4 kiwifruits (about ¾ pound)
½ pineapple
1 teaspoon fresh lime juice
1 teaspoon finely chopped fresh mint leaves
2 tablespoons water
2 tablespoons sugar

Garnish: 6 cocoa spirals (recipe follows)
   and fresh mint leaves

*available at Latino markets and some
   supermarkets
**if egg safety is a problem in your area, substitute powdered egg whites (such as Just Whites, available at some supermarkets and by mail order from New York Cake and Baking Distributors, 800-942-2539), reconstituted

Make parfaits:
Halve fresh passion fruits, if using, and scoop pulp and seeds into a blender. Blend pulp and seeds briefly (seeds should still be in large pieces). Force fruit through a fine sieve into a measuring cup, pressing on solids, and discard solids. In a bowl combine 1 cup fresh purée or thawed frozen purée and lemon juice.

Put cream in a large bowl. Split vanilla bean lengthwise. Scrape seeds into cream and reserve pod for another use. With an electric mixer beat cream until it just holds stiff peaks.

In a bowl with cleaned beaters beat whites (or reconstituted powdered whites) until they just hold soft peaks. Gradually beat in sugar and continue to beat until meringue holds stiff, glossy peaks. Fold passion-fruit mixture into cream until just combined and fold in meringue gently but thoroughly. Divide mixture among 6 conical glasses or other 1-cup molds (see headnote) and tightly cover with plastic wrap. *Freeze parfaits until frozen, at least 3 hours, and up to 3 days.*
Make coulis:
Trim strawberries and in a blender purée with sugar and lime juice. Pour *coulis* through a fine sieve

222

into a bowl. *Coulis may be made 2 days ahead and chilled, covered.*

Make salsa:

Peel kiwifruits and cut into ¼-inch dice. Core pineapple and peel. Cut pineapple into ¼-inch dice. In a bowl stir together kiwifruits, pineapple, lime juice, and mint. In a small saucepan heat water and sugar over moderate heat, stirring, until sugar is dissolved and stir into fruit mixture. *Salsa may be made 1 day ahead and chilled, covered.*

Assemble desserts:

Spoon *coulis* onto 6 plates, tilting plates to coat, and spoon salsa into center. If using glasses, before unmolding parfaits remove plastic wrap and, holding each glass by the stem, invert under hot running water a few seconds. (If using 1-cup molds, set in pan of hot water for a few seconds.) Run a small thin knife around edge of each glass or mold. Holding each parfait in place with a metal spatula, invert glass or mold on top of salsa and carefully remove spatula and glass or mold. Gently put a cocoa spiral over each parfait and garnish with mint. Serves 6.

PHOTO ON PAGE 22

COCOA SPIRALS ◓

¾ cup all-purpose flour
¼ cup unsweetened cocoa powder
2 teaspoons baking powder
⅔ cup milk
1 large egg
1 tablespoon honey
2 to 4 tablespoons vegetable oil

Into a bowl sift together flour, cocoa powder, and baking powder. In a small bowl stir together milk, egg, and honey and stir into flour mixture until combined. Transfer batter to a squeeze bottle or sealable plastic bag.

In a skillet heat 2 tablespoons oil over moderate heat until hot but not smoking. Cut a ¼-inch hole in 1 corner of sealed plastic bag, if using, and squeeze or drizzle batter into oil in a 5-inch spiral, starting in center. Cook spiral until puffed and just cooked through, 15 to 30 seconds (spiral will be soft). With a large metal spatula transfer spiral to a rack set over a baking pan to drain. Make more spirals in same

manner, adding remaining oil as necessary. *Cocoa spirals may be made 1 day ahead and chilled, stacked between small squares of wax paper, in an airtight container.*

VANILLA BEAN ICE CREAM ◓+

2 vanilla beans
3 cups heavy cream
1 cup whole milk
1½ cups sugar
3 large eggs

With a knife halve vanilla beans lengthwise. Scrape seeds into a large heavy saucepan and stir in pods, cream, milk, and sugar. Bring cream mixture just to a boil, stirring occasionally, and remove pan from heat.

In a large bowl lightly beat eggs. Add hot cream mixture to eggs in a slow stream, whisking, and pour into pan. Cook custard over moderately low heat, stirring constantly, until a thermometer registers 170° F. (Do not let boil.) Pour custard through a sieve into a clean bowl and cool. *Chill custard, its surface covered with wax paper, at least 3 hours, or until cold, and up to 1 day.*

Freeze custard in an ice-cream maker, in 2 batches if necessary. Transfer ice cream to an airtight container and put in freezer to harden. *Ice cream may be made 1 week ahead.* Makes about 1½ quarts.

PHOTO ON PAGE 65

WATERMELON ICE +

⅓ cup water
½ cup sugar
a 3-pound piece chilled watermelon
1 tablespoon fresh lemon juice

In a small saucepan simmer water with sugar, stirring until sugar is dissolved. Transfer syrup to a bowl set in a larger bowl of ice and cold water and stir syrup until cold.

Discard rind from watermelon. Cut fruit into 1-inch chunks. In a blender purée watermelon, syrup, and lemon juice and pour through a fine sieve into a 9-inch square metal baking pan, pressing hard on solids. *Freeze mixture, covered, until frozen, 6 to 8 hours, and up to 2 days.*

Just before serving, scrape watermelon ice with a fork to lighten texture and break up ice crystals. Makes about 5 cups, serving 6.

PHOTO ON PAGE 61

FRUIT FINALES

BAKED PECAN-STUFFED NECTARINES

⅓ cup pecan halves
2½ tablespoons sugar
1 large egg yolk
2 firm-ripe nectarines

Garnish: 4 pecan halves
Accompaniment: superpremium vanilla
   ice cream

Preheat oven to 425° F.

In a small food processor pulse pecans until finely ground. Add 2 tablespoons sugar and yolk and pulse until combined. Halve and pit nectarines and arrange, cut sides up, on a baking sheet. Divide pecan mixture among nectarine halves, mounding it in center, and garnish each mound with a pecan half. Sprinkle nectarines with remaining ½ tablespoon sugar.

Bake stuffed nectarines in middle of oven until pecan mixture is golden, about 10 minutes.

Serve nectarines with ice cream. Serves 2.

ROASTED SPICED PEARS AND FIGS
WITH ALMONDS

½ cup sliced almonds
4 firm-ripe pears (preferably Bartlett)
½ pound dried figs (as soft as possible;
   about 12)
½ cup sugar
½ stick (¼ cup) unsalted butter
1 vanilla bean
1 teaspoon cinnamon
¼ teaspoon ground allspice

Accompaniment: sour cream

Preheat oven to 450° F.

In an ovenproof 10-inch heavy skillet toast almonds in one layer in middle of oven until golden, about 5 minutes, and transfer to a bowl.

Halve pears lengthwise and cut each half into 3 wedges, discarding cores. Quarter figs lengthwise.

In skillet melt sugar and butter over moderate heat, stirring occasionally, until sugar is melted completely and remove skillet from heat. With a knife halve vanilla bean lengthwise and scrape seeds into butter mixture. With a wooden spoon stir in vanilla pod, cinnamon, allspice, pears, and figs until coated and roast in middle of oven 20 minutes, or until pears are just tender. Remove pod and with spoon stir in almonds until coated well.

Serve roasted fruit mixture warm with sour cream. Serves 8.

PHOTO ON PAGE 81

CARAMELIZED PINEAPPLE WITH RUM ◎

1 large pineapple
2 tablespoons unsalted butter
3 tablespoons packed brown sugar
  (preferably dark)
2 tablespoons rum (preferably dark)

Accompaniment: super-premium ice cream
  such as Häagen-Dazs

Preheat broiler and line bottom and sides of a shallow baking pan with foil.

Trim pineapple leaves to about 2 inches. Quarter pineapple lengthwise, reserving 2 quarters for another use. Cut and discard cores from remaining quarters. With a sharp knife cut fruit from rinds, keeping rinds intact and reserving them. Cut pineapple crosswise into ¼-inch-thick slices.

In a small saucepan cook butter, 2 tablespoons brown sugar, and rum over moderate heat, stirring, 1 minute. Add pineapple, stirring to coat, and cook mixture 1 minute.

Put reserved rinds in baking pan and with a fork and spoon return pineapple pieces to rinds, arranging in original shape. Spoon remaining butter mixture over pineapple and sprinkle tops with remaining tablespoon brown sugar. Broil pineapple about 3 inches from heat until slightly charred and heated through, about 8 minutes.

Serve caramelized pineapple with ice cream. Serves 2.

PLUMS IN WHITE PEPPERCORN
AND VANILLA SYRUP

1 tablespoon white peppercorns
1 vanilla bean
4 cups water
1½ cups sugar
8 plums (about 2 pounds)

With a mortar and pestle or with bottom of heavy skillet coarsely crush peppercorns. With a knife halve vanilla bean lengthwise. In a small kettle simmer pepper, vanilla bean, water, and sugar, stirring until sugar is dissolved, 10 minutes. Pour syrup through a fine sieve into a bowl and return syrup to kettle.

Pit plums and cut each plum into 12 wedges. Have ready a large bowl of ice and cold water. Bring syrup just to a simmer and stir in plums. Simmer plums just until tender, 1 to 2 minutes. With a slotted spoon transfer plums to a large metal bowl set in bowl of ice water and stir gently until cool. Boil syrup until reduced to about 3 cups and remove kettle from heat. Cool syrup to room temperature and stir into plums. *Plums may be made 2 days ahead and chilled, covered.* Serve plums chilled or at room temperature. Serves 8.

PHOTO ON PAGE 57

PINEAPPLE WITH BASIL ◎

½ ripe pineapple (about 1½ pounds)
1 teaspoon sugar
1 teaspoon fresh lemon juice, or to taste
2 tablespoons chopped fresh basil leaves

Garnish: fresh basil sprigs

Peel and core pineapple. Cut pineapple into bite-size pieces. In a large bowl gently toss pineapple with sugar, lemon juice, and chopped basil.

Serve pineapple garnished with basil sprigs.

🍃 each serving about 61 calories and 1.5 grams fat

PHOTO ON PAGE 86

WATERMELON SALAD ◎

a 2-pound piece watermelon (preferably
  seedless)
1 lime
1 tablespoon chopped fresh cilantro
  leaves
1½ tablespoons light rum, or to taste

Remove rind and any seeds from watermelon and cut fruit into 1-inch pieces. Into a bowl finely grate zest from lime and squeeze enough juice to measure 2 teaspoons. Stir in watermelon, cilantro, and rum and toss to combine. *Chill watermelon salad 15 minutes.* Serves 2 as a light dessert or a snack.

ALMOND TOFFEE BARK

3 cups (10 ounces) sliced almonds
1 stick (½ cup) unsalted butter, softened
1½ cups sugar
⅓ cup water
1 tablespoon fresh lemon juice
½ teaspoon vanilla
¼ teaspoon salt
6 ounces fine-quality bittersweet chocolate

Preheat oven to 350° F. Oil a large baking sheet.

In a large baking pan spread almonds evenly and toast in middle of oven, stirring halfway through toasting, until golden, about 10 minutes total.

In a 3-quart heavy saucepan bring butter, sugar, water, lemon juice, vanilla, and salt to a boil over moderate heat, stirring with a wooden spoon. Boil mixture, without stirring, swirling pan occasionally, until deep golden, about 12 minutes.

Remove saucepan from heat and stir in two thirds almonds. Immediately pour toffee onto baking sheet and with an offset spatula spread in a thin layer. Carefully transfer baking sheet to a rack and cool toffee.

Chop chocolate. In a double boiler or a small metal bowl set over a saucepan of barely simmering water melt chocolate, stirring until smooth. Pour chocolate over cooled toffee and evenly spread with offset spatula. Sprinkle toffee with remaining nuts. *Chill toffee, uncovered, until firm, about 1 hour.*

Break toffee into 2-inch pieces of "bark." *Bark keeps, layered between sheets of wax paper in an airtight container at cool room temperature or chilled, 1 week.* Makes about 36 pieces.

BUTTER RUM CARAMELS

1½ cups heavy cream
1 cup granulated sugar
1 cup packed light brown sugar
⅓ cup light corn syrup
½ stick (¼ cup) unsalted butter
½ teaspoon salt
2 teaspoons rum extract

Butter an 8-inch square metal baking pan (do not use glass) and set on a rack.

In a 5-quart heavy kettle cook cream, sugars, corn syrup, butter, and salt over moderate heat, stirring constantly with a wooden spoon and washing down any sugar crystals clinging to side of pan with a brush dipped in cold water, until sugars are completely dissolved, about 15 minutes. Boil mixture, without stirring, until a candy or digital thermometer registers 245° F., about 15 minutes. Remove pan from heat and add extract, swirling pan until combined. Immediately pour caramel into baking pan set on rack and cool completely. *Chill caramel until firm, at least 12 hours, and up to 1 week.*

Line a cutting board with wax paper and invert caramel onto it. *Bring caramel to room temperature, about 30 minutes.* With an oiled sharp knife cut caramel into ¾- by ⅓-inch pieces.

Individually wrap caramel pieces in wax paper or candy wrappers or layer between sheets of wax paper (do not use foil or parchment paper) in an airtight container. *Caramels keep at cool room temperature 2 weeks.* Makes about 70 caramels.

CREAMY BROWN-SUGAR FUDGE

2 ounces fine-quality white chocolate
2 tablespoons cold unsalted butter
1½ cups packed light brown sugar
1½ cups granulated sugar
¾ cup plus 2 tablespoons heavy cream
¼ teaspoon salt
2 teaspoons vanilla

Lightly oil an 8-inch square glass baking dish.

Coarsely chop chocolate and butter and chill. In a 4-quart heavy saucepan cook sugars, cream, and salt over low heat, stirring constantly with a wooden spoon and washing down any sugar crystals clinging to side of pan with a brush dipped in cold water, until sugar is completely dissolved, about 10 minutes. Increase heat to moderate and boil mixture, without stirring, until a candy or digital thermometer registers 238° F.

Remove pan from heat (leave thermometer in pan) and add chocolate, butter, and vanilla (do not stir). Cool fudge, without stirring, in pan until thermometer registers 130° F., about 30 minutes. With a hand-held electric mixer on high speed beat fudge until it turns pale, loses its gloss, and just begins to set, about 1 to 2 minutes. Immediately pour fudge into baking dish and smooth top with an offset spatula. Cool fudge completely. *Chill fudge, covered, until firm, at least 6 hours, and up to 1 week.* Cut fudge in baking dish into ¾-inch squares. *Fudge keeps, layered between sheets of wax paper in an airtight container and chilled, 1 month. Fudge must be served chilled.* Makes about 100 pieces.

PEPPERMINT PATTIES

3¼ cups (14 ounces) confectioners' sugar
2 tablespoons plus 1 teaspoon water
1 tablespoon light corn syrup
1 teaspoon fresh lemon juice
¼ teaspoon peppermint extract
6 ounces fine-quality bittersweet chocolate

Sift confectioners' sugar into bowl of a standing electric mixer or a large bowl. In a small bowl stir together water, corn syrup, lemon juice, and extract and add to sugar. With standing or a hand-held mixer beat together sugar mixture until combined.

On a work surface knead mixture into a ball (mixture will be stiff). With a rolling pin, applying pressure, roll out mixture between sheets of wax paper into a 9-inch round (about ¼ inch thick). Remove top sheet of wax paper from round and replace it loosely. Flip over wax paper–enclosed round and remove and discard sheet of wax paper now on top (this prevents round from sticking to wax paper). *Let round stand at room temperature until edges are firm, about 4 hours. Round may be made 1 week ahead and chilled on a tray, both tray and round wrapped together in plastic wrap. Bring round to room temperature before proceeding.*

Oil a large baking sheet and line with wax paper. With a 1¼-inch cutter cut out patties from round, transferring them as cut to baking sheet.

Temper chocolate (procedure follows) or chop chocolate and in a double boiler or a small metal bowl set over a saucepan of barely simmering water melt chocolate, stirring until smooth. (Tempering chocolate makes for glossier, firmer shells.)

Balance 1 patty on a fork (do not spear it) and submerge in chocolate (if necessary, spoon chocolate over patty to evenly coat). Holding patty on fork over chocolate, shake off any excess chocolate from patty and return patty to baking sheet. Submerge and coat remaining patties in same manner. *Chill peppermint patties on sheet, uncovered, until firm, about 1 hour. Peppermint patties keep, layered between sheets of wax paper in an airtight container and chilled, 1 month.* Makes about 36 patties.

TO TEMPER BITTERSWEET CHOCOLATE

In this procedure we used a metal bowl that fits snugly on top of a saucepan, but a double boiler will also work.

Have ready a 3- to 4-quart saucepan and a metal bowl large enough to fit on top. Make sure that when saucepan is filled one third full with water, bottom of bowl is not touching water.

Chop chocolate into no larger than ¼-inch dice and transfer three fourths dice to metal bowl. Fill saucepan one third full with water and bring water to a boil. Remove pan from heat. Set bowl with chocolate over pan (do not let bowl touch water) and melt chocolate, stirring, until a digital or chocolate thermometer inserted at least ½ inch into chocolate registers 118°–120° F. (If chocolate does not reach desired temperature, remove bowl, return water in pan to a boil, and repeat procedure.)

Remove bowl from pan and cool chocolate by adding remaining chopped chocolate and stirring until smooth. Let chocolate cool until thermometer registers 80° F.

Return water in pan to a boil and remove from heat. Set bowl over pan and reheat melted chocolate, stirring until thermometer registers 88°–91° F.

227

COFFEE CHOCOLATE TRUFFLE KISSES

9 ounces fine-quality bittersweet chocolate
  (not unsweetened)
¾ stick (6 tablespoons) unsalted butter, softened
½ cup heavy cream
4 teaspoons instant espresso powder*
¼ teaspoon salt
parchment paper
1 cup unsweetened cocoa powder

*available at many supermarkets and by mail
  order from Adriana's Caravan, (800) 316-0820

Break chocolate into small pieces. In a food processor pulse together chocolate and butter until chocolate is finely chopped. In a small saucepan whisk together cream, espresso powder, and salt and bring just to a boil. Pour hot cream mixture over chocolate mixture and pulse until smooth. Transfer mixture to a bowl. *Let chocolate mixture stand at cool room temperature until just firm enough to pipe, about 2 hours.*

Oil a large baking sheet and line sheet with parchment paper.

Transfer chocolate mixture to a pastry bag fitted with a ½-inch plain tip. Pipe mixture onto baking sheet to form 1- by 1-inch cones, or "kisses." *Chill kisses, uncovered, until firm, at least 3 hours, and up to 1 day.*

Into a small bowl sift cocoa powder. Working with 1 kiss at a time, roll in cocoa powder to coat. *Kisses keep, in one layer in an airtight container at cool room temperature or chilled, 2 weeks.* Makes about 64 kisses.

PISTACHIO PRALINES

These are based on the wonderful pecan pralines of noted cookbook author and columnist Marion Cunningham.

parchment paper
1½ cups (8 ounces) shelled natural pistachios
2 tablespoons unsalted butter, softened
1 tablespoon granulated sugar
2 cups packed light brown sugar
⅓ cup packed dark brown sugar
1 cup heavy cream
¼ teaspoon salt
1 teaspoon vanilla

Preheat oven to 350° F. Oil 2 large baking sheets and line with parchment paper.

In a baking pan spread pistachios evenly and toast in middle of oven until fragrant, about 10 minutes. In a bowl toss hot pistachios with butter and granulated sugar and cool completely.

In a 4-quart heavy saucepan cook brown sugars, cream, and salt over moderately low heat, stirring constantly with a wooden spoon and washing down any sugar crystals clinging to side of pan with a brush dipped in cold water, until sugars are completely dissolved, about 10 minutes. Increase heat to moderate and boil mixture, without stirring, until a candy or digital thermometer registers 238° F.

Remove pan from heat (leave thermometer in pan) and cool mixture until thermometer registers 220° F., about 5 to 10 minutes. With a wooden spoon stir in vanilla and vigorously stir mixture until creamy and beginning to lose its sheen. Working quickly, drop mixture by teaspoons onto baking sheets and top each praline with 3 pistachios. (If mixture becomes too stiff to spoon, warm it over low heat, stirring, until just workable.) *Let pralines stand at room temperature until firm, about 1 hour. Pralines keep, layered between sheets of parchment paper in an airtight container at cool room temperature or chilled, 1 week.* Makes about 60 pralines.

PRUNE KUMQUAT STICKY PUDDING WITH ARMAGNAC TOFFEE SAUCE

The rich flavors in this moist cake intensify with a bit of age—leftover cake is excellent served plain with tea or coffee. For extra height, we call for an 11-cup Kugelhopf pan (available by mail order from Bridge Kitchenware, (800) 274-3435 or (212) 838-1901). An 11-cup bundt pan makes a slightly broader cake.

1¾ cups packed pitted prunes (about
    14 ounces)
½ cup Armagnac
1¼ cups water
6 kumquats
1½ cups granulated sugar
3 cups all-purpose flour
1¼ teaspoons baking soda
1 teaspoon ginger
½ teaspoon ground allspice
¾ teaspoon salt
2 sticks (1 cup) unsalted butter, softened
1¼ cups packed light brown sugar
4 large eggs
1 teaspoon vanilla

Garnish: kumquats (preferably with leaves)
Accompaniments:
Armagnac toffee sauce (recipe follows)
Armagnac ice cream (page 220)

Preheat oven to 350° F. and generously butter an 11-cup *Kugelhopf* pan or 11-cup bundt pan.

Halve prunes and in a small saucepan simmer with Armagnac and ¾ cup water, uncovered, 5 minutes. With a slotted spoon transfer prunes to a shallow dish to cool. Boil Armagnac mixture until reduced to about ½ cup and add to prunes.

Halve kumquats lengthwise and thinly slice crosswise. In a small saucepan bring remaining ½ cup water with ¼ cup granulated sugar to a simmer, stirring until sugar is dissolved. Add kumquats and simmer 10 minutes. In a fine sieve drain kumquats and add to prunes.

Into a bowl sift together flour, baking soda, ginger, allspice, and salt. Resift mixture into another bowl. In a large bowl with an electric mixer beat together butter, remaining 1¼ cups granulated sugar, and brown sugar until light and fluffy. Add eggs 1 at a time, beating well after each addition, and beat in vanilla. Add flour mixture and prune mixture alternately in batches, beginning and ending with flour mixture and beating until just combined.

Spoon batter into pan (pan will be almost full) and bake in middle of oven 1 hour and 10 minutes, or until a tester comes out clean. Cool cake in pan on a rack 10 minutes and turn out onto rack to cool completely. *Cake keeps, wrapped in plastic wrap, at room temperature 1 week.*

Garnish cake with kumquats and serve with warm toffee sauce and ice cream.

PHOTO ON PAGES 76 AND 77

ARMAGNAC TOFFEE SAUCE

1½ cups heavy cream
1½ sticks (¾ cup) unsalted butter, softened
¾ cup packed light brown sugar
3 tablespoons Armagnac

In a heavy saucepan simmer cream with butter and brown sugar, stirring, 3 to 4 minutes, or until slightly thickened. Remove pan from heat and stir in Armagnac. *Sauce keeps, covered and chilled, 1 week. Reheat sauce before serving.* Makes about 2¼ cups.

SWEET AVOCADO MOUSSE

2 chilled firm-ripe California avocados
1½ tablespoons fresh lemon juice
¾ cup whole milk
½ cup sugar
½ cup well-chilled heavy cream

Halve and pit avocados and scoop flesh into a food processor. Add lemon juice, milk, sugar, and a pinch salt and purée until completely smooth. In a bowl beat cream until it just holds stiff peaks. Fold avocado mixture into whipped cream gently but thoroughly. Serves 4.

CHOCOLATE PUDDING ○

½ cup sugar
2 tablespoons cornstarch
4 ounces fine-quality bittersweet chocolate
  (not unsweetened)
1⅓ cups whole milk
1 large egg yolk
1 tablespoon unsalted butter
¼ teaspoon vanilla

In a heavy saucepan whisk together sugar, corn-starch, and a pinch salt. Chop chocolate and add to sugar mixture. In a bowl whisk together whole milk and egg yolk and gradually whisk into chocolate mixture. Bring mixture just to a boil over moder-ate heat, whisking constantly, and boil 1 minute, whisking. Remove pan from heat and whisk in butter and vanilla.

Divide pudding between two 8-ounce ramekins. *Chill puddings in freezer, surfaces covered with plastic wrap, until cool, about 30 minutes.* Serves 2.

SAMBUCA SOUFFLÉS WITH
WHITE CHOCOLATE ICE CREAM

To serve eight, use eight 6-ounce (¾-cup) soufflé molds; to serve ten, use ten 5-ounce (⅔-cup) molds.

½ vanilla bean
1 cup whole milk
¼ cup pure maple syrup
5 tablespoons unsalted butter
3 tablespoons all-purpose flour
2 tablespoons cornstarch
4 large egg yolks
8 large egg whites
⅔ cup granulated sugar
white chocolate ice cream (recipe follows)
1 cup Sambuca

Garnish: confectioners' sugar for dusting

Preheat oven to 350° F. Generously butter eight 6-ounce (¾-cup) or ten 5-ounce (⅔-cup) soufflé molds and coat with granulated sugar, knocking out excess sugar. Arrange molds on a baking sheet.

Split vanilla bean lengthwise. Scrape seeds into a small saucepan and reserve pod for another use. Add milk and maple syrup and bring to a simmer. In a heavy saucepan melt butter over moderately low heat and whisk in flour and cornstarch. Cook *roux*, whisking, 1 minute. Whisk in hot milk mixture in a stream, whisking constantly until smooth, and bring mixture to a boil. Remove pan from heat (mixture will be very thick) and whisk in egg yolks until combined well. Transfer mixture to a large bowl and cover surface with plastic wrap.

In a large bowl with an electric mixer beat whites until they hold soft peaks. Beat in ⅔ cup granulated sugar in a stream and beat until meringue just holds stiff peaks. Whisk about one fourth meringue into yolk mixture to lighten. With a rubber spatula fold in remaining meringue gently but thoroughly. Divide mixture among soufflé molds, filling them complete-ly. Bake soufflés on baking sheet in middle of oven 25 minutes, or until well-puffed and golden.

While soufflés are baking, arrange 8 or 10 scoops of ice cream on a chilled baking sheet and keep frozen. Put about 2 tablespoons Sambuca in each of 8 or 10 very small flameproof dishes or espresso cups and arrange a dish or cup on each of 8 or 10 chilled large plates. When soufflés have almost finished baking, arrange a scoop of ice cream on each plate, leaving room for soufflés.

Transfer soufflés on baking sheet from oven to a rack. Working quickly, generously dust confec-tioners' sugar over soufflés and with a strong metal spatula or tongs transfer to plates.

Using caution, ignite Sambuca and immediately serve desserts. Serves 8 or 10.

WHITE CHOCOLATE ICE CREAM

10½ ounces fine-quality white chocolate
  such as Lindt
2 cups whole milk
1¼ cups heavy cream
8 large egg yolks
1 cup sugar

Finely chop chocolate. In a heavy saucepan bring milk and cream to a simmer and remove pan from heat. In a bowl whisk together yolks and sugar until thick and pale. Add hot milk mixture to yolk mixture in a slow stream, whisking. Pour custard into pan and cook over moderately low heat, stirring constantly, until a thermometer registers 170° F. (do not boil). Pour custard through a sieve into a clean bowl and stir in chocolate until smooth. *Cool custard, uncovered, before chilling, covered. Chill custard until cold, at least 2 hours, and up to 1 day.*

Freeze custard in an ice-cream maker. Transfer ice cream to an airtight container and put in freezer to harden. *Ice cream may be made 1 week ahead.* Makes about 1 quart.

CHOCOLATE BREAD PUDDING

½ stick (¼ cup) unsalted butter
4 cups 1-inch cubes day-old country-style
    white bread
3 ounces unsweetened chocolate
    (not bittersweet)
1¾ cups whole milk
1 cup heavy cream
3 large egg yolks
¾ cup sugar

Melt butter and in a bowl toss with bread. Chop chocolate and transfer to another bowl. In a saucepan bring milk and cream to a simmer and remove pan from heat. Add cream mixture to chopped chocolate, whisking until smooth. Add egg yolks and sugar, whisking until combined well. Pour custard over bread. *Let pudding stand, covered, 1 hour.*

Preheat oven to 350° F. and butter an 8- by 8- by 2-inch square baking pan.

Transfer pudding to pan and bake in middle of oven until just set but still trembles slightly, about 25 minutes. Serve bread pudding warm or at room temperature. Serves 6.

GOOSEBERRY FOOL

3 cups pink or green gooseberries*
    (about 1 pound)
½ cup granulated sugar
½ cup well-chilled heavy cream
¼ cup *crème fraîche***
¼ cup superfine granulated sugar

*available seasonally at farmers markets
    and specialty produce markets
**available at specialty foods shops and
    some supermarkets

Pull off tops and tails of gooseberries and halve berries lengthwise. In a heavy skillet cook berries and granulated sugar over moderate heat, stirring occasionally until liquid is thickened, about 5 minutes. Simmer mixture, mashing with a fork to a coarse purée, 2 minutes more. *Chill purée, covered, until cold, about 1 hour, and up to 1 day.*

In a bowl with an electric mixer beat heavy cream with *crème fraîche* until it holds soft peaks. Add superfine sugar and beat until mixture just holds stiff peaks. Fold chilled purée into cream mixture until combined well. *Fool may be made 3 hours ahead and chilled, covered.* Serves 4.

MINTED BERRY GELÉES

1½ teaspoons unflavored gelatin
½ cup plus 1 tablespoon cold water
2 cups strawberries
1 cup raspberries
¾ cup minted simple syrup (page 222)

In a small saucepan sprinkle gelatin over water and let stand 1 minute to soften. Halve strawberries and slice enough to measure 1 cup. Heat gelatin mixture over low heat until gelatin is dissolved and stir in strawberries, raspberries, and simple syrup until combined. Divide berry mixture among four ½-cup molds. *Chill gelées until firm, at least 6 hours, and up to 2 days.*

To unmold *gelées*, dip bottoms of molds, 1 at a time, into a bowl of hot water 3 seconds and invert *gelées* onto 4 small plates. Serves 4.

ORANGE FOOLS

1 navel orange
3 tablespoons sugar
3 tablespoons unsalted butter
1 large egg
½ cup well-chilled heavy cream

With a vegetable peeler remove 2 strips zest from orange (each about 3 by ½ inch) and mince.

Squeeze enough juice from orange to measure ½ cup and in a small heavy saucepan simmer orange juice until reduced to ¼ cup.

Remove pan from heat and add sugar and butter to orange juice, whisking until butter is melted. Whisk in egg until combined well and cook mixture over moderately low heat, whisking, until whisk leaves distinct marks and first bubble appears on surface, 3 to 5 minutes.

Remove pan from heat and add zest to orange curd, whisking. Pour orange curd into a bowl set in a larger bowl of ice and cold water and stir until cold.

In another bowl beat cream until it just holds stiff peaks. Fold whipped cream into orange curd gently but thoroughly.

Spoon orange fool into 2 chilled goblets. Serves 2.

CHOCOLATE SOUFFLÉS WITH CREAMY CARAMEL SAUCE

¼ cup sugar plus additional for coating ramekins
8 ounces fine-quality bittersweet chocolate
    (not unsweetened) such as Valrhona,
    Callebaut, or Lindt
¾ stick (6 tablespoons) unsalted butter
2 tablespoons heavy cream
4 large egg yolks
7 large egg whites
¼ teaspoon cream of tartar

Accompaniment: creamy caramel sauce
    (recipe follows)

Butter six 1-cup ramekins (4 by 2 inches) and coat with sugar, knocking out excess sugar.

Finely chop chocolate. In a small saucepan melt butter over low heat. Add cream and bring just to a boil. Remove pan from heat and add chocolate, stirring until smooth. Transfer mixture to a large bowl and stir in yolks.

In another large bowl with an electric mixer beat whites with cream of tartar and a pinch salt until they just hold stiff peaks. Gradually add ¼ cup sugar, beating until just combined. Stir one fourth whites into chocolate mixture to lighten and fold in remaining whites gently but thoroughly.

Divide soufflé mixture among ramekins and smooth tops with a knife. Run tip of knife around edges of soufflés to aid rising. *Soufflés may be made up to this point 1 day ahead and chilled, loosely wrapped in plastic wrap.*

Preheat oven to 375° F.

Bake soufflés on a baking sheet in lower third of oven until puffed and surfaces are cracked, about 20 minutes.

Top soufflés with sauce and serve immediately. Serves 6.

CREAMY CARAMEL SAUCE

¾ cup sugar
¼ cup water
6 tablespoons light corn syrup
½ cup heavy cream
½ teaspoon vanilla

In a heavy saucepan simmer sugar, water, corn syrup, and a pinch salt, stirring, until sugar is dissolved. Boil mixture, without stirring, until a golden caramel. Remove pan from heat and add cream and vanilla, stirring until combined well, about 1 minute. Cool sauce to room temperature (sauce will thicken as it cools). *Sauce keeps, covered and chilled, 3 weeks. Bring sauce to room temperature before serving.* Makes about ¾ cup.

BEVERAGES

POIRE WILLIAM CHAMPAGNE COCKTAILS ☺

¼ cup sugar
¼ cup plus 4 teaspoons *poire William*
  (French pear brandy)
2⅔ cups chilled Champagne
1 Seckel or small Bosc pear

In a small saucepan heat sugar and ¼ cup *poire William* over moderate heat until sugar is dissolved, about 5 minutes. Remove pan from heat and cool syrup. Spoon 1½ tablespoons syrup into each of 4 Champagne glasses and add 1 teaspoon *poire William* to each glass. Add ⅔ cup Champagne to each glass and stir well.

Cut pear lengthwise into thin slices and add 1 slice to each drink. Makes 4 cocktails.

PHOTO ON PAGE 12

MINTED PINEAPPLE RUM COOLER ☺

3 tablespoons dark rum
½ cup unsweetened pineapple juice
2 tablespoons minted simple syrup (page 222)

Garnish: pineapple slices and fresh mint sprigs

In a tall glass filled with ice stir together rum, juice, and syrup until combined well.

Garnish drink with pineapple and mint. Makes 1 rum cooler.

RUM "LEMONADE" ☺

1¼ ounces (2½ tablespoons) bottled sour mix
  or Margarita mix
1 ounce (2 tablespoons) Bacardi Limón or
  other citrus-flavored rum
¼ ounce (½ tablespoon) Cointreau or other
  orange-flavored liqueur

a dash of Rose's lime juice
1 cup ice cubes

Garnish: lemon slice

In a blender blend all ingredients until mixture is just slushy. Pour drink into a stemmed glass and garnish with lemon. Makes 1 cocktail.

PHOTO ON PAGE 21

BLACKBERRY LIME MARGARITAS ☺

2 cups (about 11 ounces) blackberries
2 cups ice cubes
½ cup fresh lime juice
¾ cup white Tequila
¼ cup sugar

In a blender purée blackberries. Force purée through a fine sieve into a small bowl and discard solids. In a cocktail shaker combine ½ cup purée and remaining ingredients and shake well. Strain drink into 4 stemmed glasses. Makes 4 Margaritas.

FROZEN HONEYDEW MARGARITAS ☺+

1 honeydew melon
¾ cup white Tequila
⅓ cup fresh lime juice
2½ tablespoons sugar,
  or to taste

Remove and discard rind and seeds from honeydew and cut enough fruit into ½-inch cubes to measure 3½ cups. *Freeze melon cubes in a sealable plastic bag at least 3 hours and up to 1 week.*

In a blender purée frozen honeydew cubes with remaining ingredients until smooth. Pour drink into 4 stemmed glasses. Makes 4 Margaritas.

PRICKLY PEAR MARGARITAS ☺

kosher salt for coating rims of glasses
½ lime for coating rims of glasses
4¾ cups water
2¼ cups Cuervo gold Tequila
1 cup fresh lemon juice
1 cup triple sec
¾ cup fresh lime juice
¾ cup prickly pear syrup*
½ cup sugar

Garnish: lime wedges

*available by mail order from Cactus Candy Co.,
(888) 226-3901

Put salt on a small plate. Rub rim of each of 12 stemmed cocktail glasses with lime and dip in salt to lightly coat. In a large pitcher (about 2½ quarts) stir together remaining ingredients until sugar is completely dissolved.

Serve Margaritas over ice in glasses, garnished with lime wedges. Makes 12 Margaritas.

PHOTO ON PAGE 36

PASSION-FRUIT MARGARITAS ☺

If fresh passion fruit isn't available, substitute 3 cups passion-fruit nectar, frozen in ice-cube trays, for the strained fresh passion-fruit purée and, when ready to blend, omit the ice cubes.

1 pound fresh passion fruit* (about 12)
3 cups ice cubes
¾ cup white Tequila
¼ cup sugar

*available at specialty produce markets and
many supermarkets

Halve fruit and scoop pulp and seeds into a blender. Blend pulp briefly (seeds should still be in large pieces). Force fruit through a fine sieve into a cup and discard solids. In a blender blend ½ cup purée with remaining ingredients until smooth. Pour drink into 4 stemmed glasses. Makes 4 Margaritas.

HONEYDEW MIMOSAS ☺

3 cups honeydew juice (recipe follows)
a 750-ml bottle chilled sparkling wine

Fill each of 8 Champagne glasses halfway with juice and top off with sparkling wine. Makes 8 Mimosas.

PHOTO ON PAGE 55

HONEYDEW JUICE ☺

If serving this juice on its own, simply add 1 teaspoon fresh lemon juice, or to taste, to each batch.

a 4-pound honeydew melon
2 cups ice cubes
1 cup water
2 tablespoons sugar, or to taste

Cut melon into wedges and remove seeds and rind. Cut melon into 1-inch pieces. In a blender combine half of melon with half of each remaining ingredient and blend until very smooth. Pour juice into a pitcher and repeat procedure with remaining ingredients. Makes about 6 cups.

SOUTHSIDES ☺
LEMON GIN COCKTAILS

For simple syrup
1 cup water
1 cup sugar

1⅓ cups fresh lemon juice
¼ cup packed fresh mint leaves
6 ounces gin, vodka, or rum, or to taste
seltzer or club soda (optional)

Make simple syrup:
In a small saucepan bring water and sugar to a boil, stirring, and boil until sugar is completely dissolved. Cool syrup. *Syrup may be made 2 weeks ahead and chilled, covered.*

In a blender blend lemon juice, ⅔ cup syrup, and mint until completely smooth and add additional syrup to taste. *Lemon mixture may be made 4 hours ahead and chilled in a sealable container.*

Fill 4 glasses with ice and add liquor and lemon mixture. Top off drinks with seltzer or club soda. Makes 4 Southsides.

RASPBERRY ORANGE MARGARITAS

2 cups raspberries (about 10 ounces)
¾ cup fresh orange juice
¾ cup white Tequila
2 tablespoons sugar

In a blender purée raspberries. Force purée through a fine sieve into a small bowl and discard solids. In a cocktail shaker combine ½ cup purée and remaining ingredients and shake well. Serve drink over ice in tall glasses. Makes 4 Margaritas.

NECKER "SUNRISE"
PINEAPPLE MIDORI COCKTAIL

ice cubes
1½ ounces (3 tablespoons) Midori liqueur
½ cup unsweetened pineapple juice

Garnish: fresh pineapple slice

Fill a tall glass with ice cubes and add Midori liqueur. Holding a teaspoon bottom side up over glass, slowly pour pineapple juice over back of spoon into glass. (Pineapple juice will be suspended on top of Midori). Garnish drink with pineapple. Makes 1 cocktail.

PHOTO ON PAGE 21

TOP-SHELF MARGARITAS

kosher salt for coating rims of glasses
1 lime wedge for coating rims
    of glasses
2 cups ice cubes
¾ cup Grand Marnier
¾ cup Patron Añejo Tequila or
    other premium aged Tequila
½ cup fresh lime juice

Garnish: 4 lime wedges

Put salt on a small plate. Rub rims of 4 stemmed cocktail glasses with lime wedge and dip in salt to lightly coat. In a cocktail shaker combine remaining ingredients and shake well. Strain drink into glasses and garnish with lime wedges. Makes 4 Margaritas.

BLOOD-ORANGE MIMOSAS

two 750-ml bottles chilled sparkling wine
    (preferably California or Spanish)
3 cups chilled blood-orange juice (from about
    10 blood oranges*)
¼ cup grenadine

*available seasonally at specialty produce markets
    and by mail order from Chefs' Produce Team,
    (213) 624-8909

In a pitcher gently stir together Mimosa ingredients. Makes about 8 Mimosas.

PHOTO ON PAGE 79

ORANGEADE

6 cups fresh orange juice
4½ cups chilled seltzer or club soda

Garnish: orange slices

In a large pitcher stir together juice and seltzer or club soda and garnish with orange slices.

Serve orangeade over ice in tall glasses. Makes about 10½ cups.

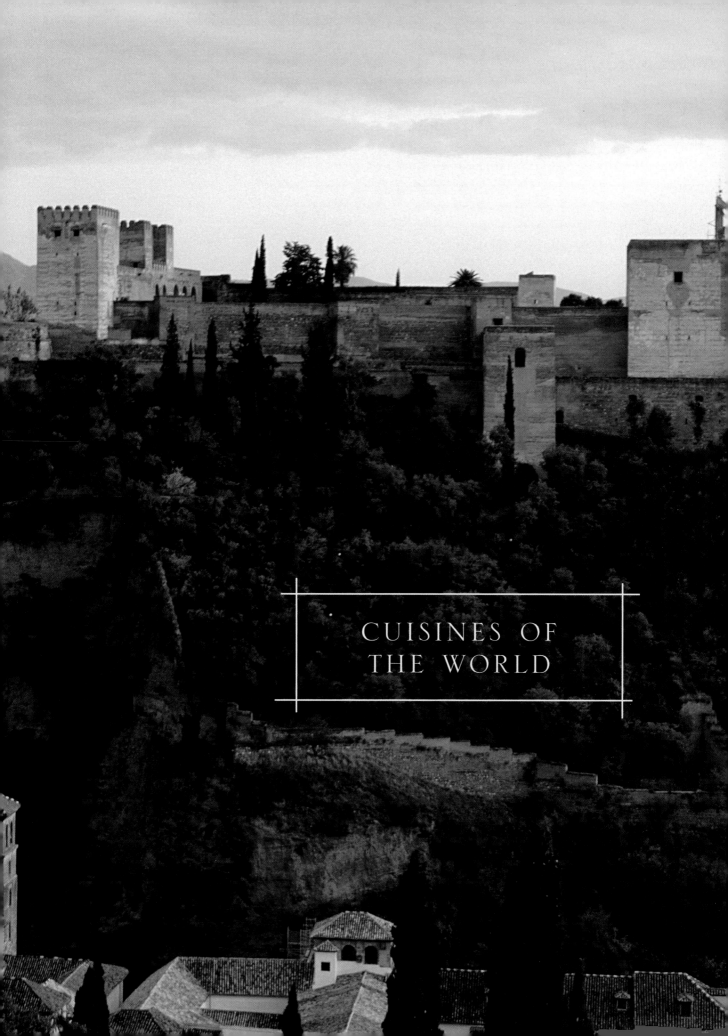

CUISINES OF
THE WORLD

SPAIN

At the southwestern tip of Europe, Spain rises from enveloping seas in a mosaic of criss-crossed mountains, white sandy beaches, cliffs, grassy meadows, forests, river valleys, wetlands, and windswept plains. Much of this peninsula climbs to surprising heights, and perhaps it is this closeness to the heavens that draws attention upwards, particularly at dawn and dusk, to breathtaking skies and remarkable light. Turreted castles, whitewashed windmills, quaint fishing villages and medieval towns as well as cosmopolitan cities with soaring cathedrals and art-filled museums further embellish the land, bringing history to life. Then, too, the Spanish people are as elegant and charming as their surroundings. Their warm hospitality and delicious regional cuisines draw forty million visitors (the same number as inhabitants) each year.

Even a short visit will reveal that these sociable people live to eat, and to eat well. Whether rich or poor, Spaniards generally appreciate fine food and are willing to pay for the most expensive ingredients. On a typical day, breakfast is followed by a mid-morning snack, and then it is soon time for early-afternoon *tapas* (snacks served in neighborhood bars with a glass of Sherry, wine, or beer). After these appetizers, many go home for three hours to enjoy the main meal of the day with family. There is yet another chance to have a sweet or more *tapas* in the early evening before dinner, which is served around 10 p.m. Customarily, meals are served at a leisurely pace in two courses—a first course (eggs, salad, vegetables, or soup) and a main course, often without accompaniments. Depending on the day, appetizers, salads, and desserts may be added. Fiestas, for example, are times of great indulgence. Although many are religious in nature, even solemn occasions, such as Holy Week in Seville, turn into fabulous parties that last well into the wee hours of the morning. Processions, bull fights, and/or traditional songs and dances along with endless meals (and often wonderful pastries) accompany the festivities.

How did the Spanish come to be such food-lovers? The answer involves a fascinating culinary history that began to unfold as early as the second century B.C. with the Romans, who then dominated "Hispania" for hundreds of years. Not only did these invaders build a solid infrastructure of roads, bridges, and aqueducts (as well as the magnificent cities of Barcelona, Tarragona, and Merida), they also brought a passion for good food. Knowing profitable land when they saw it, they cultivated the olive tree and showed Hispania how to cook with olive oil. Likewise, grapes (for winemaking) and wheat (for breadmaking) were grown with great success. Waves of Germanic tribes invaded in the fifth century A.D., and as the Roman empire broke up, Spain was exposed to various flavors from other parts of Europe. The Visigoths introduced spinach, legumes, and radishes and developed livestock farming. In A.D. 711, the Moors arrived from North Africa and, with the exception of a few Christian holdouts in the north, quickly conquered the country that they would rule for nearly 800 years. One can only imagine the impact of such a long reign. Certainly they lived in splendor, traces of which can be seen today in the Alhambra in Granada and the Mezquita of Córdoba. Over time the Moors established intricate irrigation systems, planted Middle Eastern foods that were suited to Spain's varied soils and climates, and imported herbs and spices. Rice, lemon and orange trees, eggplants, almonds, sugarcane, saffron, anise, sesame seed, nutmeg, cumin, cinnamon, caraway, cilantro, and mint—all can be attributed to the Moors. And this infusion of Eastern flavors drastically and permanently transformed the cuisine. In 1492, the Christians, having begun their quest to reunite the country early in the eleventh century, finally reclaimed Granada, the last vestige of the Moors' kingdom. This historic year also saw the discovery of the New World, and Spain, at the height of her prestige and power, acted as the European gateway for new foods arriving from America—tomatoes, peppers, corn, cocoa beans, and potatoes. Once again, Spain's palate was greatly altered.

Today, having undergone a period of isolation during a brutal civil war and Franco's right-wing rule, Spain has emerged as a peaceful, prosperous nation of seventeen autonomous regions (the Balearic and Canary Islands are included), as well as two city enclaves on Africa's north coast, all governed by a parliamentary monarchy centered in Madrid. And yet, Spain often is likened to a miniature continent made up of independent-minded people who are proud of their differences. While Spanish is spoken throughout the country, the Basque Country, Catalonia, Galicia, and Valencia have their own languages. And, although Catholicism is pervasive and controls the national calendar, Judaism and Islam are practiced in some communities. With such a mixture of cultures, topographies, and microclimates, it's not surprising that regional cuisines flourish.

Speaking in broad terms, there are seven culinary regions of Spain: The **North Coast** includes the Basque provinces, where seasoned sauces are masterfully paired with myriad seafoods (and meats). In fact, the entire coastal area provides outstanding seafood varieties, and it's apparent that a particular recipe and sauce exists for each one of them. This verdant land also produces some of the finest cattle and sheep, and the meat appears in stews, casseroles, and *empanadas* (savory ingredients wrapped in flaky pastry). Cabrales cheese, fizzy hard cider, crisp white wines, and sausage and bean dishes also are prized. The **Northeastern Interior**, both lush and desolate at times, proffers bountiful beans of many varieties and other vegetables (such as white asparagus, baby artichokes, and peppers—roasted red peppers are a specialty) that enrich sausage, lamb, and veal in hearty stews. Trout, rabbit, cured ham, salt cod, excellent cheeses, and some of the finest red wines of Spain are part of this cuisine. **Catalonia and the Balearic Islands** are best known for varied casseroles made with Mediterranean seafoods, pork sausages, rabbit, game birds of every description, and free-range chickens, often cooked with fruits and vegetables. Sauces, including *picada* (a mortar mash of almonds, hazelnuts, and/or pine nuts, garlic, and parsley) and *alioli* (garlic mayonnaise), often add a final dash of flavor to various dishes. This area is also famous for *cava* (bottle-fermented sparkling wines). The **Central and Western Interior**—an area of wheat fields, plains, and mountain ranges—has always been popular for roast baby lamb, suckling pig (less than three weeks old), and rustic stews made with *chorizo* (pork sausage) and cured ham, chickpeas (particularly the famous *cocido)*, Manchego cheese, and beans. Madrid, on the other hand, is the culinary hub of the country, serving international fare as well as all Spanish regional cuisines. Fresh seafood is rushed to this landlocked city from coastal areas in extraordinary quantities and varieties. The **Levantian Coast**, the marshy flatland of southeastern coastal Spain, is famous for untold variations of paellas and other rice dishes that often include outstanding seafoods or vegetables from the area. **Andalusia**, the southernmost region with Atlantic and Mediterranean shores, boasts an extravagant supply of seafood, while inland, olive groves stretch for miles over rolling hills. Seafood fried in olive oil, pork dishes (and local air-cured hams), *tapas*, cooling salads and gazpachos, and world-renowned Sherry are enjoyed here. Light sauces scented with saffron, cumin, and coriander are reminiscent of the days when the Moors ruled this region. Finally, the subtropical **Canary Islands**, with culinary roots in Africa, Spain, and America, have a distinctive regional flavor all their own. Avocado, papaya, pineapple, cilantro, bananas, tomatoes, potatoes, corn, and watercress thrive here. *Mojos*, uncooked sauces made with olive oil, vinegar, garlic, peppers, spices (sometimes cumin and paprika), and often cilantro are used as lively dipping sauces and marinades.

Despite regional differences, all Spanish food is simple and easily recognizable. Spices never mask the true flavors of ingredients, and dishes are, for the most part, surprisingly mild. Olive oil, garlic, and parsley play a primary role in almost every recipe, while tomatoes, peppers, almonds, and bread appear in every cuisine (ground almonds and breads thicken sauces and soups). Many dishes are simply simmered, uncovered, in a *cazuela* (a flameproof, shallow earthenware casserole), the most popular cooking vessel. But perhaps the most striking culinary similarity among regions is the outstanding quality of ingredients.

On the following pages, we offer primers that take a closer look at some of Spain's most exciting flavors: **tapas** (page 243) focuses on the national pastime of snacking and describes typical bars and the snacks they offer; **paella** (page 245) unlocks the mysteries of this favorite rice dish; and **basic ingredients** (page 247) gives useful information and mail-order sources for all the traditional Spanish foods that appear in our menus, which immediately follow.

Our Spring Family Dinner highlights a few specialties of northern Spain, and in true fashion, consists only of a few dishes. For the first course, a hazelnut sauce tops steamed asparagus. (Should you be lucky enough to find white asparagus, we urge you to try it.) The lamb stew cooks until it is fork-tender in its own juices, wine, and local herbs with smoky *pimientos del piquillo* (roasted red peppers) that form a *chilindrón* sauce. Our dense bread, full of sweet cooked onion flavor, is great for mopping up this delightful sauce. Dessert is a simple dish of strawberries in a red-wine marinade; the Rioja wine suggested for this menu complements the fruit. (Note: while pears or peaches would be more authentic, strawberries abound in American spring markets.)

Then, because *tapas* are ideal snacks to nibble with a glass of wine or Sherry, we created an hors d'oeuvre party with a collection of these little regional dishes. (Please be aware that the Spanish, while they might serve one or two *tapas* at home, typically enjoy them at their local bar. We also added a salad and a dessert, both unlikely *tapas* fare.) Most of the dishes in this menu can be made, at least partially, ahead of time.

Finally, a Summer Lunch by the Sea captures the flavors of coastal Spain and her islands with hot-weather dishes that are perfect for alfresco dining. Our chilled gazpacho, made with frozen lima beans and plenty of green grapes, pine nuts, and garlic, reinvents *ajo blanco* (chilled almond and garlic soup with grapes); it should be served in small bowls while everyone eagerly awaits the centerpiece of the menu—the paella. Few Spanish dishes are as flamboyant, and ours, brimming with lobsters, shrimp, squid, mussels, and flavored with saffron, is exceptionally bright and impressive. Lemon *alioli* adds a jolt of fresh garlic flavor to the seafood and rice. The aromatic finale, spiced caramel oranges, is refreshingly light. Both soup and oranges can be made well ahead of time, allowing the cook to devote full attention to the paella.

The foods of Spain are fresh and inviting. There is nothing pretentious here, just delicious flavors of the Mediterranean, easily combined, waiting to be savored with family and friends. Be sure to enjoy them as a Spaniard does—without rush, and with plenty of good wine and good cheer.

TAPAS

Everyday, Spaniards set aside some time to relax with friends to catch up on the latest news. And, since a drink and a bite to eat always enhance a good chat, it is no wonder that *tapas* has become a popular pastime. Sometimes at 1 in the afternoon, more often around 8 in the evening, crowds of friends, office workers, shoppers, business acquaintances, young couples, and others head to bars called *tascas* for an hour or two before they dine. There, a glass of wine, beer, or Sherry is accompanied by *tapas*, delightful morsels such as a slice of good ham, a bit of deep-fried seafood, marinated olives, or a wedge of potato omelet. Strangers are welcome and may even be offered a taste of the house specialty in exchange for their opinion on the topic at hand. Lively conversation, after all, is essential.

Mealtimes are typically late in Spain, which allows plenty of time to "do *tapas*." Larger towns offer a choice of several *tascas*, and the most popular ones in cities are easily recognized from the throngs spilling out onto the streets. Jam-packed and swirling with cigarette smoke, these places pulsate with the clamor of voices; occasionally, guitar music or an impromptu *flamenco* performance adds to the excitement. The bar itself might be contemporary or ancient, spacious or pocket-sized, elegant or an unpretentious neighborhood hang-out with a few wooden stools at low tables, but even the smallest village will have a friendly tavern that serves a glass of local wine and *pinchos*, literally "little bits of something."

Many have speculated on the origins of *tapas*, and since "*tapar*" means to cover, the usual anecdote recounts that glasses of Sherry served in taverns once were topped with a slice of ham or cheese to keep out dust. As these "lids" grew more varied to attract new customers, the art of *tapas* was born. One certainty is that the tradition began in the south during the 19th century and spread to other areas. Andalusia, particularly Seville, remains the ultimate *tapas* region, but these savory bites are popular all over. In Madrid, they have become as much a lifestyle as a meal, and fit in perfectly with the Madrileño penchant for enjoying life to its fullest.

Tapas bar fare varies from one special local dish, to a few simple offerings, to a sumptuous array with dozens of choices. In Santander, a northern beach resort, several harborside spots are popular for crisp, sweet, deep-fried squid, known as *rabas*. Nearby in San Sebastian, an elegant coastal city, stacks of intricate little canapés piled high on platters are the norm. Down south in Moorish-influenced Córdoba, one *mesón* (rustic tavern) is known for its grilled quails marinated in perfumed spices, while another is famous for a refreshing salad of octopus, pimientos, and oranges. And, in Madrid, there are several bars called *Museo del Jamón* (ham museum), where literally hundreds of regional hams can be savored.

Beverage options also can shift from bar to bar: casual *cervezerías* pour dozens of beers (*cervezas*); while upscale *xampanyeries* (pronounced champagne-yerias), mostly in and around Barcelona, pop open bottles of the sparkling wines called *cava*. Throughout Andalusia, chilled Fino or Manzanilla Sherry is favored and usually ordered by the half bottle for freshness. And in the northwestern regions of Galicia and Asturias, *sidra* (hard cider) is the typical choice. Naturally, *tapas* selections complement the beverage served.

Visitors to Spain learn that the ubiquitous bowl of olives or roasted almonds is often gratis; however, when platters of cold or room-temperature morsels are spread out on the bar, it's best to keep track of what has been eaten. Payment is often by the honor system, or a tooth-pick count may be taken by the barman. Hot choices from the kitchen are usually posted on a chalkboard, and one needs to look no further than the plates of regular patrons to discern the specialty of the house. Larger portions called *raciones* can be ordered for a group, as is often the case when friends enjoy night-long *tapas* "crawls."

Although *tapas* are traditionally enjoyed in bars, a collection of these dishes also makes a lovely hors d'oeuvres party. Our menu (page 259), inspired by traditional favorites from all over Spain, is a savory mixture of cold and hot dishes. We've even taken the liberty of adding dessert, little crunchy cookies, to accompany a glass of Sherry. *Tapas* combined with friends and good cheer provide a small taste of the good life, Spanish-style.

PAELLA

Paella, the quintessential rice dish of Spain, is enjoyed throughout the country, but the sunny, flat, fertile El Levante region along the southeastern coast is its true home. Here, over a millenium ago, the Arabs devised an elaborate system of canals to regulate runoff water and introduced *arroz*, the short-grain rice we now simply call "Spanish rice." Today, the area's endless rice fields are still maintained by the very same irrigation system.

Although "paella" refers to any Spanish rice dish that is cooked in a wide, flat paella pan, the popular chicken, meat, and seafood mixture usually comes to mind. (Levantinos never combine meat and seafood in their paellas, but acquiesce to the demands of tourists.) Throughout the Valencia region, rice is a staple of the diet, and myriad fresh local products—duck, pork, lamb, rabbit, snails, eels, sausage, garden vegetables, white beans, and chickpeas—as well as offshore catches—cuttlefish, grouper, lobsters, mussels, scorpion fish, sea crayfish, shrimp, and squid—act as accompaniments. Paella certainly has come a long way from its humble origins as an austere Lenten dish of rice and dried cod. But then, to a Spaniard, it has always been the quality and flavor of the rice itself, not the "garnishes," that really matter.

Levantinos consider paella a heavy dish and, therefore, enjoy it only at lunchtime, the main meal of the day. Traditionally, it was prepared by men in the fields over a wood fire; and to this day, it is usually a country meal prepared out-of-doors by the man of the house. In Valencia, however, tourists and locals alike rely on excellent restaurants that, more often than not, cook their paellas indoors. Aficionados insist that authentic paella can be enjoyed only in the Levante where all the essentials—the *arroz*, local water, vegetables, and Mediterranean seafood—are at hand. And, since Spaniards consider paella a national treasure, their discussions on how best to prepare it are quite serious. Most devotees agree that a wood fire is necessary to give the dish a smoky flavor and form *socarrat*, the prized brown crust that crisps onto the bottom of the pan. But then, one questions, should the fire be made with vine prunings or orange-wood? If cooked indoors, the debate turns to whether the rice should be completed on top of the stove or finished in the oven. Naturally, each and every nuance makes a difference.

Fortunately, great-tasting paella can be cooked on an ordinary stove, indoors and beyond Spanish shores, with the proper pan and ingredients (see our recipe on page 272 and mail-order sources on page 251). For best results, an inexpensive traditional Spanish paella is recommended. This two-handled, shallow, thin metal pan (preferably iron, not stainless steel) conducts heat quickly, allowing the rice to dry out properly and become al dente. To serve 6 to 8 people, you'll need a 17-inch pan (measure across the top, not including the handles), with a 15-inch base. Place the pan over two burners, turning it frequently and moving it back and forth over the burners to ensure even heat. When it comes to ingredients, short-grain rice is a *must* for proper texture and absorption of flavors. (Arborio rice from Italy is readily available; alternatively, try Calasparra or SOS rice from Spain.) It is also worth purchasing smoked Spanish paprika and Spanish saffron threads for their distinctive tastes.

Finally, after preparing our paella recipe several times, we have a few helpful suggestions to ensure al dente, moist rice that is not soupy: Most importantly, you will need to carefully watch and test the rice along the way to make sure that it reaches a certain degree of "doneness" before proceeding to the next step. Begin by *not* rinsing the rice. Once the rice is added to the vegetable mixture, boil it over high heat, stirring, until the liquid is substantially reduced, the bubbles thicken, and most of the rice appears on the surface (at this stage each grain will be hard so you cannot test by taste). After the seafood is added, the paella is put in the oven (note different oven temperatures and baking times required for gas and electric ovens) until almost all the liquid is absorbed and the rice is still somewhat undercooked (chewy, but not yet al dente—taste it here). The paella will continue to cook as it rests for 10 minutes, covered.

Few dishes are as rewarding as paella, and with just the right equipment, a few authentic ingredients, and our step-by-step instructions, it is an accessible dish. In Spanish homes the paella pan is placed in the center of the table so that everyone can help themselves. We encourage you to serve it this way—after all, paella is as beautiful as it is delicious.

BASIC INGREDIENTS

Spain's spectacular covered markets—beautiful and spacious skylit structures, such as those at the centers of Barcelona, Madrid, Valencia, Santiago de Compostela, San Sebastian, and Zaragoza—showcase only the freshest local foods. Restaurant chefs and housewives alike come here to select the finest fruits, vegetables, fish, seafood, meats, poultry, cheeses, and charcuterie. Although cuisines may differ from region to region, the quality of ingredients is never negotiable.

A walk through any one of these markets reveals a profusion of the best regional foods in season. Pristine fruits—perhaps succulent figs, fragrant melons, dates on the branch, or sweet oranges—are handled like jewels and artfully displayed. Garden vegetables—shiny eggplants, slim asparagus, wedges of cut squash and pumpkin, and leafy greens—are grouped with geometric precision. Baskets overflow with fresh beans as well as dried—chickpeas, lentils, and oversized limas. Nearby, olives in a muted rainbow of light green, violet, and black are scooped out of barrels that stand in rows. In the next aisle, fish and shellfish—hake, porgy, scallops in the shell, *langostinos*, trout, crayfish—plucked from the water just hours before, gleam on beds of ice. Exotic sea creatures, like *centollo* (a giant spider crab), tiny white *angulas* (baby eels), and *percebes* (barnacles), often fetch the highest prices. In the meats section, seasonal game, tender baby lambs, suckling pigs, veal, chicken, even bull meat might be available. Further along, an astonishing variety of cured meats hang overhead—hams still on the hoof and loops of local sausages in various shapes and sizes, including white *butifarra* sausages (Catalonia), bright red *chorizos* (Castile), and black *morcilla* blood sausages (Asturias or Castile).... And the cheese stalls are just as packed. Hand-crafted choices might include smoked *Idiazábal*, a sheep's milk cheese (Basque region); mild, creamy *Tetilla* (Galicia); or cured *Manchego* (La Mancha). With such delicious abundance, Spaniards can't help but devote so much time to enjoying fine food. Price seems of little consequence; luxury items, like cured ham, shellfish, and game, are bought routinely.

While the covered markets are splendid, *bodegas* (grocery stores) as well as supermarket chains carry fresh local seasonal products. It is evident that all Spaniards care intensely about the quality of their food, and in order to maintain high standards, especially as agriculture and food production is modernized, there are regulatory councils that grant a "seal of approval" to certain foods and wines. The *Denominación de Origen* (D.O.) guarantees that a product is from a certain area and has been produced by traditional methods. This mark is conferred upon wines, hams, cheeses, bottled roasted red peppers and white asparagus, and various other goods. D.O. approval is a source of pride to both producer and consumer alike, and an assurance of quality and authenticity.

Spanish foods and wines, such as saffron, Sherry, Sherry vinegar, and Manchego cheese, are increasingly available in the United States at Latino markets and specialty foods stores. These ingredients have no real substitutes, so we recommend buying them before cooking our menus. Likewise, *pimientos del piquillo* (roasted peppers) and Spanish paprika have distinctive smoky-sweet flavors that cannot be easily replicated. These items, however, may be more difficult to find, so we have provided mail-order sources on page 251. Not all Spanish ingredients are indispensable: Any fine Mediterranean olive oil or olives may be substituted and, when it comes to cured meats, choose the best-tasting ones available, regardless of origin. Spanish wines remain among the best fine wine bargains—those chosen for our three menus are just a few among hundreds of possibilities. Ask your wine merchant for further suggestions or consult *The Foods and Wines of Spain* by Penelope Casas.

Olive Oil (*Aceite de Oliva*)—Most Spanish olive oil comes from Andalusia, the southernmost region, where olive groves stretch as far as the eye can see. Although most is "pure olive oil" (a mild-tasting blend of refined olive oil extracted by heat or chemicals with some virgin olive oil added for taste), the best cold-pressed "virgin" oils still retain their regional character. Fragrant, fruity Andalusian virgin oils are sometimes slightly bitter; be sure to use the most aromatic ones for frying and cooking, and those with medium fruitiness for salads and gazpacho. Smooth, sweet Catalonian virgin oil has an almond aroma that is best for mayonnaise and salad dressing. While any pure olive oil can be used for cooking, salads call for a flavorful extra-virgin oil like estate-grown Nuñez de Prado from Baena, an unfiltered oil with spicy green-apple flavor.

Table Olives (*Aceitunas de Mesa*)—Olives are the quintessential *tapas* snack. In city markets, dozens of different types of cured olives from all over the country are available in plain or flavored brines. Green olives, generally bitter and tart, are usually marinated with acids (lemon juice or vinegar) and aromatic herbs; while riper violet and black olives might be flavored with sweet-sour dressings and spices. Stuffed olives, a Spanish favorite, have any number of possible fillings, such as anchovies, pimientos, or almonds. Spanish olives are increasingly available in specialty foods stores in the United States. Look for extra-large, green Manzanilla Finas, cracked green Gordals, and bitter, small, black Arbequinas, all of which can be used in our recipe for marinated olives.

Sherry (*Jerez*)—Made in a trio of towns in southern Andalusia, Sherry, a fortified wine (a neutral brandy is added before bottling), is usually considered too strong to accompany a main course. Although all Sherries are made from the same grapes (primarily Palomino), their eventual sweetness is determined during their development in the cask. Dry Sherries (*finos*, *manzanillas*, and slightly sweeter *amontillados*) are enjoyed chilled as an apéritif or with *tapas* (a freshly-opened bottle is essential). Rich, fragrant *olorosos* and sweet, syrupy cream Sherries are sipped with dessert or as after-dinner drinks. In Spanish kitchens a dose of *fino* finishes a quick pan-sauce, while *oloroso* is preferred in desserts.

Sherry Vinegar (*Vinagre de Jerez*)—Another Andalusian specialty, Sherry vinegar, which begins in the same casks as Sherry wine, is left to mature for at least six years. A few casks are aged even longer, and these vinegars have the depth and complexity to rival Italian balsamic vinegars, though they are far less sweet. Sherry vinegar has a high acidity level and concentrated flavor, so when substituting it for other vinegars, less is needed.

Cured Ham (*Jamón Serrano, Jamón Ibérico*)—Originally, *jamón serrano* (ham of the mountains) referred to any Spanish cured ham; today, the term refers to cured ham made from domestically raised European white pigs. *Jamón Ibérico* designates artisanal ham that is still made from native Iberian pigs, raised mostly in the mountainous southwestern provinces where they roam free. *Jamón Ibérico* is sometimes called *pata negra*, since these pigs have black hooves; or it may be called *jamón de Jabugo*, after one area that produces these hams. Serrano hams may also be known by the names of the towns in which they are made, such as Trevelez or Teruel. Like Italian prosciutto, all Spanish hams are air-cured, but they are more strongly flavored. After the meat is salted with coarse sea salt, it is slowly wind-cured in open lofts, then matured in cellars. The minimum curing period for serrano hams is 36 weeks, while *Ibérico* hams are usually aged for two or more years. *Jamón serrano* has a deep red color and a soft buttery texture; *Jamón Ibérico* is even more tender, since the meat is marbled throughout. Supreme *Ibérico* hams, exorbitantly expensive, are marked *bellota*, indicating that the pigs have been fattened on acorns exclusively. Few Spanish hams are exported to the United States, however, there are producers who make serrano ham domestically, in the Spanish style. Prosciutto can be substituted.

Chorizo Sausage (*Chorizo*)—Although many different sausages are enjoyed in Spain, one of the most popular is *chorizo*. Made of minced pork meat and fat, it is flavored with crushed garlic and spices, sometimes Sherry, and characteristically with paprika, which adds a strong red hue. Most *chorizos* are stuffed into sausage skins and then hung to air-dry, although some are initially smoked. As with all charcuterie products, there are countless local variations and family recipes. Some interesting regional ones include venison or wild boar *chorizos* from Castile. Depending on how long the *chorizo* has dried (how hard it becomes), the sausage can be sliced and served as a cold cut, fried and served as a *tapa*, or used to flavor a cooked dish. In the United States domestically produced *chorizos* are available at Latino markets, some supermarkets, and by mail order (opposite). (Note: Generally, Spanish *chorizo* is less spicy than the South American sausage of the same name.)

Salt Cod (*Bacalao*)—Basque fisherman have caught cod for hundreds of years, sailing as far as Greenland and Newfoundland and salting their catch to preserve it for the voyage home. Although fresh seafood is plentiful, the use of salt cod is so deeply rooted in Basque cuisine that it remains a favorite.

Cabrales Cheese (*Queso Cabrales*)—This pungent cheese is made primarily from cow's milk, with some goat's and/or sheep's milk added for tangy flavor. Aged in the limestone caves of Asturias, as it has been for centuries, Cabrales cheese naturally acquires blue-purple veining. Its distinctive richness and crumbly texture are similar to Gorgonzola, which can be substituted.

Manchego Cheese (*Queso Manchego*)—Slightly salty, piquant, and firm-textured, Spain's most famous cheese is made from the milk of hardy sheep in La Mancha (Castile). Today, the cheese is formed in wooden or plastic molds that imprint the rind with an *esparto* grass design to mimic the traditional wrapping. Finer producers make the cheese with unpasteurized milk and allow it to age to intensify the flavors. This cheese is widely available in cheese stores in the United States.

Quince Paste (*Membrillo*)—Made simply from quince and sugar cooked until reduced and concentrated, quince paste varies in color from light brown to rich, deep mahogany: the darker, the more flavorful. *Membrillo* is grainy and shiny, slightly translucent, and extremely sweet. It comes in blocks and is best sliced thin and served with salty ham or cheese (or both, as in our *tapas* recipe for toasts). Our quince *confit* (fresh quince pieces that are cooked until tender but still hold their shape) is a delicious variation on *membrillo*.

Saffron Threads (*Azafrán*)—The labor involved in hand-picking and roasting the stigmas of the purple crocus makes Spanish saffron, from La Mancha, the most expensive spice in the world. Its aroma, flavor, and color go a long way, however, and a few precious threads, dissolved in wine, are enough to flavor and gently color a whole dish (usually a paella). Too much saffron, in fact, will give a medicinal taste. Buy saffron in threads that are of a uniformly deep red hue without too much yellow, and avoid powdered saffron to ensure purity.

Paprika (*Pimentón*)—There are many kinds of paprika, but smoky-tasting, aromatic *pimentón* from La Vera in western Extremadura is truly exceptional. Locally grown peppers are hand-turned daily over oak-wood fires for ten days. The smoke-dried peppers are then ground in old stone mills at low temperatures to preserve volatile oils. This process has earned a D.O. mark, which appears on each tin. Three varieties are made—sweet, hot, and, our preference, bittersweet. This paprika appears in our oxtail stew and paella and will also add smoky spiciness to roast chicken, lentil or black bean soup, and dips and spreads.

Roasted Red Peppers (*Pimientos del Piquillo*)—Particularly sweet and tender but never mushy, *pimientos del piquillo*, grown and prepared in and around the town of Lodosa (Navarre), are relished for their smoky flavor. They may be served plain or stuffed or added to stews (as in our spring lamb stew). In order to earn a D.O. mark of quality, the peppers must be roasted over wood fires, peeled by hand without water, and bottled in their own juices. See mail-order sources or, in a pinch, use other bottled whole *pimientos* or grilled peppers.

MAIL ORDER SOURCES

Many Spanish ingredients—including saffron, Manchego cheese, Sherry vinegar, olives, and virgin olive oils—are available at Latino markets, specialty foods stores, and some supermarkets. Below is a list of mail-order sources for these items and others used in our menus that may be more difficult to find. Sherry and other Spanish wines can be found in most wine shops.

Dean & Deluca
560 Broadway, New York, NY 10012
tel. (800) 999-0306; fax (212) 226-2003
for ham, chorizo, cheeses, quince paste, rice, pimientos, paprika, dried chiles, chick-pea flour, dried lima beans

La Española Meats, Inc.
25020 Doble Avenue, Harbor City, CA 90717
tel. (310) 539-0455; fax (310) 539-5989
for ham, chorizo, cheeses, quince paste, rice, pimientos, paprika, paella pans

The Spanish Table
1427 Western Avenue, Seattle, WA 98101
tel. (206) 682-2827; fax (206) 682-2814
for ham, chorizo, cheeses, quince paste, rice, pimientos, paprika, dried lima beans, paella pans

Zingerman's
422 Detroit Street, Ann Arbor, MI 48104
tel. (888) 636-8162; fax (734) 769-1260
for ham, chorizo, cheeses, quince paste, rice, pimientos, paprika, dried chiles, chick-pea flour, paella pans

A Spring Family Dinner

Espárragos en Salsa de Avellana
ASPARAGUS WITH HAZELNUT SAUCE

Cordero al Chilindrón
LAMB STEW WITH PIMIENTOS AND CHILES

Zapatilla Encebollada
ONION BREAD

Cune Rioja Crianza '95

Fresas al Vino Tinto
STRAWBERRIES IN RED WINE

Serves 6

Banyoles, Catalonia

Below: Lamb Stew with Pimientos and Chiles.
Opposite: Asparagus with Hazelnut Sauce; Onion Bread

Espárragos en Salsa de Avellana

Asparagus with Hazelnut Sauce

For sauce
2 slices firm white sandwich bread
½ cup hazelnuts
3 garlic cloves
¼ cup olive oil
½ to ⅔ cup water
½ cup packed fresh flat-leafed parsley leaves
2 teaspoons white-wine vinegar

2 pounds thin asparagus

Make sauce:

Trim crusts and cut bread into ⅓-inch cubes. Discard any loose skins from hazelnuts and coarsely chop nuts. Thinly slice garlic. In a 10-inch skillet heat olive oil over moderate heat until hot but not smoking and cook bread, nuts, and garlic, stirring occasionally, until golden. With a slotted spoon transfer 2 tablespoons hazelnuts and a few garlic slices to a small bowl and reserve for garnish. Cool remaining mixture to warm and in a blender blend with ½ cup water, parsley leaves, and vinegar until combined well, adding enough remaining water, 1 tablespoon at a time, to facilitate blending. Season sauce with salt.

Trim asparagus and in a steamer set over boiling water steam asparagus just until tender, 2 to 5 minutes depending on thickness of stalks. In a bowl toss asparagus with sauce. Arrange asparagus on a platter and sprinkle with reserved hazelnuts and garlic. Serves 6.

Cordero al Chilindrón

Lamb Stew with Pimientos and Chiles

Pimientos del piquillo (roasted Spanish peppers) add smoky, mild heat to this favorite Northern dish.

1 large onion (about 1 pound)
4 garlic cloves
¼ pound sliced serrano ham* or prosciutto
1 ounce dried *ancho* or *pasilla* chiles* (about 2 large)
¾ cup drained *pimientos del piquillo** (a 7- to 8-ounce jar) or other whole *pimientos*
3 pounds boneless lamb shoulder or leg, cut into 2-inch pieces
3 tablespoons olive oil
2 cups water
1 cup canned crushed tomatoes
1 cup dry white wine
2 large fresh rosemary sprigs
1 bay leaf
1½ cups fresh or thawed frozen peas (optional)

*sources on page 251

Chop onion, garlic cloves, and ham or prosciutto. Wearing rubber gloves, seed chiles and with kitchen shears cut into 2- by ¼-inch pieces. Cut *pimientos* into ½-inch-wide strips.

Season lamb with salt and pepper. In a 5-quart heavy kettle heat oil over moderately high heat until hot but not smoking and brown lamb all over in 2 batches, transferring to a large plate. In fat remaining in kettle cook onion, garlic, and ham or prosciutto over moderate heat, stirring frequently, until onion is softened, about 5 minutes. Add lamb and any juices that have accumulated on plate to onion mixture with chiles, *pimientos*, and remaining ingredients except peas. Simmer lamb stew, covered, stirring occasionally, until meat is very tender, 1¾ to 2 hours. *Stew may be made up to this point 1 day ahead and cooled, uncovered, before being chilled, covered.*

Simmer stew, uncovered, until sauce is thickened to desired consistency. Stir in peas and salt to taste and simmer until peas are cooked through, about 5 minutes for fresh and 2 minutes for frozen. Discard bay leaf. Serves 6.

ZAPATILLA ENCEBOLLADA
ONION BREAD

For this recipe you will need a baking stone or 4 to 6 unglazed "quarry" tiles, available at cookware shops and by mail order from The Baker's Catalogue, (800) 827-6836.

2 onions (about ¾ pound total)
1½ teaspoons salt
¼ cup olive oil
1 cup warm water (105°–115° F.)
1 tablespoon active dry yeast
2¾ to 3 cups all-purpose flour
cornmeal for sprinkling

Chop onions and in a large heavy skillet cook onions and ½ teaspoon salt in oil over moderate heat until softened and pale golden, about 15 minutes.

In bowl of a standing electric mixer stir together warm water and yeast and let stand 5 minutes, or until creamy. Add 2¾ cups flour and remaining teaspoon salt and with dough hook attachment beat dough at medium speed 3 minutes. Add onion mixture and beat, adding enough of remaining ¼ cup flour to form a sticky dough, 1 minute. Transfer dough to a lightly oiled bowl, turning to coat, and cover with plastic wrap. *Let dough rise in a warm place until doubled in bulk, 45 minutes to 1 hour.*

Turn dough out onto a well-floured surface and with floured hands knead 2 minutes. Return dough to oiled bowl and cover with plastic wrap. *Chill dough 12 hours, or until doubled in bulk, and up to 18.*

One hour before baking bread, put a baking stone or "quarry" tiles (see note, above) arranged close together on oven rack in lowest position in oven and preheat oven to 425° F.

Punch down dough and turn out onto a well-floured surface. Cut dough in half and let dough rest, covered with a kitchen towel, 10 minutes. With floured hands roll each dough half into a 15-inch-long rope.

Sprinkle baking stone or tiles and a rimless baking sheet with cornmeal. With a long side of baking sheet closest to you, arrange 1 rope parallel to far edge and about 2 inches from it. Pat rope into a 4-inch-wide flat loaf. Shake sheet to make sure loaf will slide, sprinkling more cornmeal underneath if it sticks. Line up far edge of sheet with back half of

stone or tiles and tilt sheet, jerking it gently to start loaf sliding. Once edge of loaf touches stones or tiles, carefully pull back sheet to completely transfer loaf. Sprinkle sheet with more cornmeal. Working quickly, shape remaining dough rope and transfer loaf to front half of stone or tiles in same manner.

Bake loaves 25 minutes, or until golden, and transfer to a rack to cool. Makes 2 loaves.

FRESAS AL VINO TINTO
STRAWBERRIES IN RED WINE

The Rioja suggested for this menu or a California red Zinfandel make a lovely sauce.

one 750-ml bottle dry red wine (about 3½ cups)
½ cup sugar
2 pounds strawberries (about 3 pints)

In a 3-quart saucepan boil wine and sugar until reduced to about 1½ cups, about 20 minutes, and cool. *Chill sauce, covered, at least until cold, about 2 hours, and up to 2 days.*

Hull strawberries and cut in half. In a large bowl toss strawberries with wine sauce and chill 15 minutes. Serves 6.

A Tapas Party

Aceitunas y Pepinillos Marinados
Marinated Olives and Cornichons

**Tostadas de Jamón y Queso Manchego con
Membrillo Confitado**
Serrano Ham and Manchego Cheese with Quince Confit on Toasts

Tortilla de Espárragos, Setas, y Chorizo
Asparagus, Mushroom, and Chorizo Omelet

**Ensalada de Berros y Lechuga
al Queso Cabrales**
Watercress and Romaine with Cabrales Cheese

Pimientos Marinados a la Brasa
Marinated Grilled Red Bell Peppers

Tortillitas de Camarones con Mojo
Shrimp Pancakes with Cilantro and Green Pepper Sauce

Fritos de Bacalao y Patata
Salt Cod and Potato Fritters

Estofado de Rabo de Toro al Pimentón
Oxtail Paprika Stew

Judías Blancas con Romero y Comino
White Beans with Rosemary and Cumin

Pastas de Piñones
Pine Nut Cookies

Segura Viudas Cava Brut Reserva

Valdespino Inocente Fino Sherry

Serves 8 to 10

Bullfighters in Seville, Andalusia

Clockwise from upper left: Shrimp Pancakes with Cilantro and Green Pepper Sauce; White Beans with Rosemary and Cumin, Marinated Grilled Red Bell Pepper, and Marinated Olives and Cornichons; and Serrano Ham and Manchego Cheese with Quince Confit on Toast. Opposite: Oxtail Paprika Stew, Asparagus, Mushroom, and Chorizo Omelet, and Watercress and Romaine with Cabrales Cheese

Aceitunas y Pepinillos Marinados
Marinated Olives and Cornichons

1½ cups large brine-cured green olives
  (preferably Manzanilla)
1½ cups large brine-cured black olives
  such as Kalamata or Gaeta
1 cup drained *cornichons* (sour gherkins;
  about 6 ounces)
1 large navel orange
1 teaspoon fennel seeds
1 tablespoon fresh thyme leaves
2 bay leaves
¾ cup olive oil

In a large sieve rinse and drain olives and *cornichons* and put in a bowl. With a vegetable peeler remove four 3- by ½-inch strips zest from orange and cut into julienne strips. Juice orange and pour through a fine sieve into a measuring cup. In a small saucepan stir together ½ cup juice, zest, and remaining ingredients and heat just until warm. Pour orange marinade over olives and *cornichons* and let stand at room temperature 30 minutes. *Marinate olives and cornichons, covered and chilled, stirring mixture twice a day, 3 days. Let olives and cornichons stand at room temperature 15 minutes before serving.* Discard bay leaves. Serves 8 to 10 as part of a *tapas* buffet.

Tostadas de Jamón y Queso Manchego con Membrillo Confitado
Serrano Ham and Manchego Cheese with Quince Confit on Toasts

a 12- to 24-inch loaf Italian or French bread
a 4-ounce piece Manchego cheese*
3 ounces thinly sliced serrano ham* or prosciutto
½ cup quince *confit* (recipe follows) or a 4-ounce
  piece quince paste* (*membrillo*)

*sources on page 251

Preheat oven to 400° F.
With a serrated knife cut bread into ¼-inch-thick slices. Cut slices into thirty 1-inch pieces, reserving remaining slices for another use. On a baking sheet toast pieces in middle of oven until golden, 6 to 8

minutes. Cool toasts. *Toasts may be made 3 days ahead and kept in an airtight container at room temperature.*

With a cheese plane thinly slice cheese and arrange cheese and ham or prosciutto on each toast, cutting pieces to cover with a slight overhang. Top each toast with a piece of quince *confit* or paste (if using quince paste, cut into thin triangles to fit toasts). Serves 8 to 10 as part of a *tapas* buffet.

Membrillo Confitado
Quince Confit

1 quince (about 6 ounces)
2 cups water
1 cup sugar
2 teaspoons fresh lemon juice

Peel, quarter, and core quince. Cut quarters crosswise into ⅛-inch-thick pieces. In a 2-quart heavy saucepan bring quince, water, and sugar to a boil, stirring occasionally. Cook quince mixture, partially covered, at a bare simmer, stirring occasionally, 1½ to 2 hours, or until quince is tender (quince will be a deep pinkish orange) and syrup is reduced and thickened. Stir in lemon juice and cool to room temperature. *Quince confit keeps, covered and chilled, 1 month.* Makes about 1 cup.

TORTILLA DE ESPÁRRAGOS, SETAS, Y CHORIZO

ASPARAGUS, MUSHROOM, AND CHORIZO OMELET

10 asparagus stalks (about 1 bunch)
¼ pound spicy *chorizo** (Spanish cured sausage)
½ pound *cremini* mushrooms
1 large onion
3 medium boiling potatoes (about 1¼ pounds)
6 tablespoons olive oil
6 large eggs

*sources on page 251

Trim asparagus and in a deep skillet just large enough to hold asparagus bring 1 cup salted water to a boil and simmer asparagus 2 minutes (asparagus will not be fully cooked). Drain asparagus well and diagonally cut into ½-inch pieces.

Halve *chorizo* lengthwise and cut crosswise into ⅛-inch-thick pieces. Cut mushrooms lengthwise into ⅛-inch-thick slices and chop onion. Peel potatoes and cut into ¼-inch dice.

In a 12-inch nonstick skillet heat 3 tablespoons oil over moderate heat until hot but not smoking and cook potatoes with salt to taste, covered, stirring occasionally, until almost tender but not browned, about 10 minutes. Transfer potatoes with a slotted spoon to a bowl and cool. In oil remaining in skillet cook mushrooms and onion, uncovered, over moderate heat, stirring occasionally, until any liquid mushrooms give off is evaporated. Add *chorizo* and cook, stirring occasionally, 2 minutes, or until *chorizo* begins to give off oil. Remove skillet from heat and cool mushroom mixture slightly.

In a large bowl whisk together eggs and salt and pepper to taste and stir in mushroom mixture, potatoes, and asparagus. Let egg mixture stand at room temperature 10 minutes.

In cleaned skillet heat 1½ tablespoons oil over moderately high heat until hot but not smoking. Add egg mixture, immediately spreading with spatula, and cook, shaking skillet frequently to prevent omelet from sticking, 4 minutes, or until underside is golden brown. Invert heatproof platter or baking sheet over skillet and invert omelet onto it. Add remaining 1½ tablespoons oil to skillet and slide omelet back into skillet. Cook omelet until underside is golden brown, about 3 minutes more.

Reduce heat to moderately low and cook omelet 4 minutes more, or until potatoes are tender. Transfer omelet to a serving plate. *Omelet may be made 1 day ahead and chilled, covered. Reheat omelet on a baking sheet, loosely covered with foil, in a preheated 350° F. oven until just heated through.*

Serve omelet, cut into wedges, warm or at room temperature. Serves 8 to 10 as part of a *tapas* buffet.

ENSALADA DE BERROS Y

LECHUGA AL QUESO CABRALES

WATERCRESS AND ROMAINE WITH CABRALES CHEESE

2 bunches watercress
2 hearts of romaine
1 tablespoon Sherry vinegar
¼ cup extra-virgin olive oil
½ cup crumbled Cabrales cheese*

*sources on page 251

Discard coarse stems from watercress. Tear watercress and romaine into bite-size pieces.

In a large bowl whisk together vinegar, oil, and salt and pepper to taste until combined well. Add greens and cheese and toss until combined well. Serves 8 to 10 as part of a *tapas* buffet.

Pimientos Marinados a la Brasa
Marinated Grilled Red Bell Peppers

6 red bell peppers
3 large garlic cloves
½ cup extra-virgin olive oil
coarse salt to taste

Prepare grill.

Grill bell peppers on a rack set 5 to 6 inches over glowing coals, covered, turning occasionally with metal tongs, until charred and just tender, 20 to 25 minutes. Transfer peppers to a large bowl and let stand, covered with plastic wrap, until cool enough to handle. Peel peppers and quarter lengthwise, discarding seeds, stems, and ribs. (Alternatively, quick-roast bell peppers: Quarter peppers lengthwise, discarding stems, seeds, and ribs. Put peppers, skin sides up, on rack of a broiler pan and broil 2 inches from heat until skins are charred, 8 to 12 minutes. Transfer peppers to a bowl and let stand, covered with plastic wrap, until cool enough to handle. Peel peppers. Broiled peppers will not have a smoky flavor.)

Thinly slice garlic cloves lengthwise and in cleaned bowl toss with warm bell peppers, oil, salt, and black pepper to taste. *Marinate bell peppers, covered and chilled, 3 days.*

Serve peppers at cool room temperature. Serves 8 to 10 as part of a *tapas* buffet.

Tortillitas de Camarones con Mojo
Shrimp Pancakes with Cilantro and Green Pepper Sauce

½ pound shrimp
1 garlic clove
1 teaspoon coarse salt
3 scallions
½ cup all-purpose flour
½ cup chick-pea flour*
1 cup water plus additional for thinning batter
1 tablespoon olive oil
vegetable oil for frying

Accompaniment: mojo (recipe follows)

*sources on page 251

Peel and devein shrimp and finely chop. Mince and mash garlic to a paste with salt. Thinly slice scallions.

Into a bowl sift together flours and add 1 cup water and olive oil, stirring just until batter is smooth. Batter should have consistency of thin pancake batter; if necessary, stir in water to thin batter. Stir in shrimp, garlic paste, and scallions. *Let batter stand, covered and chilled, at least 3 hours and up to 6. If necessary, stir in enough water to thin batter to original consistency.*

Preheat oven to 200° F.

In a 12-inch heavy skillet heat ¼ inch vegetable oil over moderately high heat until hot but not smoking. Working in batches of 4, drop 1 tablespoon of batter into oil and spread batter with tip of spoon to form a pancake about 2½ inches in diameter. Fry pancakes until undersides are golden, about 30 seconds. Flip pancakes with a slotted metal spatula and fry until undersides are golden, about 30 seconds more. Transfer pancakes with spatula to paper towels to drain. Keep pancakes warm on a baking sheet in oven.

Serve pancakes with *mojo*. Makes about 36 pancakes, serving 8 to 10 as part of a *tapas* buffet.

Mojo
Cilantro and Green Pepper Sauce

1 teaspoon cumin seeds
3 garlic cloves
1 teaspoon coarse salt
1 small green bell pepper
1½ cups packed fresh cilantro leaves
2 tablespoons Sherry vinegar
½ cup olive oil

In a dry small heavy skillet toast cumin seeds over moderate heat, shaking skillet occasionally, until a shade darker and fragrant, 2 to 5 minutes. Cool cumin seeds and with a mortar and pestle or in an electric coffee/spice grinder finely grind seeds.

Mince and mash garlic to a coarse paste with salt. Chop bell pepper and in a food processor or blender purée with cumin, garlic paste, cilantro, vinegar, and oil until smooth. *Mojo may be made 6 hours ahead and chilled, covered.* Makes about 1¼ cups.

FRITOS DE BACALAO Y PATATA

SALT COD AND POTATO FRITTERS

½ pound skinless boneless salt cod
   (preferably center cut)
1 pound yellow-fleshed potatoes such as Yukon
   Gold (about 2 medium)
2 garlic cloves
1 large egg
2 tablespoons finely chopped fresh parsley leaves
vegetable oil for deep-frying

Accompaniment (optional): *mojo* (page 264) or
   alioli (page 274)

Cut salt cod into 1-inch pieces and rinse well. In a
large bowl cover cod with cold water by 2 inches.
*Soak cod, covered and chilled, changing water 3
times daily, 2 days.* Drain cod in a colander.

In a saucepan simmer potatoes in salted water to
cover by 2 inches until tender, 20 to 25 minutes.
While potatoes are simmering, mince garlic cloves.

Transfer potatoes with a slotted spoon to a bowl
and add cod to hot water. Simmer cod until it just
flakes, about 3 minutes. Drain cod and, when cool
enough to handle, finely chop. While potatoes are still
warm, peel and force through a ricer into a bowl.
Stir in cod, garlic, egg, parsley, and salt and pepper
to taste until combined well.

In a deep large heavy skillet (about 12 inches
across and 3 inches deep) heat 1¼ inches oil over
moderately high heat until a deep-fat thermometer
registers 375° F. Working in batches of 8, drop
tablespoons of batter into hot oil and fry fritters,
turning over occasionally with a slotted spoon, until
golden, 1 to 2 minutes. With slotted spoon transfer
fritters as fried to paper towels to drain. Make sure
oil returns to 375° F. between batches. *Fritters may
be made 2 hours ahead and kept, loosely covered, at
cool room temperature. Reheat fritters on a baking
sheet in a preheated 350° F. oven until hot, about
5 minutes.*

Makes about 50 fritters, serving 8 to 10 as part of
a *tapas* buffet.

ESTOFADO DE RABO DE TORO AL PIMENTÓN
OXTAIL PAPRIKA STEW

1 large onion
1 green bell pepper
1 head garlic
3½ pounds small oxtails (about 1½ inches thick)
¼ cup olive oil
1 bay leaf
1 tablespoon Spanish smoked paprika* or
    2 tablespoons Hungarian paprika
2½ cups water
1¾ cups beef broth
1½ cups dry white wine
1 cup fresh parsley leaves

*sources on page 251

Chop onion and bell pepper and discard loose papery outer skin from garlic, leaving head intact.
Preheat oven to 325° F.
Pat oxtails dry and season with salt and pepper. In a 4- to 5-quart heavy kettle heat oil over moderately high heat until hot but not smoking and brown oxtails in batches, without crowding, transferring with tongs to a plate. Pour off all but 2 tablespoons fat from kettle and cook onion and bell pepper over moderate heat, stirring occasionally, until onion is golden. Stir in oxtails, garlic head, bay leaf, paprika, water, broth, and wine and bring to a boil.

Braise oxtails, covered, in middle of oven 3 to 3½ hours, or until meat is very tender but not falling off bone. Transfer oxtails and garlic with tongs to a bowl. Discard bay leaf.

Finely chop parsley. When garlic is cool enough to handle, squeeze pulp out of skins into a small bowl and mash with a fork. Whisk garlic and parsley into sauce in kettle until combined well and season with salt and pepper. Add oxtails with any juices accumulated in bowl and gently stir to coat. *Stew may be made 3 days ahead and cooled completely, uncovered, before being chilled, covered. Reheat stew.* Serves 8 to 10 as part of a *tapas* buffet.

Judías Blancas con Romero y Comino
White Beans with Rosemary and Cumin

1 pound large dried lima beans* (about 2½ cups)
4 fresh rosemary sprigs plus 1 tablespoon fresh
    rosemary leaves
2¼ teaspoons coarse salt
1½ teaspoons cumin seeds
2 large garlic cloves
1 tablespoon Sherry vinegar
½ cup extra-virgin olive oil

*sources on page 251

In a 6-quart kettle bring beans, rosemary sprigs, and cold water to cover by 4 inches to a boil and simmer until beans are tender, 45 minutes to 1 hour. Remove kettle from heat and stir in 2 teaspoons coarse salt. Let beans stand 15 minutes.

While beans are standing, in a dry small heavy skillet toast cumin seeds over moderate heat, shaking skillet occasionally, until a shade darker and fragrant, 2 to 5 minutes. Cool cumin seeds slightly and with a mortar and pestle or in an electric coffee/spice grinder finely grind seeds. Mince garlic and rosemary leaves and in a large bowl whisk together with cumin, vinegar, remaining ¼ teaspoon salt, and pepper to taste. Whisk in oil until dressing is combined well.

Drain beans in a large colander and add to dressing, tossing to coat. *Bean salad may be made 3 days ahead and chilled, covered. Let salad stand at room temperature 15 minutes before serving.* Serves 8 to 10 as part of a *tapas* buffet.

Pastas de Piñones
Pine Nut Cookies

¾ cup plus 3 tablespoons pine nuts
    (about 6 ounces)
1 cup all-purpose flour
½ teaspoon salt
¼ teaspoon baking powder
1 teaspoon ground anise seeds
1 stick (½ cup) unsalted butter, softened
½ cup sugar
1 large egg
1 teaspoon finely grated fresh lemon zest

Preheat oven to 350° F. and grease 2 large baking sheets.

In a shallow baking pan toast ¾ cup pine nuts in middle of oven until golden, 6 to 8 minutes. Cool toasted pine nuts and coarsely chop.

Lower oven temperature to 325° F.

Into a bowl sift together flour, salt, baking powder, and anise. In another bowl with an electric mixer beat together butter and sugar until light and fluffy and beat in egg until combined well. Beat in zest and flour mixture until just combined and stir in chopped nuts.

Drop level teaspoons of dough 2 inches apart onto baking sheets and press 1 whole pine nut into center of each mound. Bake cookies in batches in middle of oven until pale golden, 14 to 16 minutes. Cool cookies on sheet 1 minute and immediately transfer with a spatula to racks to cool. *Cookies may be made 3 days ahead and kept in an airtight container at room temperature.* Makes about 90 cookies.

SUMMER LUNCH BY THE SEA

GAZPACHO DE UVAS Y HABAS
GREEN GRAPE AND LIMA BEAN GAZPACHO

PAELLA A LA MARINERA CON ALIOLI DE LIMÓN
SEAFOOD PAELLA WITH LEMON GARLIC MAYONNAISE

Martin Codax Albariño Rías Baixas '97

NARANJAS CARAMELIZADAS AL PERFUME DE ESPECIES
SPICED CARAMEL ORANGES

Serves 8

Above: Green Grape and Lima Bean Gazpacho. Opposite: Seafood Paella

GAZPACHO DE UVAS Y HABAS
GREEN GRAPE AND LIMA BEAN GAZPACHO

Although we enjoyed the coarse texture of this refreshing soup, it may be forced through a fine sieve before chilling.

two 10-ounce packages frozen lima beans
¼ cup water plus 4 cups ice water
2 pounds seedless green grapes (1 large bunch)
8 slices firm white sandwich bread
1 cup pine nuts (about 4 ounces)
4 garlic cloves
¼ cup Sherry vinegar
2 teaspoons fine sea salt, or to taste
¾ cup extra-virgin olive oil

Garnish: seedless green grapes, peeled and
   halved, and extra-virgin olive oil for drizzling

In a saucepan simmer lima beans and ¼ cup water, covered, over moderate heat, stirring occasionally, until just tender, about 4 minutes. In a colander drain beans and rinse under cold water until cool. Drain beans well.

Pick enough grapes to measure 4 cups, reserving remainder for another use, and trim crusts from bread, discarding crusts. In a large bowl soak bread in ice water 2 minutes and squeeze bread over bowl, reserving water. In a blender purée one third of beans, grapes, bread, pine nuts, garlic, vinegar, salt, and reserved water until smooth and with motor running add one third of oil in a slow stream, blending until combined well. Transfer soup to another large bowl and repeat procedure with remaining ingredients. *Chill soup, covered, until cold, about 2 hours, and up to 2 days. Whisk soup before serving.*

Serve soup garnished with grapes and drizzled with oil. Makes about 10 cups, serving 8.

PAELLA A LA MARINERA CON ALIOLI DE LIMÓN
SEAFOOD PAELLA WITH LEMON GARLIC MAYONNAISE

This recipe calls for a 17-inch paella pan, available by mail order (sources on page 251). To assure even heating, place the pan over 2 burners and frequently rotate it a quarter turn while moving it back and forth over the burners. Ingredients are added to the pan in rapid succession, so it is important to prepare them before beginning to cook (you'll need several large platters and bowls). All ingredients except the tomatoes may be prepared 6 hours ahead and chilled, covered. Ask your fishmonger to split and devein the lobsters and clean the squid.

two 1½-pound live lobsters, split lengthwise
   and deveined
1 pound large shrimp (15 to 20)
1 pound cleaned small squid
1 teaspoon fine sea salt
2 dozen small mussels (preferably cultivated)
1 red bell pepper
1 green bell pepper
3 scallions
3 medium vine-ripened tomatoes
1 teaspoon Spanish smoked paprika*
   or Hungarian paprika
8 garlic cloves
5½ cups fish stock**
¼ teaspoon crumbled saffron threads
6 tablespoons dry white wine
2 tablespoons fresh lemon juice
½ cup olive oil
3 cups Spanish short-grain rice*, such as SOS
   or Calasparra, or Arborio rice
2 tablespoons finely chopped fresh parsley leaves
½ bay leaf
½ cup fresh or thawed frozen peas

Garnish: lemon wedges and parsley
Accompaniment: lemon *alioli* (page 274)

*sources on page 251
**available at fish markets and some specialty
   foods shops or recipe on page 274

Twist off tail sections and claws from lobsters, reserving heads and legs for fish stock. With kitchen shears cut split lobster tails crosswise in half (for a total of 8 pieces). With back of a heavy knife slightly crush shells of lobster claws to make it easy to remove meat when eating and transfer lobster tails and claws to a platter. Shell and devein shrimp, reserving shells for fish stock, and transfer shrimp to a bowl. Cut squid crosswise into ½-inch-thick rings and transfer to another bowl. Sprinkle shrimp and squid each with ¼ teaspoon sea salt. Scrub mussels well, removing beards, and transfer to another platter.

Preheat oven to 400° F. for gas oven and 450° F. for electric.

Cut bell peppers into 1- by ¼-inch strips and transfer to a bowl. Cut scallions crosswise into ¼-inch-thick pieces and transfer to another bowl. Coarsely chop tomatoes and transfer to another bowl. Sprinkle paprika over tomatoes. Mince and mash enough garlic with salt to taste to a paste to measure 2 tablespoons. In a saucepan bring stock to a simmer and keep at a bare simmer, covered. In a cup stir together saffron, wine, and lemon juice.

In a 17-inch paella pan set over 2 burners heat 6 tablespoons oil over moderately high heat until hot but not smoking and stir-fry lobster pieces with tongs (oil will spatter), frequently rotating pan and moving pan back and forth over burners for even heat, 2 minutes. With tongs transfer lobster to a platter (lobster will not be cooked through). In oil remaining in pan stir-fry shrimp in same manner 2 minutes and transfer with a slotted spoon to another platter. Add 1 tablespoon oil to pan and stir-fry squid in same manner 2 minutes, transferring squid to platter with shrimp. Add remaining tablespoon oil and stir-fry peppers in same manner 2 minutes. Stir in garlic paste and stir-fry 1 minute. Add tomatoes and paprika and stir-fry 1 minute. Add rice and stir to coat with tomato mixture. Stir in parsley, bay leaf, stock, and wine mixture. Bring mixture to a boil over high heat and cook, gently stirring constantly and frequently rotating pan, until liquid is reduced, bubbles thicken, and most of rice appears on surface, about 6 minutes. (Spoon should leave a path exposing bottom of pan when pulled through center of rice mixture.)

Remove pan from heat and, working quickly, stir in shrimp, squid, scallions, peas, black pepper to taste, and remaining ½ teaspoon sea salt. Gently push lobster and mussels into rice and drizzle any juices that have accumulated on platters over rice. Bake paella in middle of oven, uncovered, about 10 to 12 minutes for gas oven and 15 to 20 minutes for electric, or until a crust forms around edge of pan, almost all liquid is absorbed, and rice has slightly more bite than desired. (If rice is too hard and paella is dry, sprinkle with 2 tablespoons water and continue to bake in oven; if rice is cooked but too much liquid remains, cook paella on top of stove over moderately high heat, without stirring, frequently rotating pan, until liquid is absorbed.) Immediately transfer paella in pan to a rack and cover tightly with foil. Let paella stand 10 minutes (paella will continue to cook). Discard bay leaf.

Serve paella in pan, garnished with lemon wedges and parsley. Serve *alioli* on the side. Serves 8.

FISH STOCK

1 onion
½ celery rib
reserved heads and legs from two 1½-pound
    lobsters and reserved shells from 1 pound
    large shrimp (see page 272)
1 small whiting, cleaned, with head on
6 black peppercorns
1 bay leaf
1 slice lemon
2 fresh parsley sprigs
1 cup bottled clam juice
5 cups cold water
¾ cup dry white wine

Chop onion and celery. With back of a heavy knife crush lobster heads. In a well-buttered heavy kettle (4- to 5-quart capacity) cook onion, celery, lobster and shrimp shells, whiting, peppercorns, and bay leaf, covered, over moderate heat 5 minutes. Stir in remaining ingredients and bring to a boil, uncovered, skimming froth. Simmer stock mixture, uncovered, until liquid is reduced to about 6 cups, about 20 minutes. Pour stock through a fine sieve into a heatproof bowl. *Stock may be made 3 days ahead and cooled, uncovered, before being chilled, covered. Stock keeps, frozen, 3 months.* Makes about 6 cups.

ALIOLI DE LIMÓN
GARLIC MAYONNAISE WITH LEMON

2 lemons
4 large garlic cloves
1 cup mayonnaise

Grate enough lemon zest to measure 1 teaspoon and squeeze enough juice from lemons to measure 3 tablespoons. Mince enough garlic to measure 2 teaspoons. In a small bowl stir together zest, juice, garlic, and mayonnaise and season with salt and pepper. *Alioli may be made 2 days ahead and chilled, covered. Season alioli with salt and pepper before serving.* Makes about 1 cup.

NARANJAS CARAMELIZADAS AL PERFUME DE ESPECIES
SPICED CARAMEL ORANGES

Although the fried orange zest garnish adds sweet crunchy bite to these caramel oranges, it may be omitted.

8 navel oranges
2 teaspoons fennel seeds
½ teaspoon black peppercorns
1½ cinnamon sticks
2 cups sugar plus additional for fried zest
¼ cup medium-dry Sherry
1 cup vegetable oil for frying zest

With a vegetable peeler remove zest from 2 oranges for garnish. Squeeze juice from 1 orange. With a sharp knife cut peel and pith from all oranges. Cut each orange into 8 chunks, discarding seeds, and transfer to a large heatproof bowl.

With a mortar and pestle or with bottom of a heavy saucepan coarsely crush fennel seeds and peppercorns. Split whole cinnamon stick in half lengthwise.

In a dry heavy saucepan cook 2 cups sugar over moderately low heat, stirring slowly with a fork (to help sugar melt evenly), until melted and pale golden. Cook caramel without stirring, swirling pan to ensure even coloring, until deep golden. Remove pan from heat and carefully add Sherry down side of pan (caramel will bubble and steam). Cook mixture, stirring constantly, until caramel is completely dissolved. Carefully add orange juice down side of pan (caramel will bubble and steam). Stir in spices and cook mixture, stirring constantly, until caramel is dissolved. Immediately pour caramel over oranges and stir to combine well. Cool oranges to room temperature, stirring occasionally. *Caramel oranges may be made 1 day ahead and chilled, covered.*

To make fried orange zest, in a 1-quart heavy saucepan heat oil over moderate heat until a deep-fat thermometer registers 375° F. Fry zest in batches, stirring, 1 minute, or until golden. (Make sure oil returns to 375° F. between batches.) Transfer zest as fried with a slotted spoon to paper towels to drain and immediately sprinkle with additional sugar.

Serve caramel oranges topped with fried zest. Serves 8.

EASY ONE-DISH DINNERS

All too often, the mere thought of planning a menu (not to mention preparing several dishes to come up with a flavorful meal) can discourage the busy cook. Before you toss another burger on the grill or order out for pizza, try our winning alternative—a one-dish dinner. Keeping ease and taste uppermost in mind, we have created 24 delicious recipes—for salads, pastas and grains, vegetarian fare, and stews—that are substantial enough to serve as complete meals on their own. Whether you choose one of our quick-and-easy 45-minute pasta recipes, a somewhat more involved salad or stir-fry, or a slow-cooked stew, you'll have the convenience of serving a satisfying dinner from a single recipe.

Not so long ago, meat, poultry, or seafood played the leading role in most meals; today, a host of fresh greens and vegetables, pastas in every shape imaginable, and various whole grains share the limelight or even take center stage. Our recipes, emphasizing seasonal produce and herbs, encourage you to expand your cooking and eating repertoire in easy, innovative ways. Many meatless suppers, like our Lentil and Rice Eggplant Bundles, Broccoli Rabe Frittata, and Sesame Noodle Salad with Salmon offer chic dining that's special enough to serve to guests. Even our chicken, beef, and lamb stews are chockful of garden freshness.

A well-stocked pantry will allow you to make many of these recipes without a lot of last-minute shopping. Ingredients to have on hand include staples from the kitchen cabinet (pasta, rice, lentils, canned beans, dried chiles, nuts, and dried fruits), the refrigerator (bacon, eggs, cheese, and ham), and the freezer (frozen peas). Our risotto then requires only a final purchase of boneless chicken thighs; and the twice-baked potatoes just need a bag of fresh spinach. Some dishes call for specialty items: Duck *confit*, smoked chicken, and Thai red curry paste, for example, add bursts of flavor and excitement to everyday dishes; while a packaged brown and wild rice mix, bean-thread noodles, and quinoa are welcome changes from ordinary rice and pasta.

Although each recipe stands on its own as a full meal, some quick accompaniments may be added. With the Garlic and Fennel Braised Chicken, for instance, we urge you to serve plenty of crusty bread to sop up the juices (first squeeze the softened garlic cloves from their skins and then smear them on the bread). Add a glass of wine and some fresh fruit or store-bought ice cream or sorbet for dessert, and dinner—for family or friends—is complete. Cooking is a simple pleasure when you have a stash of *Gourmet's* one-dish dinners at hand.

SALADS

SMOKED CHICKEN, AVOCADO, AND TOMATO SALAD

For dressing
3 tablespoons fresh orange juice
2 teaspoons soy sauce such as Kikkoman
1 teaspoon minced garlic
1 teaspoon Dijon mustard
¼ teaspoon finely grated fresh orange zest
¼ cup vegetable oil

1 whole smoked chicken breast
  (about 1 pound)
1½ firm-ripe avocados
3 Belgian endives
2 scallions
½ pound vine-ripened cherry tomatoes
2 cups loosely packed *mesclun*

Make dressing:
In a small bowl whisk together all dressing ingredients except oil until combined. Gradually whisk in oil until emulsified and add salt and pepper to taste.

Halve chicken breast lengthwise and discard skin. Cut breasts crosswise into ½-inch-thick slices. Pit and peel avocados and cut into ¼-inch-thick slices. Halve endives lengthwise and cut lengthwise into thin strips. Diagonally cut scallions into thin slices and halve tomatoes. In a large bowl gently toss salad ingredients with dressing and season with salt and pepper. Serves 4 as a main course.

SEARED SEA SCALLOPS AND WILD RICE SALAD

1¼ cups wild and brown rice blend, such as
  Lundberg Wild Blend, or brown rice
  (about 8 ounces)
4 cups water
½ pound *haricots verts* (thin French green beans)
4 scallions
½ cup dried cranberries
5 tablespoons extra-virgin olive oil
3 tablespoons fresh lime juice
20 medium sea scallops (about 1 pound)

2 tablespoons vegetable oil
½ cup sliced almonds

In a fine sieve rinse rice under cold water and drain. In a 3-quart heavy saucepan bring rice and water to a boil and simmer, covered, 40 minutes, or until tender.

While rice is simmering, diagonally cut beans and scallions into thin slices. Add beans to rice and simmer, covered, 1 minute. In a sieve rinse rice mixture under cold water to stop cooking and drain well.

In a large bowl toss together rice mixture, scallions, and cranberries. In a bowl whisk together olive oil and lime juice until just combined and stir into rice mixture with salt and pepper to taste.

Discard tough muscle from side of each scallop if necessary and horizontally halve scallops if large. Pat scallops dry and season with salt and pepper. In a large heavy skillet heat 1 tablespoon vegetable oil over moderate heat and cook almonds, stirring constantly, until golden, about 2 minutes. Stir almonds into rice mixture. In skillet heat remaining tablespoon vegetable oil over moderately high heat until hot but not smoking and sauté scallops in batches until golden and just cooked through, about 1 minute on each side, transferring to a plate.

Divide rice salad among 4 plates and top with scallops. Serves 4 as a main course.

SESAME NOODLE SALAD WITH SALMON

For dressing
3 tablespoons vegetable oil
¼ cup sesame seeds
2 tablespoons honey
2 tablespoons Asian sesame oil*
2 tablespoons soy sauce
2 tablespoons rice vinegar (not seasoned)
2 teaspoons minced peeled fresh gingerroot

5 cups water
4 ounces bean-thread (cellophane) noodles*
¾ English cucumber
1 bunch fresh chives
1 yellow bell pepper
1 pound salmon fillet, skinned

*available at some specialty foods shops and
supermarkets and by mail order from
Uwajimaya, (800) 889-1928

Make dressing:

In a small skillet heat 1 tablespoon vegetable oil over moderate heat and cook sesame seeds, stirring constantly, until golden. In a small bowl whisk together sesame seeds, remaining 2 tablespoons vegetable oil, and remaining dressing ingredients until combined well. *Dressing may be made 3 days ahead and chilled, covered.*

In a 3-quart saucepan bring water to a boil and remove pan from heat. Stir in noodles and let stand 15 minutes.

While noodles are standing, halve and seed cucumber and diagonally cut into thin slices. Cut chives into 1-inch pieces and cut bell pepper into very thin strips. Pat salmon dry and season with salt and pepper. Heat a nonstick skillet over moderate heat until hot and cook salmon until golden and just cooked through, about 4 minutes on each side. Transfer salmon to a plate and cool about 10 minutes.

Drain noodles in a colander and rinse under cold water to stop cooking. Drain noodles well and with scissors cut into 6-inch pieces. Break salmon into bite-size pieces. In a large bowl toss together noodles, dressing, cucumber, chives, bell pepper, and salt and pepper to taste. Add salmon and gently toss until just combined. Serves 4 as a main course.

CHILI LIME CHICKEN SALAD WITH MANGO

4 skinless boneless chicken breast halves
    (about 1½ pounds total)
6 tablespoons vegetable oil
2 tablespoons bottled chili sauce such as Heinz
2 tablespoons fresh lime juice
1 teaspoon minced fresh jalapeño chile
1 teaspoon minced garlic
1 firm-ripe mango
1 red bell pepper
2 bunches watercress
1 cup loosely packed fresh cilantro leaves

Preheat broiler and line rack of a broiler pan with aluminum foil.

Pat chicken dry. In a small bowl stir together 1 tablespoon oil and 1 tablespoon chili sauce and season with salt and pepper. Spread mixture on chicken and arrange on broiler rack. Broil chicken 2 to 3 inches from heat until golden and cooked through, about 4 minutes on each side. Transfer chicken to a cutting board and let stand 10 minutes.

While chicken is standing, in a small bowl whisk together remaining tablespoon chili sauce, lime juice, jalapeño, and garlic until combined. Gradually whisk in remaining 5 tablespoons oil until emulsified and add salt and pepper to taste. *Dressing keeps, covered and chilled, 3 days.*

Pit and peel mango and cut into thin strips. Cut bell pepper into very thin strips and tear watercress into bite-size pieces, discarding coarse stems. Diagonally cut chicken into ¼-inch-thick slices. In a large bowl gently toss chicken, mango, bell pepper, watercress, and cilantro with enough dressing to coat and season with salt and pepper. Serves 4 as a main course.

HAM AND CHEESE CHOPPED SALAD WITH HONEY DIJON VINAIGRETTE ○

For vinaigrette
1 tablespoon white-wine vinegar
1 teaspoon Dijon mustard
1 teaspoon honey
3 tablespoons extra-virgin olive oil

4 ounces sliced ham
3 ounces extra-sharp Cheddar (preferably white)
¼ sweet onion such as Vidalia or Maui
1 Granny Smith apple
3 celery ribs
1 medium head *radicchio* (about 6 ounces)
1 head romaine

Make vinaigrette:

In a small bowl whisk together vinegar, mustard, and honey until combined. Gradually whisk in oil until emulsified and add salt and pepper to taste.

Cut ham into thin strips and separately cut Cheddar and onion into ¼-inch dice. Quarter and core apple and cut into ¼-inch dice. Thinly slice celery. Cut *radicchio* and romaine leaves crosswise into ½-inch-thick slices. In a large bowl toss together salad ingredients with vinaigrette and season with salt and pepper. Serves 4 as a main course.

WARM POTATO, BACON, AND SPINACH SALAD

1 pound small boiling potatoes
1 pound sliced bacon
4 mushrooms
3 celery ribs
½ bunch fresh chives
¼ pound fresh spinach leaves (preferably baby)
For dressing
¼ cup mayonnaise
1 tablespoon cider vinegar
½ teaspoon Dijon mustard
¼ cup extra-virgin olive oil

In a small heavy saucepan cover potatoes with cold salted water by 1 inch and simmer until tender, 15 to 20 minutes. While potatoes are simmering, coarsely chop bacon and in a large heavy skillet cook in 2 batches over moderate heat, stirring, until golden. Transfer bacon as cooked to paper towels to drain and cool. Slice mushrooms and diagonally cut celery into thin slices. Cut chives into ½-inch pieces. If using regular spinach, tear leaves into bite-size pieces, discarding coarse stems.

Make dressing:

In a small bowl whisk together mayonnaise, vinegar, and mustard until combined. Gradually whisk in oil and add salt and pepper to taste.

Drain potatoes and while still warm cut into ½-inch-thick slices. In a large bowl toss potatoes with dressing until coated. Add bacon, mushrooms, celery, chives, spinach, and salt and pepper to taste and toss until combined. Serves 4 as a main course.

PASTAS AND GRAINS

QUINOA WITH DUCK CONFIT AND WILTED RADICCHIO

⅓ cup balsamic vinegar
1 tablespoon sugar
¼ cup walnuts
¾ cup quinoa*
2 *confit* duck legs**
1 large shallot
1 small head *radicchio*
1 tablespoon unsalted butter
2 tablespoons chopped fresh parsley leaves

*available at natural foods stores
**available from many butchers and by mail
    order from D'Artagnan, (800) 327-8246

Preheat oven to 450° F.

In a small heavy saucepan bring vinegar and sugar to a boil and simmer until reduced to about 3 tablespoons, about 7 minutes. Remove pan from heat and keep balsamic syrup warm, covered. In a baking pan toast walnuts in middle of oven until golden, about 5 minutes, and coarsely chop.

In a sieve rinse quinoa under cold water until water runs clear. In a saucepan bring 1 inch water to a boil and set sieve over pan (quinoa should not touch water). Steam quinoa, covered, until fluffy and dry, about 20 minutes.

While quinoa is steaming, arrange duck in baking pan, skin sides up, and bake in middle of oven until skin is crisp, about 20 minutes.

Finely chop shallot and chop *radicchio*. In a large nonstick skillet heat butter over moderately high heat until foam subsides and sauté shallot, stirring, until softened. Add quinoa, *radicchio*, and salt and pepper to taste and sauté, stirring occasionally, until *radicchio* is wilted and just tender, about 3 minutes. Add walnuts and parsley and toss until combined.

Serve quinoa mixture topped with duck legs and drizzled with balsamic syrup. Serves 2 as a main course.

POLENTA AND ARUGULA WITH SAUSAGE

1 small onion
1 red bell pepper
2 bunches arugula
1 pound sweet or hot Italian sausage
  (about six 3-ounce links)
6 cups water
1½ cups yellow cornmeal

Preheat oven to 400° F.

Finely chop onion and bell pepper. Discard coarse stems from arugula and chop leaves. In a 5-quart heavy kettle brown sausage over moderate heat, about 10 minutes. With tongs transfer sausage to a shallow baking pan and pour off all but 1 tablespoon fat from kettle. Increase heat to moderately high and in kettle sauté onion and bell pepper, stirring, until onion is softened. Transfer onion mixture to a bowl.

In kettle bring water with salt to taste to a boil and add cornmeal in a slow stream, whisking constantly. Cook polenta over moderately low heat, whisking frequently, until polenta is thick, about 30 minutes.

About 10 minutes before polenta is thickened, roast browned sausage in middle of oven until cooked through, about 10 minutes, and cut into ¼-inch-thick slices. Remove polenta from heat and stir in onion mixture and arugula.

Serve polenta topped with sausage. Serves 4 as a main course.

ORECCHIETTE WITH SHRIMP, SUGAR SNAP PEAS, AND SCALLION PURÉE

¾ pound *orecchiette* (ear-shaped pasta) or
  small pasta shells
1 pound large shrimp (about 20)
½ pound sugar snap peas or snow peas
4 garlic cloves
2 tablespoons unsalted butter
¼ cup dry white wine
2 bunches scallions (greens only)
2 tablespoons extra-virgin olive oil

Fill a 6-quart kettle three-fourths full with salted water and bring to a boil for pasta. Peel and devein shrimp and halve lengthwise. Diagonally cut peas into ¼-inch-thick slices and mince garlic.

Cook pasta in boiling water until almost *al dente*. Add peas and cook until pasta is *al dente*, about 1 minute more. Reserve 1 cup cooking liquid and drain pasta and peas in a colander.

In a large skillet heat butter over moderately high heat until foam subsides and sauté garlic, stirring, 15 seconds. Add shrimp, wine, and salt and pepper to taste and cook shrimp, stirring, until pink and just cooked through, 3 to 5 minutes. In a serving bowl toss shrimp mixture with pasta and peas.

In a blender pureé scallion greens with oil, ½ cup reserved pasta cooking liquid, and salt and pepper to taste until smooth. Add pureé to pasta and toss, adding more cooking liquid if desired. Serves 4 as a main course.

CREAMY PENNE WITH ASPARAGUS AND PROSCIUTTO ◔

¾ pound *penne* or other tubular pasta
1 pound asparagus
⅓ pound sliced prosciutto
½ cup heavy cream
⅔ cup freshly grated Parmesan (about 2 ounces)

Fill a 6-quart kettle three-fourths full with salted water and bring to a boil for pasta. Diagonally cut asparagus into ¼-inch-thick slices and cut prosciutto into ½-inch pieces.

Cook pasta in boiling water until almost *al dente*. Add asparagus and cook until pasta is *al dente*, 1 to 2 minutes more. Drain pasta and asparagus in a colander.

In a large nonstick skillet sauté prosciutto over high heat, stirring, 2 minutes and add cream. Bring cream to a simmer and stir in Parmesan and salt and pepper to taste. Remove cream mixture from heat. In a serving bowl toss pasta and asparagus with cream mixture until combined. Serves 4 as a main course.

TAGLIATELLE WITH ZUCCHINI RAGÚ ◔

a 28- to 32-ounce can whole tomatoes with juice
¾ pound *tagliatelle*
½ cup Kalamata or other brine-cured black olives
2 cups packed fresh basil leaves
2 medium zucchini (about ⅔ pound total)
¼ cup extra-virgin olive oil

In a saucepan cook tomatoes with juice over moderately high heat, stirring occasionally, until reduced by half, 15 to 20 minutes. Fill a 6-quart kettle three-fourths full with salted water and bring to a boil for *tagliatelle*. Pit olives. Separately chop olives and basil and add to tomatoes with salt and pepper to taste. Cut zucchini into thin rounds and stir into sauce with oil. Remove from heat and keep warm.

Cook *tagliatelle* in boiling water until *al dente*. Reserve ½ cup pasta cooking liquid and drain *tagliatelle* in a colander. In a serving bowl toss *tagliatelle* with *ragú* and about ¼ cup reserved pasta cooking liquid, adding more liquid if desired, until combined. Serves 4 as a main course.

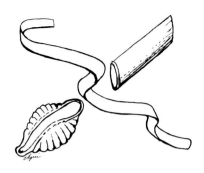

RISOTTO WITH CHICKEN, PEAS, AND THYME ◔

1 pound skinless boneless chicken thighs
1 large onion
5 cups chicken broth (preferably low-salt)
½ stick (¼ cup) unsalted butter
1½ cups Arborio rice*
1¼ teaspoons chopped fresh thyme leaves
½ cup dry white wine
1¼ cups frozen peas

Garnish: freshly grated Parmesan

*available at Italian markets and specialty foods shops

Cut chicken into ¼-inch dice. Chop onion. In a small saucepan bring broth to a simmer and keep at a bare simmer.

In a 4-quart heavy saucepan heat 2 tablespoons butter over moderately high heat until foam subsides and sauté chicken, stirring occasionally, until cooked through, about 7 minutes. With a slotted spoon transfer chicken to a bowl. Add remaining 2 tablespoons butter to pan and sauté onion, stirring occasionally, until softened. Stir in rice, thyme, wine, and 1 cup broth and cook, stirring constantly and keeping at a strong simmer throughout, until liquid is absorbed. Continue cooking at a strong simmer and adding broth, about ½ cup at a time, stirring constantly and letting each addition be absorbed before adding next, until all broth is added, about 16 minutes total. Stir in peas and chicken and cook until rice is tender and creamy-looking but still *al dente*, 1 to 2 minutes.

Serve risotto with grated Parmesan. Serves 4 as a main course.

LENTIL AND RICE EGGPLANT BUNDLES

4 carrots
3 celery ribs
1 medium onion
1 cup dried lentils
1½ tablespoons ground coriander seeds
2 teaspoons ground cumin
⅓ cup olive oil
½ cup long-grain rice (not converted)
3½ cups water
2 medium eggplants
1 cup packed fresh cilantro sprigs
For vinaigrette
⅓ cup extra-virgin olive oil
3 tablespoons white-wine vinegar
2 teaspoons ground coriander seeds

Garnish: fresh cilantro sprigs

Chop carrots, celery, and onion. Pick over lentils and in a sieve rinse under cold water. In a 3-quart kettle cook carrots, celery, onion, coriander, and cumin in 2 tablespoons oil over moderate heat, stirring often, 5 minutes. Add lentils, rice, water, and salt and pepper to taste and cook, covered, at a bare simmer until lentils are tender, about 20 minutes.

Preheat broiler.

While lentil mixture is cooking, cut eggplants lengthwise into ¼-inch-thick slices. Brush 2 baking sheets with some oil and arrange slices in one layer on baking sheets. Brush slices with remaining oil and season with salt and pepper. Broil eggplant in batches, without turning, 4 to 5 inches from heat until golden, about 5 minutes.

Chop cilantro and toss with lentil mixture.

Make vinaigrette:

In a small bowl whisk together oil, vinegar, coriander, and salt and pepper to taste.

On each of 4 plates arrange 4 eggplant slices in a fan shape. Mound one fourth lentil mixture at base of each fan and fold slices over lentil mixture to form a package. Spoon vinaigrette over eggplant packages and garnish with cilantro. Serves 4 as a main course.

CAULIFLOWER, POTATO, AND GREEN BEAN CURRY

1½ pounds vine-ripened tomatoes
1 pound green beans
a 2-pound head cauliflower
1 pound small red potatoes
2 fresh jalapeño chiles
3 tablespoons chopped peeled fresh gingerroot
⅓ cup raw cashews*
2½ tablespoons coriander seeds
2 teaspoons cumin seeds
2 teaspoons salt
1 teaspoon turmeric
½ teaspoon fennel seeds
¾ cup water plus additional if necessary
¾ stick (6 tablespoons) unsalted butter

*available at natural foods stores

Cut a small shallow X in bottom end of each tomato and have ready a large bowl of ice and cold water. In a kettle of boiling salted water blanch tomatoes 10 seconds and with a slotted spoon transfer to ice water to stop cooking. Peel, seed, and chop tomatoes. Diagonally cut beans into 2-inch pieces. In same boiling water cook beans until tender, about 7 minutes. Drain beans in a colander and transfer to ice water to stop cooking. Drain beans. Trim cauliflower and cut into 1-inch florets. Cut potatoes into ½-inch-wide wedges.

Seed chiles if desired (wear rubber gloves) and in a blender purée chiles, gingerroot, cashews, coriander, cumin, salt, turmeric, and fennel seeds with ½ cup water until smooth.

In a deep 12-inch heavy skillet with a tight-fitting lid heat butter over moderate heat until foam subsides and cook chile purée, stirring, until purée is thickened and separates from butter, about 5 minutes. Add tomatoes and cook, stirring, 5 minutes. Add potatoes and cook, stirring, 1 minute. Cover skillet and simmer mixture, stirring once or twice, 5 minutes. Stir in cauliflower and remaining ¼ cup water and cook, covered, stirring once or twice and adding more water, ¼ cup at a time, if mixture becomes completely dry, until vegetables are tender, about 15 minutes. Stir in beans and cook, covered, until heated through, about 2 minutes. Serves 4 as a main course.

TWICE-BAKED POTATOES WITH SPINACH AND FETA

4 large russet (baking) potatoes
two 10-ounce bags fresh spinach
¾ stick (6 tablespoons) unsalted butter,
    softened
½ cup whole milk
4 ounces feta

Preheat oven to 450° F.

With a fork prick potatoes and on a baking sheet bake in middle of oven 1½ hours, or until tender. While potatoes are baking, discard tough stems from spinach and chop spinach. Leave oven on.

When potatoes are just cool enough to handle, halve lengthwise and scoop flesh into a bowl, leaving ¼-inch-thick shells. With a potato masher mash potatoes. Transfer shells to baking sheet and brush insides with 2 tablespoons butter. Season shells with salt and pepper and bake in middle of oven until golden, about 20 minutes.

While shells are baking, in a 3-quart saucepan heat remaining 4 tablespoons butter over moderately high heat until foam subsides and sauté spinach, stirring, until wilted, about 2 minutes. Season spinach with salt and pepper and stir in mashed potatoes. Stir in milk and remove pan from heat. Crumble feta and stir into potato mixture until combined well.

Spoon potato mixture into shells and bake until heated through, about 10 minutes. Serves 4 as a main course.

PORTABELLA OPEN-FACED SANDWICHES ☺

1 medium vine-ripened tomato
1 tablespoon balsamic vinegar
3 garlic cloves
1 large shallot
⅓ cup extra-virgin olive oil
2 medium zucchini
6 large portabella mushroom caps
8 ounces smoked mozzarella
6 slices crusty Italian bread

Prepare grill.

Quarter tomato and in a blender purée with vinegar and salt and pepper to taste until smooth. Mince garlic and shallot and in a small bowl stir together with oil. Cut zucchini lengthwise into ¼-inch-thick slices. Brush mushrooms and zucchini with oil mixture and season with salt and pepper. Coarsely grate mozzarella.

On a lightly oiled rack set 5 to 6 inches over glowing coals grill mushrooms and zucchini until just tender, about 5 minutes on each side for mushrooms and 2 minutes on each side for zucchini slices. (Alternatively, grill mushrooms and zucchini in a lightly-oiled well-seasoned ridged grill pan over moderately high heat in same manner.) Toast bread and spread with tomato mixture. If desired halve mushrooms crosswise. Top tomato mixture with mushrooms, cheese, and zucchini. Serves 6 as a light main course.

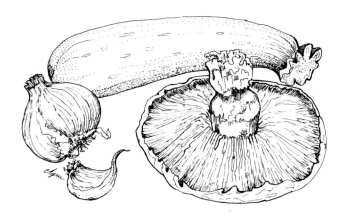

Asparagus, Jícama, and Shiitake Stir-Fry

1 pound asparagus
1 large red bell pepper
a ½-pound piece *jicama*
1 pound fresh *shiitake* mushrooms
1 bunch scallions
a 2-inch piece peeled fresh gingerroot
2 large garlic cloves
¼ cup soy sauce such as Kikkoman
1 tablespoon sugar
2 teaspoons cornstarch
¼ cup water
3 tablespoons vegetable oil

Accompaniment: rice

Diagonally cut asparagus into 2-inch pieces, separating tips from stalks. Cut bell pepper into 2- by ¼-inch strips. Peel *jicama* and cut into ¼-inch-thick slices. Cut slices into thin sticks about 2 inches long.

Discard stems from mushrooms and cut caps into ½-inch strips. Diagonally cut scallions into ¼-inch-thick slices. Finely chop enough gingerroot to measure 2 tablespoons. Finely chop garlic cloves and in a bowl combine with mushrooms, scallions, and gingerroot.

In a small bowl stir together soy sauce, sugar, cornstarch, and 2 tablespoons water.

Heat a wok or 12-inch nonstick skillet over high heat until a bead of water dropped on cooking surface evaporates immediately and add oil, swirling wok or skillet to coat evenly. Add asparagus stalks and stir-fry 1 minute. Add asparagus tips and bell pepper and stir-fry 1 minute. Add mushroom mixture and stir-fry 2 minutes. Add remaining 2 tablespoons water and cook, covered, 2 minutes, or until asparagus is just tender. Add *jicama* and stir-fry 30 seconds. Stir soy sauce mixture and add to wok or skillet. Stir-fry mixture 30 seconds, or until sauce is slightly thickened.

Serve stir-fry with rice. Serves 4 as a main course.

Broccoli Rabe Frittata

½ pound broccoli rabe
1 large onion (about ½ pound)
2 garlic cloves
1 large russet (baking) potato
¼ cup olive oil
1 teaspoon salt, or to taste
4 ounces fresh mozzarella
4 large eggs

Accompaniment: green salad (optional)

Discard coarse and hollow stems from broccoli rabe and coarsely chop stalks and leaves. In a large saucepan of boiling salted water blanch broccoli until just tender, about 3 minutes, and drain. Rinse broccoli under cold water to stop cooking and squeeze out excess moisture.

Chop onion and mince garlic. Peel potato and cut into ¼-inch dice. In a 10-inch nonstick skillet cook onion and garlic in 2 tablespoons oil over moderate heat, stirring, until softened and pale golden. Add potatoes and salt and cook, stirring occasionally, until potatoes are tender, about 10 minutes. Remove skillet from heat and cool mixture slightly.

Coarsely grate mozzarella. In a large bowl lightly beat eggs. Stir in broccoli rabe, potato mixture, mozzarella, and salt and pepper to taste.

Preheat broiler.

In cleaned skillet heat remaining 2 tablespoons oil over moderately high heat until hot but not smoking. Add egg mixture and cook over moderate heat, without stirring, shaking skillet once or twice to loosen frittata, until underside is golden but top is still wet, about 5 minutes. Cover skillet handle if not oven-proof with a double layer of foil and broil frittata 3 inches from heat until top is just set and golden, about 2 minutes. Slide frittata onto a plate and cool to warm or room temperature.

Cut frittata into wedges and serve with salad. Serves 4 as a light main course.

PORK AND PINTO BEAN CHILI

3 ounces dried *ancho* chiles* (4 to 6)
1 fresh jalapeño chile (optional)
a 14- to 16-ounce can whole tomatoes
   including juice
2 cups fresh orange juice
¼ cup packed fresh cilantro leaves
1 tablespoon salt, or to taste
3 pounds boneless pork shoulder, cut into
   1½-inch pieces
2 tablespoons olive oil
1 large white or sweet onion (about 1 pound)
4 garlic cloves
1½ tablespoons ground cumin
2 teaspoons dried oregano (preferably Mexican)
2 cups water
3 cups drained canned pinto beans
   (about two 15-ounce cans)
about eighteen 6-inch flour or corn tortillas

Garnish: chopped fresh cilantro leaves

*available at Latino markets, specialty foods
   shops, some supermarkets, and by mail order
   from Kitchen Market, (888) 468-4433

Heat a dry griddle or heavy skillet over moderate heat until hot but not smoking and toast *anchos*, 1 or 2 at a time, pressing down with tongs, a few seconds on each side to make more pliable. Wearing rubber gloves, remove stems, seeds, and veins from *anchos* and jalapeño and in a blender purée chiles, tomatoes with juice, orange juice, cilantro, and 1 teaspoon salt until smooth.

Pat pork dry and season with salt. In a 5-quart heavy kettle heat oil over moderately high heat until hot but not smoking and, working in batches, brown pork on all sides, about 3 minutes per batch. Transfer pork as browned to a bowl.

Chop onion and garlic and cook in fat remaining in kettle over moderately low heat, stirring, until softened. Add cumin, oregano, and remaining 2 teaspoons salt and cook, stirring, 1 minute. Stir in pork,

chile purée, and water and simmer over low heat, covered, stirring occasionally, until pork is tender, 1½ to 2 hours. Rinse and drain beans and stir into pork mixture. Simmer chili until beans are heated through.

Preheat oven to 350° F.

While chili is simmering, wrap stacks of 6 tortillas in foil and heat in oven until hot, 8 to 12 minutes. Unwrap packages and transfer tortillas to a cloth-lined basket. Keep tortillas warm, covered.

Sprinkle chili with cilantro and serve with tortillas. Serves 6.

BRAISED CHICKEN WITH GARLIC AND FENNEL

3 whole chicken legs
4 chicken breast halves
2 large heads garlic
3 carrots
3 fennel bulbs (sometimes called anise,
   about 1½ pounds total)
1 pound new potatoes (about 1½ inches
   in diameter)
two 2½- by ½-inch strips orange zest
1 tablespoon salt, or to taste
1 teaspoon freshly ground black pepper
1 teaspoon fennel seeds
6 tablespoons extra-virgin olive oil

Accompaniment: hot crusty bread

Preheat oven to 350° F.

Cut chicken legs into thighs and drumsticks and remove skin. Skin chicken breast halves. Remove outer papery skin from garlic heads and separate cloves without peeling. Diagonally cut carrots into ½-inch-thick slices.

Chop enough fronds from fennel to measure 1 tablespoon and reserve for garnish. Trim fennel stalks flush with bulbs, discarding stalks, and discard any tough outer layers. Halve bulbs lengthwise and cut halves lengthwise into ¼-inch-thick slices.

In an ovenproof 5-quart heavy kettle with a tight-fitting lid toss together chicken, garlic, carrots, fennel slices, and remaining ingredients until coated with oil. Cover kettle and bake until chicken is cooked through and vegetables are tender, about 1½ hours.

Stir in reserved fennel fronds and serve stew with bread. Serves 6.

Beef and Mushroom Stew with White Wine and Mustard

2 large onions (about 1 pound total)
4 garlic cloves
2 medium leeks (white and pale green
   parts only)
10 ounces mushrooms
two 14- to 16-ounce cans whole tomatoes
   including juice
3 pounds beef chuck, cut into 1½-inch pieces
1½ teaspoons fresh thyme leaves or ½ teaspoon
   dried thyme, crumbled
1 bay leaf
2 teaspoons salt, or to taste
2 tablespoons olive oil
1 cup dry white wine
½ cup brandy
½ pound sliced bacon
2 tablespoons Dijon mustard

Accompaniment: noodles or rice (optional)

Preheat oven to 300° F.

Cut onions into 1-inch pieces and thinly slice garlic. Diagonally cut leeks into ¾-inch-thick slices. In a large bowl of cold water wash leeks well and with a slotted spoon transfer to a colander to drain. Quarter mushrooms. In a sieve set over a bowl drain whole tomatoes, reserving juice, and quarter tomatoes. Trim excess fat from beef if necessary.

In a very large bowl toss together onions, garlic, leeks, mushrooms, beef, thyme, bay leaf, salt, pepper to taste, and oil until combined well. Stir in tomatoes with reserved juice, wine, and brandy.

Cut bacon into 1-inch pieces. Cover bottom of an ovenproof 8-quart heavy kettle with a tight-fitting lid with bacon. Pour beef mixture over bacon and bring to a simmer, uncovered, over moderately high heat, without stirring. Cover kettle and bake mixture in middle of oven until beef and vegetables are tender, about 2½ hours.

Discard bay leaf and stir in mustard. Serve stew with noodles or rice. Serves 6.

Thai Curried Shrimp with Peas

2 pounds large shrimp (about 40)
1 cup packed fresh basil leaves
1 cup packed fresh cilantro sprigs
1½ tablespoons Thai red curry paste*
1 tablespoon vegetable oil
a 13.5-ounce can unsweetened coconut milk*
4 teaspoons Thai fish sauce (*naam pla*)*
2 to 3 teaspoons packed brown sugar, or to taste
a 10-ounce package thawed frozen peas

Accompaniment: rice (preferably Jasmine)

*available at Southeast Asian markets and many
   supermarkets

Peel and devein shrimp. Finely chop basil and cilantro.

In a 5-quart heavy kettle cook curry paste, oil, and ¼ cup coconut milk over moderate heat, stirring, 1 minute. Stir in remaining coconut milk and simmer until slightly thickened, about 5 minutes. Stir in fish sauce and brown sugar and cook, stirring, 1 minute. Stir in shrimp, basil, and cilantro and cook over moderately low heat, stirring occasionally, until shrimp are almost cooked through, about 4 minutes. Stir in peas and cook, stirring occasionally, until peas are heated through, about 2 minutes.

Serve curried shrimp with rice. Serves 4 to 6.

LAMB AND EGGPLANT STEW WITH GREMOLATA

1 pound vine-ripened tomatoes
   (about 3 medium)
two 1-pound eggplants
3 red bell peppers
1 pound onions (about 3 medium)
4 garlic cloves
3 pounds boneless lamb shoulder, cut into
   1½-inch pieces
1 tablespoon olive oil
2 teaspoons salt
For gremolata
2 garlic cloves
2 teaspoons finely grated fresh lemon zest
2 tablespoons coarsely chopped fresh
   flat-leafed parsley leaves

Accompaniment: rice or hot crusty bread
   (optional)

Preheat oven to 350° F.

Peel and seed tomatoes (procedure follows) and cut into 1-inch pieces. Quarter eggplants lengthwise and cut quarters crosswise into 1-inch-thick slices. Cut bell peppers and onions into 1-inch pieces. Thinly slice garlic.

Trim lamb of excess fat. Pat lamb dry and season with salt and pepper. In an ovenproof 7- to 8-quart heavy kettle with a tight-fitting lid heat oil over moderately high heat until hot but not smoking and brown half of lamb on all sides, about 5 minutes. Transfer browned lamb to a large bowl and brown remaining lamb. Return lamb in bowl to kettle and stir in vegetables, garlic, and salt. Cook mixture, stirring, 2 minutes. Cover kettle and bake in middle of oven 30 minutes. Stir lamb stew and bake, covered, until lamb and vegetables are tender, about 30 minutes more.

Make gremolata:

Mince garlic and in a small bowl stir together with zest and parsley.

Sprinkle *gremolata* over stew and serve with rice or bread. Serves 6.

TO PEEL AND SEED TOMATOES

Cut a small shallow X in bottom end of tomatoes. In a kettle of boiling salted water blanch tomatoes 10 seconds, or until skin starts to curl at X. Transfer tomatoes with a slotted spoon to a bowl of ice water and let stand until cool enough to handle. Remove skin. Halve tomatoes crosswise and with a small spoon scoop out seeds.

ITALIAN SAUSAGE AND WHITE BEAN STEW

2 onions (about ¾ pound total)
2 large garlic cloves
a 14- to 16-ounce can whole tomatoes
   including juice
2 pounds sweet Italian sausage
1 tablespoon olive oil
1 cup chicken broth
½ cup dry white wine
1 teaspoon chopped fresh rosemary leaves
½ teaspoon salt, or to taste
3 cups drained canned white beans
   (about two 15-ounce cans)

Halve onions lengthwise and cut crosswise into ½-inch-thick slices. Finely chop garlic. In a sieve set over a bowl drain tomatoes, reserving juice, and chop.

Discard casings and cut sausage into ¾-inch-thick slices. In a deep 12-inch heavy skillet heat oil over moderate heat until hot but not smoking and brown half of sausage, turning gently, about 5 minutes. With a slotted spoon transfer sausage to a bowl. Brown remaining sausage and transfer to bowl. In fat remaining in skillet cook onions and garlic over moderately low heat, stirring, until softened. Stir in sausage, tomatoes with reserved juice, broth, wine, rosemary, salt, and pepper to taste. Bring mixture to a simmer and cook, covered, over moderately low heat, stirring occasionally, 15 minutes.

Rinse and drain beans and stir into sausage mixture. Cook stew, uncovered, stirring, until beans are heated through, about 5 minutes. Serves 4 to 6.

GUIDES TO THE TEXT

GENERAL INDEX

———

Page numbers in *italics* indicate color photographs
☺ indicates recipes that can be prepared in 45 minutes or less
☺+ indicates recipes that can be prepared in 45 minutes but require additional unattended time
🍃 indicates recipes that are leaner/lighter

TABLE SETTING ACKNOWLEDGMENTS

To avoid duplication below of table setting information within the same menu, the editors have listed all such credits for silverware, plates, linen, and the like in its most complete form under "Table Setting."

Any items in the photograph not credited are privately owned.
All addresses are in New York City unless otherwise indicated.

Back Jacket

Berry Tart with Mascarpone Cream: See Table Setting Credits for Lunch among the Hydrangeas.

Frontispiece

Peach Raspberry Top-Crust Pie (page 2): English dessert plate (with pie and ice cream), circa 1890—Pantry & Hearth, (212) 532-0535.

Table of Contents

Necker "Sunrises" (page 6): See Table Setting Credits for Buffet by the Sea on Necker Island.
Blueberries with Yogurt and Maple-Blueberry Syrup (page 6): "Kirsty" earthenware cereal bowl; "New Kings" sterling silver spoon; "Cottage Lane Floral" cotton napkin—The Ralph Lauren Home Collection, (212) 642-8700.
Spiced Chicken Breast with Couscous Salad; Pickled Red Cabbage with Toasted Sesame Seeds; Coconut Tempura Shrimp on Banana Caper Relish (page 7): See Table Setting Credits for Buffet by the Sea on Necker Island.

The Menu Collection

Table Setting (page 10): See Table Setting Credits for Lunch among the Hydrangeas.

Fireside Dinner

Poire William Champagne Cocktails (page 12): Champagne flutes designed by William Yeoward—Bergdorf Goodman, 754 Fifth Ave. Cocktail napkins—ABC Carpet & Home, 888 Broadway.
Table Setting (page 13): "Les Amours" porcelain dinner plates by Ancienne Manufacture Royale—for stores call Bernardaud, (800) 448-8282. Creamware pudding dish (soup), circa 1810—Bardith, 901 Madison Ave. Glass plate (cheese toasts); wineglasses, designed by William Yeoward—Bergdorf Goodman (see above). "Cardinal" silverplate flatware—for stores call Puiforcat, (800) 993-2580. Silver-plate julep cups; horn salt and pepper dishes and spoons—William-Wayne & Co., 850 Lexington Ave. Sterling-and wood-handled toasting fork made in 1911—James II Galleries, 11 East 57th St. Cashmere and wool tablecloth with suede trim—ABH Design, 153 East 61st St. Lusterware pitcher, circa 1815; porcelain spill vases, circa 1840 (on mantelpiece)—Bardith (see above).
Ginger Cakes with Molten Chocolate Centers (page 15): Wedgwood creamware dessert plates, circa 1810—Bardith (see above).

Superbowl Sunday Buffet

Buffet Setting (page 16): Earthenware baking dish—for stores call Emile Henry, (302) 326-4800. 5½-quart enameled cast-iron "French oven" by Le Creuset; red cotton towels (napkins) by Primrose Bordier for Le Jacquard Français—Gracious Home, 1220 Third Avenue. Earthenware plates designed by Barbara Eigen—to order call Connoisseur, (913) 677-9667. "Uginox" stainless-steel flatware—Ad Hoc Softwares, 410 West Broadway. Wood bowls—Dean & DeLuca, 560 Broadway. "Column" wineglasses; wood tray—Crate & Barrel, 650 Madison Avenue. "Romantica" linen cloth—for stores call Anichini, (800) 553-5309. "Dyonisos" crystal decanter (dressing)—Baccarat, 625 Madison Avenue.
Herbed Bean Spread with Baguette Toasts (page 17): Stainless-steel coffee table—Troy, 138 Greene Street. Metal-alloy bowl by Nambe (bean spread)—Bloomingdale's, 1000 Third Avenue. Woven-reed place mats—for stores call Dransfield and Ross, (212) 741-7278.

Brunch in the Shade on Necker Island

Porch Setting (page 18): Highball glasses—Frank McIntosh Home at

314

Saks Fifth Avenue, (800) 347-9177. Linen napkins—for stores call Necessities, (718) 797-0530. Reed-matting pillows—for stores call Dransfield & Ross, (212) 741-7278. All other items credited below.

Fruit Salad (page 19): Metal bowl—Pottery Barn, 117 E. 59th St. "Tahiti" sterling-and-bamboo flatware—Buccellati, 46 E. 57th St. Coaster with coral decorations—Dransfield & Ross (see above).

Mixed Greens with Asparagus and Morels Topped with Poached Eggs and Hollandaise (page 19): Wood plate—Bergdorf Goodman, 754 Fifth Avenue.

Buffet by the Sea on Necker Island

Buffet Setting (page 20): Frosted glass plate (red cabbage salad)—Pottery Barn, 117 E. 59th Street. Woven-straw chargers—Bergdorf Goodman, 754 Fifth Avenue. "Bamboo"-edged plates by Este—Barneys New York, Madison Ave. at 61st St. "Sumatra" bamboo-handled flatware by SCOF—for stores call Mariposa, (800) 788-1304. "Seashell" linen-and-cotton napkins with shell edges; split-bamboo runner—Dransfield & Ross, (212) 741-7278.

Necker "Sunrises"; Rum "Lemonade" (page 21): "Bellini" wineglass and highball glasses—Mariposa (see above). Split-bamboo tray—Dransfield & Ross (see above).

Lazy Day Lunch on Necker Island

Chilled Pumpkin and Lemongrass Soup with Crab Meat; Frozen Passion-Fruit Soufflés with Kiwifruit-Pineapple Salsa, Strawberry Coulis, and Cocoa Spirals (page 22): Fuchsia silk napkin by Kim Seybert—Frank McIntosh Home at Saks Fifth Avenue, (800) 347-9177. Reed-matting neck roll (pillow)—Dransfield & Ross, (212) 741-7278.

Grilled Mahimahi with Crushed Potatoes, Orange Vinaigrette, and Cilantro Pesto (page 23): Pink faience service plate—Gucci, 685

Fifth Ave. "Natalie" wineglass—Crate & Barrel, 650 Madison Ave. Ochre silk napkin by Kim Seybert—Frank McIntosh Home at Saks Fifth Avenue (see above).

A Rustic Italian Dinner

Table Setting (page 24): "Piombino" square ceramic plates (pasta) and bowl (artichokes) by Barbara Eigen; "Piazza" ceramic dinner and salad plates; "Bosso" wood-handled flatware; "Rufa" stemmed glasses; "San Martino" tumblers; straw runner; "Gianni" linen guest towel by Anichini (bread); pillar candles—Tuscan Square, 16 West 51st Street. "Dunbar" orange cotton napkins (as place mats)—for stores call Fallani and Cohn, (800) 666-0055 or (914) 365-3535. Seventeenth-century English red velvet chair—Newel Art Galleries, 425 East 53rd Street.

Savoy Cabbage and Arugula Salad; Lattice-Topped Apricot Crostata (page 25): "Prato" salad bowl; "Peltro" porcelain-and-pewter espresso cup and saucer—Tuscan Square (see above).

A Cheese Tasting Party

Table Setting (page 28): Stoneware dinner plates and bowls—Takashimaya, 693 Fifth Avenue. "Hammered Antique" stainless-steel flatware by Reed & Barton; cheese tray; bread basket—Wolfman • Gold & Good Company, 117 Mercer Street. "Marcel" wineglasses by iittala; frosted glass tumblers—Ad Hoc Softwares, 410 West Broadway. Linen napkins; horn cups and bowls; cheese knives (on tray)—William-Wayne & Co., 850 Lexington Avenue.

Exotic Mushroom Broth (page 29): Salt-glaze tureen, lid (not shown), and platter, circa 1760—Bardith, 901 Madison Avenue.

Cheeses and Accompaniments (page 30): Wood bowl (pears)—Ad Hoc Softwares (see above). Glass salad bowl—William-Wayne & Co. (see above). "Normandie" crystal

Sauternes glasses—Baccarat, 625 Madison Avenue.

Apple, Apricot, and Prune Tart with Crème Fraîche (page 31): Cake stand—Curly Willow, East Hampton, N.Y., (516) 324-1122. Mother-of-pearl spoon—William-Wayne & Co. (see above).

Easter Sunday

Table Setting (page 32): "Epoch" white ceramic salad plates—Crate & Barrel, 650 Madison Avenue. "Herb Garden" porcelain buffet plates by Laure Japy—for stores call Blachere Group, (800) 641-4808. "Bamboo" flatware by Guy Degrenne—for stores call The Zrike Co., (212) 686-3991. "Bamboo" crystal wineglasses by Tharaud—Cardel, 621 Madison Avenue. Etched water glasses—William-Wayne & Co., 850 Lexington Avenue. "Shirred Edge" linen napkins (on chair backs) by Angel Zimick—for stores call Metropolitan Design Group, (212) 944-6110. French wicker-and-bamboo table, circa 1870—J. Garvin Mecking, Inc., 72 East 11th Street. French *faux*-bamboo side chairs (from a set of 10), circa 1880—Newel Art Galleries, 425 East 53rd Street.

Radishes with Goat Cheese (page 33): Ceramic leaf plate—for stores call Great Impressions Ceramic Design, (510) 526-6019. Wineglasses—William-Wayne & Co. (see above).

Rack of Lamb with Spinach Pine-Nut Crust; Baby Carrots and Asparagus (page 34): "Herb Garden" porcelain platter by Laure Japy—Blachere Group (see above).

Pineapple Rum Trifle Cake (page 35): American milk-glass cake stand, circa 1890—More & More Antiques, 378 Amsterdam Avenue. Glass hobnail dessert plate—William-Wayne & Co. (see above).

A Barbecue at the Phoenician

(Pages 36 through 39): Photographed at The Phoenician, Scottsdale, AZ, (800) 888-8234.

315

Mother's Day at the Ritz-Carlton, Chicago

(Pages 40 through 43): Photographed at The Ritz-Carlton, Chicago, IL, (800) 621-6906.

To the Lighthouse

Picnic Setting (page 44): Nineteenth-century pine trunk—Wayne Pratt, Inc., (508) 228-8788.

Lobster Salad with Corn, Sugar Snap Peas, and Basil-Mint Oil; Gingered Watermelon and Yellow Tomato Salad; Peppered Pita Crisps; Nectarine Lime Curd Tart with a Brown Sugar Crust (page 45): "Chaîne d'Ancre" porcelain plates; "Attelage" stainless-steel flatware—Hermès, (800) 441-4488. White cotton piqué napkins—Bergdorf Goodman, (800) 218-4918. Brass lamp; rope (around napkin)—E & B Marine Catalog, (800) 262-8464.

Sunday Dinner

Table Setting (page 47): "Parchment" white ceramic dinner plates; "Pristine" white ceramic service plates; "Torsade" acrylic-handled flatware—Wolfman•Gold & Good Company, (212) 431-1888. "Capri" white ceramic bowls; "Crackle" blue ceramic bowls; "Lido" blue tumblers and blue double Old Fashioned glasses—Pottery Barn, (800) 922-5507. "Splash" blue glasses (on counter)—for stores call Izabel Lam, (718) 797-3983. "Beach" linen napkins—ABH Design, (212) 688-3764.

Grilled Flank Steak; Twice-Baked Potatoes with Basil and Sour Cream; Spinach and Sprout Salad (page 48): Silver-plate serving fork; ceramic cake stand (potatoes); ceramic platter—Wolfman•Gold & Good Company (see above). "Pomfret" glass salad bowl—Simon Pearce, (212) 421-8801.

Lemon-Blueberry Ice-Cream Cake (page 49): "Ellipse" blue ceramic plates—Pottery Barn (see above).

Lunch among the Hydrangeas

Table Setting (page 51): Aqua glass salad plates; stardust-blue glass dinner plates; "Ice" goblets by Cristina Salusti—for stores call Fossilglass, (212) 966-2798. "Ripple" glass service plates—for stores call Annieglass, (800) 347-6133. "Tunisia" aqua frosted all-purpose glasses—Frank McIntosh Home at Saks Fifth Avenue, (800) 347-9177. Frosted-handled acrylic flatware—Bergdorf Goodman, (800) 218-4918. Napkins—Nantucket Trading Emporium, (508) 325-0714. "Florentine" glass and metal table—for stores call Brown Jordan, (626) 443-8971, ext. 221.

Summer Brunch

Buffet Setting (page 54): "Saybrook" painted wood table; "Kirsty" earthenware cups and saucers; "Vineyard Check" cotton napkins; "Kalahari" wing chair covered in "Cottage Lane Floral" cotton fabric; white canvas with "Starfish" embroidery pillow (on wing chair); "Landon" glass bowls (11 inches and 5 inches); "Atlantique" stainless-steel serving spoon—for stores call The Ralph Lauren Home Collection, (212) 642-8700. Wicker basket—for stores call Crate & Barrel, (800) 996-9960. Wicker-covered carafe—William-Wayne & Co., (212) 288-9243.

Corn and Basil Egg Roulade with Yellow Tomato Coulis; Sliced Black Forest Ham (page 55): "Emma" pressed-glass tumbler (daisies) and goblets; "Handkerchief" earthenware teacups and saucer (on top of stacked plates); "Handkerchief" and "Button-down" earthenware plates (stacked); "Breezeway Stripe" cotton napkins; "New Kings" sterling forks—The Ralph Lauren Home Collection (see above).

Grilling by the Pool

Lamb and Red Pepper Kebabs; Shrimp and Onion Kebabs; Bulgur, Parsley, and Mint Salad (page 56): Glass dinner plates by Pinkwater—Bergdorf Goodman, (800) 218-4918. Wineglass—Dish, (888) 347-4827.

Frozen Pistachio Halvah Pie; Plums in White Peppercorn and Vanilla Syrup (page 57): Apilco porcelain pie plate—Gracious Home, (212) 517-6300. "Fandango" glass plates—Crate & Barrel, (800) 996-9960.

Flavors of Japan

Table Setting (page 58): White onyx dishes (fish); porcelain leaf dishes (eggplant)—William-Wayne & Company, (800) 318-3435. Lacquered leaf dishes (cucumber salad); ceramic pouring bowls (rice); chopsticks; linen napkins—Takashimaya, (212) 350-0100. "Yoshino" square crystal plates (under cucumber salad); crystal sake carafes—The Hoya Crystal Gallery, (212) 223-6335. Square green capiz shell trays—Carnevale, (800) 548-9979. "Contour" striped crystal glasses by M.A.P.—Frank McIntosh Home at Saks Fifth Avenue, (800) 347-9177. "Splash" frosted glasses—for stores call Izabel Lam, (718) 797-3983.

Crab and Egg Maki with Tobiko; Edamame (page 59): "Slab" rectangular and square glass dishes—for stores call Annieglass, (800) 347-6133. "Dom Perignon" crystal Champagne flute—Baccarat, (800) 777-0100.

Watermelon Ice (page 61): Wire-wrapped glasses; lacquered spoons—Takashimaya (see above).

Family Reunion

Goat Cheese and Tomato Tart (page 62): Cutting board—Crate & Barrel, (800) 996-9960. Vintage blue-and-white checked napkin—Pantry & Hearth, (212) 532-0535. Hickory high chair, circa 1930—Zona (212) 925-6750, ext. 15.

Table Setting (page 63): "Canyon Road" white earthenware dinner plates; "Grafton Stripe" cotton blanket—for stores call The Ralph Lauren Home Collection, (212) 642-8700. Tin dinner plates—Pottery Barn, (800) 922-5507. Vintage wineglasses; nineteenth-century spongeware bowl—Pantry & Hearth (see above). Wood-handled flatware—Ad Hoc Softwares, (212) 925-2652. Blue-and-white striped linen napkins—Mecox Gardens, (516) 287-5015. Late-nineteenth-century sterling napkin rings—More & More, (212) 580-8404. Yellow sap bucket; "Fat Lady" pine table with painted base by El Paso—Zona (see above).

Peach Raspberry Top-Crust Pie; Vanilla Bean Ice Cream; Buttermilk Cupcakes with Two Frostings (page 65): Wire mesh food cover—Wolfman•Gold & Good Company, (212) 431-1888. Straw pail with aluminum liner—Ad Hoc Softwares (see above).

A Southwestern Thanksgiving

Spiced Pumpkin Seed Flatbread (page 66): Glass vase—Takashimaya, (212) 350-0100.

Table Setting (page 67): Matte earthenware plates—Luna Garcia, (800) 905-9975. "Round" stemware and beakers (water)—Simon Pearce, (212) 421-8801. "Telluride" stainless-steel flatware; "Southern Plains Serape" striped cotton place mats—Ralph Lauren Home Collection, (212) 642-8700. "Dunbar" cotton napkins by Fallani & Cohn—call ABC Carpet & Home, (212) 473-3000. Glass vase—Takashimaya (see above).

House designed and built by Servais Design & Construction, Inc., (510) 548-8453.

Thanksgiving in the City

Caramel Nut Tart; Ginger Ice Cream; Cinnamon Nutmeg Tuiles (page 71, top): Spode silver lusterware dessert plate, circa 1840—Bardith, (212) 737-3775.

Vine Leaf-Wrapped Sheep's-Milk Ricotta with Fennel and Olives (page 71, bottom): Silver-plate tray—S. Wyler (212) 879-9848. "Mmmmm..." linen napkin by Angel Zimick—Frank McIntosh Home at Saks Fifth Avenue, (800) 347-9177.

Table Setting (pages 72 and 73): "Khazard" Limoges plates (dinner

and presentation) by Jean Louis Coquet—for stores call Lalique, (800) 993-2580. Georgian-style octagonal silver-plate dishes (covers not shown), circa 1860—James II Galleries, (212) 355-7040. Silver-plate tray—S. Wyler, (212) 879-9848. "Round English" hand-forged sterling flatware; "Round English" hand-forged sterling relish spoon—James Robinson, (212) 752-6166. "Damier" crystal stemmed glasses—for stores call Hermès, (800) 238-5522. Velvet-trimmed linen napkins—for stores call Dransfield & Ross, (212) 741-7278. Silver lusterware goblets (with roses), circa 1830—Bardith (see above). "Thistle Scroll" linen and metallic throw (used as tablecloth)—Donna Karan Home Collection—Neiman Marcus (selected stores), (800) 365-7989. "Cab" leather chairs—Cassina, (212) 245-2121.

Christmas Dinner

Crab with Dill on Cayenne Toasts; Roquefort Dip with Apple, Endive, and Celery Hearts (page 74): Neale & Wilson creamware platter, circa 1790—Bardith, (212) 737-3775. "Eve" crystal Champagne flutes by William Yeoward Crystal—for stores call (800) 818-8484.

Rib Roast with Roasted-Garlic Thyme Sauce; Creamy Cabbage, Parsnip, and Potato Casserole with Robiola (page 75): English ironstone platter, circa 1870, and vintage horn-handled carving set—More & More Antiques, (212) 580-8404. "Country French" metal bowl by Wilton-Armetale—for stores call (800) 826-0088.

Table Setting (pages 76 and 77): "Carat" Limoges service plates by Philippe Deshoulieres—for stores call Lalique, (800) 993-2580. "Early English" hand-forged sterling flatware—James Robinson, (212) 752-6166. "Brummel" crystal water glasses—Baccarat, (212) 826-4100. Glass rummers, circa 1840—Bardith (see above). Glass vases (pinecones and pears)—Collectania, (212) 327-2176.

"Windsor" glass candlesticks and glass hurricane lamp (pinecones)—Simon Pearce, (212) 421-8801. Amaryllises and wreaths—Zezé Flowers, Inc., (212) 753-7767.

Holiday Brunch

Table Setting (page 78): "Eve" crystal Champagne flutes; "Myrtle" green glass goblets—for stores call William Yeoward, (800) 818-8484. Glass bonbon dishes; "Woodstock" glass serving bowl (roasted pears)—Simon Pearce, (212) 421-8801. "Lombardi" pewter flatware—Ad Hoc Softwares, (212) 925-2652. Amaryllises—Zezé, (212) 753-7767.

Popover Pudding with Irish Bacon (page 80): 3½-quart enameled cast-iron casserole—Le Creuset, (800) 827-1798. Scottish stoneware plates, circa 1870—James II Galleries, (212) 355-7040.

Grilling on the Light Side

White Grape Granitas (page 82): Shot glasses—Fishs Eddy, (212) 873-8819. "Quadrille" porcelain salad plate—Dan Levy, (212) 268-0878. Stainless-steel demitasse spoons—Crate & Barrel, (888) 249-4155.

Grilled Pork Tenderloin with Chili Maple Glaze; Papaya and Red Onion Salsa; Grilled Zucchini and Bell Pepper Couscous (page 83): Earthenware dinner plate—Dan Levy (see above). Wineglass—Simon Pearce, (212) 421-8801. "Tabriz" linen napkin by area—for store locations, call (212) 924-7084. "Moon" lacquered stacking tables—Crate & Barrel (see above).

Dinner on the Light Side

Spinach and Endive Salad with Lemon-Ginger Dressing and Crisp Won Ton Strips; Red Snapper with Spicy Soy Glaze on Sautéed Vegetables and Sweet Potato (pages 84 and 85): Hand-painted Limoges dinner and salad plates by Fabienne Jovin—Bergdorf Goodman, 754 Fifth Avenue. "Chop" bronze flatware—Pottery Barn, 117 East 59th Street.

317

Dinner on the Light Side

Cilantro-Stuffed Chicken Breast with Poblano Chile Sauce; Rice, Bean, and Corn Salad; Pineapple with Basil (pages 86 and 87): "Helios" Limoges dinner and dessert plates by Ancienne Manufacture Royale—Bernardaud, (212) 371-4300.

A Recipe Compendium

Corn and Basil Egg Roulade; Baking Powder Biscuits; Sliced Black Forest Ham (page 88): See Table Setting Credits for Summer Brunch.

A Spring Family Dinner

Strawberries in Red Wine (page 253): "Bellini" cobalt dessert glasses—Mariposa, (978) 526-9244.

Asparagus with Hazelnut Sauce; Lemons (page 254): "Uva" octagon dinner plate; "Barocco Blu" serving bowl—Vietri, (800) 277-5933.

Lamb Stew with Pimientos and Chiles; Onion Bread (page 255): "Puccinelli" cobalt bubble wine glasses; "Barocco Blu" oval platter and dinner plates—Vietri (see above). Cobalt vase—Anthropologie, 375 West Broadway. Oval platter and candlestick (in plate rack)—Bazaar Sabado, 54 Greene Street.

A Tapas Party

Pine Nut Cookies (page 259): White Verona Galouchi napkins—Wolfman • Gold & Good Company, 117 Mercer Street.

Oxtail Paprika Stew; Asparagus, Mushroom, and Chorizo Omelet; Watercress and Romaine with Cabrales Cheese (page 261): Rim soup bowls; salad servers, fork, and spoon—Wolfman • Gold & Good Company (see above). Pewter flatware—Zona, 97 Greene Street.

Summer Lunch by the Sea

Green Grape and Lima Bean Gazpacho (page 270): Napkin—Bazaar Sabado, 54 Greene Street.

Seafood Paella with Lemon Garlic Mayonnaise (page 271): "Puccinelli" classic wine glass; "Isabelle's Garden" dinner plates—Vietri, (800) 277-5933. Small green glasses—Tuscan Square, 16 West 51st Street.

CREDITS

Grateful acknowledgment is made to the following for permission to reprint recipes previously published in *Gourmet* Magazine:

The Phoenician: A Barbecue at the Phoenician (page 36) was created by:
James Cohen—executive chef;
Kevin Gay, Michael Snoke, and **Alessandro Stratta**—*chefs de cuisine*;
Richard Ruskell—*chef-pâtissier*;
Judy Capertina—pastry chef;
Dale Sparks—cellar master (wines)

Necker Island: Brunch in the Shade (page 19), Buffet by the Sea (page 21), and Lazy Day Lunch (page 22) were created by:
Troy Smith: Chilled Pumpkin and Lemongrass Soup with Crab Meat (page 114); Coconut Tempura Shrimp on Banana Caper Relish (page 126); Sambuca Soufflés with White Chocolate Ice Cream (page 230).

Jay Wesley: Rum "Lemonade" (page 233); Necker "Sunrise" (page 235).

Scott Williams: Grilled Mahimahi with Crushed Potatoes, Orange Vinaigrette, and Cilantro Pesto (page 116); Spiced Chicken Breasts with Couscous Salad (page 141); Mixed Greens, Asparagus, and Morels Topped with Poached Eggs and Hollandaise (page 154); Pickled Red Cabbage with Toasted Sesame Seeds (page 189);

Celery Root and Apple Salad with Creamy Mustard Dressing (page 189); Fennel Confit and Tomato Salad (page 190); Frozen Passion-Fruit Parfaits with Kiwifruit-Pineapple Salsa, Strawberry Coulis, and Cocoa Spirals (page 222).

The Ritz-Carlton: Mother's Day at the Ritz-Carlton, Chicago (page 41) was created by:
Sarah Stegner—dining room chef;
En-Ming Hsu—executive pastry chef;
Steven Laude—wines/dining room manager.

David Shack and Judith Sutton: Sautéed Quail with Paprika Sauce and Moroccan-Spiced Vegetables (page 146). Copyright © 1998 by David Shack and Judith Sutton. Reprinted by permission of the authors.

Nina Simonds: Chicken Fried Rice with Fermented Black Beans (page 166); Chinese-Style Rice (page 167); Shrimp Fried Rice (page 168); Vietnamese Fried Rice (page 168). Copyright © 1998 by Nina Simonds. Reprinted by permission of the author.

Zanne Early Stewart: Dark Chocolate Brown Sugar Pound Cake with Chocolate Glaze (page 201); Brown Sugar Sour Cream (page 201). Copyright © 1998 by Zanne Early Stewart. Reprinted by permission of the author.

Grateful acknowledgment is made to the following *Gourmet* readers for permission to reprint recipes previously published in *Gourmet* Magazine:

Jerome Eisner: Beef Wellingtons with Gorgonzola (page 128).

Elizabeth Alling Sewall: Pot Roast with Root Vegetables (page 130).

Colleen and Richard Deon: Lobster Bisque (page 113).

The following photographers and organizations have generously given permission to reprint photographs. Some of these photographs have previously appeared in *Gourmet* Magazine.

Antonio de Benito ICEX for Spain Gourmetour: Flamenco Dancer (page 7) ©1996.

Tina Gehring: Bullfighters in Seville, Andalusia (page 258) ©1996.

Julian Neiman: Banyoles, Catalonia (page 252) ©1995; Fishermen, Canary Islands (page 268) ©1995.

Jane Strong: Spanish tiles (pages 257, 263, 265, 266, 273, and 274) ©1998.

Romulo Yanes: The Alhambra, Granada (pages 236 and 237) © 1992; Camariñas, Galicia (pages 238 and 239) © 1992.

If you are not already a subscriber to *Gourmet* Magazine and would be interested in subscribing, please call *Gourmet*'s toll-free number, 1-800-365-2454.

If you are interested in purchasing additional copies of this book or other *Gourmet* cookbooks, please call 1-800-438-9944.